# MONEY and MADNESS at LEHMAN BROTHERS

A TOUCHSTONE BOOK
PUBLISHED BY SIMON & SCHUSTER
NEW YORK   LONDON   TORONTO   SYDNEY   NEW DELHI

# STREET
# FREAK

## A MEMOIR

## Jared Dillian

Touchstone
A Division of Simon & Schuster, Inc.
1230 Avenue of the Americas
New York, NY 10020

This work is a memoir. Events, actions, experiences and their consequences have been retold as the author presently recollects them. Some names and identifying characteristics have been changed, and some dialogue has been recreated from memory.

First Touchstone hardcover edition September 2011

TOUCHSTONE and colophon are registered trademarks of Simon & Schuster, Inc.

For information about special discounts for bulk purchases, please contact Simon & Schuster Special Sales at 1-866-506-1949 or business@simonandschuster.com.

The Simon & Schuster Speakers Bureau can bring authors to your live event. For more information or to book an event, contact the Simon & Schuster Speakers Bureau at 1-866-248-3049 or visit our website at www.simonspeakers.com.

Designed by Renata Di Biase

Manufactured in the United States of America

10  9  8  7  6  5  4  3  2  1

Library of Congress Cataloging-in-Publication Data

Dillian, Jared.
  Street freak : money and madness at Lehman Brothers / Jared Dillian.
    p.   cm.
  1. Stock exchanges—United States. 2. Financial crises—United States. 3. Global Financial Crisis, 2008–2009. 4. Lehman Brothers. I. Title.
  HG4910.D535 2011
  332.6′20973—dc22                                              2011011938

ISBN 978-1-4391-8126-3
ISBN 978-1-4391-8128-7 (ebook)

# CONTENTS

# STREET
# FREAK

# PROLOGUE

Back in 1999, when the world was brimming with optimism, when there were purple Yahoo! taxicabs patrolling the streets of San Francisco, I was a clerk on the options trading floor of the Pacific Coast Options Exchange. It was there that I learned how the financial markets worked. I spent much of my time standing in the back of the Intel-Oracle pit with the other clerks and stock jockeys; that is, the area where traders in Intel and Oracle options congregated.

There was a trader in the pit named Jack Taylor. Jack was six four, 240 pounds, with no concept of personal space. He spent half his day in a personal fast market, almost as though he was on crack, trading everything in sight: "BUY YOUR BOOK, JAN 30 CALLS, 20 LOT! SELL YOUR BOOK, DEC 25 PUTS! SAGEOLA! SAGEAROONI!" He was all arms and legs, thrashing his crumpled-up risk reports, crashing into other traders in the pit, eating lobster and steak burritos, passing gas all over the rest of the crowd, and heading out back to have sex with one of the female exchange clerks behind the Dumpster.

I wanted to be like Jack.

I wanted to be like Jack because he seemed to be one of God's simplest and most beautiful creations. Make money, good. Lose money, bad. Burrito, good. Hangover, bad. My life seemed terribly complicated, and if I could boil down my existence to this primordial level, then it would be an existentially freeing experience.

But I was wrong. Jack's wild personality was a smoke screen, a defense mechanism that he had created to convince other people (and perhaps himself, too) that his life really was that uncomplicated. He was not a simple guy but a rather complex one: a smart kid who had graduated from an Ivy League school, who had made deliberate and rational choices about what to do with his life, and who was now having second thoughts. His acting out was his way of coping, his way of distracting himself from the reality that the financial markets are a cruel way to make a living.

Jack now owns a sandwich shop in Chicago: Jack's Sandos.

All traders go through what Jack went through. They learn to cope with the idea that they are expendable. If you ever take a trip to an investment bank's trading floor, look around. Try to find the rare and elusive silver fox. Try to count the number of traders over forty. You won't find many.

Partly this is because of mathematics. If the markets are mostly a zero-sum game, then the winners stick around and the losers find other things to do with their lives. The likelihood of somebody lasting ten years is only about one in five hundred.

The bigger reason that you don't see old farts on trading floors is because people self-select. After a number of years in the business, they say enough is enough, hand in their company ID, and they go raise alpacas outside of Spokane.

The important detail is that all traders are capitalists of one stripe or another. Some of them are even supercapitalists, staunch libertarians, politically well to the right of even the Republican Party. And capitalism requires a dedication to the pursuit of reality. A rock is a rock is a rock. A rock is not a tree, no matter what mental gymnastics you perform. Profits are profits. Losses are losses. And there is no *evading* losses. You see your P&L every day, and the negative number stares you in the face.

Back in the civilian world, people permit themselves to evade reality. If the market is down, they won't open the brokerage statement. They will stop investing. They will give up. They will *hope* that things come back.

Being a professional trader allows no such evasion. Hope is not a strategy. If you have a loss, you had better figure it out, or you are out on your ass.

That is a hell of a way to live.

But only if you can get to work in the morning. Seven years of this.

*I'm late. Again. Did I lock the front door?*

If you're a trader, it is important to exercise the illusion of control, because the reality is that you're not in control of anything. The smartest man on Wall Street, after months and months of research on a single trade, has no control over the outcome. In the short term, his position can move against him and force him to liquidate the world's best idea, only to make him watch as it appreciates 200 percent over the next six months.

*I definitely turned the coffeemaker off. But I'm not sure I locked the front door.*

Traders deal with probabilities. There is a probability distribution for interest rates, for the log return of stock prices, and for cheating on your spouse without getting caught. The world is filled with uncertainty, and you try to model it. You quantify it. I model the likelihood that someone will break into my house if I forget to lock the door, and I determine that it is infinitesimally small. But not small enough.

*I'd better turn around and check the front door.*

It is true that in the absence of trade, there is war. But trade is just a different kind of warfare: buyers continually demand lower prices, and sellers want more for what they're selling. A transaction occurs when— for a brief moment in time—buyer and seller can agree on a price. You'd think that both parties would be satisfied at this point, but in practice, they're more pissed off at each other than they were before. Everyone thinks he's getting screwed. A trading floor is filled with unhappy people, because nobody is ever satisfied.

*Okay. Here we go.*

Unlock, unlock.

Step outside. Turn around.

Lock dead bolt. Test doorknob. Push against door. *Feel* that it's locked.

Lock doorknob.

Lock dead bolt again. *Five, four, three, two, one.*

Lock door again. *Five, four, three, two, one.*

Lock dead bolt again. *Three, two, one.*

Lock door again. *Three, two, one.*

Lock dead bolt again.

Lock door again.

Jiggle doorknob. Locked. *Five, three, one. Five, three, one.*

In most of the world's markets, prices are sticky. The price of milk does not change on a second-by-second basis. It does not *tick*. Neither do the prices of air conditioners, coffeemakers, or MP3s. But a share of GE stock is worth more than it was just a second ago. In the financial markets, quoted prices are good for an instant; after that, they're stale. Numbers change, and there are consequences. People start yelling. In fact, traders yell all the time. Sometimes it's because they're angry with you, but mostly it is to convey a sense of urgency. *Five bid for ten thousand, immediate. Higher, now!* I've seen kids out of college who were completely unprepared for the brutality of trading. Someone yells, and they crumble. They literally shake. Trading is not for the weak, the indecisive, the passive, or the homeschooled.

*Damn it.*

Back to the house, all the way from the bus stop.

*Forgot to check the refrigerator.*

*This is madness. The madness. It's back again, isn't it?*

Intimidation, I found, works pretty well, but only to a point. It can get you the extra penny, the balance of the order, and the price adjustment. But it is not a necessary or even sufficient condition for success. There is the guy in the pit with the glasses that nobody pays attention to. He buys when other people are selling. He steps aside when a big order comes through. He's cordial. He keeps up appearances, but it is impossible to tell if he is having a good day or a bad day. It is impossible to tell if he is having a good year or a bad year.

He is having a very good year. He is up $3 million.

*The refrigerator's closed.*

Back upstairs.

*I can't stand this.*

Windows. Bathroom windows, office windows, bedroom windows.

Computer off, printer off.

*Concentrate.*

Coffeemaker off. Lights off.

Porch windows.

*Ready.*

It is more important to be smart than it is to be big, or fast, or a jerk. And on Wall Street, there are all kinds of smart. There are mathematicians, people who can find the flaws in Nobel Prize–winning options pricing models. There are computer geeks. There are poker players. There are the social psychologists, like me, who know that human behavior runs in patterns over time. Any or all of them can get rich. The people who don't are the people who don't ask questions, the people who consider it a birthright to act as a tollbooth attendant, taking their nickel from the market, not a care in the world.

*Different pattern this time. Nine, eight, seven, six, five, four, three, two, one.*
Lock door.
Lock dead bolt.
Jiggle doorknob. Locked. *Nine, five, one. Nine, five, one.*
*Remember that. And catch your bus.*
*This is a choice. You can choose not to do this.*

There are those who think it is terribly unproductive to have an entire class of people dedicated to buying and selling money. They say that buying and selling money doesn't actually produce anything. It's just moving wealth around from one pile to the next. Even if that were true, it doesn't mean that anyone should care: to most people, making money is an end in itself. There are those, however, who spend their entire career on Wall Street and can't explain what it is they do for a living when they go home to their children at night. They're embarrassed for themselves, because they feel that they're not a force for good in the world.

To me, making money was an end in itself. But beyond that, it is important for any economy to have deep, liquid capital markets. Lost in the debate about the credit crisis—about whether or not it was good for banks to be lending money to people who would have great difficulty paying it back—is the concept that these people, for the first time, had *access* to capital. Without the existence of capital markets, without people like me and Jack Taylor, none of the dot-com companies, even the so-called good ones, like Amazon, would have been able to raise capital on such attractive terms. The same can be said for just about every bubble, every capital markets phenomenon. In markets, people make mistakes. But for every mistake made, someone, somewhere, benefits.

*Did I lock the door?*
*You locked the door. You did nine-five-one.*
*I can remember doing nine-five-one, but I can't remember locking the door.*
*So get off the bus.*

Being a trader, to me, meant that for the first time in my life, I was looking out for myself. Me looking out for myself was a good thing. Because I was looking out for myself, because I sought to buy low and sell high, good things were happening in the world. A money manager was able to sell something at an inflated price, and his clients—dentists and teachers and bus drivers—all benefited. But I didn't care. I just wanted to get paid.

This came with a price.

For most people, it is their sanity. Go to a casino late at night and observe. Money at risk brings out the worst in human behavior. There is the plainly shitfaced man in his fifties who is betting $2,000 on a single hand of blackjack, ignoring his wife's calls, the phone vibrating incessantly in his pocket. There are the prostitutes. There are the counters, also known as the "advantage" players. All of these creatures exist in the capital markets in one form or another. Their behavior is excusable when there is money at stake. But it makes for a short career.

*Again.*

Back windows. Front windows.

Coffeemaker off. Lights off.

Porch windows.

*This is going to be it. I'm not coming back again.*

*Plastic utensils and Velcro shower curtains are in your future if you keep this up.*

I would be the exception, I thought. I was perfectly suited to trading. A former military officer and math whiz, thoughtful yet aggressive, intellectual yet vulgar, I could survive—no, thrive—in any trading environment. I remembered prices like they were yesterday. I saw patterns. And I was brutal enough to fight for the last penny. I wasn't going to be one of those guys who bailed out after a few years and went to something soft and forgiving, like consulting. I wasn't going to leave the business and write a book about how awful Wall Street was. Pussies.

I walked through life knowing that what I was doing was right. My insides matched my outsides. There is nothing so precious in this world as a man who is in the right place at the right time; who knows that he is doing what he is meant to be doing; who knows that if God exists, He placed him here on this earth to be a trader.

*Oh no.*

On the bus. Almost in the tunnel now.

*Not again.*

But take a hundred people and put them in separate rooms, each with a computer terminal and no windows, and allow them to trade futures. Give them each a million dollars. Don't let them come out for a week. Ninety of them will lose everything. Nine of them will manage to break even, maybe making a few hundred thousand dollars in the process. One of them will get rich.

All of them will go insane trying.

*I thought this was supposed to get better. I thought this was supposed to go away.*

I had gone mad trying. But then, everyone goes mad trying. Lehman Brothers was too small to be an investment bank and too large to be an insane asylum. The difference between me and everyone else was that I was man enough to admit it.

Off the bus and running down the street, back to the house.

*Just tell yourself you're being crazy. That's all it is. This isn't real. It's all in your head.*

Sweating through my suit.

*But when I get like this, I can't tell what's real and what's not.*

*That's why it's called crazy.*

People staring at me.

*Did you remember your meds? I remembered my meds.*

This is a hell of a way to live.

## 1

## Spartacus | October 2, 2007

The market has its own intelligence. It has a sort of malignant omniscience that dictates that the market will do whatever fucks over the most people at any given moment in time. It knows your positions, and it knows your fears. You are a sinner in the hands of an angry God, and your positions are going to pay. Like Santa Claus, sort of, except that the market doesn't care who's been naughty or nice; more often than not, naughty wins. The market cares who is the most exposed, who is the most out over his skis, and who has taken the most risk at any given moment. And once the market has ascertained the point of maximum pain, it will move, violently, in that direction, causing the greatest number of people to lose the most money.

It was moving that way for me today, having just been lifted on two million shares of IWM, an exchange-traded fund that tracks the fortunes of small capitalization stocks. The perpetrator this time was Spartacus, a monstrous hedge fund that managed billions of dollars in assets, run by only a dozen men and boys. Their trading desk consisted of a few Staten Island kids who had walked bass-ackward into a pot of gold, and was led by a Snidely Whiplash character, an evil genius Russian named Yevgeny. Yevgeny was rumored to have earned $50 million last year by picking off slowpoke retard ETF traders like me, hoovering money out of my P&L and into his in a brutal daily transfer of wealth.

Yevgeny didn't give a damn that he was trading small cap stocks. He didn't have an opinion as to whether small cap stocks would outperform large cap stocks on an economic basis. He was not making a strategic investment for the fund. For all he knew, he was trading May wheat. He cared about small cap only because it moved more than large cap; it was more volatile. And with greater volatility comes more opportunities to fuck people over. His trade was causing about $170 million to be rammed into two thousand tiny stocks, increasing the price of each of them by about .2 percent, getting two thousand CEOs momentarily excited for their companies' prospects as they watched their tickers turn green on Yahoo! Finance—that is, until Yevgeny decided to turn around and sell.

This particular trade was already turning into a shit show, because when the fastidious, obsessive sales trader Andrew Duke quoted me, I thought I heard him ask for a price on one million shares. When the ticket arrived electronically on my screen, it read twice as much:

B  IWM  2,000,000  SPRTC  M048392049832

I knew I was in big trouble. I had lost $140,000 before I'd even printed the trade, given that the ETF had rallied several cents, and being short two million shares, I was losing $20,000 a tick. This was going to be an exercise in stuffing ten pounds of shit into a five-pound bag.

D.C. and I looked at each other. We had been working together long enough to be able to communicate by visual semaphore.

When I first met D.C., I didn't like him. He was one of those perfect Ivy League mannequins, all J.Crew and hair helmet. He was also a Garden City guy. Garden City amounts to a massive Wall Street cult on Long Island, where any able-bodied male born within the city limits has a birthright to a job at a major investment bank. My disdain, at the beginning, was barely concealed. But D.C. was no ordinary cake eater. He was, literally, perhaps the best lacrosse player in the country. At five nine (generously) and 150 pounds, you wouldn't figure him to be the world's greatest athlete. He barely lifted weights and managed only the occasional run around Central Park. But he was, quite simply, the most coordinated human being on earth, and nearly ambidextrous at that. People who are gifted in one way are often gifted in others, and as a trader, D.C. was the silent assassin.

Once I began working with him in 2004, I liked him instantly. In addition to his physical gifts, he was the most competitive person I knew. I would occasionally tire of the Hundred Years' War with the sales force. D.C. never backed down. He fought to make money on every single trade. And he was profoundly disappointed when he didn't.

Perhaps the most interesting thing about D.C. was that he was exceedingly uninteresting. He had no deep, dark secrets, no skeletons in his closet, no illicit romances, no addictions, no nothing. It was impossible to believe that someone, especially in this business, could be that well adjusted. He was also a notoriously private person, so even if he was doing lines off a hooker's fake tits at two in the morning in the W Hotel, I was never going to find out. In a way, his profound dullness made him just as much of a misfit as everyone else.

We were a great team: I had the raw smarts and the passion for finance, and he had the trading dexterity and the persistence. Occasionally, however, someone would sneak one past the goalie, and we would have to clean up the mess. This time, it was Spartacus, and this time, it was a million-dollar mess.

"Holy shit," says D.C. I shrug. We'll figure something out.

The market has its own chemistry, its own pressure. Traders, after enough time, learn to trade a market by feel. A trading floor is a room full of dogs, cats, and squirrels that can sense an oncoming storm. All morning, stocks had been like a manhole cover rattling around on the pavement, hinting at some imminent terrific explosion. When Yevgeny bought, the manhole cover shot up into the air.

I bought a million shares as fast and as sloppy as I could. Satisfied with my handiwork, I sat and trembled slightly as I watched IWM trade 20 cents above where I'd offered it. I lost $70,000 on the first million that I covered, and I was out $200,000 on the second million, which I hadn't even touched yet. This is important, because I'd have to buy even more IWM in order to trade out of the dangerous position, and that would only make the losses worse. If you have one hundred thousand shares to buy, you'll have to buy it at progressively higher prices to fill your order. The purchases you make at 10:30 drive up the cost of purchases you make at 10:35.

I was trying to restrain myself. The old me would have been pounding on the desk until I bruised the heels of my hand, and yelling, "*Goddamn motherfuckers!*" at the top of my lungs. But no matter what Spartacus or any of my other customers did, I was determined to act professionally and to not lose my cool. I had embarrassed myself one too many times with a hurricane of a temper tantrum on the trading floor, which was always followed up by an emotional hangover on the way home. The market, along with its malignant intelligence and chemistry, now had the new me: the cooler-than-the-other-side-of-the-pillow me, the future senior vice president and general sizeola Lehman Brothers trader.

I had two choices. I could hedge the trade now and lock in a sure $270,000 loss, which would destroy any profits we'd make for the rest of the day. Or I could wait to see what the market did and hope to buy back my IWM at a lower price later. The problem was, if I used a binomial tree to model each and every possible outcome, the likelihood of breaking even was less than one in twenty.

The probability was actually worse than that, given that it was Spartacus. The hedge fund was big enough and determined enough to push the market in their direction. When Spartacus bought, they didn't buy just from one bank, they went around Wall Street and bought from everybody. I saw the prints going up.

*09:52:02* IWM 1.0M 85.44 T

Only forty-two seconds later, another IWM transaction with another bank, and then another, each one driving the price higher . . .

*09:52:44* IWM 2.0M 85.47 T
*09:53:30* IWM 1.0M 85.55 T
*09:54:11* IWM 2.0M 85.61 T

This is what we called "getting steamrolled" or "shitting on our print." It meant that Spartacus had an order that was too large to give to a single counterparty, so they were splitting it up and spreading it around. It is good etiquette to give the entire order to one broker and let him work it over time to get the best price. It is bad etiquette to spray the street with your order flow like that—bad enough behavior to get you cut off from most places—but Spartacus denied it every time. They lied about their trades, even when there was a gargantuan pile of evidence against them. They were bad guys.

I turned to D.C., whom I always consulted in times of stress. "What do you think?" I asked him. He shook his head solemnly. This was out of his realm of experience, taking a $250K hickey before a trade was even half over.

"Okay," I said to the speechless D.C., "I think Spartacus is trying to bully this market higher, and I think it's going to run out of gas. No way am I buying back these IWMs—not until they get back to scratch."

When I am in a losing trade, my body undergoes a physiological reaction. I cannot leave my seat; I feel chained to it. I hunch over my desk, staring at the screen, watching the chart go higher, tick for tick. I don't really sweat, but I do tremble with fear and rage. I curse my life, and I hate myself in spite of the hundreds of thousands of dollars that I make. I am sick of being the doormat for all these arrogant hedge fund punks. I want to choke the living shit out of the sales trader that brought in the trade. I desperately need a drink. I feel the urge to verbally destroy the first person that talks to me. I start to think that torture is too good for some people. I hate everything and everybody, I see nothing but darkness, and the only thing that makes me feel better is even more hate; a higher, more cynical form of revulsion.

I watched the P&L on my GPM, the software which gave me a real-time view of my P&L: ($330,000). ($375,000). ($420,000). *This is getting ridiculous. Am I just being stubborn? Or do I have a rational explanation for why I think the market is suddenly going to reverse in my direction? I can't lock in a $420,000 loss. It can't possibly get worse.*

It gets worse. The market rallies more: ($610,000). ($700,000).

I had lost $700,000, and I hadn't touched a share of the stock.

D.C. looked at me. "This is a disaster," he said. "Yes," I agreed, but I was frozen in my hunched-over position, staring at the chart, and I couldn't manage to say much else. I felt like I'd swallowed a medicine ball.

It's one thing to get run over on a trade. It's another thing altogether to get run over for a whole *percent* in fifteen minutes. It's unlikely for even entire asset classes—stocks or bonds as a collective entity—to move a percent in fifteen minutes. Such is Spartacus. You can't just take the other side of their trades; you have to buy with. Once their trades start hitting the tape, every little weasel watching sees the prints and the price action and starts pushing it higher.

Then something miraculous happened. The market stopped going up. It began to consolidate. It seemed like it *wanted* to go higher, but it couldn't. It was possible that Spartacus had bullied the market one too many times.

IWM started to trade lower. And lower. Now, the first instinct a trader has when he's lost $700,000 is to close out the trade at down $600,000 and declare victory. I repeated to D.C., "I am not buying back a share of this thing until it gets back to unch."

Now, *unch*, short for "unchanged," is kind of an arbitrary level to aim for. Behaviorists, like the Nobel Prize winner Daniel Kahneman, believe that markets are driven by decision theory and information biases, and they call this "anchoring." Nobody likes to lose money on a trade, so they'll risk losing even more—an infinite amount—just to break even. It makes no sense to choose the price at which you got lifted as an anchoring point; in fact, it's completely arbitrary. But this is what I was doing, and I knew it. I was ashamed of myself, but I was tired of losing money to these bastards, and I was going to break even on a trade if it killed me.

The P&L started to move my way: ($550,000). ($490,000). ($425,000). I began to ease the death grip on my mouse. I sat back in my chair a little bit. My neck muscles began to relax.

In some areas of the financial markets, it's possible for both the buyer and the seller to make money on a trade. That may seem counterintuitive, but it happens quite a bit. In ETFs, however, it's a zero-sum game. Stock goes up, buyer wins, seller loses. Stock goes down, seller wins, buyer loses. It turned my customers, even the friendly ones, into my enemies.

Every day I went to work and went to war with Spartacus. It was a war we could not win; most of the time we got run over on their trades, and if we ever made money on a trade, Spartacus would demand a price improvement, threatening to pull their business if we didn't acquiesce. Heads I win, tails you lose. All I could do was try to minimize the damage. The fund had paid us $6 million in commissions this year, and we had lost all of it and then some; we found ourselves trying to use other customers to subsidize Spartacus's losing business. I wanted them to just go away.

Andrew Duke didn't want them to go away. He was the sales trader who had the unpleasant task of covering Spartacus within his larger book of bastards. He was a human shield. Tall and competent, Duke had worked his way up from being an "admin," a glorified secretary, into a sales role. He was grumpy, and deeply cynical, like me. I liked him. But we were not friends. Wall Street had made us enemies.

Duke was compensated based on how much his customers traded with the firm. Whether they traded stock, ETFs, or options, his customers paid commissions. The more his customers traded, the more Duke got paid. Duke didn't want Spartacus to go away. He wanted them to keep trading, even if it meant that, on balance, Lehman Brothers lost money to them. I was compensated by the profit and loss of my cozy little ETF desk, and I had no interest in losing money. It didn't matter how much I complained to Duke that Spartacus was a loser—he was going to keep picking up the phone anyway.

Duke looked over at me. We made eye contact. He looked away. Duke knew that we'd gotten hosed on the trade, and he didn't particularly want to have a conversation about it.

Meanwhile, IWM continued to fall. I started to jiggle my legs, which is what I did when I was happy. We were close to breaking even on the trade.

*Enough is enough.* I had a million shares to buy, and I started to bid, 100,000 shares at a time, in penny increments. *Figure bid for a hundred. Ninety-nine bid for a hundred. Ninety-eight bid for a hundred.* The market continued to fall. *Come to Butt-head.* I beckoned.

I finished buying stock. I looked up at GPM: ($70,000). We received $60,000 in commissions on the trade, so I had lost $10,000, which was essentially breaking even.

I high-fived D.C., which was sad, because we were high-fiving each other about losing money. I then walked over to Duke and stood behind him.

"How bad was it?" he asked.

"Take a guess."

Duke winced. "I can't even imagine," he said. "Sorry about the mix-up, but I thought I pretty clearly said two million—"

"We lost ten grand," I stated flatly.

Duke stood up and held out a hand. "Now, that is some trading. *No way* I would have been able to stay short that long."

"Guess that's why they pay me the big bucks." In all honesty, Duke probably got paid more than me just to pick up the phone.

But I had gutted out a near seven-figure loss and made it all the way back to scratch, staring down one of the biggest hedge funds on the street. If trading had a hall of fame, I would be in it for that trade alone.

I got up from my desk. I had to hang a whizz—I'd swallowed down a giant coffee and been glued to the screens, white-knuckling the IWM trade for the better part of the morning. I walked down the aisle of salespeople and looked over their shoulders at their screens. A few had ESPN.com up. Takeareport.com. One girl was shopping for shoes.

*Lazy.* As I opened the door to the men's room, I thought about how much money we could all make if people put in an eight-hour day. Here was a group of highly intelligent, highly educated people, with all the resources, all the information, all the market data in the world, all the tools and the talent necessary to suck money out of the market, and people chose to spend their days shoe shopping. Theories on market efficiency had killed people's work ethic. If you can't beat the market, then why try? *But you can win,* I thought. *The market can be beaten.* And here you had people sitting there dicking the dog and waiting for the phone to ring. How about making outgoing calls? How about looking up a list of institutions and cold-calling accounts? How about doing some technical analysis? How about coming up with some trade ideas to send to clients? This was the most passive, spoiled, unmotivated group of motherfuckers I had ever come into contact with.

I stepped up to the urinal. At that moment, I was hung like a seahorse. Risk kills libido. The reason hedge fund traders hang around clubs for "models and bottles" is because it is a substitution effect for their sex drive, which evaporates when exposed to huge amounts of risk on a daily basis. I was like a neutered cat. Most weeks, I would forget to whack off. I didn't even have any blood flow. I was worried about atrophy. Christ.

Back on the trading floor, the buzz from earlier that morning had died down. The sun was starting to come through the windows facing Seventh Avenue. Analysts were starting to compile lunch runs. Trading, like sailing, is 95 percent boredom and 5 percent sheer terror. Activity comes in spurts, and most of it happens in the first hour after the open. There is a perception that it gets busy around the close, but it really doesn't. Dozens of traders were milling about the floor, each one making at least a million bucks, and they were getting paid for about a half hour of work.

Before I even sat back down at my desk, I could tell from the pinched look on D.C.'s face that we had been picked off once again. I didn't even have to ask—Spartacus. D.C. pointed at a chart of XLE on his screen, the energy ETF. It looked like a monstrous priapism.

*Goddamnit.* I looked at the CTI. Sure enough, there was a buy ticket for 500,000 XLE. I looked at the quote monitor—there were three other orders being printed outside of Lehman. Normally, when the market moves one direction, stocks are generally correlated; that is, they all tend to move in the same direction. Right then, energy stocks were moving up while the rest of the stock market was going down. Spartacus had a knack for being long the one sector that was going up or being short the one sector that was going down. Either they were astute investors, or they were using predatory trading techniques to force the market their way. Either way, it was impossible to trade with someone who was *always right.*

The more I thought about it, the angrier I became. The vast majority of our customers were good citizens, and we had one assface that was fucking things up for everybody. I spent hours trying to trade proprietarily to make a little extra scratch, and these guys would put mustard on it and eat it. And there was an additional cost, too: the time and psychic energy we spent managing Spartacus's bombs was time that we could have spent actively trading on our own behalf. The time I spent that morning staring at IWM, I could have spent looking for a spot to get short the market; D.C. and I might have been able to share a high five that actually meant something.

"Duke!" I yelled. He looked at me. "What the fuck? Didn't I just talk to you about this?" He shrugged. It was useless yelling at him; he was just the order taker, the conduit, the traffic cop.

"Fucking piece of shit! Motherfucker!" People were beginning to pay attention to us, waiting for another famous Dillian blowup. I wasn't going to give them the satisfaction. I was a new man. No more hothead Dillian. I was Buddhist Dillian.

Marty, my boss, turns around from his robot wars with the futures and asks me what's going on. Marty can't stop trading. He looks like Tom Hulce playing Mozart in *Amadeus*, who can't stop composing music, turning green while thinking up the Requiem on his deathbed.

"Fucking Spartacus again. They blew our heads off on IWM this morning, and they're doing it again on XLE. Look. Whole market selling off, XLE in our face."

"Trades going up outside of us, as always," adds D.C.

Marty puts on his sober manager hat. "Have you talked to Duke yet?"

"Talk to him? I talk to him all the time! He can't do anything about it. This is a bigger issue than Duke. This needs to go all the way up to the Snake. Or higher."

Marty is pursing his lips, preparing to speak the truth. "You can't have that conversation, because on the structured flow side, they've been buying worst-of call options like they're going to the electric chair, and we've been printing money off the business. We're making a lot more money in worst-ofs than you're losing in ETFs."

This was a familiar theme. ETFs are intended to be the loss leader. The missile sponge. We are supposed to give away capital for free so that people will trade sexier products with more edge. On the football team of trading, we are the left tackle. No glorious touchdown passes for us, just the daily grind at the line of scrimmage, and an unimpressive high-six-figure salary to go with it.

So we were stuck with Spartacus. It was like having the ugly stripper follow you around and sit in your lap all night. You can't exactly tell her to go away without causing a scene.

The more I thought about it, the more depressed I became. I went into trading to become a rock star, to make triple-digit returns, to become fantastically wealthy, and to be the envy of the financial community. What I was, in effect, was one of the snails that cleaned the fish tank of the financial markets. I spent most of my time playing defense, trying to prevent disasters while making tiny amounts of money on the margins. I was a janitor. And here we all were, with our Ivy League educations and our social class and our pedigrees and our friends, and we were all in one big room on a daily basis pissing into the wind. The number of people who were true financial decision makers on Wall Street was frighteningly small. The Soroses, the Falcones, the Paulsons—there were only a handful of people that truly influenced financial markets. I was not one of them. And I was never going to be one of them.

What made it worse was that the sell-side trader was held in such low regard. We were all considered to be whores, basically; but beyond that, even the cash equities trader or the credit default swap trader garnered some respect. They were experts on individual companies: they knew and understood their stories of success or failure, were intimately familiar with sector trends, and had a near monopoly on investment flows. They were in high demand from the buy-side community because every buy-side trader wanted to pick their brains on who was long, who was short, and what they thought stock XYZ was going to do. Conversely, nobody wanted to talk to an ETF trader. An ETF trader was not an expert on individual stocks; he was an expert on liquidity. He was an expert on decidedly unsexy liquidity. He had the brains and the tools of a program trader and the dirtbag customers of an options trader. He was a wannabe, a nobody, an orphan.

*I am never going anywhere in this organization.* ETFs fell under volatility trading. The next logical promotion I could get would be head of volatility. But an ETF trader can't become head of volatility; that's like having a paralegal get nominated for the Supreme Court. I was condemned to a life of mediocrity.

I hate my job.

Duke yelled over to us. "A million SPYs, how?"

He was asking for a two-way market on a million shares of SPY, the S&P (Standard & Poor's) 500 exchange-traded fund. It was for Spartacus. Again. Ugly stripper. I was supposed to show him a price where he could sell one million SPYs, and a price where he could buy one million SPYs, his choice. This was a reasonably big trade, about $135 million.

D.C. fielded the trade. "Twenty-eight at thirty-two!" D.C. was telling him he could sell them at twenty-eight cents or buy them at thirty-two. The "big number," or the "handle," was not relevant to making a market, whether it was $135.32 or $136.32.

"*Sold!*" yelled Duke.

Simultaneously, the market lurched lower. The price was now $136.20, before we even had a chance to hedge. Like that, $80,000 just disappeared.

*What the fuck.*

I snapped.

I grabbed a tape dispenser, lifted it high above my head, and slammed it into the desk with all my might.

"I'm gonna have his BALLS IN A JAR!" I yelled at Duke at the top of my lungs. Except, all anybody heard was "BALLS IN A JAR!"

Silence.

An undercurrent of *"ballsinajarwhat'sthatsupposedtomeanidon'tknowpret tyfunnyballsinajar"* spreads across the floor.

Meanwhile, a cloud of dust settled around me. The tape dispenser had been filled with sand for weight. There was sand all over my suit, in my hair, on my glasses, my keyboard, my turret, and everywhere else. There was also a pool of blood forming on the desk, mixed in with the sand, where the serrated edge of the tape dispenser had nearly sliced off my pinky finger. I was standing there, trembling with rage, covered in blood and sand, all over having failed to prevent an $80,000 loss.

Now, $80,000 may sound like a lot. But what I didn't know was that the mortgage desk had risk several orders of magnitude larger. I didn't know that the leveraged loan book was big and toxic. I didn't know that Lehman's real estate portfolio was absolutely pornographic. There were assholes on every floor in the building who'd built up massive Captain Jack positions that they were unable to liquidate, and they were pissing money into the street. Our leaders were completely ignorant of the last eighty years of financial history, seemingly unaware of the fact that markets go through cycles of boom and bust, and that twenty-five years of credit expansion had led the financial markets to the edge of disaster.

I might have been able to save $80,000, but I wasn't going to be able to save Lehman.

## 2

Drive | September 11, 2001

In all the time I'd spent staring at the World Trade Center, not once had I imagined what it would look like on fire.

I don't see well at night when I'm not wearing my glasses. I was driving, and where we were, there were no streetlights. The George Washington Bridge was closed, as well as the Tappan Zee. We were headed to Bear Mountain, the only other place to make a Hudson River crossing.

We were going to visit my mother. We didn't know for how long—hopefully, no more than a couple of days. Within a week, I thought, this would all be sorted out, and I could get back to work. Our associate class at Lehman Brothers was in the middle of rotations, the process where new associates find out which trading desk they're going to work on, and that day, I was supposed to have met with the corporate bond traders. I'd been nervous about it—very nervous—because they had the only viable trading job being offered to the entire class.

Competition was going to be fierce. Already I knew I was going to have to fight off at least ten other guys for the seat. And I had very little competitive advantage. I didn't know anything about credit. Other people did. It was a long shot.

My wife was with me, and the cat. Both were quiet. There wasn't a lot to say. It had been a profoundly shitty day. Hours earlier, I had volunteered at the police department to help the people coming back from the city. I stood at the ferry terminal and handed out towels. I expected them to be grateful. I expected them to be relieved. Instead they were angry. They were furious. They took the towels, scowling, without looking at me.

The Bear Mountain Bridge, I would eventually learn, stands next to Bear Mountain State Park, which has a zoo, of sorts, and lots of grass for tossing around a Frisbee. Years later, I would hike through the park and over the bridge, along the Appalachian Trail. There were signs posted along the footpath, with free telephones, talking you out of jumping, persuading you not to commit suicide. Don't jump. At the time, I had no intention of jumping.

I was relying on my wife for directions. This was a new route for me. Usually we took the George Washington, then went north up the Saw Mill River Parkway, then east on the Cross County Parkway, then north up the Hutchinson River Parkway, which merged into the Merritt Parkway, which was how we avoided the traffic on I-95. The Bear Mountain detour was taking us well out of our way. I'd thought we would get there by midnight, but now it was looking like two at the earliest.

This wasn't really what I had in mind when I gave up my Coast Guard job to come to Wall Street. On a recruiting trip the year before, I'd happened upon one of the street vendors selling New York City souvenirs to unsuspecting tourists. There were hundreds of these street vendors all doing the same thing around the city, but this particular street vendor was *mine*. He was selling photographs of both the World Trade Center and the World Financial Center. I bought a portrait of the towers that had been taken from the street, looking up at their vastness, with wispy clouds in the background, and another of the World Financial Center, with the twin towers in the background, taken from the middle of the Hudson River on a clear day. I took them home and hung them in my living room as a testament to the possible, so that I would be reminded on a daily basis of the superiority of American capitalism. *There* is where I am going to work, in those important buildings with all those people and all that money. You people think too small. I am going to work with people who think big.

I spent a few years of my childhood living on Governors Island, and I could see the twin towers out the front window of our apartment. I'd spent my childhood worshipping them. I used to wonder what kind of industry or commerce was going on that could possibly employ enough people to fill up those two massive structures. Over time, I learned that things of great consequence happened in those buildings, and that playing cops and robbers on the high seas was of piddling importance compared to the amount of capital being moved through the towers every single day. The people who worked in those buildings were the most important people that you had never heard of, and they paid more taxes in one year than most people managed to save in a lifetime. I learned that the World Trade Center was the center of the financial universe, that I had grown up right across the street from it without really understanding what it meant, and that it was my destiny to experience it.

My father was a Coast Guard aviator, and my mother, a teacher and substance abuse counselor. They were unhappily married and would divorce when I was seven, and my memories from that particular period in time are not pleasant. But I was attending one of the most prestigious private schools in the city, which let me skip grades in my course work, and to live in New York at even the age of six or seven is to learn that anything is possible.

After the divorce, I moved to an unfortunate town in southeastern Connecticut with my mother, and I navigated school-yard politics poorly. I was the class nerd, and I was bullied a little, and I struggled with weight—although by today's standards, I was downright slender. And it is difficult to be the smart kid in the class, the musician, picked third to last for kickball teams, in an anti-intellectual rural school, but I managed.

Ever since I was a child, I have been fiercely competitive. I lack natural athletic ability, but I *try* harder than everyone else. I run out grounders. I dive for balls. If I try something, anything, whether it is a spelling bee, or a marching band competition, or a wrestling match, I will win. That didn't carry over to academics, though. In college I would be a solid B student; not because I got B's, but because I would typically get all A's and an F. I made a conscious decision that I would rather get an F than a B, because to get a B meant that you had tried and failed, and an F meant you didn't even try, so nobody would know if you'd failed or not. So I spent an equal amount of time on dean's list as I did on academic probation.

It turned out that finance was full of people like me; people who were exceptionally good at standardized tests (I may not know the right answer, but I can pick it out of a lineup); people who didn't care so much about jumping through all these stupid hoops to get straight A's. If they did, they did without trying. Finance attracts people like that because, as a trader, it doesn't matter if you show up on time for class or take notes or kiss ass, as long as you are making money, because that is the only thing that is important. And making money isn't a function of *work*, it is a function of *intelligence*.

There was no history of ardent capitalism in my family. On both sides of my family, it was mostly public servants.

I went to the Coast Guard Academy because I saw my dad's yearbook. These cadets looked like supermen. Washboard abs, doing push-ups, picking up girls in Europe while on the Coast Guard Training cutter *Eagle*, smiling, sunburned—they had it all. I guess I wanted to be masculine more than anything. That was an incredibly bad reason to go there. I hadn't realized until my first week of swab summer that I would actually someday have to go to sea.

I was restless in the Coast Guard. It was anti-intellectual, and I felt like my brain was atrophying. I was also uncomfortable with the rewards system that the service had set up: pretty much everyone was promoted on schedule as long as you didn't screw up, and everyone pretty much got the same medals and awards. It was difficult to distinguish yourself. How you distinguished yourself was through *politics*—getting the choice billets, managing your career—and I didn't have any appetite for that.

Supposedly, when I was in the military, I was in harm's way. I guessed that I had done dangerous things. I had carried a gun. With my gun, a standard-issue nine millimeter, I had boarded vessels looking for drugs, and found none. The probability of something bad happening was infinitesimally small—a shot hadn't been fired in anger in the service for years. But I was one of the loyal German shepherds: the highly trained individuals with short haircuts who worked to make the country safe. Then I had decided that making money was more important. Now look what happened.

Earlier that day, I had been outside the World Financial Center, across the street from the World Trade Center, reading the newspaper. Actually, I was studying the newspaper, trying to memorize what was going on in the markets. After six weeks of Lehman Brothers training classes on bond mathematics and option volatility, and a lot of cocktail parties with Miller Lites and chicken on a stick, the rotation period had arrived. It's a mating dance, and it's as much about personality as it is about ability; nearly everyone who has been hired, by that point, is competent. Rotations were about making sure that you picked someone you wanted to sit next to for five years, whose personal habits you'd come to understand with a shocking level of intimacy: how they acted out when they lost money, how they smelled when they were hungover, and how they tried to conceal their personal conversations. The rotations were about *fit*. To me, fit was an elusive concept. I wasn't one of the countless Ivy League resumes. I was not a lacrosse player. I had an unusual background, and I was going to stick out like a—well, like a poor kid at Lehman Brothers.

I'd picked an assortment of desks where I wanted to interview—really, anything with a trading job—and the desks had gone through a gargantuan pile of resumes and picked out the candidates that *they* wanted to interview. I received all five of my picks and nobody else, which meant that there was zero demand for my services among the business units. They were bastards, anyway. But I had only five rotations, while some of my classmates had twelve or thirteen. Frankly, I was a little hurt, but not surprised. I might as well have graduated from Okeechobee Swamp Community College. Nobody had heard of the Coast Guard Academy, nobody knew what it was or that it was one of the most selective schools in the country, and nobody really cared that I had just put myself through grad school at night while working two jobs. But I was here to tell my story. I was here to tell the corporate bond traders that I was an animal, that I could function for days without sleep, that I had a near limitless capacity for hard work, that I could hustle, and that I could brute-force my way into making money even if I didn't possess the proper credentials. At Lehman, this should have been an easy argument. The firm was known for its scrappiness. What I didn't know was that the firm was also known for its elitism.

I had spent the better part of the week cramming my head full of facts on credit, but, realistically, I wasn't going to become an expert in only six or seven days. And while I knew the basics about corporate bonds, I knew very little about how the market was changing, how credit default swaps were just beginning to gain in popularity, and I knew next to nothing about CDOs (collateralized debt obligations), synthetic CDOs, or any of the other structured credit products. I didn't know anything about correlation trading. I didn't know anything about the indices. When the credit folks came down to talk to the associate class, I didn't understand a word they said—I understood only that they were hiring precisely one trader and that I wanted that trader to be me. The old fierce determination to win was coming back. I was going to get this job.

At least until the building caught on fire. In case you were wondering what happens when somebody yells "Bomb!" after a loud explosion, let me tell you. People start running around in circles. That's what I did; I dropped my coffee and started to run. First I ran south, then I ran east, then I ran west. I was in the middle of a cloud of overpaid, free fucking electrons, at the marina outside the World Financial Center. Then I noticed that other people were looking up. So I looked up too.

I was annoyed. I was supposed to come into Lehman Brothers and get this job. Now the goddamn World Trade Center was on fire. What the fuck.

I listened to the crowd around me. Some people were talking about a plane. Had a plane done this? I wondered if some jackass with one too many Bloody Marys in his system, and maybe a death wish, had decided to take a swan dive into the fucking twin towers. It seemed highly improbable, a one-in-a-trillion shot. Pilot error doesn't get you to T-bone the World Trade Center. If someone did this, it was a suicide job.

*That's a big fire.*

The fire was burning out an entire floor, a few floors down from the top, and was now spreading higher. This was all happening relatively quickly. It occurred to me that more than a few people had died, or were dying in there. This was kind of serious. Who knows if they will still have rotations? I figured they still might, considering that it was just some little Cessna that had crashed into the building. I had a contact number for the credit desk, but I didn't have a cell phone. I had to go inside.

What I didn't realize was that even though the markets hadn't opened yet, they were reacting: futures on stock indices trade around the clock. When the plane hit, the futures dipped, then gyrated. As a trader, I would learn that liquidity disappears when the market receives news that it doesn't understand. Nobody wants to trade. Bids and offers vanish. There were those who thought that the collision was just a fluke, and they were buying. There were those who were convinced that it was something more sinister, and they were selling. Furthermore, stocks open later than just about everything else. Bond traders get in to work earlier than the equities guys, and their markets were already open. Everything was going nuts. If you want to know when something important in the world happens, don't watch the news, watch the markets. Even if I had gone inside to talk to my interviewers, they wouldn't have been in a position to speak with me. They were really, really busy.

*That fire is getting bigger.*

I walked back to the table where I'd been sitting, picked my coffee cup off the ground, and took a gulp. I began to pack my things. I was going to find my point of contact and make sure that this interview was still on.

A gasp went up from the crowd. Somebody jumped.

I looked up. I'd missed it. This was serious now. People were getting hurt, and here I was, an able-bodied twenty-seven-year-old male, freshly out of the military, about to walk past a disaster on his way to a meaningless interview. I resolved to help out. I swallowed the rest of my coffee, threw away my newspaper, and jogged toward the World Trade Center.

There was a group of men standing on the northwest corner and a group of women sitting on the sidewalk at the southwest corner of an intersection a block away from Two World Trade Center. There was a solitary policeman, telling people to move back. He looked like he was shitting his pants. They were all looking up.

I looked up too. I didn't like what I saw.

The signs on the Bear Mountain Bridge footpath read: "Life is worth living." Is it? What if you are about to be burned to death? What if you have to choose between being consumed by flames and a few seconds of terror, then nothing? Signs on bridges don't cover every scenario. In some cases, it is acceptable to jump.

As I drove toward the Hudson, I tried not to think about the things that I'd seen. But there was one image that I couldn't get out of my mind: the image of the second plane crashing into the second World Trade tower right over my head, exploding into a big, *red* fireball. God, was it red. I tapped the brakes and felt a pain in my shins. I'd sprinted away from the building at full speed, in dress shoes, and my feet, my shins, and my calves were still on fire. It was the fastest I had ever run.

The Bear Mountain Bridge is the lowest point along the entire Appalachian Trail.

I remembered running toward the water. I didn't want to stand next to any buildings. It was clear by that point that we were under attack. I listened to the crowd. Some people had heard about an attack on the Pentagon too. I thought about jumping in the river. Safer there, maybe. But I made my way to the ferry to get home. Some people were still showing their IDs. They were trying to find comfort in simple routines.

On the top level of the ferry, I saw a familiar face. A convertible bond salesman. I couldn't remember his name.

"You hear about Cantor Fitzgerald?" he asked me.

I shook my head. I didn't know who that was.

"They were on the top floors of the first building. Their phone lines were open. You could hear them screaming."

I wondered when I would get back to work.

It all depended on how the buildings collapsed. Our headquarters was right across the street. Was Lehman Brothers dead? Was I still going to have a job? Did I leave the military for nothing? Was this all a huge mistake?

My wife had heard about the attack, but there was no way for her to get ahold of me. She'd walked down to the water to look at the burning buildings and imagined the worst. When she returned home, there was a message from some unknown guy on the answering machine. It said, "I'm sorry to tell you that—well, that . . . fuck it."

She thought I was dead.

I drove. I drove away from my job, my new apartment, and my new life. I drove back home, to my childhood. The next day, in search of a connection, I would materialize on my high school campus, talking to teachers, talking to students, telling them my story.

I rolled down the windows in the car. I was a survivor, I thought. I was going to make it.

Just keep driving.

## 3

## Vice Asshole | Fall 2001

I'm a fucking security guard. Doop dee doo.

The one thing I learned about investment banks in the fall of 2001 was that they exist nowhere. The physical space they occupy is irrelevant. Sure, they're headquartered in fancy buildings with lobbies carved out of Italian marble and exotic Russian women acting as corporate security. Sure, they house thousands of souped-up desktop computers, real atom splitters, and tens of thousands of flat-panel monitors. There are stacks of prospectuses, there are trade tickets, there are Lucite deal toys, but none of these gadgets turns a street address into an investment bank. An investment bank is people. The real assets of the firm walk out the front door at the end of the day.

If the plane had flown eight hundred feet to the west, we would have been like Cantor Fitzgerald: literally nothing left. But while it was heartbreaking, devastating, and, above all, infuriating to lose our world headquarters—and more importantly, our brand-new trading floor—to a pickup basketball team of pusillanimous peckerheads, in the end, it was a *nyah-nyah-nyah* moment because the surviving employees (one had been killed) could simply board rubber rafts and row across the Hudson River to our offices in Jersey City. In many ways, we were lucky.

There was still plenty of work to be done, though. The backup facility, 101 Hudson Street, was the tallest building in town at the time, but it was little more than office space, occupied by an abandoned colony of information technology geeks. To house Lehman's trading floor, it had to be outfitted with the fastest, biggest networking cable imaginable. And it had to be done fast. Guys wearing shirts that were any color other than white worked around the clock to make it happen.

There were aesthetic improvements that needed to be made as well. The room had been one giant cube farm. Dudes with hacksaws came in and sawed the shit out of the cubicles, lopping off the top halves to create something of a vista across the makeshift trading floor. You can't have prairie dogs peeking over the tops of their cubicles to buy and sell. Computers were hauled in, though people were going to have to make do with only one or two monitors instead of the usual three, four, or five. The primitive telephones (practically rotary dial) had to be replaced with the ubiquitous trading turret, a state-of-the-art contrivance that houses hundreds of phone lines to exchanges, clients, and other traders within the firm.

They did not, unfortunately, improve the shitters. At eight thirty in the morning, there was already a full house—long lines of uncomfortable men gripping the *New York Post*, waiting for the can.

I was a spectator to all this. Actually, I wasn't even a spectator. I was sitting at home, drawing a paycheck, which I found bewildering after spending so many years getting paid virtually nothing to bust my ass. Because there was room for only so many MBAs in the new (but really old) building, our associate class was instructed to stay home and wait for further instructions. In the meantime, we were getting paid a lot of money to wait. I spent my time sleeping (twelve hours a day), drinking (thirty-two-ounce plastic cups full of Jack and Coke), and rolling up the windows whenever I drove by Newark International Airport. (I no longer liked the sound that airplanes made.)

And I went surfing. Boogie boarding, rather. With Dave Lane.

Dave and I were fast friends. This means little, because Dave was fast friends with everyone. Then again, I was fast friends with approximately no one, so maybe it meant a lot. Dave was an expansive personality, a gregarious WASP whose meager resume (started and failed at his own business, MBA from a top school, no GMAT scores) said more about him than an impressive one ever could have. Dave knew, or at least appeared to know, that he was the rising star in our associate class—the guidon bearer, the unofficial leader—and he was ready to bleed Lehman green, without feeling compelled to list some trivial accomplishments on a piece of paper. He wore the right things in the right way (crisp shirts and pressed slacks), and he said the right things (always speaking clearly, smiling, displaying an impressive vocabulary) without trying very hard. When he used his cell phone, he held the mouthpiece up to his face, with the other end pointing toward the sky, saying things like *"you fucking guy."* This was to show that he was talking and not listening. He was an easy person to get to know, and a very difficult person to get to know well. Most people reserve a corner of themselves, keeping it hidden from view, for privacy's sake. For all his extroversion, Dave hid more than most.

So we went surfing. I was flattered that he asked.

He picked me up in his Jeep, and off we went to the Jersey Shore—a real beach town, a surfer town, on a cloudy day in October. The Garden State Parkway was sparsely populated. There were very few people out by the water, and the ones that were there had long hair, hard, knotted deltoid muscles, and wet suits. The air was heavy with the potential for rain. Dave had a long board, a short board, a wet suit, a surf shirt, an extra wet suit, an extra surf shirt, a dog (which he'd left at home), wax, surf shoes, and three pairs of sunglasses, not including the ones he would eventually buy at the surf shop. I had a boogie board, $30, and my bad self.

I had always been too clumsy to surf. I had also been too clumsy to play on monkey bars, climb trees, navigate an obstacle course, and do backflips off a diving board. I kept the training wheels on my bicycle for a long time. I was a cautious child who had grown into a cautious adult. I would never ride a motorcycle or go bungee jumping or skydiving. I would work on a trading floor, develop a soft abdomen, and avoid physical contact with others.

We spent the afternoon bobbing around on our boards beyond the break as the sun tried and failed to burn through the gray clouds. A light rain appeared and spattered the water around us. When you are surfing, I discovered, you don't care if you get any more wet. You are as wet as wet can be. We talked about credit spreads: "Do you think that Wal-Mart paper could ever trade inside of US Treasuries?" I asked. He called me a zucchini. We talked about our jobs: "Do you think there are going to be layoffs?" I asked. He called me a baboon. I wondered which desk I would end up on. Dave already knew. I wondered if there would be another terrorist attack. Dave had no idea. I felt like the yippy Chihuahua in orbit around Spike the Bulldog in the Hanna-Barbera cartoon. I didn't mind. I was happy to have a friend. I went home and had a king-size Jack and Coke and slept for twelve hours, then woke the next day, trying not to think about my job or 9/11 or anything else.

There was a group beginning to coalesce around Dave Lane, and I was proud to be a part of it. Things came easy for us. It was becoming clear that the associate class was splitting in two: those that were able and those that were unable. There were athletes and nonathletes. I was, for once in my life, hanging out with the cool kids.

We went out to dinner once, my whole crew of newfound friends and I, at Churrascaria Plataforma. I was unfamiliar with the concept of a Brazilian meat bonanza. Red means stop, green means go. Someone ordered fruity, fizzy, unpronounceable drinks. Mine was small. Dave Lane was at the head of the table, of course, where he pointed his fingers in the air and did a little birthday dance. Brad Young was there, a geology PhD who had left the cozy but political world of academics for the pursuit of filthy mammon. He was tall, blond, and handsome, and alternated between brilliance and absentmindedness. He showed up forty-five minutes late, as was his custom. Adam Cohen arrived on time, along with his limp; I learned later that he had lost a leg to cancer at the age of nine. His impassioned knowledge of sports, particularly 1980s baseball, was pretty impressive; he was a younger version of Howard Cosell. Chris Vincent, a sunny Californian and metrosexual of questionable orientation had come, as had Wilson James, a grizzled thirtysomething who tended to speak in streams of consciousness, and who was the only one of us mature enough to have children. There were girls too; a skinny, nervous former accountant and an earnest, affectionate Eastern European who we referred to as the Romanian Nightmare.

It would be the most expensive dinner of my life. Dave ordered every appetizer in sight and several bottles of wine, taking out his cell phone occasionally to yell *"you fucking guy"* into the mouthpiece while smiling. When Adam cleaned his plate four times in succession, Dave Lane announced to the group that he had a hollow leg. I was worried about money, but nobody else looked terribly concerned—they seemed to have a limitless capacity for financial pain. I tried to remember that I'd walked away from my $45,000 of military pay into a job that paid me $85,000 a year, plus a $25,000 signing bonus, plus a $10,000 relocation bonus, plus a $30,000 year-end guaranteed bonus. But these other kids had grown up in the rich suburbs of New York and Chicago and thought nothing of dropping $100 on dinner. I had been raised by my divorced mother on $10,000 a year. I could have lived for two weeks on $100. I ordered another $10 fizzy thing.

We went drinking, a lot, back then. There was nothing quite so enjoyable in those post-9/11 times as a stiff Jack and Coke, particularly the first one. The first one I would drink in the daytime, in a dark bar where the sunlight intruded, preferably in a highball glass the size of a fifty-five-gallon drum, and it would be so strong that my facial muscles would contract upon tasting it—squinting, grimacing—until I finally swallowed the whole thing down. The second one would be easier. For me, after the third, all the worries about getting laid off would melt away, all the memories of watching people die would disappear, I would get warm, my muscles would expand, and I would start to talk faster and faster instead of standing on the outside of the group, lurking, sulking. For a night, I would stop being the poor kid, the knuckle-dragging ex-military guy. I could talk anyone out of his or her shoes.

Sometimes things would get out of hand. I threw pennies at Dave Lane until he punched me in the head. I body-slammed Chris Vincent on the sidewalk after getting shooed out of a gay bar. I was asked to leave Hogs & Heifers after getting a little too revved up.

It is hard to get too revved up in Hogs & Heifers.

But there we were, throwing back shots and slamming the glasses down on the bar, which was cracked and splintered from too much dancing and being set on fire too many times. Hogs & Heifers, you see, is a biker bar, tamed in a New York way for Wall Street cake eaters like me. If you show up at the door wearing a tie, they cut it off. There were pool tables, if you wanted to play pool with a three-hundred-pounder sporting a ZZ Top beard, and there were female bartenders wearing tank tops who pounded shots right along with you, girls who never seemed to get drunk, who got more and more aggressive, who could pour drinks all night and dance on the bar and shout at people and then take you home and maul you while you watched amateur porn on her ten-year-old television set in a apartment filled with beer bottles and ashtrays and a glass coffee table dusted with cocaine. It was dark outside, but it was darker inside, and we were there to show that we were men, because we worked in a masculine profession, and if we were going to be jackasses during the day, we were going to be jackasses at night.

Dave Lane and I were having a drinking contest. We were hammered, and we were giving each other purple nurples as hard as we possibly could. I was cranking away on Lane's right nipple, twisting it around 360 degrees, pulling it away from his body, trying to get him to flinch. He was staring back at me and inflicting an incredible amount of abuse on my left nipple. We both grinned.

Afterward, I slammed a shot glass on the bar with a little too much gusto and was asked to leave.

The next day, I had enormous black bruises all over my chest. In a week, they would turn yellow. It could have been from Lane, but it also could have been from whatever had happened between leaving the bar and passing out in the subway station.

My three-month suicide mission came to an end when the pretty girls in recruiting and the human resources department finally found something for us to do. We would be security guards.

There was still no room for us to become salespeople or traders, and there was already security in the lobby, but in the midst of post-9/11 paranoia, Lehman wanted to protect against the possibility of some disaffected Muslim from a nearby sleeper cell taking an express elevator upstairs and wiping out an entire trading floor of capitalist infidels with dynamite strapped to his chest. Ostensibly, it was the job of the MBA to tackle the guy and smother the blast, taking one for the team. We were cheaper than traders.

In practice, all we did was check IDs. This was less than helpful, because a trader getting paid a stick a year ($1 million) would never be terribly enthusiastic about shifting his newspaper, his coffee, and his firm research from one arm to the other to show his ID in the lobby and then a second time just to get on the trading floor. This was an inconvenience, a burden. I was pissing off the very people who I would eventually ask to hire me. It wasn't a good situation.

Some of my classmates were indignant. "I didn't shell out a hundred grand for business school to be a fucking security guard." *Fine*, I thought. That kind of attitude was going to get them nowhere. To work on Wall Street, I thought, you have to be willing to do absolutely anything. You have to be willing to hustle trade tickets. You have to be willing to answer phones. You have to be willing to suck dick for money. I was going to be a trader if it killed me. I didn't give up my military pension to get all sniffly about being a security guard.

*This is something that I can do,* I thought. I'm an ex-grunt. I'll shine my shoes so you can read a newspaper in them and stand there at fucking parade rest all day. I can look intimidating. I have broad shoulders and a square jaw. I have big pecs from doing lots of decline. I can chase down some rich punk for his ID. I can kick him in the common peroneal nerve and watch a sympathetic nerve reflex collapse him to the carpet. *People are going to feel safe on my floor.* Commerce can proceed as usual.

Each trading floor had two entrances, one on the east end of the elevator bank and one on the west end. While on security guard duty, I had a partner—another associate from the class—who usually sulked his way through the bare minimum. I did my best to make him look as foolish as possible. I held the door for people, calling them Sir or Ma'am, saying Good Morning and Good Afternoon as I checked their IDs. I dressed like I was on the Presidential Honor Guard. I didn't take bathroom breaks or lunch breaks, and I never, ever left early. I guarded the floor like I was standing watch on the DMZ.

Nobody noticed. In fact, nobody even made eye contact with me as I held the door for them; they knew I was surplus dead weight that the firm had hired.

Then some people noticed. A handsomely dressed middle-aged man with a pocket handkerchief and a fantastic New Jersey accent introduced himself as Billy McCarthy, head of Listed Trading, after I had opened the door for him, standing at parade rest, chest puffed out, shoulders back, for the sixth or seventh time.

Now we were getting somewhere. I looked over at my partner. He was sitting in a comfy chair, half asleep. *You snooze, you lose, buddy.*

I was longing for interaction with these people. I wanted them to notice the outstanding job that I was doing, to take me on the trading floor and share their wealth of information, to tell me something that would help me edge out one of my classmates. I needed a mentor. I needed someone to be generous of his time, to think about someone other than himself for just one second. Then I realized that on Wall Street, that was utterly impossible. What I really needed was an angel.

J. C. Gonzales appeared in my elevator bank. I'd met him the year before when I'd flown across the country to take part in an "informational interview." An informational interview is not really an interview at all, or at least it's kind of a reverse interview, where the job seeker asks questions of the employee, really intelligent ones, like, "What is it like to be a trader?" or "What is your average day like?" The whole purpose of the informational interview is face time. You try not to make yourself look like an idiot so that when they decide who to hire, the guy you sat with will say something like, "Yeah, he wasn't too much of an idiot." Nearly all hiring decisions are based on the level of someone's interest, since many candidates are equal in ability, so you try to act really, really interested in the job. You lean forward in your chair. You ask questions, even bad ones, because bad questions are better than no questions at all. But then, as a general rule, nothing of substance takes place during an informational interview because the interviewer is already in the middle of a trade or on the phone with a client, and, furthermore, has little interest in listening to some dumbass MBA for a half hour. For the interviewee, it's a lot like talking to a television set.

J. C. Gonzales was kind to me last year; he tore himself away from the market long enough to answer a single question. He was a thoughtful, deliberate associate, an ideal hire for any investment bank, a guy who answered the phone on the first ring, and, for all intents and purposes, he was a white male with an ethnic-sounding last name. He sold equity derivatives to hedge funds. I thought it didn't get much sexier than that.

"What's going on in the market?" I asked him.

A simple "up" or "down" would have sufficed. What I got was a filibuster on things like "nondefense capital goods," "housing starts," "the ECB," and something called the "Tankan." It was bewildering. J.C. had misplaced his patient, helpful demeanor and was trying, for some reason, to blind me with science. It was working. I realized that even though it was only a frosted glass door that separated us, nothing would bridge the gap in our understanding of the market. The elevator came, and J.C. left to grab a chicken parm sandwich.

I sat back down in my chair, crestfallen. I was never going to get a job.

About an hour later, a guy who bore a striking resemblance to ALF (the TV space alien from the planet Melmac) bounced into the elevator bank. I was still at parade rest. "You look a little bored out here. Want to come in and learn a few things?"

*OhmyGod.* This could be the big break. But then, a soldier doesn't leave his post. I froze.

"I'm sure it will be fine," he said, reading my face. I didn't need much more convincing.

ALF brings me back to his desk and plops me down in a chair next to his computer. I am sitting in a sea of pissed-off looking people. He shows me a piece of paper that says "Risk Bid" on it, and it's full of numbers. He's going on and on about "liquidity" and something called "average daily volume." I can't hear anything. I'm overwhelmed by the people around me who *do* know what they're doing. How did they get to this point in their careers? Did some guy who looked like ALF take them under his wing too? Did they spend hours and hours parked at their desks, learning this shit, pulling all-nighters? It all looks terribly complicated.

I glance back at "Risk Bid." I try to make sense of it and can't. ALF looks at me. He's figured out that I'm a dim bulb. He ejects me from his seat and back out into the elevator bank to check IDs.

I was conscious not only of the fact that I couldn't make sense of the trade but also that everyone was looking at me; everyone was judging me. Wall Street was full of picky people, I had been told. Did I have the right glasses? Was I wearing the right shoes? I was thrown out into the elevator bank like a human body rejecting a transplanted organ. Get the fuck out of here.

I don't belong. Too poor. Too dumb.

I hate myself.

I've been doing such a good job as a security guard over the past month that they're probably going to make my position permanent.

For now, I've decided that I no longer give a rat's ass about getting hired, that all my shoe shining and ass kissing has gotten me nowhere. Besides, I'd been hearing reports that my slimy classmates had already been pinning down jobs by breaking the rules and walking onto the trading floor to grip and grin. Nowhere in my Wall Street reading material did it say that I was going to have to be a politician just to get by.

But today I'm excited because I've been invited up to a cabin in New

Hampshire with the lads from Churrascaria Plataforma, our crew of coolguys. The cabin was built alongside miles and miles of hiking trails in the White Mountains. Some of the guys were Dartmouth grads and had been tooling around up there for years, drinking, playing cards, and generally fucking around. I had few expectations. I was told only to bring booze.

I would be the last to arrive. I'd pulled security guard duty, so I had one more day of screwing the pooch in an elevator bank between me and the mountains. The others had pulled duty too; they'd just blown it off. I was beginning to learn that on Wall Street, a lot of the rules are optional, particularly the ones that don't pertain to making money. More importantly, the more money you make, and the more *size* you are, the more optional the rules become. Rules are for the stupid, the clueless, those who cannot be trusted to do the right thing.

I sat in the elevator bank, filling up with self-loathing, when Sam Grossman appeared in front of me with a bacon, egg, and cheese bagel. It was surplus. "Take it," he said. On Wall Street, people buy three times as much food as they can possibly eat, give some of it away, and dump the rest. You could feed five homeless shelters a day off of Lehman Brothers's leftovers. Beside Sam was a man with a giant head. It was the biggest head I had ever seen. I couldn't decide if I would rather win the Powerball or have this guy's head full of nickels. Big Head was smiling at me, looking like he knew something about me, like he knew what section of the adult DVD store I shopped in.

I didn't know anything about Big Head, but I knew Sam's story. He was one of the lucky ones: he'd been a summer associate the year before—an intern, essentially—and his desk, Program Trading, had liked him so much that they invited him to come back full-time the following year. More accurately, his desk hired him a whole year in advance; signed the paperwork and everything. Sam, a fast talker with a head full of numbers, was nonchalant about it. "They're futures traders," he said, referring to the programs desk. "They hedged forward."

Now Sam was in the catbird seat while the rest of us poor bastards had to fight it out in the trenches. Sam already had his job; he was Ben Cohan's right-hand man, his piss boy. Ben Cohan ran program trading, but his real love was proprietary trading—that is, trading on the firm's behalf—which he did using something he called "systematic strategies." Algorithms. He wrote programs to take money out of the market. While the rest of us mere mortals were trying to fuck each other over with telephones and paper tickets, Cohan was sucking up dollar bills with a giant Zamboni. Nice work if you can get it, but it seemed to me to take a lot of the fun out of it.

Sam had attached himself to this money making robot and is grinning from ear to ear, and possibly further. He introduces me to Big Head, whose name is Mike Ingram. Sam is talking, and I figure out that Big Head works with him, at least tangentially. We should get to know each other, says Sam, because we're both ex-military. Ingram was in the navy, a submariner, though I don't know how he'd get that melon through a hatch.

I shake hands with Ingram. *Look at that monstrosity.* Finally, I'm feeling good vibes from a potential employer. Ingram exudes ex-military honesty. "I'm actually looking for somebody," he says, "so we should keep in touch."

*Really.* "What do you do?" I ask.

"Index arbitrage."

Cooooool.

I had a sleeping bag, a change of clothes, and a shitload of booze. No toothbrush.

I was on a night mission without night vision goggles, driving up Interstate 91 from Massachusetts into Vermont; I was trying to figure out how fast I could go without getting pulled over. For a speed limit of sixty-five, I decided that was seventy-eight. It didn't matter; there weren't any cops. There were probably fewer than a thousand law enforcement officers in the entire state. It was dark, and I was fast. There were no streetlights. There were very few cars on the road. There was no moon, and I could barely make out the black outline of the mountains surrounding me. My car, a dinky Toyota Tercel, didn't have a CD player, but I'd brought a portable one that was wired into the tape deck, blasting old electronic music that nobody seemed to like but me. I had one Gatorade bottle full of warm piss sloshing around on the floor, and I was readying a second one. I wasn't stopping for nobody or nothing.

I was trying to get to the cabin quickly to make up for lost time. The guys would already be several beers deep, and I was going to have to catch up. I was brimming with optimism about my lead with Big Head, and I wanted to crow about my newfound skills in political maneuvering. On second thought, maybe I'd stay quiet; I didn't want my classmates getting a piece of my action. I didn't want them horning in on Big Head and his precious associate trading job in equities.

Turns out there was little danger of that. The others had already sniffed out the caste system in the firm; we all watched the trading desks give presentations to the incoming class, and the equities guys were not impressive. The cash equities guys, for instance, wore double-breasted suits with heavy pinstripes and shiny gold ties, and they spoke with Jersey accents. They had last names that invariably ended in vowels. They said things like "take a report," and "put a trade-along on that," that made them sound like they had a tip on a horse. Meanwhile, the fixed-income people were older, calmer, more intellectual. They had kids in school. They had large houses. They did not have New Jersey accents. They were mathematicians, or at least were masquerading as mathematicians. They were politically ambiguous. They were winners.

Historically, at Lehman Brothers, equities (stocks) had been an afterthought—or, more accurately, an afterbirth. Lehman traded bonds (debt) because it was profitable. The firm traded stocks because everyone else did, and it had to keep up appearances. It is important to note that Lehman's leadership—all of it—was bond traders. This is common among Wall Street firms because, under normal market conditions, equity risks are plain vanilla and linear. Stock go up, stock go down. There is nonlinearity at the extremes (low-priced stocks are seemingly overvalued because they trade with an option value), but for the most part, it doesn't take an Ivy League graduate to trade fifty thousand shares of Campbell's pork and beans. That Ivy League graduates do says something about the pay structure. Conversely, all bonds, even plain vanilla Treasury bonds, have curvature. The rate of change in price isn't linear. And most credit instruments, such as corporate bonds, and mortgage-backed securities in particular, have extremely complex options embedded in the structure that are extremely difficult to price. When Lehman Brothers was spun off from American Express in 1994, the equities division was little more than a gang of Italian Americans chunking around blocks of stock in quarters and eighths. (There was actually an area on the floor referred to as "Little Italy.") Bonds, on the other hand, with all their nonlinearities and their complex mathematics, were being traded upstairs by the caviar crowd. Fixed income flew first class, equities flew coach. Fixed income was in the luxury box, equities sat with the rabble. Fixed income ate in expensive restaurants, equities got asked to leave expensive restaurants. Over time, though, Lehman figured out that there was real money to be made in stocks, so it started to focus a little more attention in that direction.

That summer, the effort was just beginning. Equities was hiring lots and lots of MBAs, trying to diversify away from bachelor's degrees out of fourth-tier schools. And not just MBAs, but real rocket scientists, too; our class included a Caltech computer science PhD whose curriculum vitae was entirely incomprehensible.

But Dave Lane and his crew had rooted out the class differences, and while there should have been nothing in their chromosomes to make them genetically predisposed to trade fixed income over equities, they had seen their share of summer homes and fancy dinners and decided that they wanted nothing of the sweaty goons in stocks. Chris Vincent was the sole exception: he was willing to sell anything that wasn't nailed down and would travel anywhere there was a party.

I refueled in White River Junction and poured the piss out onto the pavement.

From there, the directions were a little sketchy. Follow this road for nine miles (watch the odometer), take a right, turn off at the No Camping sign. I was going fifty-five in a thirty-five and making myself carsick with all the hairpin turns. It was pitch black, and I was not bashful about using the high beams. If I hit a deer, I'd be burger.

NO CAMPING. I ambled my Toyota down into a ditch and onto a primitive dirt road with deep ruts. My car bottomed out a half-dozen times on the way to the cabin. The road was surrounded by woods with that special horror movie feel; the second I ran out of gas, I was almost certainly going to be dismembered by a chain saw. The directions didn't say how far I had to go. So I just kept driving and prayed that something would appear.

I didn't see the light from the window of the cabin until it was upon me. I wheeled my Tercel behind the manly SUVs and killed the engine.

The boys filed out of the cabin, headlamps bobbing in the dark, and gave me a resounding cheer.

"We weren't sure you were going to make it," said Brad.

Dave nodded. "There were some markets going around on when you'd show up, if at all."

Traders trade everything, not just stocks or bonds. They like to assess probabilities, and they'll bet on the outcome of just about anything. Football and basketball are obvious choices, but later, in 2005, there was a robust market in Michael Jackson suicide futures. Trading hundreds of millions of dollars of risk isn't enough. You have to go to a casino. But just going to the casino isn't enough. You have to get a tip on a horse. And once you realize *that* isn't enough, you start betting on *Dancing with the Stars*. I was flattered that money had changed hands over my car ride.

I shook hands and slapped backs, without bothering to notify anyone of the piss I had splashed on myself. "Give the kid some credit for finding the cabin," said Dave Lane. I was happy. I wasn't retarded after all.

"If you hadn't found it," said Brad, "it would have been a small problem."

"Why is that?"

"No cell phone reception up here," Dave said, "and it's too late to go around knocking on doors and asking for directions. You would have had to go back to White River Junction and get a hotel."

"Oh. Well, I don't have a cell phone anyway."

They looked at me like I had a cabbage for a head.

"Okay," said Dave, "then *you* are *clearly* a piece of work."

I was indeed retarded.

The cabin had a wood stove in the middle of the room, three bunk beds, and a loft overhead where you could sleep more—probably ground zero for a lot of Dartmouth freshman sex. There was a counter and a sink, where the bags of chips and pretzels were stacked. There were coolers of beer outside. There were several large jugs of water.

There was a privy.

There was an assload of candles. Dave and company hadn't thought to bring a lantern. Good thing I'd picked one up in my in my miniature tornado around the apartment seconds before I hopped in the car. I brought it out with a flourish, like a magician, to cheers. It took six D batteries and spit out about as much light as a dim flashlight, but it was something. I hung it on a nail sticking out of the wall. My small contribution.

We were all seated around the table, gnawing on tortilla chips. *This is it.* I had spent my entire life trying to fit in with one clique or another, and failed. But these were smart guys. Lehman Brothers was like nerd camp all year round. In all likelihood, it was a roomful of valedictorians (except for me—I ran out of steam senior year, victim of the "fuck-its"). And the best part was, these were the handsome, athletic, well-spoken smart kids—not exactly Eagle Scouts, but kids with leadership skills who never found an organization worth leading. Not the socially inept, pimply faced vampires pulling all-nighters as grad students in a computer lab, drinking Mountain Dew and furtively jerking off under a desk.

I felt compelled to tell a story. To take a chance and reveal something personal. I took a breath. "When I was in the military, I decided to go to business school. I took the GMATs during an inport period, one of the computer-based tests, and got a 680. I thought that was pretty good, so I put it directly on my resume, thinking it would help me get a job. Then, as we were sitting there in Windows on the World during 'One Firm' week, they announced the class average SAT score."

Grand pause. "686."

Dave Lane and Adam Cohen were fucking rolling. I had never seen them laugh so hard. Chris Vincent volunteered his score: at 710, he had the second lowest in the group. Wilson and Adam were silent, but I had already seen their resumes; they were in the mid-700s. Brad, a nonfinancial person, had probably skipped the GMATs but in all likelihood had a sparkling GRE.

Dave Lane kept laughing, but said nothing. He often said more that way.

I took another swallow of Jim Beam from the flask I'd brought up with me. This one I felt in my fingertips as my blood turned to alcohol. I was, for the first time in my life, *below average.* Maybe this was some weird extension of the Peter Principle: if you keep getting smarter and smarter people in a room, eventually one of them is going to be dumb. I wasn't the least bit embarrassed; I was starting to get used to the fact that my brain moved a little bit slower, measured in milliseconds, than everyone else's. I had a hard time keeping up with the conversation. I didn't always get the jokes. There was always something I wasn't being let it on. I didn't realize that on Wall Street, this could be an asset.

I could feel the alcohol-fueled talking jag coming on, and I was trying to suppress it. The guys were making easy, effortless small talk, shooting the shit on just about every imaginable topic *besides* work, and it was neither the time nor the place to bring up my minor victory in the elevator bank. It was an unwritten rule not to talk about 9/11, for sure, and not to talk about getting a job on a desk. Most of us wanted to trade, and we were all fighting for the same spots. I sat silently and played with a rivulet of wax that had slithered from a candle onto the wooden table.

Eventually the conversation turned to women. I perked up. I offered an opinion on the skinny accountant (sold), the Romanian Nightmare (buy), the tall, ambitious blonde (one-by-two call spread), and just about everyone else in our class, including the recruiters. Oddly enough, I was attracted to precisely zero of the women in our associate class. Sure, every once in a while, one of them would wear a sheer blouse, and I would look up momentarily from my modified duration, but for the most part, they belonged to a species of female that was not merely insensitive but seemed to be incapable of experiencing a feeling of admiration for a man. They were transactional. They would love you if you didn't get fired, they would love you if you brought home your bonus, conditionally. If you didn't, then they would find someone who would. There were no after-school romances, no love notes or illicit emails, no sex in public places. They were boring in a cheap sort of way.

Worst of all, they had expensive tastes.

The conversation inevitably turned to actresses. I said I was in love with Claire Danes, recalling how, during my informational interviews the year before, I'd walked around the city and drooled at the *Mod Squad* billboards. We discussed Natalie Portman, Jessica Alba, Beyoncé, Mena Suvari, Julia Stiles, Rosario Dawson, Brooke Burke, and Monica Bellucci. I extolled the virtues of short, dark, buxom women. Dave Lane liked them skinny. We could not be reconciled.

"Jesus, did you drink that whole thing?" asked Lane.

I looked down at my flask. I was so excited to be in a cabin talking about pussy that I'd lost track of my drinking. I looked around the table and was shocked to see that everyone else was drinking soda.

"Uh, yeah."

"Strong like *bull*," said Lane. "We haven't even started the drinking games yet, and the kid gets a huge head start."

I beamed with pride. 680 GMAT, but I can drink.

"What drinking games?" I asked.

"Asshole," said Wilson. Like I was supposed to know.

I had never much seen the point of drinking games. I didn't like to be told when I could and couldn't drink. Drinking games were for amateurs, girls, and frat boys who needed an excuse to get drunk. I needed no excuse. I would drink the same amount with or without a drinking game. I could get drunk faster without a drinking game and have more fun.

"You know how to play?" asked Brad.

"No clue."

"That's okay, neither do I," said Chris. The lines had been drawn. Winners and losers. I was no longer part of the group. There was an "in crowd," and it consisted of Dave, Brad, Wilson, and Adam. Wilson, the party promoter, started pouring Jack and Cokes. Chris pulled his chair up next to me. I felt like I was in remedial swimming class.

"In 'asshole,'" begins Dave, "there is a president, a vice president, a vice asshole, an asshole, and some guys in between. The president can tell anyone what to do. The vice president can tell everyone what to do except the president. And so on. The asshole has to deal the cards and pour drinks."

"At the beginning of every round," he continues, "the president can make a rule. The rule can be anything: like, everyone has to drink on doubles." He starts dealing.

Chris and I are staring at two piles of cards. We're expected to pick them up.

"So how do you play?" I ask.

"You'll see," replies Dave. I pick up my cards and look at them. I am trying not to be pissed off. I am trying to trust in the process.

Dave reaches across the table, folds over my cards, and looks at them. "You're screwed," he says.

Terrific.

I play without knowing how to play. After the first round, I'm the vice asshole. Chris is the asshole. We take the designated asshole and vice asshole seats, in the asshole ghetto near the window. Dave Lane is the president, Brad is the VP, and Wilson and Adam are in the middle.

I am told to drink.

Eventually I learn that twos are the high card, followed by aces, followed by kings. Doubles can be played only against doubles. Jokers trump. The problem is that the asshole has to give his two best cards to the president, who gives his two worst cards to the asshole. The vice asshole has to give his best card to the vice president, who gives his worst card to the vice asshole. It is like a country with a perfectly regressive tax system, reinforcing the class differences rather than breaking them down. But the game has turned into a perverse reflection of real life: Who came from money, and who didn't. Who went to an Ivy League school, and who didn't. Chris and I are the assholes, and I am thankful that he is the bigger asshole, as I take a long swallow from my Jack and Coke and set about refilling it.

"Hey," says Dave, "the asshole gets drinks. You want a drink, tell him to get you a drink."

I feel like I am in a concentration camp. Chris pours me a drink.

It is getting louder. I am talking louder. I look at the bottles. We still have a lot of work to do.

There is an ideal level of intoxication, usually after about five or six drinks, where you're perfectly buzzed. You can bullshit and tell stories and hang with the best of them. I'd crossed that threshold about a half hour ago. My brain is getting wet. I am starting to miss parts of the conversation while staring into my drink. I look up occasionally and wonder what the hell is going on.

At one point, President Dave tells Asshole Chris to run around the cabin in his underwear. *How old are we?* I think, but Chris is up to the task. He whoops and hollers as he crunches the snow with his bare feet.

The game dies off, but I'm still holding my cards. Chris tries to go to bed, but we throw ice at him. I tell several people to go fuck themselves.

"You have enough to drink there, Dillian?" asks Adam.

"Sit on your thumb," I say.

Wilson is stoking the stove. It's hot enough already—we had long ago stripped down to our T-shirts, even though it was well below freezing outside—but Wilson is in charge of the fire, and one way or another, he's going to cram an entire tree's worth of wood into that thing. The stack is emitting ten tons of carbon dioxide, and the stove is starting to glow.

The others are taking out sleeping bags. I stand, knocking over three drinks as I stumble into the table. Nobody notices. Being careful not to fall on the stove, I walk over to the bed. I am the vice asshole, so I get a top bunk. So does Chris. I heave myself into it, nearly stepping on Brad's head in the process. I rip off my shirt and lie there on the dirty mattress, with no sleeping bag and no pillow, both of which I have forgotten to bring in from the car. The room is spinning, and my temples are pulsing. Dave is blowing out the candles.

*If I have to puke, there is no way I'm going to make it outside without killing myself.*


*Fuck, it's hot.*

I can't breathe. I pucker and gasp like a fish. Superheated air fills my lungs. I'm drenched with sweat, or alcohol, or both. My brain is boiling. I feel like I am a caterpillar some kid put in a microwave.

The cabin is dark, but the stove is glowing white hot. It looks like it is about to melt. Goddamn Wilson cranked that thing with too much wood.

I heave my legs around the side of the bed. *Here goes,* I think, and then crash to the wooden floor. *Door. Must find door.* I slam into the table, knocking over another colony of bottles and plastic cups. *Okay, that's the table.* I feel along the edge of the table until I get to the end, then reach out and feel something solid. *Door. There's no handle. How the hell do I get out of here?*

I really can't breathe now—it feels like I'm underwater, like a live lobster dropped in a pot. Next comes the spasm, and the death rattle. I feel along the door until I find a horizontal board; this has to be it. I squeeze my fingers underneath it and pull as hard as I can.

"Unnnngghhh!"

*Crack!*

The others are starting to stir. I feel hands on my shoulders. "This way."

It's Brad. Together we shuffle off to the other corner of the cabin. I feel a rush of cold air. I fall to my hands and knees.

"Jesus Christ!" Dave is awake and running the show. "Wilson, what the fuck? What did you do to the stove?"

Chris crashes to the floor. "Holy balls, it's hot in here."

Wilson puts on his oven mitts and harasses the fire with a poker. "I didn't think it would get this hot."

"This is ridiculous." Dave has stepped over my lifeless body and has dragged his sleeping bag out to the front porch. I lift up my head. "You're going to sleep outside?"

"I'll be miserable," he says, "but not as miserable as I'd be in here. This thing is rated to fifteen degrees." Camping boy has everything.

All the doors to the cabin are open, and the windows too. Chris moves down to the bunk vacated by Dave. People are still pissing and moaning about Wilson.

I stay where I was, collapsed on the floor in a crumpled heap, my ass in the cabin, on fire, and my head outside, freezing. On average, I am happy.

*Bacon.*

I could hear Wilson yammering away in one of his Spalding Gray monologues about how cabin breakfasts taste better than regular breakfasts. He seemed to be talking to himself.

I was still on the floor. My body had contorted to form an imaginary chalk outline, as if I'd been dropped from the top of a building and landed face-first, limbs splayed. My brain was stewing. I lifted myself up off the floor and turned around to see Wilson pouring a can of bacon grease into a frying pan, with his headlamp still on. The others were getting dressed in brightly colored outdoor gear.

"Hey, there he is," Dave said. I was surprised to see him in the cabin instead of on the front porch in his sleeping bag.

"What time is it?" I asked.

"Eight thirty. We're going hiking."

*Christ.* Under normal circumstances, this would have been a waste of a day spent padding around the apartment in boxer shorts, sipping strong coffee. I was a fucking wreck. I tried counting backward from one hundred by sevens. I could do it, slowly.

Wilson served us eggs and bacon and toast. I gnawed on it slowly. I was not part of the conversation.

"Hey, look at that!" exclaimed Chris, pointing toward the window.

The windowsill was cracked and split down the middle.

Everyone laughed. Oh, I get it. That was me. What I'd thought was the door was actually the windowsill. Choking on the sauna blast, I had practically ripped it off the wall the night before.

The others were roaring. "*Unnnngggghhh . . . let me out!*" I smiled.

I trudged up Mount Moosilauke, heaving and panting and sweating and farting. I was sent to the back of the pack because I was asphyxiating everybody with my ass, which was incapable of processing a liter of alcohol. I wore Dave Lane's fleece because, when I got dressed, he looked at me and said, "You—are a disaster." Cotton is the enemy, he told me, and I would sweat through it on the way up the mountain and then it would freeze when I got to the top. He and Brad, mountain man, gave out more clothes to Chris. Asshole and vice asshole, we were wearing secondhand clothes.

The sun, reflecting off the snow, was making my headache worse. I needed one of Dave's many pairs of sunglasses. *This is what I do to fit in*, I thought. This is what Wall Street guys do. They drink themselves silly and then go do something physically demanding the next day, as long as it isn't a plebeian sport like football or basketball. I was game. I was ready to shit my pants.

Brad and Dave looked down the hill, waiting for me. *I'm coming*. I was sweating bucketloads of pure booze.

When we got above tree line, my pants froze, according to plan. They were icy cylinders. I tapped on them, and they made a thudding sound.

Above tree line, there were only cairns sticking out of the snow to guide us. The wind was howling. I was starting to perk up. The steep part of the climb was over, and we were hiking along the ridge, looking down at the valley.

There was a monument at the top. We made it. Dave and Brad started pointing out all the other mountains in the distance and telling us their names. Chris, camera nerd, took out a digital camera and started snapping pictures. He fixed it to the monument and set the timer. We posed.

I patted Brad on the shoulder while Dave looked on. Wilson had his hands on his hips. I was grinning broadly. There was nothing but blue sky in the background.

Chris dropped the lens cap. *Clink, clink, clink* it went down the mountain, like a pachinko machine.

Chris lunged after it, trying to bushwhack down the icy slope. Sage old man Wilson restrained him, and said, looking off in the distance, *"let it go . . ."*

The flash went off. The moment was captured for posterity.

In the picture, I am giggling.

## 4

## Found Money | Winter 2002

I had been deathly afraid of interviews. And for good reason. During my first round at Lehman Brothers, I met with a former navy officer who was clearly deranged.

"Did you ever paint the ship?" he asks me.

"Come again?"

"You were the first lieutenant. Did you ever paint the whole ship?"

"Well, we never painted the *whole* ship; we never went into dry dock during my tour, we—"

He leaves.

I sit, thinking about how I can change the subject.

He is back.

"Do you like managing people?"

"Well, I—"

"It's a yes or no question. Do you like managing people, yes or no?"

"It's not really a yes or no question—"

"YES IT IS."

"Look, I had a lot of guys working for me, and there were some good times and some bad times—"

"DO YOU LIKE MANAGING PEOPLE, YES OR NO?"

"*Yes.*"

"Well, I *hated* it. That's why I became a trader, so I wouldn't be responsible for other people's fuckups."

He leaves again, the word *fuck* hanging in the air.

Then there was the time with an interest rate volatility trader.

"So before we begin," he says, "we need to clear something up."

"Okay."

"What is *this*?" He points at my resume.

It reads, "Encrusted with Top Secret Clearance."

He launches into a tirade. "You wouldn't believe the shit that I see, people traveling across the country for an interview, and their resume is all fucked up. How does that happen?"

My ears are on fire. "I don't know," I say.

I feel like I am going to cry.

He laughs. "Man, I'm just messing with you. I changed it in Microsoft Word. Your resume is fine. I just wanted to see how you would react."

So after getting past these guys, I figure I can survive Ben Cohan.

Kissing Big Head's ass paid off. I'd been granted an interview with the rare and elusive Cohan, the sphinx-like chief of algorithmic trading—the grand poobah of index arb. This time, I was determined to *control* the interview and not let it control me. I had an agenda: I was going to tell Cohan how hard I could work, and he was going to be fucking impressed.

I sat in a folding chair on the dimly lit Jersey City Lehman Brothers backup trading floor, next to the Man in Charge. It was obvious that he was conducting an interview—I was hunched forward, completely tense in my neck and shoulders—so his underlings had scattered. Cohan was probably in his fifties, but he had fat, youthful cheeks, which made him look happy most of the time. And he *was* happy, as long as he was surrounded by people who were as smart as he was, or smarter. But if he was like any other Lehman Brothers managing director, he also saw the value in hard work.

"Why do you want to be a trader?"

I had my speech prepared.

"Back when I was in the Coast Guard, I was stationed out of a small town in Washington State. There wasn't much to do there but read, so I haunted the local used-book store, and that's where I picked up *A Random Walk Down Wall Street* by Burton Malkiel. I was a math major, so it sounded interesting."

Malkiel's book argues that markets are perfectly efficient, so it's impossible for anyone to make money over the long run. It's Dadaism for finance—what's the point, we're all fucked anyway, that kind of stuff. But unlike Dadaism, efficient market theory actually has a following.

"I read the book, decided it was loathsome, nihilistic, academic bullshit, and set out to spend the rest of my career proving it wrong.

"I went to business school part-time—I had to, I was still in the military—and I also got a job on the trading floor, on the Pacific Exchange. I would get up at three forty-five in the morning, make it down to the trading floor by quarter of five, work until twelve, head back to my day job in the Coast Guard, work until ten at night, then come home and study until twelve or one. I was working twenty-two hours a day toward the goal of getting a job on Wall Street.

"*Nobody* can work harder than me. Nobody is willing to put in the hours that I will put in. I am *insane*."

Cohan was silent.

"What do you know about index arbitrage?"

"I know that futures will temporarily be synthetically mispriced to cash, and that an arbitrageur can buy cheap futures and sell the index, or vice versa."

Cohan was silent.

He went on to ask me a handful of questions, all of which he responded to with silence. I must have blown him away.

At the very least, I think I did okay.


"I wish I could take both of you."

I'm in an office, interviewing with the head of government bond trading, a bespectacled Indian man who had lectured our class on things like "wolatility" and "wariance" in a high-pitched voice, making Chris Vincent all giggly. He was a former math professor who liked his hires to know their shit forward and backward. I've just fumbled a Taylor rule expansion on his desk and salvaged it with my "nobody can work harder than me" speech.

But he's telling me he can't take me.

"I just gave away the job five minutes before you came in," he says, pointing at his phone.

"You can't take on somebody extra?"

He thinks about it. "No. I can't. Good luck."

I shake his hand and turn to leave. Wilson James is standing outside, grinning.

"It was you?"

"What?"

"*You're* the one he gave the job to?"

Wilson looks down. "Oh, man, I'm sorry."

It figures. Wilson actually *was* a math teacher, or a physics teacher, or something. He and Gautam were two nerd peas in a pod.

I wouldn't have been in this position if Ben Cohan hadn't told the recruiters he was "not blown away" in my interview. His exact words: not blown away. Not blown away is code for "dumbass," I surmised. Not blown away is code for "a little slow." He was looking for someone who could talk, like Sam Grossman. Someone a little more refined.

I couldn't be Sam Grossman. I was a grunt. The index arbitrage job was mine to lose, and I'd lost it.

The recruiters had pointed me toward bond trading after an extra slot opened up, but I'd blown that too. Now I had nothing. I was a stateless vessel.

I picked up a desk phone and called Stacy, a recruiter, and told her my problem.

"Well, that's okay, because I think you'll be going to index arbitrage."

"How? I thought Ben Cohan was 'not blown away'?"

"I don't think Ben has a lot of say in the matter."

So that was it. I was getting jammed.

This happened to associates who couldn't find a job. Lehman couldn't just fire them, so it jammed them in a desk. The orphaned associates got to stick around, but not without suffering a little professional embarrassment first. Now Ben Cohan had another mouth to feed whether he liked it or not. My goal would be to start feeding myself, and others, before he had an opportunity to shit-can me.

But the track record for jammed associates was exceptionally poor; within six months to a year, most of them were out on their ass. Interestingly enough, I was getting jammed somewhere I actually wanted to be.

The old, fierce determination to win came back. People who bet against me were often made to look very, very foolish.

They never learned.


Index arbitrage—which was going to be my new playground—involves derivatives, which have been around since the beginning of time as a way for producers and consumers of commodities such as corn, wheat, and oil to manage the risk that the price of a commodity will change adversely over time. A farmer who oversees ten thousand acres of corn production has a lot of risk. He makes decisions such as how much corn to plant, based on information he has today, like the current price of corn. If corn is $4 a bushel today, and his fixed costs are $3 million, he knows that he will be profitable if he plants a million bushels of corn: he can eventually sell it all for $4 million. But what if the price of corn changes by the time he brings it to market? What if it falls to $2 a bushel? He is ruined. The farmer has to declare bankruptcy, sell off his farmland and his tractors, live in a flophouse, and drink bathtub gin.

What the farmer needs is a way to lock in the price that he would get for his crop *today*. Theoretically, it's possible that he could sell his entire crop today, except for the fact that the corn has yet to be grown and whoever will buy it doesn't have the money. But if he could find a buyer for the corn, maybe he could enter into an agreement to sell the corn at a specific price at a specific date in the future. He would be selling his corn *forward*.

There are risks on the other end too. Think of a consumer of corn, like a miller or flour producer. The miller knows that he'll be profitable if the price of corn stays at $4 a bushel. But what if the price rises, and he has to pay $5, $6, or $7 a bushel? He won't be able to meet his production costs, and he too will be drinking bathtub gin. He wants to be able to buy his corn today, at $4 a bushel, without having to worry about the price rising by the time the farmer brings it to market. He wants to enter into an agreement with the farmer to *buy* the corn at a specific price at a specific date in the future. He can't buy it today because he doesn't have the money yet. He couldn't pay the farmer today even if he wanted to. But when he enters into an agreement with the farmer, there's no cash involved—at least, not until the agreed-upon date when the miller writes a $4 million check to the farmer and gets his big pile of corn in return.

This agreement between the farmer and the miller—this *forward contract*—is what's known as a derivative. Notice that during the period of time that the derivative is in effect, either the farmer or the miller may end up looking like an idiot. If the price of corn falls to $3 a bushel, the farmer will be happy because he locked in his price; he is effectively *short* corn at $4 a bushel and has made $1 million on his forward trade. But the miller will be kicking his own ass all the way down the street, because if he had only waited until corn fell to $3 a bushel to buy the forward contract, he would have made an extra million bucks.

This works fine when the farmer and the miller know each other personally. Maybe they live in the same community, go to the same church, and to the extent that there is corn farming on Long Island, their kids play on the same lacrosse team. Each is a man of integrity, and they both trust that the other will make good on his obligation, even if the price moves against him. But what if the farmer or the miller mismanages his business to the point that he goes bankrupt and can't perform on the forward contract? And what if the farmer has more than one customer? What if he has dozens? What if the miller buys from dozens of different farmers? Does he have agreements with each of them? Do either of these guys have the time and the inclination to be sitting around writing up forward contracts all day?

Maybe, they think, there should be a special public meeting place where all the farmers and all the millers congregate, and they could take care of this all at once. This place is called an *exchange*.

An exchange is a public place where people who need to hedge their risk forward, either as a buyer or a seller, can transact in a public marketplace. Now, instead of the farmer dealing with the miller, he deals directly with the exchange, which employs something called a *futures contract*—essentially a standardized forward contract.

When it's time for the farmer to deliver his corn, he brings it to the spot where the exchange tells him to deliver it, where the miller will pick it up. When it's time for the miller to pay for the corn, he doesn't pay the farmer, he pays the exchange instead, which in turn pays the farmer. Now the farmer doesn't have to worry about the miller going tits up and not paying him, and the miller doesn't have to worry about the farmer going tits up and not delivering the corn—they only have to worry about the exchange going tits up, which is several orders of magnitude less likely.

At Lehman Brothers, on the index arbitrage desk, we traded futures on stock indices—that is, futures on baskets of stock, like the S&P 500 index or the Dow Jones Industrial Average. These futures contracts were the direct descendants of the corn futures that the farmer and the miller used to mitigate their risk, only now they were handled by fast-talking, genius Wall Street traders—people who blew away Ben Cohan.

Luckily, my boss ended up being a direct descendant of the farmer.

There is no reason to get up early in Jersey City. There is nothing to do there.

In the morning, its financial district looks like some Chinese government stimulus project gone awry. There are buildings, but nothing happens. Real traders trade in New York, not in New Jersey, which is why half of Goldman Sachs engaged in a minor revolt when the firm announced plans to build the tallest facility in the state across the river. Ahoy, polloi. No partner could be convinced to travel from Scarsdale to Jersey Fucking City. So in the mornings, there are tumbleweeds. The local businesses had yet to figure out that they could get rich selling coffee and bagels to Lehman refugees, so for now there was only the Au Bon Pain, with its surly employees.

I arrived at my first day of work, dodging the tumbleweeds, at zero dark hundred, wearing the same pair of black loafers in which I'd sprinted away from the World Trade Center. I'd shined them into mirrors the night before. I was alone, except for the television, which featured Emma Crosby of CNBC and her lovely British accent giving the report on European markets. I watched her, rapt, then muted it when she was through. It occurred to me that there was absolutely nothing I could do. I couldn't even log into Ingram's computer for him—I didn't have his password.

People began to trickle in. I looked at them hopefully, like a cat waiting for a treat. *I am the new member of your team. Please talk to me.* They ignored me. They sat down and began to work on Lord knows what. I should have been working too, maybe checking on overseas markets, but I didn't know how to work the Bloomberg terminal. I read the *Wall Street Journal* instead.

Mercifully, Mike Ingram appeared, smiling. He gave me a healthy farm boy handshake, which I returned enthusiastically—he was just as excited about me being there as I was.

Ingram, an ex-navy submariner, started his career assisting an Indian rocket scientist on the STRIPS desk, where fragments and pieces of government bonds are bought and sold. He was deeply analytical, and he programmed spreadsheets and trading tools, building out much of the infrastructure for the desk, but he was never given the keys to the car, not even after three years. Just because you work on a trading desk doesn't make you a trader, and it doesn't mean that you're going to make any money. At the time, equities were in a colossal bull market, and Treasuries were plainly out of style—the government was running surpluses as far as the eye could see, and it was beginning to look like there wouldn't be any government debt left to trade. Just as there are bull and bear markets in asset classes such as stocks or bonds, there are bull and bear markets in jobs. It is not enough to be on Wall Street, or to be on Wall Street at the right time—you have to be on Wall Street at the right time and in the right place when your pet financial product comes into favor. Motivated by pure greed, Ingram jumped to equities, having been hired by Ben Cohan, who was happy to give up index arbitrage in order to trade proprietarily. But Ingram was finding that he'd bitten off more than he could chew; he needed a clerk to handle all the trade support and bookkeeping. I was willing to drag my bare balls through a half mile of broken glass just to lick the tire tracks of the garbage truck that hauled away the trade tickets, so I was the man for the job. What I didn't know was that Cohan was trading his career just like we all were; he abandoned index arb because he didn't see much of a future for it in the age of electronic trading.

I also didn't know that Cohan was a legendary trader. If he was selling, I shouldn't have been buying.

"What can I do?"

"Relax," said Ingram. "Just watch for a while."

Christ. I wasn't getting paid $130,000 a year to *not* make money.

"Okay."

Ingram and I share a single desk—a repurposed cubicle, with the top sawed off. He has access to the computer, the turret, and the Bloomberg. I have access to his giant head. We're sitting so close together that I can feel his body heat. He's talking on the phone. He's laughing—it sounds like he's been friends with this guy for years. He calls him Ronnie. He's making some notes on a piece of paper; all sorts of numbers and figures. I can't figure out what any of this has to do with index arbitrage, and the market hasn't even opened yet.

Ingram leans over to give me a quick explanation of index arb, most of which I already know: about how futures are priced and how there is a fair value and how you try to buy them cheap and sell them dear. Then comes the stuff I *don't* know. He's talking a lot about "balance sheet," which I thought was exclusively an accounting term—I didn't realize it had anything to do with trading. We have $x$ amount of S&P balance sheet and $y$ amount of Nasdaq balance sheet and $z$ amount of Russell balance sheet. He tells me that we're being asked to put on some more Russell balance sheet. I'm playing along, nodding with enthusiasm, but there's a comic strip question mark above my head—when are we going to get around to scalping futures?

This is not what I had in mind. I'd pictured myself as an option trader, negotiating trades in a maddeningly complex series of steps involving calls, puts, strikes, expirys, delta, gamma, theta, and vega. I'd pictured myself as a hybrid between the intellectual financial engineer and the bruising, street-smart floor trader. To me, trading options required a combination of pure aggression and raw intelligence. The leverage was massive, the risks enormous, and the rewards often random and capricious. To be a *delta one* trader—a trader who trades without taking any nonlinear risk—somehow seemed beneath me. Vol traders were clever. They'd discovered a more interesting way to make money. Then again, at least I was trading *something*, and the amount of capital Ingram and I had at our disposal was tremendous. I didn't know if index arb was profitable, and I decided I didn't really care. I was about to become an expert in *something*.

The market opens. The makeshift trading floor comes to life. Ingram's on the phone, and the button labeled MERC INDX is lit green. It's 9:29.

"Hey, Meat."

I try to imagine what a guy named Meat looks like.

"Happy Monday to you too."

Ingram's legs are jiggling. It's 9:30.

"Four on ten."

He waits.

"Three on ten."

He's watching an Excel spreadsheet. There's a boldfaced, highlighted number, and it's flickering.

-1.45.

-1.67.

-1.81.

Ingram's head is obscuring the rest of the spreadsheet.

Suddenly, he says, "Got it!"

Then he writes something on a trade ticket, says "two on ten," and goes back to watching the spreadsheet.

Meanwhile, people are yelling at one another. "Broadcom Jan thirty calls, two way!" "Oracle Feb 15 straddle, show me a bid!" I've been working on the Lehman Brothers trading floor for three hours—a dream come true—and I'm already jealous. Ingram is waging his own private war with the market, whereas everyone else is taking part in a larger conversation. The other people seem important. Ingram and I don't seem very important at all.

Someone who looks like the Pillsbury Doughboy with perfectly parted hair stands up and makes a lot of noise. "Five hundred Q's, how? *Sold!* Five hundred more, how? *Sold!*" He looks like he could bench-press maybe eighty-five pounds. He looks like, in a previous life, he'd been repeatedly stuffed into his own locker. This little Pudding Pop is, momentarily, the king of the trading floor.

I'm sensing tension from Ingram. He's not saying "three on ten" anymore, he's hung up the phone, and he's staring at his screen. His shoulders are up around his ears. Traders very quickly become experts at reading body language; they know that when someone's losing money, it's best to leave him in silence. But I'm having a tough time figuring out what could possibly have gone wrong in a trade that's a pure arbitrage. Arbitrage is when you buy copper in Shanghai for $400 and sell it in London for $500, paying $50 in shipping costs. You can't screw it up. But Ingram looks beaten. He finally tires of this, clicks the mouse a few times, and the tension leaves his body. He writes down something on a trade ticket and turns to me.

There is a profound sadness in his face. I can't figure out why. This is the best job in the world—free money—so what's there to be unhappy about?

• • •

After a few days of my watching, Ingram let me calculate his P&L. I figured this would require the use of some complex internally generated Lehman Brothers software, but I was wrong. He wasn't even using a spreadsheet. He ran his P&L with pen and paper.

I was appalled. The third-largest investment bank in the world did its P&L by hand? What had I gotten myself into? Everywhere I looked, all around the trading floor, there were software applications: applications to calculate risk, applications to calculate market impact, applications to calculate option greeks. Nowhere did I see anyone doing anything on paper except taking notes. I asked Ingram if our P&L system had been destroyed on 9/11. He said no, he'd simply never had one.

This was unacceptable, and Ingram knew it. As an ex-military guy, one who had been responsible for every last penny in his collateral duties, he wanted to know where every dollar was going, whether it was being made or lost in the arbitrage, or EFPs (exchange for physicals), or interest rate movements or dividend changes. He needed me to right the ship.

But for the time being, I was sitting right behind Ingram, practically dry humping him, sweating, peeking around his head to see the trades and calculate the damage. It was basic arithmetic; I knew the multiplier for the futures (250), so the only other numbers I needed were the prevailing interest rate; the level at which he bought or sold the futures, which I could read off his trade ticket; and the index level at which he bought or sold the basket of stocks, which I could read off the program trading terminal just over his right shoulder.

In his first trade, he bought S&P March futures, at 1161. He sold the basket at 1165.23. In ten seconds, I figured out that he'd made $1,122. But he was already onto the next trade. Bought at 1160. Sold at 1164.01. A $998 profit.

Then he made $765, $1,009, $1,045, and $888.

Then $1,497. That was a good one.

Then $605, $790, and $1,055.

Then Ingram was silent.

I calculated what I had so far: $8,562. Not bad for about eight minutes of work. But Ingram was stuck on something. Shoulders around the ears again. I knew enough not to ask.

I looked around. The ETF trader, Chuck Monaghan, was pissed in an understated kind of way. There had been some disagreement about price on a very large trade. He was sniping at Pudding Pop guy. "Three cents on a million," he said. I did the math in my head. Three cents, a million shares, $30,000. That was a lot of money to lose on a careless error.

That was a lot more money than Ingram and I were making.

Finally, Ingram clicked his mouse in frustration. I looked back at the screen and the ticket. He'd sold futures at 1152 and bought the basket at 1158.65.

He'd lost $11,563.

I looked at Ingram. He looked at me.

"It's not as easy as you think," he said. "It's not a true arbitrage. You have to leg into it."

"What do you mean, 'leg'?"

Ingram was flushed. "It means you can't execute the basket and the futures simultaneously. There's no true arbitrage anymore. You have to sell the stock first and then buy the basket second. In between, you have risk."

I thought about this. On the one hand, I was relieved that index arbitrage involved actual *skill*. This meant that the markets were, for the most part, efficient. There ain't no such thing as a free lunch. Other index arbs around the street were bidding and offering futures, conspiring to limit the arbitrage profits of the other players.

On the other hand, I was disappointed. I'd seen Ingram go through this routine of tension and release for the past few days, but it turned out he had been spinning his wheels the entire time. No wonder Mike hired me in a panic. He'd inherited this beast and needed help making money with it.

*I never lose*, I thought. This can't be an intractable problem. There are profitable index arb traders all over Wall Street.

I wanted to trade as quickly as possible.

Ingram had something else in mind for me. Recognizing how medieval his pen-and-paper P&L was, he told me that I'd have to program a P&L spreadsheet before he let me trade.

This was more difficult than it sounds. My peers at the top business schools were all Microsoft Excel ninjas, as was just about everyone else on Wall Street. I was not an Excel ninja. I was a donkey.

First I needed a computer. I was still dry humping Ingram and had only a pad of paper to my name, so I talked Ingram into getting me a laptop. It involved more bureaucracy than I expected.

Then, one morning, a gift: a laptop sitting on my half of the desk. It was dark outside, and Emma Crosby was on TV again, with her bedroom talk. *Let's plug this bad boy in.*

I knew there were outlets in the floor, I just didn't know where. Plug in hand, I crawled under the desk, felt a depression in the floor, and followed it.

*Zap!*

I stood bolt upright. Ingram had just arrived. "You all right?" He was laughing.

"Um, I think I just electrocuted myself."

"You going to try again?" asked Ingram.

"Nope, it's all you. I'm outta here."

When I got back, the laptop was set up. Now I had to build the goddamn spreadsheet in between writing down Ingram's trades on paper.

Luckily, I had a template. A summer associate had been set on this project the year before and had made good headway—he'd solved the database problem but hadn't been able to figure out the financial arithmetic. After a few days of discomfort, I untangled the programming and tortured the spreadsheet until the database confessed. Ingram was now running his P&L on his desktop, and it even included an implied interest rate calculation.

"Can I trade now?"

He said no.


Slowly, I began to acquaint myself with the other animals on the floor.

Delee, Herb, and Vikesh were Lehman Brothers's program traders. They were always fucking around and wasting time. In between fucking around and wasting time, they made a lot of money.

Herb was a Russian Jew with a top drawer full of unpaid cable bills. He was the type of guy who always had a tip on a horse. He wore appallingly tight pants and blousy shirts. He would vacation in Las Vegas and take pictures of himself in clubs, wearing a white suit with gold chains. Later we called him Uday.

Delee was a wisecracking Asian American, the king of the one-liner, who spoke perfect unaccented English when he verbally shredded senior management, Herb and Vikesh, or new guys like me. He wore expensive clothes and had a penchant for pinstripes, which looked fine framed against his small waist. He smelled good. He came from Goldman Sachs. The smell was success.

Vikesh, who we called Vic, got a late start in life after finding the world philosophically disagreeable and spending an extra year or two in the SUNYs. He demolished every Indian stereotype: he was tall, handsome, and an infamous womanizer. He was the fastest motherfucker on a spreadsheet I'd ever seen. He could accomplish in ten seconds what would take me fifteen minutes. Once a year he would disappear for two weeks and climb Mount Kilimanjaro.

The three of them, with the possible exception of Herb, had SAT scores that would make your teeth hurt. Ben Cohan, their manager, had little to do. With Delee, Herb, and Vic on board, the program desk ran itself. Cohan was free to delight in his proprietary trading.

Sam Grossman, who had so courteously offered me the breakfast sandwich back in my security guard days, worked behind me. All afternoon he shouted things like "Get down there!" and "Mack truck! Beep Beep!" It sounded like fun, but I was usually too busy calculating P&L to find out what he was up to.

One afternoon I got sick of the arithmetic and walked over to his screen. He was staring at a spreadsheet called "Trade Pressure." There were lots of colors and a little animation switching from red to green and back to red.

"What's that?"

"It's one of the projects our quants have been working on," said Grossman.

"What does it do?"

Grossman chewed on his lip. "Basically, instead of looking at just the size of the best bid and offer, it looks at all bids *below* the best bid and all offers *above* the best offer, and tries to derive some kind of . . . pressure that will drive the market higher or lower."

This all sounds a little fantastic, but I'm trying to keep an open mind.

"Does it work?"

"We're still testing it out. I'm supposed to sit here and watch it all day, buying futures if the pressure says the market's going up or selling futures if it says the market's going down."

"What do you think?"

Grossman paused. "It might work. We don't follow the model blindly, though. I can override it if I think it's wrong."

I was shocked. "Doesn't that kind of defeat the purpose?"

Grossman straightened up in his seat. He was asserting himself. "Not really. If you think about it, the quants build these models in a vacuum—they don't have any trading experience. You want the Russian mad scientists building your models, not trading your book, and you need an experienced trader to use human judgment from time to time."

"You mean a trader with three months' experience?" I was sorry I'd said it as soon as the words left my mouth.

Grossman wasn't offended. "Okay," he said, "but three months is better than nothing. You know I've been trading spooz this whole time."

"Spooz," I knew, were S&P futures. Everybody knew that.

Grossman continued. "Ben told me to lose as much money as I possibly could. When I made money my first day trading, he was pissed. He wants people to learn from their mistakes."

"So you just day-trade?"

"I suppose. I talk to Meat at the Merc. I trade in the pit. I started off with five lots, and now I'm up to ten lots. If this goes well, I'll take it up to twenty lots." Twenty lots—twenty futures contracts—was about a $6 million trade.

I didn't know whether to be jealous or not. Day trading seems so vulgar—fit for aimless, restless, pathetic fifty-five-year-old men; amateurish, balding capitalists; degenerate gamblers; and born losers. "How have you been doing?"

"Not bad, actually—I've made about four hundred thousand dollars in two months. I figure if I can make two million a year, I'll be paying for myself, and Ben won't mind keeping me around."

It was like getting punched in the kidneys by Buster Douglas. I needed to earn my keep. Lehman Brothers, coming off the best year in the firm's history, had hired busloads of MBAs. In the middle of his speech to us in Windows on the World, Joe Gregory, Lehman's number two, cackled and roared that we were the "last ones in." The goal was not to get shitcanned.

But Lehman had overhired, and there were too many bodies for too few seats—it was only a matter of time. If I could get a P&L attached to my name, and if I was profitable consistently, I would be safe. I couldn't just show up to work every day and watch Ingram chop himself to bits. We'd been making money, but not enough; barely six figures in the time we'd been working together. I couldn't help but wonder how this was a sustainable business. We were barely paying our own salaries, let alone the millions that Lehman needed to feed the managing directors.

The money had to be coming from somewhere.

I asked Ingram, "Can I trade yet?"

He said no.

My last five years had been all about Wall Street—all about becoming a trader. Every waking thought, every action was meant to further that goal. It was an obsession, and an unhealthy one at that. I'd completely missed out on my twenties; that feeling of being young and invincible. For what? Money? It wasn't really about money. It was about getting from A to B.

What I didn't realize was that trading is a journey, not a destination. So you're a trader. Now what? Trading is a constant process of intellectual and emotional growth, and people who trade for twenty years are still learning what to do and who to be when they finally hang it up. I was so focused on *becoming* a trader that I was missing out on the good stuff inherent to the process, like building spreadsheets and electrocuting yourself.

I knew I could do it. I knew I could do it *now*. Why wait?

Ingram was in a good mood. He'd put together a sparkling run of trades, and we were up about $30,000 for the day, our best day so far for the month of January. Then he'd bought me a delicious chicken Parmesan sandwich from up the street; it weighed at least two pounds. I sat next to him, bloated and happy.

He was telling me about baling hay. Ingram had grown up in Kansas, where it was good money for a big, thick, high school football player. It was also, according to Ingram, one of the hardest jobs in the world.

"Me and two other guys—all football players—used to ride around in the back of the truck. All we'd have is some water and a radio playing country music. One of us would haul the bales into the back of the truck, and the other two would stack them. That sounds like an easy enough job, but lifting even *one* of these things is a total nightmare. They each weigh about a hundred pounds, and the twine digs right into your hands. Once you start stacking them and lifting them over your head, it's ridiculous. But you should have seen the biggest of us, an offensive lineman at Oklahoma State. He was close to three hundred pounds, and he had no trouble at all—he whistled while he worked.

"I can't tell you how many people came out for that job and walked away after one day. 'No thanks. I'm never coming back.' Ninety degrees, in the sun, killing yourself."

*My boss baled hay in Kansas. I love him.*

Ingram was really getting into it now. He still weighed about 240 pounds, maybe 255 with the head. He started gesturing with his big paws.

"Then, after loading up the truck, we'd drive back and start stacking in the barn. This was the hard part. It was hot in that barn. *So* hot. And you had to get these bales all the way up to the roof, thirty feet in the air. With the sun beating down on the roof, it had to be a hundred and thirty, a hundred and forty degrees up there. Maybe hotter. You'd sweat out twenty pounds of water. Once the barn was full, we'd come outside, and we'd be *freezing*, because of the temperature change."

Ingram rolled himself up into a little ball, giggling. "We'd leave the truck running and huddle up in front of the engine block, trying to stay warm. And it was ninety degrees outside!"

I was in love. Everyone around us was a fucking Ivy League effete snob, but I was working for a real man; a guy who'd baled hay for an entire summer. If anyone can succeed on Wall Street, it has to be the guy who baled hay.

"Mike!"

We both turned around. It was Ben Cohan. He looked pissed. "Did you get that?"

"Get what?" asked Ingram, still smiling.

"GODDAMMIT!" Cohan pounded the desk as hard as he could. The entire row of cubicles shook.

I looked at the Bloomberg. We had a chart of the market. There was a line going straight down and a line going straight back up again.

Ingram turned white.

"That kind of shit happens once a year! You missed a *fucking gold mine!*"

The floor began to murmur. People were trying to figure out why Ingram got his ass chewed.

I already knew. There must have been an error—some drunk probably sold thousands of futures inadvertently. He'd entered in two thousand instead of twenty, or put in a market order instead of a limit order, or a combination of the two. He'd crushed the futures down twenty full handles.

This is an index arb trader's dream. He'd buy the futures from the error and sell stock simultaneously, making tens of thousands of dollars on every trade until he'd bought enough futures and sold enough stock to push the market back into line.

Ingram was still trying to figure out what the fuck had happened. He didn't even know what hit him.

Nobody talked to us for the rest of the day. No one even *looked* at us—they just stepped over our corpses. Cohan had a famous temper, but his treatment of Ingram was particularly harsh; you speak to someone that way only if you think he's a moron. Cohan wasn't impressed with Ingram, and I started to wonder if the last few months were taking their toll. He must have seen our P&L.

I was guilty by association. I was a new hire, which meant that I was already scum, and if Ingram was a political lightning rod, I'd need to get away from him as quickly as possible. On the other hand, he was the best boss I'd ever had. He taught me everything I needed to know, and he was full of kindness at the same time. My classmates, Dave Lane included, weren't so lucky. They were getting coffee, running errands, and being yelled at on a regular basis. Ingram was a decent human being.

If only I could get him to mint gold coins.

• • •

I eventually found out where all the money was coming from.

Ingram had been making noise about us having to roll our futures. Futures expire; with stock index futures, they expire quarterly. If you have a position in March futures, you have to roll it to June, or else it's going to disappear. For an index arb trader, this is of crucial importance—if you're long stock and short futures, and your short futures suddenly disappear, then you're simply long stock. It's a myth that traders are often *only* long or *only* short in a stock, cheering when the market goes up or down. That's almost never true. Traders are almost always long one thing and short something else against it. For us to be long, our stock inventory without a futures hedge would be unthinkable.

We had $7 billion of stock. If for some reason we forgot to roll our futures, and the market was down 1 percent the following day, we'd lose $70 million.

Ingram and I were religious about hedging our stock position, right down to the discrepancies caused by tiny daily changes in interest rates and variation margin. Rolling futures on a $7 billion position was a big deal. You don't want to fuck it up. And it was up to me to figure out how many futures we needed to roll.

Ingram emailed me a spreadsheet. I glanced at it, then discarded it. I hated spreadsheets. All I needed to know was the delta of both the March and June futures. Delta, a function of interest rates, is a measure of exactly how much stock a futures contract hedges. It was an easy calculation. I wrote it down on a piece of paper and handed it to him.

"What about the spreadsheet?"

"Eh."

He looked concerned.

"I like doing things by hand." And left it at that.

The mechanics of rolling futures are pretty simple. We were short March futures, so we needed to buy back our March futures and sell June futures simultaneously. Ingram sent me another spreadsheet, called "spreadpricer.xls." I entered the price of the spread—the difference in price between March and June futures—and it spit out an interest rate as a spread to LIBOR, or London Interbank Offered Rate, a benchmark interest rate. Ingram told me to let him know when the spread got near LIBOR plus 25.

I spent an entire week staring at spreadpricer.xls. The spread started at LIBOR plus 21, went down to plus 19, and then back up to plus 23, where it stayed.

"Mike. It's been at LIBOR plus twenty-three for a while now, and that's as high as it's gotten." I might as well have been speaking Swahili—it had no meaning to me. Ingram thought about this and said, "We'll do the roll tomorrow."

Ingram spent the next day on the phone with the floor of the Merc. "Three thousand at double, with a tick. Three thousand at sixty, up above. Two thousand at sixty-five." The floor would call him back with fills, or executed orders, which Ingram would write down on a ticket before time-stamping it and handing to me. I didn't know what to do with the tickets, except to stare at them. I assumed it was my job to do the P&L, but I couldn't figure out how to reverse engineer it.

"Here." Ingram forwarded me "spreadspnl.xls," which had highlighted cells where I was supposed to enter the futures fills. There was a March price and a June price, and the spreadsheet spit out an implied forward interest rate for each transaction. Once everything was entered to my satisfaction, I hit F9 and recalculated the spreadsheet. An orange cell at the bottom listed the total P&L.

It read $6,232,019.

*Wait a minute, there has to be an error in here somewhere.* I checked the contract multiplier. I checked for "fatfinger errors." I couldn't find a discrepancy.

"Hey Mike," I offered, "check this out."

Ingram looked at $6,232,019. "Yeah, that looks about right."

"How the fuck did we just make six million dollars?"

Ingram in his James Earl Jones voice said, "Ah, young grasshopper."

"Come on. You're not serious."

Ingram settled in. "I am serious. Think about what index arbitrage is. We're money market traders. We're borrowing and lending money. We lend at a higher interest rate, and we borrow at a lower interest rate. When we roll spreads, we're locking in the rate that we're lending at for the whole term—in this case, until June. We fund our stock balance sheet on an overnight basis, meaning that we borrow money on an interest rate that changes every day. So this isn't a *true* P&L, because we won't know how much money we made until June. But if overnight rates stay relatively steady, then, yeah, we'll make six million bucks."

It was all starting to make sense. Index arbitrage was a fucking gold mine. "So we could basically show up and do nothing for the next three months and make six million bucks?"

"That's right," said Ingram. "In fact, there's an index arb trader at another firm, Cupcake, who signed himself up to a performance-based contract. He was allowed to keep ten percent of what he made, so he ballooned the balance sheet up as big as he possibly could, rolled spreads every quarter, and made a hundred million dollars, ten million of which he kept for himself."

Fuck. "Why can't we do that?"

"I don't know, why not?"

So I hadn't really been hired to scalp a few hundred bucks out of stock index futures. I'd been hired to manage this leviathan we called the "balance sheet," which was full of thousands of stocks, all the way from 1-800-Flowers.com to General Electric to Lehman Brothers itself. We were there to manage the index, to perform additions and deletions, to keep track of dividends, and, above all, to pay a great deal of attention to interest rates. Since we were funding on an overnight basis, if short-term interest rates rose, we'd be in trouble. But if short-term interest rates fell, we'd be very happy.

"So we need the Fed to keep cutting rates?" I asked.

"That's right. And what do you think the Fed is going to do next? Hike or cut?"

"Cut."

"Right again. So we just let it go."

Declining interest rate environments are nectar to arb traders. It's like riding your bike downhill. Who needs brakes? Just let it go faster and faster.

"So what do we do when the Fed starts hiking rates?" I asked.

Ingram shrugged. "Overhedge, I guess. We'll figure it out."

It made no sense to worry about tomorrow. We'd just made six large.

"Can I trade yet?"

"No."

Ingram handed me a beer. A plain vanilla Budweiser. "You earned it."

"What's this for?"

"Last day in the building. We're moving to the new headquarters in February."

I wondered why I hadn't heard about this before. What I *had* heard about was the new dress code—back to suits. Dick Fuld, our scowling, humorless CEO, had acquiesced to business casual at the height of the tech bubble, against his will, and saw the flagging economy as a way to impose his will back on the worker bees. Fuld was old school and wanted an army of young employees in expensive suits. Instead I spent the previous weekend at Men's Wearhouse picking up a week's worth of $300 and $400 suits, along with a $99 pair of shoes and a handful of horrendous ties. I wasn't even dimly aware of how bad it was going to suck wearing shitty suits every day.

I wasn't the only one with a beer. Ben Cohan was yukking it up with Delee, Herb, and Vikesh. The sales guys were all smoking and joking. They were acting like crash survivors. Maybe that's what we were, in a sense, but most of us seemed more relieved about ditching our Jersey City shithole than we'd been about surviving a terrorist attack.

Ingram still hadn't given me the keys to the car, but I was at least looking forward to having my own desk and four screens to decorate it with. Screens were a status symbol, and most traders had four, while salespeople had three, research salespeople had two, and administrative assistants had one. A natural pecking order. Some traders would even install a fifth screen, and I thought that was the sexiest thing I'd ever seen.

I'd visited the new building, at 745 Seventh Avenue in Times Square, a few weeks prior. It was a little bit modern, and a little bit industrial—distinctive, but not quite out of place. There was a world map on the facade, with a clock, and a giant screen saver, designed to comply with Times Square signage regulations. The lobby was marble, or at least looked like it, and when you walked through it, you had the sinking feeling that you were supposed to be wearing a tie. We'd purchased it in a not-quite-distressed sale from Morgan Stanley, which had found itself long not one but two pieces of prime real estate right in the heart of midtown Manhattan—the next logical target for a terrorist attack. Lehman was willing to move anywhere, but to have a building that was trading floor–ready was a godsend. They paid $750 million. It would be worth every penny.

Beer in hand, I felt like a baseball player who'd labored for years in the minor leagues—riding buses, staying in cheap hotels—and finally been called up in the middle of the season. Our new address was Yankee Stadium, and I was in the starting lineup.

Batting ninth.

## 5

Jay Knight | Winter 2002–Spring 2002

In the military, and especially in the sea services, there are officers, like I was, and there are enlisted. The officers dine in the wardroom, with cloth napkins on their laps, looking over the rims of their glasses. The enlisted, out on the mess deck, throw more food than they eat. They're responsible for all the "work" of the ship—they scrape, they paint, they chase turds. They cook dinner. They receive messages, they work on engines, they navigate. The officers, on the other hand, don't do anything in particular—they *manage*. But the enlisted are proud to be the ones getting their hands dirty. The Coast Guard has a Marxist reverence toward physical labor, and it's worth more than the money they're not being paid.

On the trading floor, everyone's pretty much an officer. Analysts are ensigns. Associates are lieutenants, junior grade. Vice presidents are lieutenants or lieutenant commanders. Senior vice presidents are commanders. Managing directors are captains. And very senior managing directors, the executives of the firm, are admirals.

The enlisted are harder to spot. They're the IT support people, the programmers, the middle- and back-office people, the HR girls and the secretaries. They're enlisted because they don't have the *upside* that people like me had—no matter how hard they work, there is a limit to how much they get paid. The officers of the firm face no such limit.

If you interact with nothing but morons all day, you're enlisted. If you work for a college-educated effete snob, you're enlisted. If you deal with the tangible world, and not ideas, you're enlisted. Meat, Lehman Brothers's man on the floor of the Chicago Mercantile Exchange, was definitely enlisted.

His was an endangered habitat—physical trading floors worldwide were dropping like flies, as one exchange after another went electronic. By 2003, all the European stock exchanges had gone paperless. Germany, France, the UK, and Japan—all electronic. It was the United States that had refused the metric system, and it was the United States that was stubbornly clinging to open-outcry trading.

Meat inhabited this world, a world where being as obnoxious as possible is a competitive advantage. He spent all day placing orders for Lehman traders, thrashing his vocal cords, trying to get the best prices among the throngs of howling, screaming baboons.

The last thing he needed to worry about was a bonehead new associate.

"No, start over, that's not how you do it."

I felt a slow burn coming on. Ingram had given me his futures tickets to check out at the end of the day with Meat on the floor of the Merc. Meat was a futures industry veteran; he'd spent the better part of the last fifteen years clerking on the floor, next to the S&P pit, for Morgan Stanley, and then for Lehman Brothers, getting his hands dirty. We'd never met. I knew only what Ingram had told me, which was that Meat was hard-nosed, unfailingly professional, and not the type to suffer fools or tolerate mistakes. I hit the direct light and said, "Meat, it's Jared," and he said, "Jared, speak up, I can h*arrr*dly hear you," with the hard *R*, the hallmark of a Chicago accent. I pictured a giant, 250-pound bald butcher with a blood- and grease-stained apron, holding a cleaver. I wanted to know why people called him "Meat."

Now was not the time. Now I was getting a lecture on how to check out futures fills, the process of checking your work for errors. "When you're buying futures," Meat said, "you give the price first and the quantity second. You say, 'Paid *five* on *ten*.'"

"I know."

He ignored me. "And when you're selling, you give the quantity first and then the price. 'Sold *ten* at *five*.' You say 'on' for buys, and you say 'at' for sells. You have to get the language down, or else there's going to be confusion, and there's going to be an error."

"I know, I know." But if I knew, then why did I get it backward?

"Well, if you know, then why did you get it backward?" Meat asked.

Okay. We're not off to a good start.

Meat paused. "So I hear you're going to be trading the index arb?"

Another sore point. I'd been asking Ingram if I could trade for weeks on end, and I still hadn't stepped up to plate. "Eventually, I guess."

"That's good." Meat sounded hopeful. "You're next in a long line of great arb traders at Lehman. But I have to tell you, the way these minis are growing, the good days are long gone. Ben Cohan used to make money hand over fist. Before you know it, it'll all be electronic, and they'll shut this floor down."

Three years earlier, in the midst of the dot-com boom, the Chicago Mercantile Exchange had decided to blast itself out of the Stone Age of paper tickets. It developed an electronic version of the S&P futures contract, called the "e-mini," which was one-fifth the value of the big, institutional contract, which was five hundred times the value of the S&P 500 index in dollars. The idea was to attract retail investors to index futures, but to date, all the e-mini had accomplished was to create a brisk arbitrage between the big contract and the e-mini, open to the vultures who sat around the top of the pit with handheld computers and laptops.

"You're not really worried about that, are you?" I asked him. "I mean, most of the volume still goes through the bigs."

Meat disagreed. "We're fucked. We're dinosaur*rrs* down here with our hand signals, and sooner or later we're going to be extinct."

If that were true, it would be too bad. A Chicago trading floor was one of the last places on earth where any asshole could walk into the room and make a pile of money. Sometimes, any asshole did. But it took all kinds—there were math PhDs and pizza delivery boys standing shoulder to shoulder, screaming, sweating, and spitting on one another's necks. A public exchange trading floor is a sight to behold. In extreme chaos, there is extreme beauty.

Where I sat, there was a more elite, refined sense of beauty. We'd moved into the new building in Times Square, and I finally understood what everyone was complaining about back in Jersey City. This was a real Wall Street trading floor, with a vast ocean of computers and monitors, sturdy desks with pictures of young children lined up on top, people in white shirts, and blue shirts, and the occasional burgundy shirt with a silver tie (worn by one of the IT guys). The carpets were green, the walls were green, the mouse pads were green. Surrounding the floor were glass offices occupied by managing directors who made unholy amounts of money. There was a glass conference room too, which we called the fishbowl. Beyond that: Seventh Avenue, with herds of chubby blond people from Missouri milling about the street vendors and the amateur rappers, the ghetto dancers, and Zamfir copycats with their Pan flutes. Little did they know that zillions of dollars were zipping around just twenty feet over their heads. Little did they know that nearly every single warm body on the second floor of the building they'd just walked by was a millionaire.

I worked on the second floor, but I was not a millionaire yet. I had some work to do.

Luckily for me, even though I was paid next to nothing, at least by Wall Street standards, there were psychic benefits. At hypothetical cocktail parties, I could tell people that I was a *Lehman Brothers trader*, an exotic, expensive breed of cat. I was, by default, upper class, whether I had any money or not. My intelligence and my abilities had been spoken for.

Lehman Brothers had a code of conduct and an employee manual covering things such as vacation days and maternity leave. The company had a dress code too, but it wasn't written down for someone like me to find. I'd just invested a couple thousand bucks on a week's worth of suits, and I was experiencing regret. I didn't look like everyone else. I didn't realize that most people spent on one suit what I'd spent on five. I hadn't yet heard the names Joseph Abboud or Hickey Freeman. And I was always on the losing end of something called "The Lehman Handshake."

Everyone on the trading floor had these funny little brightly colored ties with cutesy prints. The narrow end of the tie would stick out every now and then to reveal a diagonal slash and a tiny label. I could never get close enough to read them, but everyone had them, Ingram included. His tie was brown, with pineapples and naked dudes all over. It was the ugliest thing I had ever seen. Ingram, the Kansas farm boy, looked perfectly ridiculous in any tie, let alone the tropical variety. But it was the uniform, and I might as well have been wearing a barrel with suspenders. Matt Liebman, a sharp-dressed, salesman and sartorial snob, gave me the once-over every morning as soon as I arrived. He'd shake his head, hands on hips—*you are a piece of work*.

One day I wore a black tie with gold spots, picked up from the Men's Wearhouse on sale for $10. Liebman grabs the tie, turns it around, and stares at the label. It reads "IV Front." I am a piece of work.

That's your "Lehman Handshake."

• • •

The central planners had failed to anticipate the potential synergies of sitting index arb next to program trading, so Ingram and I were an island in the middle of cash guys.

In equities trading, *cash* doesn't refer to money. A cash trader isn't a money market trader, even though that's exactly what it sounds like. Cash traders trade individual stocks. They call it cash because you need the cash to buy the stock—not the case with the derivative, which is just a contract created out of thin air. The cash guys I was sitting next to were "US Cash," not to be confused with "European Cash" or "Asian Cash." The head of US Cash was John Smith, an impossibly masculine trader, a walking molecule of testosterone who'd captained the Penn State football team to a national championship under Joe Paterno. He patrolled the aisles, rotating his shoulders and practically his entire torso just to tell people to go fuck themselves. We thought he had a neck injury.

The cash business followed Smith's leadership. It was a masculine place to work and to live. US Cash was fast cars, money, steak, cigars, boobs, *Maxim* magazine, football, gambling, weightlifting, more boobs, and scotch. And golf. I was books, electronic dance music, art, literature, light jogging, frugality, *Details* magazine, and baseball. Actually, we had boobs in common, but I was mostly out of place.

I sat back-to-back with the mad genius of the cash business, Hank Hsu. He was ex-Navy, like Ingram, but the similarities ended there. Ingram was a classic submariner, quiet and thoughtful, a poster child for the silent service. Hsu was a loud surface sailor who liked to blow shit up. He had, indeed, blown a lot of shit up in the first Gulf War. He liked to play videos on his computer of missiles being launched off destroyers set to Sousa marches and AC/DC.

While running Ingram's P&L, I'd listen to Hsu talk poker with his buddy Johnny B. The conversation was an unintelligible hodgepodge of flop, preflop, river, ace, king, trip threes, and nut straight. It was also impossible to get a sense of the money that was changing hands, though I guessed it was somewhere in the hundreds. I was wrong. If they weren't talking poker, they were talking college basketball, and on more than one occasion I saw Johnny B. display an envelope of cash.

Hsu was unquestionably intelligent. He was, in fact, too smart to be trading cash, but he wasn't qualified for derivatives—he couldn't sit still. So he used 5 percent of his brain to trade, 45 percent to surf the Internet, and 50 percent to play video games. In the morning, he would arrive bleary eyed, having spent the whole night blowing shit up in a multiplayer online universe, then he'd spend the rest of the day punting around stocks such as CSCO and QLGC.

But even with only 5 percent of his brain, Hsu was a superstar. John Smith would occasionally drop by to menace him while he surfed bikini girls, but he'd let it go. Hsu was making him rich.

In the meantime, I'd gotten in the habit of listening in on Ingram's phone calls. Not his personal calls, which mostly consisted of hushed exchanges with his wife, but his conversations with Meat. On a trading floor, anyone can listen to anyone else's phone calls. Turrets have dozens of outside lines and direct lights; if one of them is lit green, it means there's a conversation taking place, and if you're trying to figure out what the hell's going on all around you, you can simply hit the button and eavesdrop. If you don't want an underdressed MBA listening in, there's a Privacy button that'll box him out. Sometimes it's necessary to ask "Are you on privacy?," especially if you're gearing up to whisper about the assistant's jugs.

I'd been working Ingram over nonstop, twisting his arm into letting me trade, and I was beginning to make some progress. He'd finally broken down and let me *listen* to him trade. I hit MERC INDX and picked up in the middle of the call.

Meat: "These Bank One guys are looking at me."

Ingram: "What are they looking at you for?"

Meat: "Fuck if I know. I think they're waiting to see if you'll put in a bid."

Ingram: "Are they bidding?"

Meat: "Not yet. Clerk's looking at the currencies now."

My phone had a mute switch near the earpiece, and I played with it as I listened to the trading floor. It didn't sound like a sporting event. It didn't sound like a concert. It didn't even sound like a bunch of people talking at the same time—strange, considering that's exactly what it was. Sure, dudes were yelling at other dudes, but there was something else—their voices held a certain *urgency* that materializes only when the thing being yelled about is money, and lots of it.

Ingram: "Eight on ten."

Meat: "Working eight on ten. Eight bid at ten. Eight bid light. Offered at ten. Thirty on the offer. At nine now."

Ingram: "Down to seven."

Meat: "Down to seven, working seven. Seven bid. Jax offering nines. Bank One bid with. Seven bid. Working seven on ten. At eight. *Filled.*"

Ingram: "Got it. Six on ten."

And so on. Ingram had been doing much better lately: there was volatility in the market and tons of natural flow in the futures pit. When a big order comes into the pit, it splatters the locals (the traders in attendance) against the walls and leaves a wave of index arbitrage in its wake. In the absence of natural flow, there isn't much for the locals and the arb guys to do except sit around and pick each other off, making infinitesimal trades just to steal money from their next-door neighbors. But if the big boys are playing, things get fun.

I scan the floor. Delee, Herb, and Vikesh are huddled around Ben Cohan, looking like they are working on a difficult math problem. Cohan, with his high forehead and unruly hair, hands a piece of paper back to the three musketeers and with his body language says something like, "I don't give a fuck what you do with this trade; just don't make us look bad." Liebman is hanging out by the offices, across the floor, sucking up to the head of cash sales. John Smith is threatening to grab one of the cash sales guys by the neck, sending him scuttling down the aisle. I can hear things like "Buy fifty Oracle," and "twenty-five UPS, with volume," and "small penis."

*Small penis?*

Hank Hsu stands up behind me, hands on his hips, looking out across the floor. "You want to talk about small penis?" It's like he's missing the piece of his brain that restricts certain kinds of public speech. He is, in the naval sense of the word, a loose cannon.

On Hsu's right are two female Chinese quants, part of Ben Cohan's miniature *Star Trek* convention. On Hsu's better days, they can barely conceal their disdain. Now they're sitting in shock, mouths wide open.

"I don't care what you motherfuckers say about small penis. I'm half

Chinese and half Irish; who do you think has a small penis? Sleep with me, and you can *definitely* ride a bike around Central Park in the morning."

Even Ingram, engrossed in the Nasdaq futures pit, turns around, aghast. I don't know whether to shit or go blind. We're both trying to hide under the desk. The female Trekkies are pissed. They're beyond pissed. They're shooting daggers. I figure we're about twenty seconds away from a major HR violation, and I don't want to be around if the HR goons came down to throw Hsu in HR jail.

What I do want is to be like Hsu. Except for the small penis.

Times Square, even under the best of circumstances, is a toilet. It's a giant hole filled with tourists, drug dealers, and prostitutes, and I walked through it every morning on the way to work. For the first few months, after we moved into the new building, I'd start out going east on Forty-second Street, then head north through Times Square up to the Lehman building at Forty-ninth and Seventh Avenue. This was fine in the mornings, if not almost agreeable—there was no foot traffic, and the only tourists in the vicinity were lined up smartly outside *Good Morning America*. In the winter, it was plainly surreal. Big fucking signs with big fucking lights on all the time, 24/7, with howling winds and blowing trash. The homeless were hustled out of the area and put to bed on the steps of St. Mary's, but occasionally the weirdness broke through. I walked right into the middle of a posse of rappers in fur coats outside the Viacom building one morning. They looked like Digital Underground.

Eventually I learned to avoid the kooks. There was a shortcut, of sorts—I could walk up Eighth Avenue to Forty-fourth, hang a right, then make my way to Shubert Alley, crossing up to Forty-fifth, through the taxi pickup at the Marriott Marquis. It saved me about a minute. The trade-off was that it had me walking up Eighth for a few blocks, where all the porno shops had migrated after being kicked out of Times Square. Boobs at six in the morning are awkward.

It was hard to stay warm. As a kid, I never wore gloves or a hat. Scarves were for sissies. But the fifteen-minute walk from the Port Authority Bus Terminal in the middle of winter was pure torture. It felt like it was well below freezing every day, and once I got to my desk, it would take me a half hour just to thaw out my fingers and ears. Ingram wore these fancy earmuffs that wrapped around the back of his head. I thought they were pretty gay. As it turns out, *I* was the one who was gay. I'd picked up an overcoat at the Men's Wearhouse (where else?) with an albedo. It was shiny. It reflected light. And it had a belt, of sorts, around the waist, which I would tie in a bow, inching myself closer and closer to bathrobe territory. It was a combination of Northern New Jersey organized crime and Hugh Hefner. People told me I was looking sharp. I silently told them to go fuck themselves.

Ingram arrives, wearing his gay earmuffs. "So, are you ready?"

"Ready for what?"

"Want to give it a shot today?"

*Finally.*

In the midst of watching Ingram carefully over the last few weeks, I'd achieved a sense of momentum—I could tell when the market was simply farting around and when it was going to make a big move. I was beginning to understand greed as it exists on Wall Street, as well as the concept of overstaying your welcome in a trade. I also developed a feel for the gamesmanship of the futures pit, the staring contest with the other index arb desks, particularly Bank One. Although Bank One itself didn't have an index arb desk, it provided the futures support for Royal Bank of Canada, which had the biggest index arb desk in the world. You were always fighting it out in the pit with the Bank One guys, stepping ahead of their orders, playing chicken with the stock. But they always played bigger—twenty lots to our ten.

I called Meat to tell him the good news.

"That's great!"

"Yeah, but let's take it slow."

"You tell me what you're comfortable with. I'm just here to help."

It was clear to me that Meat took a great deal of pride in clerking futures. We both knew that he was an integral part of the index arb team and that his execution speed could represent the difference in hundreds of thousands of dollars over the course of the year, but the firm viewed him as a cost center, not a revenue center. Ingram had told me privately (it's not polite to talk about how poor somebody is) that guys on the Merc aren't particularly well paid. We got all the glory, and they were down in the trenches, sweating it out for us in the name of God, the Holy Spirit, and Dick Fuld. I was touched.

Ingram had also informed me that I was going to be trading the Nasdaq arb. When most people think of a Nasdaq index, they think of the Nasdaq Composite. But the Nasdaq Composite is an index of *every single stock* listed on Nasdaq, including the shitty little microcaps that trade by appointment. The Nasdaq 100 is a smaller but much cleaner index. It has only large companies—the top one hundred nonfinancial companies in the Nasdaq Composite. And there are futures listed on it too—during the bubble, it was more addictive than crack cocaine.

So I was the junior varsity index arb trader, trading the Nasdaq 100. I didn't mind. The fills were faster and cleaner, and while it wasn't the granddaddy of the indices, it would suffice.

I had a futures ticket. I had my fastcash, which told me if futures were trading rich or cheap to the index. And I had DPT—my program trading terminal—on a Unix machine. Hot stuff. At 09:28:30, I called Meat.

I could hear the noise of the crowd in the background. Crowd noise, to me, was like music—a synced-up sound track. You knew when the crowd was bored, when the crowd was excited, when a big order hit the pit, when there was a fight. After a few months of index arbitrage, I could trade blind—I needed only my ears.

It sounded like Meat was multitasking—he was talking to me, but he was also quoting S&P futures over the loudspeaker (which we called the box) and studying the S&P pit, reading the hand signals to see who was trading what. You and I look at a crowd of exchange locals, and we see an uncoordinated army of hairy men waving their arms, like they're all signaling to their very own rescue helicopter. Meat looks at it and sees a conversation—a hectic but civilized debate carried out in a massive gathering of sign language—and he knows exactly what's going on. "Thirty bid at seventy. At seventy light. Bache offering sixty, now. Twenty bid. Goldman sells twenty at twenty, Floz buys them. Covellos bidding forty now. At sixty. At seventy now. Bank One at seventy." Meat did this all day. He was clearly not being paid enough.

All of a sudden, the noise started to take a different shape, like I was running through the tunnel and onto the field at Giants Stadium.

I began to lose my nerve. I was a man. I had a penis. I'd done plenty of manly things in my lifetime—I'd been in the armed services, I'd done two thousand push-ups in a single day, I'd piloted a ship through eighty-knot winds and thirty-five-foot seas. But I felt like I was being led into prison, in handcuffs, for the first time. I was going to be somebody's bitch. There was something wrong with my insides.

"Meat."

"What?"

"I gotta take a shit."

Meat laughed. "You gotta take a shit, now?"

"Um, right now."

"Ha. Okay, talk to you in a few minutes."

It was an emergency. I was crowning. But another wonderful thing about the new Lehman Brothers building was the bathrooms, built with a trading floor in mind. They were enormous, and there were at least twelve stalls, each of them completely and utterly necessary, and each of them filled to capacity by eight thirty in the morning, after all the sales guys had read their morning research, which was enough to make any asshole dilate. The tiled floor was littered with market letters and research, and several copies of the *New York Post*. I ducked into a stall, in extremis.

I'd been itching to trade for months, and here I was in the bathroom, taking a smash out of sheer nervousness. I was a mess.

I ran water over my hands, bypassed the soap, and burst out onto the trading floor. It was alive. A sea of stupid ties. The cash guys were yelling at one another.

Ingram looked at me. "Everything okay?"

My ears reddened. I mumbled something about something I ate.

MERC INDX.

"Meat."

"Everything come out all right?"

"Peachy. Let's go. Nasdaq."

"Nasdaq . . . two bid at four." Meat quoted the market.

I stared at the fastcash. Right now futures were 0.79 rich. .85. .99. 1.10.

I knew I could effect an arbitrage between 1.20 and 1.40 away from fair value. I could *leg* into the trade, as Ingram often did, sending the stock basket first and waiting to be filled on the futures, or I could wait to get my order filled and *then* send the basket.

1.15. Not yet.

"At four," said Meat.

1.24. Still not yet.

"Three bid now light." The market was starting to rise.

1.33. Getting richer.

"Three bid." Just a little bit higher . . .

1.41.

*"Filled."*

*Crap.*

I clicked the mouse on the Unix computer, sending basket IABUY0305A to the marketplace. Across the street, one hundred stocks scattered out into space, lifting the offers of one hundred separate traders. One hundred traders' eyes dilated, watching their short positions increase. One hundred traders responded by moving their markets higher. The entire stock market rose, imperceptibly, on account of my mouse click.

To the extent that I'd ever fantasized about my first trade, I'd always pictured it small—a quiet but not entirely inauspicious beginning—but I'd never imagined it as a complete abortion. After three months of watching Ingram, learning what *not* to do, I'd gone and done it, fumbling my first trade.

It was all nerves. My heart was racing; I was doing something forbidden and exciting, sneaking out of the house, tiptoeing across the creaky floor, closing the door softly behind me. It was like the first time I walked up to a craps table, being told repeatedly to throw the money on the felt, but not hearing the dealer through the noise in my ears. I could prepare for this moment, but there was no accounting for the jitters.

I wrote "10 1454" on the sell side of the ticket, hands shaking, and next to it, "BUY A." I called the database from the spreadsheet, pulling the basket with its fills into row 19. I'd just purchased about $1.5 million worth of stock. I typed in -10 and 1454 into the sell side of the spreadsheet, then hit F9, and looked at the P&L.

$452.

*Fuck.*

I'd made money on my first trade. But I needed to be averaging about $1,000 a trade to even begin to approach a worthwhile existence. I'd been too cautious, too conservative in waiting to get filled on the futures before I sent the basket. The first rule of wind walking is that you don't let go of what you've got until you've got hold of something else. But if I obeyed the first rule of wind walking, I was never going to make any money.

I didn't think it would be this hard.

Meat stopped quoting the box for a minute to check up on me. "You okay?"

"Yeah."

"You make money?"

"Yeah."

He understood. "Okay, well, try it again."

I took a deep breath. "Ten at seven," I told him.

"Working ten at seven. Five bid."

I concentrated on the fastcash: .65. .75. .91. It was like surfing—you find a wave, and you paddle like hell to catch up to it.

1.01.

1.19.

*Buy.*

I launched IABUY0305B. One hundred stocks sprayed across the city. I looked back at fastcash.

1.05.

.89.

.67.

*Fuck.*

"At seven. Nothing yet. Nothing *yet.* At six now, working sevens."

*Christ.*

"*Unable.* Four bid."

I was offering ten futures contracts at 1457, which I had failed to sell. The market was moving away from me.

I was still offering sevens. I could wait to see if the market would rally back and buy my seven offer. I could try offering sixes, but I would still be on the seven offer, waiting to get filled. And if I waited any longer, the market could move even *further* away from me. This is what happened to

Ingram when I was doing his P&L with pen and paper. He'd wipe out ten winning trades with one loser. But I didn't have ten winning trades to wipe out.

I had to sell.

"Meat, down to four."

"Working fours. *Filled* . . . sold ten at four." Meat reflected my emotions back at me. He knew which trades were profitable and which were sinkholes; I didn't have to tell him.

"Goddamnit."

I called the database, filled in the sell side of the spreadsheet, then hit F9.

$(2,623).

I was mortified. After the first two trades of my life, I was down money. This was the fast track to getting laid off. I'd be eating out of Dumpsters by the end of the week.

Ingram interrupted my suicide plans. "Harder than it looks, isn't it?"

He was gloating, just barely, and I allowed it. It was true—this was much harder than it looked.

I spent the rest of the day digging myself out of a small hole. At the end of the day, I had enough money to buy a Yugo.

I showed my P&L spreadsheet to Ingram. "Not bad, not bad. You'll get better."

I was exhausted. I felt like I'd earned $4,000 by collecting eighty thousand cans and bottles from the trash cans in Times Square. But I was also energized. I was overstimulated, like I had been playing video games for eight hours, drinking strawberry Quik mixed with Coke. My muscles had expanded. My hands were stronger. I wanted to fuck something. I wanted to trade index arb all night.

I looked at Ingram. "You want to go out for a drink?"

"Gotta go home to the wife, sorry."

I didn't want to go home. I knew what was going to happen at home. I would eat dinner, spend some time with my wife, then I would go to bed, and I would stare at the ceiling for hours. Unable to tolerate the ceiling any longer, I would go downstairs and make myself a drink, or three. Then I would go back to bed and stare at the ceiling.

I thought this was normal. I thought this is what Ingram meant when he said, "Gotta go home to the wife, sorry." I didn't find it at all unusual. So I passed out at 0200 after a half-dozen Jack and Cokes.

The next day I made about $8,000. Ingram gave me a farm boy handshake and a healthy pat on the back. I had difficulty sleeping again.

In my time watching Ingram, I'd noticed what looked like an opportunity. Economic indicators are released periodically throughout the week, most of them before the market opens at 0830, like jobless claims, for example. But some of them are announced during the trading day, such as consumer confidence, at 1000, or the Philadelphia Fed index, at 1200, and when *those* numbers come out, the market spazzes and rips in either direction.

Specifically, the market reacts to the economic data as it moves relative to the market's *expectations*. It's not hard to figure out what the market's expectations are—they're published by Bloomberg. For example, the market might expect 450,000 claims for jobless benefits in the coming week. When the data are released, they appear on the screen—*boink*—right next to the survey number. If the number is positive relative to expectations, the market rallies, and if the number is negative relative to expectations, the market sells off—pretty much without exception.

I wondered what would happen if I bought (or sold) a basket of stock right on the release of an indicator, then sold futures a few minutes later when it was done going up (or down). I wanted to trade one *really big* index arb, but the market reacted quickly, so I needed to react quickly too; I'd have to hit the button at light speed. It seemed risky, but it also seemed worth a shot.

In a perfectly efficient market, a strategy like this would never work. Efficient market theory says that the arrival of news in the marketplace is immediately and perfectly disseminated, and no one person acting independently can get ahead of it. But I'd spent days watching this. It was like staring at the clock, waiting for 11:59 to turn to midnight. The number would come out—*boink*—and for a *split second*, nothing would happen. This tiny period of time, a half second, maybe, was enough of a window for me to send out an index arb basket and move the market before anyone else did. It was a delay that could be exploited (let alone discovered) only by someone with exceptionally fast reflexes and exceptionally acute concentration. A freak like me.

This is what Lehman Brothers hired new MBAs to do—spot market inefficiencies. And if you start herding the smartest of the smart into a single room, eventually they're going to figure out how to make money. Some of them will use mathematics. Some of them will use structuring and sales. And some of them, like me, will be little more than sophisticated video game players with a competitive streak.

That morning, I scratched around in a handful of trades with Meat, basically going nowhere. I was waiting for consumer confidence at 1000.

"Meat, consumer confidence coming up."

"Okay, you want to call me back?"

"No, stay on the line. Keep quoting."

Meat paused to think. Usually we shut down when economic data came out. "What are you up to?"

"Just stay with me. I'm going to try something new."

Consumer confidence was expected to come in at 57.2 that morning. I figured that if it came in at 61 or higher, this would send the market into orbit, and I would buy stock, selling futures a few minutes later and collecting a huge profit. Conversely, if it came in at 54 or lower, I would run the opposite play: selling stock, buying futures later. My hunch was that it would come in higher. People had been unfailingly optimistic in the midst of this bear market rally.

One minute to go before the number. I started to experience the same sense of doubt I'd felt before my first trade. The crowd was silent, like there'd been an injury on the field.

"Meat."

"What?"

"I gotta take a shit again."

"Jesus H. Christ," he said, "what the hell is wrong with you? You want to call me back?"

"No." I was straining. "I'll stay on. Keep quoting."

"Oh bid at two. Oh two. Nothing going on. Everyone's hands down. Oh two."

I watched the wall clock tick down to 1000. 09:59:51. 09:59:52. 09:59:53.

I looked back at the screen. *Come on, 61, 61, 61.*

1000.

*Consumer confidence: 65.*

*Buy!*

I clicked off two baskets in DPT. I'd traded twice the size I was used to, a twenty lot instead of a ten lot.

"One bid! Two bid! Three, no, four—no, six bid! Seven bid!"

The Nasdaq was spinning off into space. I was making a shitload of money. But I didn't want to get greedy.

"Meat, ten at nine."

"Working ten at nine. Seven bid, eight bid, *filled*. Sold ten at nine."

I was still long stock.

"Oh bid."

"Two bid." *Money.*

"Five bid."

"Seven bid." *More money.*

This was too good.

"Eight bid." *Time to sell.*

"Meat, ten at two."

"Nine bid, oh bid, one bid, *filled!*"

My hands were shaking, but my insides had settled down. I struggled to tap in the futures fills on the spreadsheet. F9.

$22,898.

*Holy shit.*

"How'd you do?"

"Meat, it's a lot of money."

"How much?"

I told him.

"Nice job! Look, you sold the top tick too; it's trading fives now."

I looked at the chart. I'd sold the tippy top. The index had declined seven points.

"I've never seen that before, someone selling the top tick on, what? This is your third day?"

"Yup."

I was full of myself. I was in search of a gold star. "Mike! Ingram!"

Mike was in lost in thought, daydreaming out the window. "What?"

Ingram stared at the spreadsheet. His eyebrows rose. "What the hell?"

"I learned a new trick. I'll show you."

I could see Ingram cycling through his emotions. First he was pleased. Then he was dismayed—months of frustration in trading index arb, and he still hadn't figured out the secret sauce. Then he was pleased again, thinking that he'd just hired a money-printing machine.

I traded like a champ for the rest of the day, with a faint erection. I was on fire. Bidding and offering, buying and selling, stock and futures. I went back to the pantry for a third cup of coffee. My brain had never moved faster. I was working two orders at the same time, with two baskets, cueing up a third and fourth. I was an animal. I was a perfectly genetically engineered index arbitrage trader.

At the end of the day, I'd made about $40,000—a huge showing. Ingram flags down Chris Masters, the head of equity derivatives trading. Chris intimidates me. He's huge, and ripped, and mean looking. He's a former track-and-field athlete, but he looks like a Division II basketball player who can bench four hundred pounds.

"Chris, Jared made forty thousand bucks today!"

Chris looks at me like I have Down's syndrome. Then he thinks about what Ingram just told him. "Very respectable," he says with a smile.

I think it is more than respectable.

But I have no idea how much money these people actually make.

I settled into a routine. Ingram let me run with the Nasdaq arb, and I was consistently profitable. Once the initial awkwardness was out of the way, Meat and I became fast friends, and I was spending my days whipping around Nasdaq futures and stock, squeezing, on average, about $30,000 out of the market every twenty-four hours. In essence, I was a bottom feeder, a sea cucumber nibbling up leftover pieces of fish food off the seafloor. The only reason this money existed was because everyone else was too slow or too busy with other shit to notice it. The macro hedge funds weren't concerned about market efficiency—they just wanted to get their position on. While the big guys feasted on porterhouse at the table, I gathered up the crumbs.

There were, of course, social consequences. In any society, the people who go around picking up garbage can't be the cultural elite. They smell like urine. They're unpleasant to look at. We tolerate them and throw them little tokens from time to time. If they're crazy, we haul them away. I was a mentally ill homeless garbage picker wearing a Men's Wearhouse suit. But I loved my job.

In fact, it was the perfect job for me. I knew it the moment I sat down behind Ingram in Jersey City and watched him trade. Back in business school, I decided I might as well become a trader simply because I could square large numbers in my head. I was a mathematical magician. I didn't know shit about finance; I just wanted to create money out of speed and pure intimidation. And in the early moments of my career, I wasn't terribly concerned with high-level economics, trade theory, or market philosophy. My brain, atrophied from years of military service, wasn't ready for that—not yet. All I wanted to do was *do*, to take action. That's index arb. The thinking would come later.

When I traded, I entered the psychic autobahn. Before long, I was trading over 10 percent of the volume in Nasdaq futures. I fought with the Bank One guys. We would both be on the bid, me with ten futures and Bank One with twenty futures. Meat called them "*carrrs*," from the old days when an agricultural future was a carload of grain. I would blast the stock and scoop up the arb, sending the Bank One traders running for cover. I would crush the market over and over again, trading five or six clean arbs and leaving the Bank One trader with none. We could not coexist peacefully, I thought. I was going to put them out of business.

Meanwhile, I was a magnet for useless knowledge. I became an expert on Nasdaq liquidity. I studied Eurodollar and Fed funds futures for the day when we would actually have to hedge interest rates. I became an amateur Fed watcher, scrutinizing each member of the board of governors and the regional presidents, divining whether they were hawkish or dovish, and determining how they would vote at the next FOMC meeting. I was a strange hybrid of exchange local and money market trader. I learned about EFPs and how Lehman used them to manage our balance sheet. I could tell you all about futures fair value and predict how the basis was going to perform based on interest rate movements and dividend changes.

But I never knew what the market was doing. After work, at a bar, someone would ask me what the market did that day.

I had no idea.

Whether the Nasdaq futures rallied to 1475 or sold off to 1425 was of no consequence to me—I made money either way. I had a vague idea that we were still in a bear market, even though we'd rallied some, but beyond that, I hadn't the slightest notion. Relatives asked me for free investment advice. I had nothing to offer. The only thing I could really say for sure was which way short-term interest rates were headed.

As it turns out, there's a lot of money to be made with that particular intuition.

I knew the Fed would never hike interest rates. We'd just been through a terrorist attack, for Christ's sake, which had distorted spending and savings patterns and hit the economy when it was already on its ass, victim of an imploding stock market bubble. The Internet economy encouraged overinvestment in computers and routers and networking cable, and the economy was choking on overcapacity. The effects were *deflationary*, and it was extremely unlikely that the Federal Reserve would hike interest rates at any point in the near future. It felt like the Fed was giving us a free option—rates could go lower, but they couldn't go higher. I wanted to find a trade perfectly suited to the situation at hand.

Eurodollar futures—futures on interest rates—are complicated, but you're really fucked when you get to *options* on Eurodollar futures. If you've been living in a world of alcohol, tobacco, and pot, and one day someone introduces you to cocaine, that's what it's like encountering options. It accelerates your trip to rehab.

Options are *nonlinear* ways to gain exposure to price movements. If you buy a stock, and the stock goes up, you make money; the stock goes down, you lose money. It doesn't work that way with options. If you buy a call option on a stock and it goes up, you make money, and if it goes down, you break even or lose only a little bit of money. That might sound like a great deal, but you need to get the timing as well as the direction right. Put options are the same, just in reverse.

Since I didn't think rates would be going any higher, I wanted to sell put options on Eurodollar futures. Simultaneously, I wanted to use the proceeds of the puts that I sold to buy call options on Eurodollar futures. The trade was cash neutral. If rates went up significantly, I would lose money. If rates went down significantly, I would make money. In between, I'd break even. This particular trade was known as a *risk reversal.* The guys on the trading floor called it a "squash."

I showed the trade to Ingram. I drew a few hockey stick diagrams (he understood little about options), explained what our risks were, how much we would stand to make if we were right, and how much we would stand to lose if we were wrong.

Ingram thought about it.

"Okay," he said.

*My first real prop trade.* I called Calvin, who was our clerk in the Eurodollar pit. He was Meat's brainy equivalent, with an equally corrosive Chicago accent.

I pushed the CME EURO button on my turret. "Calvin, please."

"This is him."

Nerd noise came through the phone.

"Hey. Got something to do in the options."

"Really? What are you thinking?" Calvin was probably surprised and impressed that some kid in equities had suddenly taken an interest in a complicated interest rate derivative.

I explained the trade.

"Funny you should say that—we've seen some similar trades going through lately. Lots of put selling. We did some call flies this morning, about ten thousand times. What strikes are you looking at?"

"I'm looking at the seventy-two, eighty-five squash in short June. Buying call, a thousand times."

"Let's see . . . the seventy-two, eighty-five squash is two bid at three, calls over. Want to work a two bid with a tick?"

Eurodollar trading was so gentlemanly compared to the spooz. There were no shenanigans, no tomfoolery, no hooligans, and no semiorganized crime. Things moved slower. Instead of thugs, you had mathematicians. Meanwhile, I felt like I needed to put on a condom before I traded in the Nasdaq pit. I cursed myself for not becoming a bond trader.

"No tick. Just pay three." Ticks were fancy, and dangerous. I didn't want to fuck around with this trade.

"Working a three bid, and . . . filled. Bought a thousand short June seventy-two eighty-five squash, paid three."

"Put it in account EQ-02, please."

"You got it."

I hung up the phone and thought about what I'd done. I was expressing a view, not just on interest rates but also on forward interest rates, through a cash-settled future. Furthermore, I was doing so in a nonlinear fashion, using options on futures. I'd used a derivative of a derivative to express a view on an imaginary concept. It was downright magical.

It didn't matter that we were equities traders. It didn't matter that we were without a risk management system. It didn't matter if our gamma and our vega were complete unknowns. All that mattered was that the trade went into a futures account, because now we could take credit for the P&L. In a modern investment bank, anyone can take risk, as long as he thinks it'll make money—even the new MBA, even the bathroom attendant. Lehman Brothers was a wonderful place—you could use your brain to print dollar bills, and if you bungled it, nobody was going to fault you for trying.

To a point.

Good thing the trade worked out.

A few months later, I was still doing the Nasdaq arb, churning out about $30,000 a day. I was happier than a puppy with two peters. It was becoming less and less likely that I'd be fired. They wouldn't dump someone making $30,000 a day, would they? They wouldn't kick me out on the street if I was whipping around Eurodollar options for fun and for profit, right? I'd finally arrived. I was the next big thing. One week, I was trading Nasdaq futures. The next, Eurodollar futures. Who knows, maybe after that, it would be live hog futures, credit default swaps, and the equity tranches of CDOs.

I mean, people did this for a living. People expressed unhedged views in the market all the time. Would I ever be one of those people? Or was I condemned to taking half seconds of risk on arb trades for the rest of my career?

"Hey Mike, why don't we just trade prop full-time?"

Ingram laughs. "You say that now because you're making money."

"I can't make money all the time?"

He laughs again. "Only if you're Jay Knight."

"Who's that?"

Ingram draws a breath. "Jay Knight was a kid who graduated from Harvard and started on the rates desk as a sales guy. Nothing special, just a sales guy. He was the assistant to an old-timer, someone who'd been in rates his whole career—twenty-five years on the same desk—and the old-timer set out to teach Jay everything he knew about bonds. Guess he figured the knowledge would just die if he didn't pass it on.

"It was great for Jay. The kid's right out of college, and he's sitting there with this treasure chest some grizzled veteran left behind. He walked ass-backward into a completely epic pad of accounts, the kind of thing that could have provided him with a comfortable living immediately, and for years to come—that is, until Lehman asked Jay to be the new two-year note trader.

"Trading twos, for Jay, was a step down. Twos don't move around all that much, and they're especially sleepy when rates are stable, like they were back then. The twos trader can expect to make only about four or five million bucks for the firm every year, meaning the trader himself is only bringing home, at most, about three or four hundred thousand dollars. Compared to the ten-year note trader, that's tiddlywinks.

"So Jay spends his first year trading twos. The day before the end of the fiscal year, he tells the back-office guys to release a bunch of P&L. Wham! He'd made a ridiculous amount of money, but he'd been keeping it in reserve until the last possible moment. Instead of making four or five million, he'd made *twenty* million.

"Now, the managing directors were happy, naturally, but they wanted to know where all that money came from. So when they sat down for Jay's bonus discussion, they asked him.

"Jay says, 'Well, I did some prop trading on the side. A little of this, a little of that, and it started to add up.'

"So the MDs look at him and say, 'Well, that's nice, but we really would like you to cut that out and focus on trading twos.'

"Jay says, 'That's too bad. Actually, I was hoping to trade prop full-time.' The MDs tell him that's not going to happen.

"So Jay says, 'Okay, fine, *I'm out of here.*'"

This is incredible. "He threatened to leave? Just quit?"

Ingram is smiling, like he's proud of Jay Knight in some paternal way.

"Yup. So the MDs said, '*Whoa, whoa,* sit down, maybe we can talk about this.'"

"So what happened?"

"They let Jay trade prop. But since he was only twenty-four years old, they took another MD, Jim Reston, and put him in charge of a prop group—basically just him and Jay. So Jay did his thing and made money, and Jim made a lot of noise about running this big prop group and basically chopped himself to bits trying to whip around Eurodollar futures.

"The thing was, Jay didn't do much during the day. He'd show up and stand on the trading floor, saying stuff like, 'Hey, you see that game last night?' Just shooting the shit, killing time. He'd do all his trading at night, which leads me to believe that he was conducting most of his trades overseas. The whole thing was a big secret operation. He had his own back office guy, he had his own P&L guy, and everybody was sworn to secrecy. Not even Jay's closest friends knew what was going on.

"So at the end of the year, out comes the P&L, and it turns out Jay made *sixty million bucks.*"

"No fucking way."

"Yes. So Jay walks into the office with these guys for the bonus discussion, and they say, 'Nice work this year, Jay. Keep it up.' Jay says, 'Actually, I was going to ask you guys if I could trade from Miami.'

"They're like, 'No fucking way are you trading from Miami! Are you fucking crazy?' So Jay says, 'Okay, fine, *I'm out of here.*'"

"He threatened to quit *again?*"

"Sure, why not? He was gonna make big bucks no matter where he went. In this business, if you can make a lot of money, you can do whatever the fuck you want. Jay figured that out while he was still young."

"So what happened?"

"Jay went to Miami. And he cut a deal that paid him a percentage of what he made for the firm. I don't know what it was—ten, probably fifteen percent. Last I heard, he was making eighty million bucks for Lehman, and that was a few years ago. He's probably over a hundred million now. So what's fifteen percent of a hundred million? There's some twenty-five-year-old making fifteen million bucks a year, living in Miami. He comes back to the office every now and then, in a white suit and flip-flops, looking like Don Johnson. But I haven't seen him in a while."

"Why not?"

"He's not even part of fixed income anymore. He has his own division. He reports directly to the Executive Committee. He reports directly to Dick Fuld."

*What the fuck.* I didn't even know this was possible. I was trying to comprehend it, trying to get my arms around the fact that the bank I worked for had a man in his twenties making $15 million a year. In Miami. Why? Because he had a special skill. I wasn't even sure what that skill was, but society had rewarded him with enough money to hire a dozen high-priced hookers, pleasuring him 24 hours a day, 7 days a week, 365 days a year. Or whatever he wanted to do with the money. There was no limit to what your imagination could come up with.

"So what kind of trades is he putting on?" I ask Ingram.

"Nobody knows. I've gotten bits and pieces of information over the years. I think they're three- or six-month trades. I'd heard from some repo guys they had to lock his stuff up for term. Probably convergence trades. But I think it takes a lot of balance sheet. I'm not sure he'd be able to replicate it at a hedge fund."

"So why don't we do that?"

"Pardon?"

"Why don't we be Jay Knight?"

"I made the mistake of telling my wife about Jay Knight. She said the same thing. 'Why don't you do that?' I told her it wasn't that easy."

"What if it is that easy?"

"How's that?"

"What if it's just a matter of trying? I mean, we spend all our time screwing around with the arb and interest rates, but if we could trade anything we wanted, *anything*, then we might be able to generate the same results, right?"

"Beats me. You want to trade some more Eurodollars?"

"Sure. Something. Anything."

I wanted to be Jay Knight. One thing I'd noticed in my time at Lehman was that the people were highly intelligent, entrepreneurial, and hardworking, and they had all the resources in the world—market data, computing power, research—but they were content to make their high six figures and call it a year. If you're already making $800,000 a year, why exert yourself? Why take risk? If you can take orders or sling stock or price programs or trade index arb and make $800,000 a year, then why risk it all?

People were *comfortable*. The money was good enough.

But not for me.

I wanted to *win*. I wanted to be the best. I wanted to have a top secret trading operation in Miami. I wanted to wear a white suit and flip-flops. I didn't want money, I wanted *freedom*. I'd chafed against military discipline. Now I was chafing against investment bank bureaucracy. It wasn't that I resented having to show up at work on time with a tied tie and shined shoes. I didn't. It wasn't that I resented my boss. Ingram baled hay, and I loved him for it. It was that we had to sneak around just to trade in Eurodollar options. Lehman Brothers gave us the freedom to think up new ways to make money, but only to a point. There were rules. There were limits. I hated limits. I wanted to do whatever the fuck I wanted to do. It was the only thing left that I wanted that I couldn't have.

## 6

Primate of the Year | Summer 2002–Fall 2002

**How does one look for a job on Wall Street?**

If you are desperate, like I was, then any bank will do.

This is the wrong approach.

Not all investment banks are created equal. To work at Goldman Sachs, you need to have graduated with a 4.0 from an Ivy League school. You need the resume of Zeus. And that only gets you in the door. Then you're subjected to multiple rounds of painstaking interviews. In fact, you're grilled by the entire bank, from the twenty-two-year-old assistant research analysts on up to the managing director partners. You have a better shot at hitting two grand slams in a single inning than you do at getting hired by Goldman Sachs. Of course, once you get the job, your genetic superiority goes unquestioned. You no longer have trouble getting dinner reservations. You can bowl a 225 in your sleep. Children and small animals like you.

It's almost as difficult to get a job at Morgan Stanley. There, it's not so much about your resume as it is your effusive personality. To work at Morgan Stanley, you need to be able to *talk*. You need to make the dull sound interesting. You need to make the unpleasant sound exciting. You need to make mediocrity sound absolutely fucking wonderful. And you need to pay someone to shine your shoes at least three times a week— preferably at the trading desk, while you're talking on the phone, with your feet up. You need a lot of kids, who in turn will need a lot of school, a lot of lacrosse equipment, and a lot of fashionable, color-coordinated clothing. Your wife needs to be hot. You will want to have sex with other women, but it's still important that your wife be hot. And if you get divorced, you need to step up your golf game. You need to be able to *sell*.

At Bear Stearns, longtime CEO and chairman Ace Greenberg used to say that he liked hiring "poor, smart, and determined." This appealed to the average person's sense of fairness and the capitalistic ideal of a pure meritocracy. But in practice, when you hire "poor, smart, and determined," your firm becomes *low class*. Your employees use their silverware incorrectly. They don't shake your hand, look you in the eye, or tell you what they want you to hear. They buy suits from Men's Wearhouse, which is easy, because there's one right across the street from Bear Stearns's front door. Wall Street tends not to hire poor people because you can't send poor people to pitch the CEO of an S&P 500 company on a merger deal. Class is important, because your clients are rich, and nobody wants to deal with a schlocky broker. The equity finance desk at Bear Stearns was the epicenter of Wall Street schlock. They handed out pinky rings with the employment package.

I suppose I could have fit in at Merrill Lynch—it seems to hire a lot of ex-military personnel. This is probably because military folks are comfortable with (or at least used to) authority, clear chains of command, and lots and lots of bureaucracy. I had an informational interview with Merrill back in 2000 and met a young associate named Tom, who told me that trading options upstairs was nothing like floor trading. "We aren't in it for teenies and eighths," he said. "We take big risk. Big *delta* risk." My eyes widened. But I wasn't going to get a job at Merrill. While meeting with the twenty-eight-year-old female head of converts, I was accused of delivering a limp-wristed handshake and checking out tail on the trading floor. I was probably guilty as charged. But that's a hell of a way to lose a job offer. To this day, I crush women's hands.

If you can't get a job at one of the big, bulge-bracket firms, there are other opportunities: smaller places like Needham & Company and C. E. Unterberg, Tobin, where the focus is on small cap stocks. In fact, there are *hundreds* of broker-dealers. It turns out that opening a broker-dealer is easier than opening a sandwich shop. Apply for the license, get the license, pass some exams, start churning out research, and charge commissions on trades. Only a fraction of these firms have decent reputations, but nearly all of them pay their employees more money than teachers, police officers, or even lawyers and doctors earn. The most mediocre Wall Street trader, with a BS in economics from Hofstra University, with a 2.7 GPA, who's read fewer than ten books in his entire life, can make a very good living. Once you're hired, you're in.

But getting hired is the difficult part. Wall Street recruiters receive thousands of resumes every single year. Most of them, they round file. Virtually *zero* jobs are awarded on the basis of a mailed-in resume. Instead the recruiters *recruit*. They travel to colleges and business schools and find people they want. They set up a system—an obstacle course, of sorts—that the students have to negotiate in order to land a job. To succeed simply by mailing in a resume is a million-to-one shot. If you go to an Ivy League school, it's one in twenty. If you're a white male lacrosse player from Long Island at an Ivy League school, it's about one in two.

I didn't know any of this. I didn't go to an Ivy League school. I got my business degree at the University of San Francisco, which I attended part-time because I was in the military. The University of San Francisco is actually a good school. I learned everything I needed to know, and then some, because I spent my free time in the library reading books on option pricing and bond mathematics. It is not, however, a good school in the eyes of the Wall Street recruiters. There are no obstacle courses at USF. There are no cocktail parties with Miller Lite and chicken on a stick. And there are no Wall Street alumni. During my tenure, most of the graduates were entrepreneurs scattered around Silicon Valley. There is no shared tradition of finance. Unless I wanted to get hired as a midlevel poseur working at a profitless dot-com, the job center was going to be of little help.

Through the military grapevine, I caught wind of a fellow Coastie who'd made his way to Wall Street. His name was Ryon Williams. I called him. Ryon told me that I was an idiot and that I had no shot at Wall Street. But beyond that, if I was still willing to try, he told me that I had to have a *story*. If I managed to land an interview, I'd need to convince whoever was listening that I'd been dreaming of Wall Street for my entire life, and that every action I'd ever taken was taken to achieve my goal: becoming a size trader. He told me that having an MBA from the University of San Francisco wasn't enough. Then he hung up the phone, expecting (and possibly hoping) never to hear from me again.

I understood instantly what my story was going to be. I'd say that I was an insane motherfucker. I was willing to do *anything* to get hired. I'd work two jobs and go to school at the same time. I'd get up at three forty-five, head down to the exchange floor at five, then work until twelve. I'd take the train back to my other job at one, and work until ten. I'd come home and do homework until midnight, then study some more, possibly until two. I'd stay up twenty-four hours a day, if necessary. I'd work all day, every day, including weekends, then spend more time in the library on the side to learn about trading, option pricing, and finance. I wouldn't go to bars. I wouldn't go to parties. I wouldn't go to baseball games. My entire life would be dedicated to trading—the theory, and the practice. I was willing to sacrifice anything: my relationships, my health, my sanity. My story: *I am an animal. I will do things that no other trader will do.*

It never occurred to me that most banks wouldn't want to hire an insane motherfucker. It never occurred to me that most banks liked to hire profoundly unexciting people. It never occurred to me that I could work too hard, stay up too late, or drink too much. I was willing to do anything, but they didn't want someone who was willing to do anything. Some things are just off-limits.

I started calling in favors—friends, then friends of friends, then friends of friends of friends, then people I just plain didn't know. I cold-called. I wanted to find an internship. First I sat with some institutional sales traders at the San Francisco regional office of J.P. Morgan. My interviewer, a true cake eater, sat slumped down in his chair, with a Hermés tie slung over his shoulder. I proposed that I work for J.P. Morgan on Tuesdays and Thursdays. He looked at me like I had a cabbage for a head.

I tracked down a USF alum, a trader on the floor of the Pacific Coast Options Exchange, also known as the P. Coast. If the upstairs pukes wouldn't have me, then I'd try the floor. Rob agreed to meet on Montgomery Street at ten and reminded me that the trading floor wasn't actually in the exchange building but around the corner, on the second floor of a nondescript building—with all the weirdos in trading smocks hanging out front, synchronizing their cigarette breaks just to watch the marketing chicks in sheer blouses pass them by in the chilly morning air.

The receptionist was a fiendishly gay, no-nonsense man named Rupert. I asked for Rob, and he came bounding out, minutes later, Hawaiian and round headed, wearing a trading smock. He spent most of his waking hours in the Sun Microsystems pit, but he offered to show me the entire floor.

It was a dark, musty cave, filled with TV monitors and kids like me. The monitors had pink, purple, and green numbers all over them. There was a lot of shouting. Nobody was wearing a tie, that's for damn sure. Sneakers and jeans and ripped cargo pants. People were scarfing down gigantic burritos. After all, they'd been at work for five straight hours already.

Whatever Rob was saying, I didn't understand it, but I gathered from the sound of his voice that he was struggling to make money. I was just taking it all in, standing at the edge of what Rob called the Microsoft pit. Someone walked into the crowd and shouted, then the crowd shouted back. The guy who walked into the pit started making allocations, giving one guy a hundred, two other guys fifty, then scraps for the rest. I had no idea what he was handing out, but everyone wanted it. They were like carp. I stayed clear of the feeding frenzy.

Rob was tugging on the sleeve of my shirt, which I'd ironed specifically for the occasion. He had to get back to work. I asked him if I could look around for a while.

Farther away from the pit, there were rows of desks with partitions—booths, really—and above each booth was a sign. I had pen and paper, so I circled the trading floor and wrote down the name of every single firm in sight. Timber Hill. Group One. LETCO. My plan was to leave the floor armed with information and approach each of the firms one at a time.

I ducked to avoid a water bottle whizzing past my head. A short man with the disease of the same name turned to the bottle thrower, pointed in my direction, and said, "That guy's going to fucking kill you! He's a fucking marine!" He must have been referring to my high-and-tight haircut.

I chuckled and went back to taking notes. Short man came over and asked if I was in the military. "Coast Guard," I said.

"No shit. I was in the Navy. You looking for a job?"

I nodded.

"Okay. I'm going to take you to a guy. His name is Tom Johnson. He's looking to hire. Shake his hand, take his business card, and tell him you'll call him tomorrow."

Short man walked me over to a middle-aged, red-haired man of about forty who was tapping his huge teeth with his fingers. I shook his hand, took his business card, and told him I'd call him tomorrow.

A week later I'm interviewing with two of Tom Johnson's traders.

"Let's play a game," one of them says. "You roll a six-sided die. If a one comes up, you win one dollar. If a six comes up, you win six dollars. The number of dollars you win directly corresponds to the number on the die. How much would you pay to play that game?"

*You've got to be kidding me.*

"Well," I replied, "the expected value of that game is three-fifty. So I would pay three dollars to play, but not four. At three-fifty, it's a push."

I was hired.

I'd arrive at the floor in complete darkness, the streets deserted, and I'd check trades for breaks, buy/sell errors, and fuckups. I'd spend my days taking absurdly complicated lunch orders (a lightly toasted sesame seed bagel with one egg over easy, avocados, onions, and sliced bananas) without being permitted to write anything down, entering trades into a program known as MicroHedge, and printing out risk reports before running them back to the pit. During my time on the P. Coast, I watched the Nasdaq Composite rise through 3000, up to 5000, and sink back down to 3000. I clerked for Courtney, a mad chess genius and options whiz, on the day that Qualcomm got a $1,000 price target from Walter Piecyk of Paine Webber. I entered 169 trade tickets by hand and was paid $100 for my efforts. Courtney made $625,000.

He was my age.

I did not begrudge him his wealth. I was being paid $10,000 a year to learn, and I learned everything there was to know. I learned about put-call parity, then about spreads, ratios, and butterflies. I learned about implied and realized volatility, what a "pickoff" was, how to trade stock, and how to intimidate people in the pit: I stood at parade rest and looked pissed off.

It was not uncommon for me to go days without sleep. I felt like fucking Superman. I was lifting weights and could bench-press 325 pounds. I ran a marathon. I was the coach of a softball team. I built my own obstacle course and then destroyed it. There weren't enough hours in the day. I loved life, I loved living, and it was a major drag that I had to close my eyes, even for a second, and miss what was going on all around me. I couldn't drink enough, I couldn't learn enough, I couldn't exercise enough, and I couldn't have enough fun. I was going to be wildly successful. I was going to make it to Wall Street.

After enough time had passed, I decided I'd written my story. In between both jobs, and going to school, and studying for exams, I flew myself to New York every couple of weeks for informational interviews. If I'd known the incredibly steep odds I was facing, I might have stopped right then and there. The actual mathematical probability of a non–Ivy League, nonaffluent, non-Northeastern, nonminority candidate getting a Wall Street trading job is so infinitesimally small, it's immeasurable. If I'd known the math, I would have quit instantly and stayed in the Coast Guard. But I thought I had a real shot.

I weaseled my way into several interviews. Some banks told me they weren't interested. Some looked down the ends of their noses at me, the unwashed sailor with a Marine Corps haircut. One woman, a well-known head of recruiting, looked over her reading glasses and her copy of the *Wall Street Journal* and asked me what I thought about the yield curve. I nearly wet my pants. I knew only about options. I felt her eyes on my back as I left the trading floor, dejected.

Lehman Brothers hired me, and to this day, I'm not sure why.

Maybe they were insane too.

It's 0835, and I'm loading spreadsheets when Ingram catches me mid-nose-pick. A meeting has been called by Chris Masters for everyone in derivatives and program trading.

The office we file into ends up being a poor choice—it's butts to nuts once everyone's crammed in. Masters is nowhere to be found, but there's a speakerphone, and a deep voice coming out of it.

"I felt it was important for everyone to get this information out as soon as possible."

Masters sounds menacing even over the phone. I imagine him at the other end of the line, glowering.

"A deal was finalized last night. We're going to have a new head of derivatives sales."

Silence.

"His name is Frank Segal, and he's coming over from Morgan Stanley. This is a big, strategic hire for us, and we think he's the kind of person who will be able to take our business to the next level. Any questions?"

There aren't any.

"Okay, thanks."

I didn't see how this affected me. I was a proprietary trader, of sorts. I didn't deal with the salespeople. The salespeople dealt with external clients, who came to Lehman to access the markets. Ingram and I accessed the markets ourselves.

Then I remembered—I'd been working next to an empty seat for the last six months.

"That's fucking *bullshit!*"

I slam down the phone. For the third time that day, I am hung when I clearly should be filled. The locals are fucking with me. Do they not understand? There's something called a symbiotic relationship. I provide liquidity when they need it. They provide liquidity when I need it. What is wrong with these people? I'd been a hothead before I started trading, even as a child, but index arbitrage exacerbates it. I have a low-grade blowup at least twice a day. People look at me. Ingram provides cover. He tells them what he'd told me—he wanted someone with a little fire in his belly.

There's a minor commotion in the row in front of me. Chris Masters is standing there, smiling instead of glowering, and there's a funny fat man with a toothpick, trying not to shake hands with people and pulling up his pants.

Somebody goes in for a shake, he gives a little wave, then he pulls up his pants and adjusts the toothpick. This goes on until Masters is satisfied that he's freaked out each of the senior people in the row.

"Who's that?" asks Ingram.

"I think it's our new head of sales."

Some personal effects had arrived, transported by Hot Blonde Secretary to the desk right next to mine, earlier that afternoon. I can't figure out what is going on with his pants. They are practically falling off. He isn't exactly a thin reed to begin with—probably 250 pounds—but these are like clown pants. Zubaz. He looks like King Hippo from the old-school video game Mike Tyson's Super Punch-Out!!, who you'd punch in the belly in order to make his trunks fall down.

He makes his way toward my desk. He is an unlovely creature. He sits down, logs into Bloomberg, and walks away. I peer over at his screen to see what a size hitter from Morgan Stanley has on his Bloomberg. There's a market monitor (one of the generic ones that shows up before you customize it), some well-known stocks, like MSFT, a sliding ticker, and a few charts. Nothing special.

There was heavy speculation as to how much Segal was getting paid. I guessed $2 million. Ingram guessed $3 million. Most people thought the number was closer to $4 million. But nobody was happy about some whale coming in and swallowing up half the bonus pool. I figured I would withhold judgment until I saw exactly how much he actually produced.

Frank Segal spent a lot of time on the phone, that was for sure. I figured he was calling clients, telling them to lose Morgan Stanley's number. I was wrong.

"Yeah. Yeah. I used to be a bond tradah. Did you know that? Yeah. I used to trade bonds. What about these Hudson County bonds? These sewah bonds? Give me a couple of those."

This guy used to be a municipal bond trader? Anyone who can work across asset classes must have his shit together.

"Yeah. Yeah. These are rated triple-A. Yeah. I know they're insured; what did you think I was thinkin'? Yeah. Those bonds. Give me some of those."

Frank Segal spent much of his first three weeks at Lehman Brothers trading municipal bonds in his personal account. I didn't hear him call a single client. I didn't see him open up a single software application, save for his default Bloomberg screen.

It was difficult to say exactly how much he was trading, but I guessed that he was dealing with a high-net-worth broker and that he was trading institutional size—somewhere in the millions, at least. What would compel somebody to rip around a few million of municipal bonds during his first three weeks on the job?

Answer: that somebody just got paid about $4 million, guaranteed, no matter what he did.

Segal had a thing for gum. He could hear people chewing it, like a high-pitched noise that only dogs can hear, halfway across the trading floor. In the middle of the afternoon, he would stand up and yell, "Cut it with the gum!" At which point a hapless vice president would motion, *Who, me?* then spit it out in the nearest trash can. Dipping didn't seem to bother him, so I chewed tobacco with reckless abandon.

His personal habits were atrocious. If there was a big lunch print, where a broker orders lunch for the desk, Segal would walk by, pick a piece of broccoli off the pizza, smell it, and put it back. I'd been trying not to pass gas in the vicinity of the head of derivatives sales. Farts on a trading floor are common. It's a big space, and it's well ventilated, but I figured I'd been sentenced to an eternity of gas cramps. This guy wasn't getting paid four sticks to smell other people's asses. I couldn't take it anymore. I relaxed, and pushed.

Segal got it instantly, sucking it in. "What the fuck? Did *you* do that? You dirty *bastard!*" He had an outrageously thick Long Island accent. It came out strongest when he was pissed.

"I can have you *fired* for that!"

An empty threat.

He also didn't care much for my occasional blowups. I'd yell "God-*damn* it!" and slam the phone, and he would reflexively bounce into the air and hover momentarily, startled, like an overweight cat. "Cut it with that shit!" he'd say.

I didn't care. I'd already pegged Frank Segal as an impostor. An amusing, harmless impostor, but an impostor nonetheless.

I actually sort of liked him.

Segal was the biggest hire that year, but there were others. Ben Cohan shipped in a middle-aged expat from Tokyo named Ting. Ting smiled a lot but didn't say much. He sat between Ben Cohan and Sam Grossman.

I asked Sam what Ting was supposed to be doing.

"Trading."

Okay. "Trading what?"

"Trading spooz."

"We brought over an MD from Tokyo just to trade spooz?"

"Dude. This guy is the master. Wait and see."

So Ting traded S&P futures every day on his computer. He never called the floor, not once. He was a robot.

Grossman was right. I started looking at the Program Trading P&L over Vikesh's shoulder. There was a line in the spreadsheet that said "Ting P&L." The number was unfailingly $300,000, $400,000, and sometimes $600,000. He made several million dollars in his first month.

"What's his secret?" I asked Grossman.

"Beats me. He's fucking Yoda."

Yoda he became, levitating over his desk, trading with the force.

It is the time of year where it is too hot to go outside.

"Hey Mike."

"Yeah."

"Okay. So you and I both think interest rates are going lower and the curve is getting flatter, right?"

"Right."

"And we both know that if we put on a position in Eurodollars that big, management would freak out, right?"

"Right." We were index arb traders, not interest rate traders. If we opened up a massive (or even midsize) Eurodollar futures position, Chris Masters would give us the body slam.

"*So*, why don't we just sell the S&P futures spread? It's the same thing, with dividends. We're *supposed* to be trading S&P futures. It's a matched book. We'll be long spooz and short spooz. There's no delta. Nobody will notice if we put on a synthetic Eurodollar trade."

Ingram thinks about this. Nobody would notice. *Nobody*, not even the risk managers. An interest rate trade, executed with equity index futures instead. It was genius. Ingram begins to glow.

"You haven't told anybody about this?"

"No, I only mentioned it to you just now."

Ingram thinks some more. "Which spread?"

"We should go out as far as we can, as long as there's liquidity. I know there's never any liquidity in the way-back contracts, but we should give it a try."

I think Ingram has an erection. "How big should we do it?" he asks.

"I don't know, man, that's up to you. I'm just giving you the idea."

Ingram immediately calls Meat and starts in on the submariner speak. He gets a ticket. He writes something on the ticket. Can't see it. He's whispering. He's the silent assassin from the silent service.

This goes on for at least an hour. I leave, get a sandwich, and come back, and Ingram is still making love to Meat over the phone. Finally, he plops a ticket on my desk.

Ingram has sold *twelve thousand* June-Sep S&P spreads.

"Mike."

"Yeah."

"Are you sure about this?" I'm sweating.

"Sure about what? You like the trade, I like the trade—why not do it as big as we can?"

"Dude. This is too big."

"Ahhhhh, come on." Ingram is positively overjoyed. He's done what he's always wanted to do. He's put on a king-size trade like he's the proud owner of a king-size dick.

"You know how much rho risk is in this thing?" I do some mental calculations. "This is at least four *billion* notional. We're probably making or losing fifty, sixty, maybe a hundred thousand a basis point."

"Like I always say, go big or go home."

He did always say that, but coming from an index arb trader, it's preposterous.

Ingram tells me later that there was no liquidity in the spread. He did some calculations, based on interest rates, of where the spread should be and got Meat to display an offer. Magically, within seconds, another broker responded with a bid. Feed the ducks when they're quacking. Ingram fed him a thousand spreads, then stuffed him with another thousand, then another *ten thousand* until the ducks stopped quacking. The trade was so huge, Meat carried the ticket around with him for a year, glowing with pride.

I asked him who bought the spreads.

"I don't know," he said, "but they're going to be sorry."

Almost instantaneously, the shit hit the fan. In the interest rate world, bad is good and good is bad. Eurodollar futures, Treasury bonds, and other interest-rate-sensitive instruments go up when there is bad news and go down when there is good news. If the economy sucks, then the Federal Reserve might lower interest rates, and the rest of the yield curve—the relationship between short-term and long-term interest rates—would follow.

The economy started to suck.

And so did the stock market. The negative economic reports started to roll in, and, right on cue, stocks started to roll over. And more importantly, interest rates started to go down, *forward* interest rates started to go down, and the *exact* forward rate that we were short went down the most. We made $600,000 on the first day. It was a home run.

I couldn't really take credit for the trade. Sure, it was my idea, but if Ingram had let me take the steering wheel, I would have put it on one-tenth the size, at best. This was Ingram's baby now. I liked seeing the big numbers in the P&L, but it was more important to Ingram than it was to me. He was the one under the gun. He was expected to make $20 million that year between the two of us, and we weren't getting there by chopping ourselves up in the index arb.

But I had been doing more of that lately—chopping myself up. When you chop yourself up, you trade a lot on the way up, and you trade a lot on the way down, only to outsmart yourself into a tiny P&L. There was only so much money I could make trading the Nasdaq—that number was starting to look like $40,000 a day. I had another idea. What other indices could I trade?

The Midcap 400 index was an obvious candidate.

In the stock world, there are big stocks, there are small stocks, and there are medium-size stocks. Some of the Midcap 400's medium-size stocks end up being promoted to the S&P 500, and some of them get demoted to the Smallcap 600, when the price goes low enough, but they're not terribly liquid. More importantly, the futures market is practically nonexistent.

If you're going to make a bet on the stock market, you do it on something that is big, liquid, and that trades a lot. You don't do it in some fucking backwater.

Hedge funds don't care about Midcap futures. Pension funds don't care about Midcap futures. Maybe the odd index mutual fund cares about Midcap futures, but that's it. I cared about Midcap futures precisely *because* it was a backwater; precisely *because* all the other arbs had left it alone. But if I was going to be trading Midcap arb, I was going to have to deal mostly with the locals: the sole proprietors who traded for their own accounts in the futures pits.

In the meantime, Meat was working like a one-legged man in an ass-kicking contest. Ingram and I were trading the arb constantly, and Meat needed more help fielding our calls, so he hired a nervous Nellie named Rory. A former floor trader, Rory had apparently been dividing his time between delivering pizzas and losing his wages trading futures. He had plenty of experience, Meat said. I'd be getting the same service to which I'd grown accustomed.

Meanwhile, I was about ready to get the Midcap arb up and running. I'd created a spreadsheet with all the Midcap stocks loaded in it, along with their dividends, and I had a futures account set up, and a stock account, and baskets built into the program trading system, called DPT. I was sorry that I'd no longer be working with Meat. I'd spent hours on the phone with him. And if I was going to be trading Nasdaq and Midcap arb at the same time, there was plenty of potential for confusion. I needed safe hands.

MERC INDX.

"Jared?"

"Rory?"

"What's up, *eehhhhhh*. Meat told me a lot about you."

"All good things, I hope."

"*eehhhhhh*."

"Beg pardon?"

"*eehh*. All good things."

I couldn't tell if Rory was nervous or if he'd been doing poppers.

"What's going on over in that Midcap pit?"

"*eeeeeeehhhhhhhhhh*. The clerk over there is Doris."

"Is she hot?"

"No!"

"Is she ugly?"

"*eehh*, no."

"So she's average?"

"*eeehhhh*, not really."

"Help me out here, man."

"I don't know! She's not ugly, but she's, *eehhh*, awful!"

"Awful how?"

"I can't describe it! Come out to Chicago, you'll see what I mean."

"What is she wearing?"

"*eehhhh*, a *Playboy* bunny T-shirt."

"Oh, she's the Playmate of the Year?"

"*eeehhhhh*, more like *Primate* of the Year."

I laughed. "Okay, Rory, what's in there?"

"*eehh . . . eeeehhhhh . . .* come on, Doris. Dunce. There we go—three bid at four."

"Work a three bid." I lined up MSELL0401A on DPT, and when the market built up a head of steam, I fired it off.

I watched the index tick lower and lower, and still no fill. "Rory."

"Uh-huh?"

"What's going on in there? Are they asleep or something? It's bid fifty cents above fair value."

"*eeehhhhhhhhh.*"

"Fuck!"

"Filled!" Rory said, relieved.

I jammed the trade in the spreadsheet and hit F9: $3,500. Pretty fucking good for one trade. But this was like trading in slow motion, I was the human highlight reel. I could do five Nasdaq arbs in the time it took me to do one Midcap arb.

No matter. It was extra money.

Over time, however, the Midcap pit started to wear on me. The locals were thieves. If I was bidding for futures, and the market went down, they would refuse to trade with me. Sometimes the index was two full points below the futures, and they *still* wouldn't trade with me. The fucks.

I was becoming increasingly volatile, along with the market, in the summer of 2002. I'd been making more money, sometimes $50,000 or $60,000 a day, and the Eurodollar trades were making money, and the spread trade was making *millions*, and I felt like I'd earned the right to be a jackass. I'd sit in my seat, neck muscles bulging, in a rage. I hadn't slept in days, and these motherfuckers were taking money out of my pocket. Didn't they know who they were dealing with? I was the best fucking arb trader on the street. These laid-off construction workers were trying to pick my pocket for $500, when I made a hundred times that in a single day. I'd teach them.

"Rory, *are we filled yet?*"

"*eeeeehhhhhh!*"

"GODDAMMIT! You tell those fucks I'm going to take them out with the fucking *trash!*" Phone slam. Storm off the floor. Ingram looking at me.

After taking a walk around the block, I'd sit back down.

MERC INDX.

"Hello?"

"Hey, it's Meat."

"Hey, Meat."

"What the fuck did you do to Rory? I thought he was going to cry. He's a wreck."

"Ah, it's these fucking Midcap guys. It's a racket."

The truth is, I didn't know what was wrong with me. There I was, doing what I'd always wanted to do, trading enormous sums of money on Wall Street—and things were not better. They were worse. I was jacked up all the time, like I was when I was in San Francisco. But it was different, in a malignant sort of way. I thought about trading, money, and fucking—constantly. Sometimes I noticed that I even smelled different, like musk, or hormones. I was the Trader of Perpetual Outrage. On any trading floor, there are one or more hotheads; that was nothing new. But I was outraged about everything. Pen goes missing, flip out. Make an error, pound the desk. Ingram gets hung, slam the phone. Everything was a problem.

Back when I was looking for a job on Wall Street, I had my story down pat. I was an insane motherfucker.

It was a good story.

But now I was turning over in my subconscious the idea that although I'd wanted this job because I felt insane, I was actually *entitled* to it because I was insane, it wasn't functional to be insane as a brand manager for Procter & Gamble or as a sales rep for a radio station or as a mortgage broker at XYZ subprime shop. It made no sense to be insane as an Army lieutenant colonel. It made no sense to be insane as an accountant.

There are very few professions left in the world where it pays to be insane—rock star, actor, priest, and politician.

And trader.

I was attracted to Wall Street because in order to get things done, you had to act irrationally. Only insane people who do insane things make money. Only insane people buy when everyone else is selling. Only insane people do exactly the opposite of what common sense tells you to do.

Being insane as a trader was working for me—to a point. Sometimes, after blowing up and slamming down the phone, I would say to myself, *Something is wrong. Nobody else is slamming phones. Nobody else is yelling at their phone. Nobody else is trading the same way that I am.*

Ingram never said a word. If there had been complaints about my behavior, they weren't getting back to me. As long as we were making money, I was safe.

But when the firm stopped making money, there were problems.

It's a common misconception that investment banks make money when the stock market goes up and lose money when the stock market goes down. That's only partially true. Investment banks have dozens of different business lines, and some are countercyclical—they make money when other parts of the business are losing money. But it's generally the case that in a true bear market, an investment bank will perform poorly.

In the summer of 2002, just about everything went wrong at once. September 11 had set off—counterintuitively—a flurry of consumption and spending. It was patriotic to shop. The inevitable conclusion to a bursting equity market bubble had been delayed for nine months. But big bear markets aren't over until euphoria for stocks has turned into revulsion. Bear markets aren't over until everyone, absolutely everyone, thinks that stocks are completely worthless and unsuitable as a destination for the investment dollar.

As it turned out, index arbitrage was one of those countercyclical businesses. The lower the stock market went, the more volatility there was. The more stocks and futures ripped around, the more money we could make. Furthermore, interest rates were plummeting. This would have been good even without our extracurricular activities, but with the massive spread trade and the Eurodollar trade we'd made—by that point, several million dollars—Ingram and I were strutting around the floor like peacocks. We were kings.

But every investment bank on Wall Street was heavily exposed to the well-being of the stock market, and Lehman Brothers, as a whole, was getting crushed. Initial public offerings went to zero, as did secondary share issuances. Enron blew up, as did WorldCom, and public confidence in accounting practices and the securities markets went to pieces. In addition, the business model of collecting trading commissions based on research of dubious quality was jeopardized by a group of analysts who weren't entirely straightforward in their buy and sell recommendations. Retail confidence in the markets ebbed to an all-time low.

The market went down every day.

It's difficult to describe to a nonpractitioner what it's like to sit in your seat and watch the destruction of wealth on a daily basis. In the derivatives market, money isn't actually made or lost, it just changes hands. But in the spot market—the market for stocks—wealth is actually created and obliterated. A lawsuit against a tobacco company will wipe a few billion dollars off the face of the earth, never to be seen again. An accounting requirement, like the Sarbanes-Oxley Act, which is supposed to restore confidence in the markets, has the opposite effect, because of the costs of compliance and the threat of legal action.

When the market goes down every day, you see your livelihood go with it. It would be as if you were a doctor and people suddenly stopped getting sick, or if you were a defense attorney, and, inexplicably, people stopped committing crimes. When the market goes down every day, you think about the money that is lost, and the money that you will lose personally. But it's more than that. It is a soul-destroying, endless black hole, a sucking vortex of hate and discontent. It eats at you emotionally, spiritually, and physically. It becomes impossible to get out of bed in the morning. Nobody wants to go to work and see the market get fucked for the thirty-ninth day in a row.

Abruptly, I stopped caring what happened to the market. I stopped caring about *anything*.

At first, I thought it was laziness. I would no longer fight every trade for the last nickel. I would no longer abuse Rory about the Midcap guys.

I started to think that making $40,000 a day was good enough. Maybe the extra $1,000 wasn't worth the hassle. And maybe I was losing my edge.

But it was more than that. Instead of checking out overseas markets, I went to bed. Instead of listening to my CD player on the bus, I left it at home. Instead of reading the newspaper, I simply carried it around with me. Instead of reading Bloomberg News, I sat there and stared at the screens. Instead of looking around at all the lighted signs in Times Square, I looked at the ground.

I wondered what it meant to stop being interested in life. I used to rise smartly at 0500. Now I hit the snooze as many times as I could. I used to spend as much time in the office as possible, even when I'd finished the P&L. Now I was out the door when the market closed. I wanted only to go home, make myself a giant Jack and Coke, and get slowly stoned while staring at the wall.

I noticed changes in the market too. There were a lot more e-mini futures trading than there used to be. It used to be that the pit-traded futures were the dog and the e-minis were the tail, but now the tail was wagging the dog. Meat confirmed my suspicions. "Yeah, all the locals do now is stand there and stare at the e-minis. We're going to be out of business in weeks." I hated the e-minis. I thought they were for robots and nerds and introverts like Ting, who were too sullen or too lazy or too geeky to pick up the phone and call the floor. But now, any asshole with a futures terminal, anywhere, could click a mouse and play along with the pros. It offended me.

It wasn't affecting my profitability. Yet. If anything, I was making even more money, because when the market went down on a straight line, it was an easy arb. I just crushed stocks and waited for the futures to come to me.

One miserable morning, after I'd told Rory to tell the Midcap guys to go fuck themselves for the hundredth time, I looked up. There were girls everywhere.

As a general rule, there aren't many women on the trading floor, and the ones who *are* on the floor tend not to be investment professionals.

Most of them are secretaries. And investment banks aren't in the business of hiring ugly secretaries.

I turned to Ingram. "What's going on?"

"I don't know." There had to be a hundred women milling about. They were all looking at the fishbowl.

Herb clued us in as he walked by. "It's Ashton Kutcher. He's in the conference room."

I had to be told who Ashton Kutcher was. At that point in time, I didn't own a television. I read financial books instead.

Sure as shit, there he was, in the fishbowl, with a couple of guys in suits.

There was only one logical reason that Ashton Kutcher would be in a conference room at Lehman Brothers—he had to have been a high-net-worth client. And whoever offered out the fishbowl in the middle of the trading floor had to be a complete donut. He had to have known it would cause pandemonium.

Across the floor, I saw a girl with outrageous cans. Ingram knew her and was friendly with her, from his fixed income days. It wasn't clear to me what she did, but I guessed she was in sales.

Look at those things. They looked like two cats in a bag. "Hey Mike, get her over here. Yeah, her. Trust me."

I had a fan on my desk. A big turbo fan, which I usually ran at full blast to cool me off when I got pissed at the Midcap guys. Ingram had two, one for his face and one for his nuts. He called it the ball fan.

Two Cats in a Bag comes over to our desk. She's all smiles. She starts talking up Ingram about Ashton Kutcher. It's hot in here, so I decide to give her a little fan action.

"*Oooh*, that feels good," she says, with her hair blowing in the wind. "Do you think Ashton will notice my hair?"

*No, but he'll notice something else*, I think.

The high beams are on, and the mechanic had recently aimed the headlights. It is unmistakable. Ingram is trying to keep a straight face. Meanwhile, dudes across the floor are standing up and staring. The trading floor is one giant orgy of sexual tension, with a hundred girls staring at Ashton Kutcher, and a hundred guys staring at the high beams.

A few hours later, Ingram tells me that I'm the best employee ever.

• • •

"Look what Zog do!"

I turn away from my war with the Midcap futures locals. It's Dave Lane standing over my shoulder. He's wearing his jacket, in August.

"Dude, I've been watching you for the last five minutes. This is you trading: *Zvvvzvbt! Zvvvzvbt!*" He's making fun of how fast I talk.

"Yeah, I'm kind of fast."

"You're *ridiculously* fast. Jesus. Not like that where I work."

"Slower?"

"Much slower."

"How's it going up there?"

He winces. "It's . . . suboptimal."

"Why, what's going on? You headed outside?"

"Yes. And no. I'll tell you about it later."

Lane. An enigma. "Okay. What are you doing after work? Drinky drinky?"

Winces again. "Guy. I get here at six, and I leave at nine. No time."

I am the opposite of jealous. I get in at seven and leave at five. "What the hell do they have you doing?"

"You name it. Prospectuses. Busywork. Crap."

"Are you trading?"

"I sit next to a guy I don't like who trades. Is that trading?"

This sounds bad. Dave Lane, the guy who got his job offer directly from Dick Fuld—did I not mention that he got his job offer from Dick Fuld? Dick came up to him at a recruiting event and asked him if he had any other offers. Lane told him he had a few. Dick extended his hand and said, "Why don't you join our team?"

There is only one answer to that question.

So Dave carries the guidon for our associate class. He is affable and fiercely intelligent. He has the Zeus resume. Lehman Brothers doesn't hire Lane; Lane hires Lehman Brothers. He easily secures the best job, trading corporate bonds. But now it's beginning to sound like a bait and switch.

"No, that's not trading," I say. "Who's the guy you don't like?"

"Jeff Fisher. He trades utilities and telecom."

"Is he a dick?"

Lane reveals little. "The relationship is . . . suboptimal."

I fear the worst. "You aren't going to get laid off, are you?" Our associate class was bloated. You didn't want to be the antelope with a limp. "How could they lay off the guy who got the job offer from Dick Fuld?"

"Guy, it's—never mind. We'll talk later. And, by the way—that suit is—it's terrible."

I am still retarded.

The trading floor has its own sounds. It has a sound when it rallies, and it has a sound when it sells off. It has a sound for bull markets, and it has a sound for bear markets. During bear markets, it sounds like a jet warming up its engines. There's a whooshing in your ears as the market collapses. It literally growls. The sound is simply made up of other sounds, the noises that the traders and the sales traders make. Sales traders get more urgent—the market is moving quickly, and the customers need to be done. The traders get angry—they're getting hit on bids that evaporate and leave them with a hole in their P&L. Even the managing directors are pissed—the hull is leaking fast, and they're doing their best to shore things up. The unidentified cash trader sings, "Kill the market, kill the market!" It sounds like death. It sounds like god-awful psychological black death.

Ingram and I are in the middle of it. There are traders and salespeople shouting all around us; everyone sounds like he needs a single-malt scotch and a Xanax. But I've stopped listening. Besides, all the noise is cover for me yelling at Rory and the Midcap pit.

Ingram hasn't stopped listening. He isn't deaf to office politics. He knows that nobody gives a rat's ass about index arb, and his job is no safer than mine. We're making a shitload of money—every day the P&L comes back with a few hundred thousand dollars in interest rate gains—but it's not enough. Ingram wants the guts and glory. He wants to be an ETF trader.

ETF stands for exchange-traded fund, a variation on the plain-vanilla mutual fund. When you buy a mutual fund, you write the management company a $1,000 check, and it gives you shares of the fund. With an ETF, only "authorized participants"—that is, big banks—are allowed to *create* or *redeem* shares of the fund, and they can do so only fifty thousand shares at a time. It's a product that retail investors like and big boy institutional investors love.

ETFs don't sound very sexy. But they are. Before ETFs, there wasn't much a big trader could do to get exposure to an index, outside of using futures. But now there were ETFs on every sector imaginable. And you no longer had to decide between Intel and Texas Instruments; you just bought SMH, the semiconductor ETF. ExxonMobil or ChevronTexaco? Just buy XLE, the energy ETF. These were the brightly colored plastic toys ETF traders played with every day.

Ingram began to spend his afternoons vulturing around Chuck Monaghan, the head ETF trader. Chuck had been an option trader, and a very good one at that, but Lehman's management had enough foresight to see that ETFs were primed for big business, so it put Chuck in charge of building them out.

Chuck was the perfect person for the job. He was a mathematician and a semiprofessional computer jock and could automate any process. Sick of doing P&L? Chuck writes a program. Sick of entering in trades? Chuck writes software to link up your trading terminal. Chuck even wrote a program that told you *how to trade*, called the impact pricer, which shows a market maker exactly how wide his market should be in any ETF under any circumstances. Chuck could write a program to tell you what color tie to wear, and he probably would have if he were paid enough money. Chuck was a perfectly rational robot, but a very nice robot.

Chuck also had an assistant, Chandler, who was not a robot. He was a tennis-playing Muppet, with a reputation for being an exceptionally fast, if not terribly thoughtful, trader. Without Chuck, Chandler would have been stuffed in a locker by the sales guys. And without the Molloy Brothers, Chandler wouldn't even have been employed.

The Molloy Brothers were a client of the firm who had reportedly made a fortune in hot dogs. In Ireland. Or haggis, in Scotland, or something like that. It was unclear. Fortunes are made and lost everywhere, so why not hot dogs in Ireland? The brothers had a direct line to Chandler—they didn't even go through the sales traders. Furthermore, Chandler charged them only three-quarters of a cent commission, which was breathtakingly low. In return, they could trade as much as they wanted.

The Molloy Brothers were Chandler's gravy train. All they ever wanted to trade was the Q's, the Nasdaq ETF, ticker QQQ. They would trade millions of shares every day and utterly destroy themselves in the process. The Molloy Brothers, bit by bit, were handing over their haggis fortune to Chandler, three-quarters of a penny at a time. Chandler was merciless. Chuck sponsored it. Ingram wanted a piece of the action.

Ingram, in my opinion, was embarrassing himself. He was, ostensibly, trying to find out if there were any "synergies" between the index arb desk and the ETF desk. And there were. If we could arb SPY and QQQ along with our baskets of stock, it would give us another angle. If the ETF desk could use our fastcash spreadsheets and our knowledge of futures, they could price their trades better. But with Ingram sitting over their shoulders, looking like a lost puppy, it was never going to happen. And it was never going to happen anyway. Once you come across a stream of revenue on Wall Street, you hang on to it and you don't let go. Chuck would no sooner give Ingram the secret sauce than he'd gift him his bonus check.

Another day, another dirtnap. Futures were down hard preopen, again. It had been like this for weeks. I was beginning to wonder if it was actually possible for the market to go to zero. As it was, the S&P 500 was trading in degrees Kelvin.

I sat at my terminal, unable to muster up the effort to log in. I sat and let the air-conditioning evaporate the sweat from my skin.

I'd been toying with the idea of making a directional bet. Arbitrage without the arbitrage. Speculation. "Speculatrage!" This is what all good arbs do eventually. They get used to the rhythm of the market, then they put on bets of their own.

Meat had asked me the other day if I'd gotten long in front of a rare, gargantuan rally. I had not. But apparently the Bank One guy's arb trader had—he said it was the easiest trade in the world—and made $150,000 in the process. It was unusual for someone to give out specific P&L details to an acquaintance. There's something inherently unlucky about it. Just when you go around buying a round of drinks for everyone at the bar, a piano falls on your head.

I thought about it. The trade hadn't been terribly obvious to me. But sometimes the trade *was* obvious to me. There were times when I'd stretched out an arb—instead of taking one handle out of the futures, I'd taken two or three. This was a directional bet, in a way. I thought I should make more of them.

The market opened and promptly shat itself. It was selling off because it was a bear market, yes, but it was also selling off because nobody could trust an accounting statement anywhere. It wasn't just a bear market, it was an indictment of the entire accounting profession, Wall Street research departments, and capitalism in general. It was not a good time to be a trader.

I joined the party. As the market took the Metamucil all morning, I crushed stock and was hit on futures. That bear market noise was filling up the trading floor again. It was louder than it had ever been. It sounded like we were in hell, like souls being tortured with pitchforks.

What the fuck.

Suddenly, the trapdoor opened, and the market fell through it. Stocks were in free fall, and people were selling stocks, futures—anything—as fast as they could. The line on the intraday chart was nearly vertical.

*I'm going to take a shot at my first prop trade.* Not once in my short career had I placed anything like an unhedged bet. This was it. There was no turning back from here.

I steadied my mouse over my futures terminal and clicked.

*Boink.*

I'd just sold one tiny futures contract at 767.25. For every point the market moved, I would make or lose $50. It was a trade that was too small even for someone's personal account, but it seemed absolutely massive to me.

Ingram leaned over. "Chris is buying spooz."

"What?"

"Chris just got long the market. Size."

"Come on. This market's going to zero."

"Go look at his ticket. It's on his desk."

I had to see for myself. There was a paper ticket that verified it—he had indeed purchased a hundred big S&P futures at 768.

Chris Masters thought that the market was going higher. He expressed his opinion five hundred times the size that I'd expressed mine. For every point the market moved, he would make or lose $25,000. Chris was known for these heroics. He'd made a living off of buying when nobody else wanted to buy.

If the market declines too much in a single day, the futures become what's known as *limit down*. They don't necessarily stop trading, but limit down means that trades can't occur at a price below the preordained daily limit. There are loads of people offering futures at that level, because it's essentially free money, as long as you can sell futures higher than the level stocks are at.

Back in the crisis of 1998, during the Long-Term Capital Management blowup and the Russian debt default, the futures were limit down after a heart-stopping decline. Everyone was losing money. Chris Masters worked for a medium-size option market-maker firm at the time, and everyone was getting rinsed. Chris strapped one on, stepped in, and started buying S&P 500 futures over and over and over again until the market began to rise.

It rallied the rest of the day, in a stunning reversal. Chris reportedly made millions and single-handedly saved his firm, or so went the mythology.

And now he was doing it again. The ink wasn't even dry on his ticket, and the market was starting to rip. "Rip, rip, rip, see how they rip," sang the unidentified cash trader. I scuttled away from Chris's desk before he came over to kick my ass.

*Fuck this.* I clicked my futures terminal and got out of the trade. I lost $300. The price I sold, 767.25, was the low of the day.

It was also the low of the week.

It was also the low of the month.

It was also the low of the year.

It would be the low for nearly seven years.

If I'd hung on to my one-lot future until 2009, I would have made money.

For today, I was the worst trader in the world.

• • •

The phone was ringing. I didn't recognize the number.

It was Chris Vincent.

"Did you hear? Dave Lane got shot."

I wasn't hip to the lingo. "You mean he actually got *shot?*"

Chris giggled. "No, you dumbass, he got laid off!"

Apparently, they *would* hit a guy with glasses.

There ought to have been a clause in the employment contract that getting hired by the diabolically handsome Dick Fuld gives you no-firing immunity for five years. Who were they going to put on the recruiting posters now that Dave Lane had been shot?

"We're going to his apartment after work. Want to come?"

Dave lived in a small but, in all likelihood, expensive apartment on the West Side. The *far* West Side. I was in a different area code. It was plenty windy there.

There was a friendly black dog and a shitload of outdoor gear. Lane probably got thousand-dollar dividend checks from REI, the outdoor superstore. There were piles of backpacks and jackets and skis and snow-boards. There were also books—lots of highly intellectual books—but I was happy not to see any Umberto Eco.

Dave arrives. He's not crying. There are no holes in the soles of his shoes. He isn't wearing a barrel with suspenders. His chin is up, and he is defiant as ever.

"Clearly"—he gives us a grand pause—"I could have kissed a lot more ass."

We laugh. Dave tells us the story. It confirms my suspicions. The credit guys he worked with were heaping abuse on him. Dave has a chip on his shoulder. There was friction.

Dave worked directly for a bully named Jeff Fisher. The man tells Lane he's a moron on a daily basis, but Fisher has problems of his own, having accumulated reams and reams of telecom paper—bonds that were in big trouble because of the WorldCom bankruptcy. Fisher knows it won't end well, so he gets nervous and starts looking for a job. Fisher *finds* a job and bails out the day before his entire portfolio is blown to smithereens by Qwest. The losses are on the order of $20 million.

It wasn't Dave Lane's problem, but it became his problem. Even though he wasn't directly or even indirectly responsible for the losses, it didn't look good. Lane spent the next few weeks cleaning up the positions, and once he was done, he was unceremoniously ejected.

It wasn't just Dave Lane. This was 2001 associate class genocide. Dozens of associates across the firm—from sales and trading to research and investment banking—were taken out and shot, including several in equities, where I worked. It was even more bewildering considering the fact that the fifty or so associates who got axed could have been saved if only five fat-ass managing directors had been shot. So to speak.

Dave already had irons in the fire, including one with an asset manager in Boston. I wasn't worried for him, or his dog, or his snowboard. The unemployment rate for people with nearly perfect GMAT scores who speak unaccented English was precisely zero. But I was worried about the general level of cynicism in the universe. It had just increased appreciably. I was beginning to learn that on Wall Street, it isn't enough to be talented. It isn't enough to be good at your job. Shockingly, it isn't enough to make money. You have to know how to work the system.

I had a lot of learning to do.

I was in front of Lace, the strip club, a block away from work, and I burst into tears.

Lately, I hadn't been doing so well. The bear market was taking its toll. Maybe I'd made a mistake walking away from what could have been a distinguished military career, and a pension that would have lasted me the rest of my life. I was a *bad trader*. I'd sold the lows of public service and bought the highs of the private sector. I was a mook.

But that wasn't quite it. Throughout most of my adult life, I'd always felt that I experienced things differently from other people. I *felt* more. Instead of getting sad, I would get *really* sad. Despondent. Instead of being happy, I would be delirious. I would laugh, and everybody would turn around to look at the crazy man. Now here I was, crying in the middle of Seventh Avenue.

But there was no reason for the crying. I was just walking down the street, and I fell to pieces.

I thought about Dave Lane. The kid gets eighty-sixed, and he's grinning from ear to ear. I'm trading up a storm, and I'm coming unglued on the sidewalk.

*Pull yourself together, for heaven's sake.* I had one block to wipe the tears off my face and off my glasses before I arrived at my desk, fresh as a daisy.

I was a fucking mess.

## 7

Dark | Fall 2002–Winter 2003

The anniversary was coming up.

Friends and relatives told me that I was exhibiting signs of post-traumatic stress disorder. I would dive under the sofa whenever a plane roared overhead. I'd suffer through terrible nightmares about planes crashing. I was pretty sure that I was going to get blown to smithereens in the middle of the Lincoln Tunnel while riding to work one day. I was advised to seek counseling. It's not a big deal, I said. Man up.

But I completely avoided ground zero. Lehman had moved up to Midtown, so I figured there was no reason for me to go back. The only people who went downtown were the goddamn tourists, the sick fucks taking pictures of a hole in the ground. I had no business there. But when my mother came to visit, she told me that she wanted to see the site, and I blanched. As soon as we arrived, I burst into tears and had to be led back into the subway station.

Politically, there was no doubt about which side of the issue I'd taken. I became, for the first time in my life, a hawk. I felt that our response to 9/11 in Afghanistan was insufficient. The terrorists hadn't been particularly discriminating about avoiding civilian casualties, and I didn't see why we had to restrain ourselves. I thought we should have given Afghanistan seventy-two hours to get the women and children out of the country, then nuked it into glass, strapped fatback on our feet, and gone ice skating.

But I didn't hang an American flag on my back porch or stick one in the window of my car. I was scornful of magnetic yellow ribbons, too. I didn't need to be reminded to never forget. 9/11 was mine. *I was in possession of it*, and in my version, there were no American flags. I had my own memories.

Meanwhile, September 11 was quickly becoming part of the Lehman Brothers mythology, and I had mixed feelings about it. It's true that we were blasted out of our headquarters. It's true that we were set up to trade, only days later, in the Jersey City building. It's true that not a single employee was laid off (at least for several months). It's true that we gained market share and came out stronger. I was proud of our firm and the conduct of its employees following the attack. I was simply uncomfortable with how much management liked to talk about it. I was uncomfortable with the motivational flyers posted in the elevators.

But Lehman Brothers had its own peculiar culture, separate and distinct from those of Goldman Sachs and Morgan Stanley. We were rich intellectual snobs just like them, but we were scrappy too. The firm could have taken a direct hit from a ballistic missile, and we *still* would have come out swinging. *Fuck with us, you'll come back with a bloody stump.*

Lehman had been playing second fiddle to Goldman Sachs for at least a century, all the while thriving on its underdog status. They had talent, but we had balls, and we knew that one day we'd beat them at their own game.

Ultimately, 9/11 only cemented the difference in character between Lehman Brothers and the other Wall Street firms. Because of our proximity to the World Trade Center, Lehman employees saw things that nobody else saw. The firm had lost its innocence, and lots of us were suffering silently, myself included.

I just wanted to be left alone.

The market begins to levitate.

It's September 10, 2002. It's been a nothing day. I've barely scratched up $10,000, and I've been sitting around trying not to pay attention to the news. It's nonstop 9/11.

Tomorrow there will be a ceremony and a moment of silence held on the exchanges. The New York Stock Exchange, the Nasdaq, the CME—every US stock and derivatives exchange will halt trading for sixty seconds. I'm wondering if I'll be able to hold it together.

But here it is, September 10, and the market starts to rally. It's gained some ground since the panic lows in July, but nobody's convinced. Most of us feel that the bear market is going to take stocks all the way to zero—right now it's just taking a break.

The S&P 500 futures are at 905. 905.50. 906.

907.

It's three thirty in the afternoon. I'm in no condition to be trading. Every television and every computer screen was tuned to the ceremonies at ground zero that morning, and the audio's still clattering around the room. My nerves are jangly, and I've been trading like shit. I haven't spoken to Meat or Rory in over an hour. Ingram is on the phone with his wife.

908.

There's a crowd forming, a debate about some structured-vol trade with a client I've never heard of. It's starting to piss me off. I hate it when people camp out behind me and shoot the shit. They might be looking over my shoulder.

909.

The market's getting ready to close. I cut and paste my futures fills and start to run the P&L.

910.

Those fucking *assholes*. Those were *my* buildings. This was *my* city.

910.

I had no specific after-work plans. I was filled with a sensation, condensed into a single word: *out*. I wanted to get out, go somewhere, drink something, do anything other than stay trapped in this building, not trading, the day before 9/11.

910.

Stock index futures trade for fifteen minutes after the stock market closes. This is a throwback to the 1980s, when the exchange kept the futures open for the release of money supply data. I can't arb anything after four o'clock, because there's no stock to trade. All I can do is square up my positions.

911.

Son of a bitch.

MERC INDX.

"Hey, Meat."

"Yeah?"

"Futures are trading 911."

"What?"

"911 the day before 9/11."

"Jared, hang on a minute."

The crowd noise sounds different.

"Jared, you won't believe what's going on down here."

"What?"

"Floz and the Covello brothers told everyone in the pit that they were going to break some fucking necks if anyone printed a single trade at any price other than 911."

911.

911.

*The women were crying hysterically.*

911.

*A man jumped from the window.*

911.

*He was wearing a plaid shirt, untucked, and as soon as he was in the air, his arms and legs began to flail. He had sandy hair and his mouth was open. This was his last second alive. He accelerated and disappeared out of view.*

911.

Every trade is going up at 911.

Chris Masters figures it out. He stands over me. "You see this, Jared?"

"Yes."

911.

I look around the room. Nobody is paying attention. Nobody but me.

911.

I'll manage to make it through the ceremonies tomorrow morning. I'll make it through "Taps." I'll make it because I allowed myself to become the tiniest bit cynical about 9/11, to protect myself from further harm. Now it's all coming back.

If I exhaled, that was it.

911.

*Another man jumped. He was wearing a suit, without the jacket. And a red tie.*

911.

*I looked up.*

*Red. A giant fireball ballooned over my head.*

911.

Fuck the ceremonies at ground zero. This is the best remembrance of all, from a bunch of floor monkey knuckleheads. The falling bodies, the screams, the charred metal, the destruction—no words from any elected official were ever going to make it better.

All we could do was remember.

911.

911.

911.

911.

911.

911.

I lost it.

There are some changes for the new fiscal year.

For one thing, Ingram and I have a new boss. Ben Cohan is shedding the program trading and index arbitrage businesses and is now focusing solely on proprietary trading. This suits him. He hasn't touched a program trade in weeks, so Delee, Herb, and Vikesh are running the show. Ingram and I had been orphans, and now we have a daddy again.

Our daddy's name is Lonnie Baines. Lonnie used to run the risk arbitrage desk, which is an entirely different world from index arbitrage. Risk arbitrage is trading mergers and special situations—when one company acquires another, there exists a mathematical relationship between the two stocks, implying a probability that the deal will go through. You can bet on the deal, or against the deal, or just trade the probability. It sounds simple, but in practice, it's extremely complicated, especially where optionality is involved. I was jealous of the risk arb guys because of how intellectually engaging their business was, but I vowed never to become one because their business was too cyclical. Every time the economy hit a bump, mergers would dry up, and half the desk would get laid off. I had a safer job, and it was at least more intellectual than my old one, squeezing life jackets and counting signal flares.

Lonnie was in his late forties, but he looked about sixty-five. He ate cigars, and drank scotch, and Lord knows what else. And he had a curious habit of carrying around an insane amount of cash. A huge roll of hundreds, wrapped up in a rubber band. There had to be at least $10,000 in there. Maybe $20,000. Occasionally he would peel off one of them to buy lunch for Delee, Herb, and Vikesh. Who the fuck carries that much cash? Some pimp was going to roll him and put a down payment on an apartment.

It was getting near bonus time. We find out what our bonuses are in December, toward Christmas, and we actually get paid them at the end of January. I wasn't terribly excited about it. I knew what I'd be getting, approximately, and it wasn't much. I'd been paid $30,000 the year before, but that was all part of the one-year employment contract I signed after I joined the firm. This year, I could be paid twice that. Or nothing. But for a low-level associate, the range of compensation wasn't very wide. The important thing was to be at the high end of the spectrum, no matter how measly the numbers were.

For Ingram, the bonus was crucial. The only reason he came downstairs from fixed income was to get rich. Now some fuck with twenty large in his pocket was the gatekeeper. Ingram had to prove to Lonnie that we were worthy of big checks.

The first rule of getting paid on Wall Street—get along with your boss. Nobody who calls his boss a fuckhead is getting a big bonus. But that's basically what happened—Ingram and Lonnie had it out in the fishbowl, with the normally soft-spoken Ingram flapping his arms and pointing his finger and clearly mouthing things like *BULLSHIT* while dancing around the room. Lonnie had apparently called him a liar, which was a big mistake. You never call a military man a liar.

It was, in part, a cultural difference. Ingram was a hay-baling military farm boy. He'd never seen $20,000 in his life, let alone carried it around in his pocket. And Lonnie was a creature of Wall Street. To his credit, he knew what the fuck he was doing. Lonnie had traded just about everything under the sun. He knew exactly how index arbitrage worked. And that's why it was puzzling when he didn't call us geniuses for putting on the spread trade, which had made, by our best estimate, nearly $10 million.

Lonnie was doing what all good traders do. He was looking out for himself. The less he paid the people who worked for him, the more he could pay himself. That's one thing Lehman was guilty of—a very lopsided compensation scheme. The managing directors paid themselves handsomely, and everyone else got scraps. Though I suppose that happens everywhere.

The key was figuring out how to become a managing director.

• • •

I got $40,000.

So did Brad Young. So did Adam Cohen. Wilson James was the king. He got $45,000.

Chris Vincent got $15,000. He got sconed.

It was taboo to talk about your bonus. It said it right there on the piece of paper they handed you—you were not to tell a soul. But the six of us (five of us, now—Dave Lane had moved to Boston to punt around bonds for a small broker-dealer) had taken a blood oath that we would tell one another what we got paid. No hard feelings. This was good, because it gave me information. It was bad only if you got an embarrassing number.

It was December, and it was dark. Really fucking dark. The trading floor was plainly surreal this time of year, because darkness would descend before the trading day was even over, and the giant screen saver that stretched around the building would reflect back at us from the building across the street, glowing green and purple and orange. When there were clouds or rain, it looked like a nebula. I thought we were in Tokyo.

I asked Ingram about his bonus after he came out of Lonnie's office. He just shook his head. He didn't get rich. He was beginning to wonder if his move downstairs was a huge mistake.

I saw my friend Rick Williams across the floor, sitting with his head in his hands. Rick was a Harvard Law graduate whom the firm had asked to examine the antitrust implications of mergers. He was not a trader. He was a research dude, and a highly educated one at that. But Rick was one of my all-time favorites at Lehman. Occasionally we would leave work together and navigate the crowd of clueless Iowans on our way to the Port Authority, talking the whole time.

I'd complain about my property taxes, which were four times higher than they'd been in California for a similarly sized property. "This is bullshit," I'd say. "Property taxes essentially negate all property rights. I don't own my house, the city does. I just rent it from them."

Rick would look at me and say, "You're right."

He'd go on to tell me that the government made laws, enforced laws, and founded the whole legal framework that our society rests upon, and that all property, in essence, was owned publicly. I was in complete horror. *This is what they teach at Harvard Law.*

We had ideological, not political, discussions, which is an important distinction. With politics, people's feelings get hurt. Rick and I were just having fun being smart.

Now Rick looked at me, the screen saver reflecting off his smudged glasses, his face a pale shade of green. He looked like he'd eaten rat poison.

"What's going on?"

Rick could barely speak. "This is ... complete ... bullshit."

Uh-oh. Bad bonus.

"I think I'm the first person in the history of the firm who ever lost money in a bonus discussion."

"Come again?"

"I have to *pay* the firm. I got a *negative* bonus."

"How is that possible?"

"You remember how our bonus last year was structured like a forgivable loan that would be forgiven $10,000 a year? Well, I got a $5,000 bonus, $1,500 of which went to taxes. They told me that $3,500 would be applied to the forgivable loan, and I had to write a check to Lehman Brothers for $6,500."

"Are you going to do it?"

"*Fuck* no." It was the first time I had ever heard him drop an F-bomb. Rick was typically cool as a cucumber. He could have argued in front of the Supreme Court. Now he was coming unglued. "Fuck that shit. I'm not writing a check. They can fire me if they're going to fire me."

He went on. "*Dude.* I have like a hundred thousand dollars in school loans. I went to school for three years, not two. All my friends are working at law firms. They're all getting paid. What the fuck am I supposed to do? I can't even feed my family! You can't live here on eighty-five thousand a year! What do they expect people to do?"

I felt awful for Rick, but I was signaling that I wanted to end the conversation. I put my hands on my knees. I drummed my fingers. Rick was going on and on.

I wasn't about to tell him about my $40,000.

I went home, in the darkness, feeling a little bit rich.

Come on, 51.

*51, 51, 51, 51.*

It's ten o'clock.

51.3

*Sell!*

I was at it again, having continued my trading tricks into 2003, launching stock right after economic data were released, this time with the ISM. The Institute for Supply Management, formerly the National Association of Purchasing Management, compiles a survey on manufacturing activity. I expected it to suck, which is to say that I expected a few hundred piddling factory managers with greasy shirts and comb-overs to be marginally more pessimistic about the prospects of their firms and their employment. It sucked, indeed.

But instead of watching the market collapse and collecting my $20,000, I saw it gobble up my stock and begin to rally.

*What the fuck.* I lifted futures as fast as I could.

"Mike, you see that?"

He grimaced. He was playing the same game. "I did. What was that?"

"That makes no sense. ISM sucks, and the market rallies."

"I guess that would make it the Costanza trade."

"Huh?"

"You never watched *Seinfeld*?"

"I don't own a TV."

Ingram laughed. "Well, there's this one episode where George Costanza decides that his life is all fucked up, so maybe if he does the *opposite* of what his instincts tell him to do, things will work out better. Like, he tells George Steinbrenner to go fuck himself, and then he gets promoted."

"Uh-huh."

"So the Costanza trade is when a piece of data comes out, and you think it's going to make the market go down, but it goes up instead."

"Uh-huh."

"It's hilarious. You gotta see it."

I was scornful of television. TV was for people who wanted to turn their off brains. I wanted to have mine on, always. But the Costanza trade was born.

From that day on, the reaction to economic indicators ran in reverse. Right was wrong and wrong was right. Up was down, for that matter. I was accustomed to making about $50,000 a week off of economic releases. Now that money had disappeared.

Once I thought about it, the Costanza trade began to make sense. If there's an outsized reaction to an economic statistic, due to people like me ripping stock, then other opportunistic traders will come along and play the reversion. They'll sell the market when it gets too high. And if they're successful, they'll keep doing it. Eventually you have more traders playing the reversion than the initial reaction, so when the auspicious economic data are released, the market goes down, not up.

I could have responded like George Costanza and done the opposite of what my instincts told me to do. I could have purchased stock on a bad economic number. It would have been a profitable trade. But my mind wouldn't accept the contradiction.

This, combined with the e-minis, was conspiring to limit our profits. The electronic futures were trading more often, to the point where the locals in the pit were making one-point-wide markets instead of two. I had to work twice as hard to make money. Those damn e-mini futures were getting in the way.

I realized that I was becoming a victim of technology. If both futures and stocks are traded electronically, you can replace labor with capital. You can instruct a computer to do a human's job. It would be a very basic program, one that an intern could write.

Technology was adding liquidity to the market. The pit was becoming increasingly irrelevant. *I* was becoming increasingly irrelevant. I'd just gotten a job making buggy whips as the first automobile was rolling off the assembly line.

How stupid can you get?

I needed to cancel my subscription to the *Wall Street Journal*. I was getting sick of reading bad news on the way to work. It was March 2003, and there was nothing but death and misery in the newspaper.

But I was beginning to have second thoughts about TV. The latest shows, *American Idol* in particular, were a constant topic of conversation at Lehman. If it were possible, I was feeling even more left out.

I just didn't like the idea of coming home from work every day and staring at the tube. My time was better spent doing something, anything else. Even drinking.

Meanwhile, interest rates had gone about as low as they could possibly go—there was no money left for us to make. This was not a good time to be running out of ideas, but that's what I was doing. I'd already survived one round of layoffs, but the bear market was stretching out, and there were rumors of a second round, this one even more severe. If I was profitable, I was safe, but now the diabolical index arb robots had taken over my trade, and there was nothing clever for me to do.

I resigned myself to the fact that the market was going down forever. The bear market trading floor noise was still there, but it was missing the element of panic—now it had resignation. *Just fucking sell 'em.* A fatalism had pervaded the trading floor. Sooner or later, we were all going to be manning newsstands and hot dog carts. Everyone felt the same way.

Sometimes I'd make it through an entire day at the office without speaking to another human being. I didn't say hello to the security guard outside the building. I didn't make eye contact with the people in the elevator. I didn't acknowledge anyone else in my row as I walked to my seat. I gave Ingram the left-hand wave. I looked at the ground when I bought my bagel and coffee. I got my own lunch and ate it in silence. I worked on a trading floor with three hundred other people and talked to nobody. I didn't laugh—ever. I felt completely powerless. I felt that the market, the firm, and the world were completely out of my control, and I had little choice but to sit in pain and wait for the inevitable to happen.

Mornings were the worst. I struggled to stay busy. I wrote down futures levels. I printed out my charts. I read the news. Even the bad news. It was either that or spend time alone with my thoughts. These days, the inside of my head was a bad neighborhood—I didn't want to go in there without a flashlight and a shotgun.

For Ingram, the mornings were fine. He'd head off to the fishbowl for a strategy meeting with the rest of the senior people. It was nice that they invited him, given his lowly delta-one status. I followed the meeting from a distance—Ingram talks, and nobody pays attention. Lonnie talks, and nobody pays attention. Ben Cohan talks, and everyone pays attention. He's really getting after it this morning. Something important is being said.

Ingram came back smiling.

"What was going on in there?"

Ingram laughed. "Cohan. He's nuts."

"What?"

"Cohan says we're going to have a big rally today."

"Why?"

"Because they found Elizabeth Smart."

Elizabeth Smart was the Mormon teenager who'd been abducted from her bedroom some months ago. This morning, the only thing the cable channels were talking about was that they'd found Elizabeth Smart, the blonde Mormon harpist. Even CNBC. You couldn't get financial news. It was nonstop Elizabeth Smart.

"Ben Cohan said that?"

"He was totally serious. He said that it's been nothing but bad news for weeks, and that the market needed good news—*any* good news, even if it had nothing to do with the market."

It was nuts. But so was Ben Cohan.

Ben Cohan didn't like Ingram because a theory like that wouldn't make any sense to a linear thinker like Ingram. Cohan was interested primarily in market psychology; he had no objective, rational reason to think that the market would go up. He believed that people were inherently irrational and would act in nonsensical but predictable manners. If you could predict people's behavior, you could make money.

I resolved to take what Ben Cohan said at face value. The idea had some merit. When I walked in that morning, I was ready to eat a gun, even before I sat down at my desk. *Kaboom!* Already Elizabeth Smart was making me feel better.

Ingram continued. "Nobody in the room agreed with him. They went around the table. First me, then Chris, then Lonnie, then everyone else. We all said the market was going to zero. Cohan was the only one who disagreed, and everyone told him that he was out of his tree."

Son of a bitch, look at that. The futures were already perking up.

The market was like a roller coaster, but just the part where the machinery takes the coaster up a big hill. *Chug, chug, chug.* It was a grab-a-thon all day, and it never got out of control. Steady buying. It made for easy index arb. Buy stock now, sell futures later. Out of the corner of my eye, I saw Ingram fighting it, and losing.

Ingram was sour grapes. "I ever tell you about Cohan?"

"No. What?"

"Search for his name on the NYSE website."

I looked him up. Cohan had been disciplined by the NYSE a while back for, for the best I could tell, a massive market-on-close buy program, that he then turned around and reversed. Violation or not, it was the work of a fucking genius. No mere mortal could have come up with a scheme of that magnitude. Sending a billion-dollar order to the market just to make it go higher? Then doing the same thing in reverse? It was insanity. I was not worthy.

For a second, I wondered how in the hell Cohan could get a job after that. You're standing tall before the man, you get a mark on your U4, your official record, it's hard to find employment. But I realized that it's one thing to be stealing customer funds and quite another to be bigger than the entire market. Any head of trading at any firm could appreciate what Cohan had done. Wall Street won't hire miscreants, unless their offense was absolutely brilliant. But in the process, Cohan had violated one of the central tenets of trading—never try to be bigger than the market. Either you will lose, or the goons will come and get you. He had to learn the hard way.

I looked over at his desk. Cohan was all smiles. Likely he'd strapped on a big one and was watching the market do the work for him.

The rally continued. It got downright pornographic. It opened on the lows and closed on the highs. The market made a nearly three standard deviation move. At the end of the day, someone yelled over the hoot, the internal intercom system, "STOCKS!"

Ingram was in a shitty mood. He'd been punting around futures lately, with mixed results, and he was *definitely* on the wrong side of this one. I tried to ignore him. I wanted the brain of Cohan, with the humanity of Ingram.

Cohan was smoking and joking with Chris Masters. It was a big day for the trading floor. Soon Cohan would be moving upstairs to the fifth floor to carry out his secretive prop operation. He was taking my classmate Sam Grossman along with him, as well as his *Star Trek* convention.

It was hard not to be jealous of Sam. He was talented, to be sure, but it was more important for him to stay close to Cohan, the moneymaking machine; he'd picked the winner and stuck to him like flypaper. And he'd been awfully smug around bonus time. Wilson James had brought down $45,000, but I imagined that Sam's number was much higher. Cohan had also gotten Herb promoted to vice president, which was incredible, given that Delee and Vic had taken to calling him Uday for his choice of suits. If you were under the Cohan umbrella, you were golden.

If Cohan was long, the market went up. If he was short, the market went down. If he was long a deal spread, it compressed. If he was short an index rebalance, it was a winner. He was right punting around futures and he was right on risk programs. He liked to say that he was wrong 80 percent of the time, but that was pure bullshit. He was too good to be lucky, and he was too lucky to be good.

In all my time at Lehman, Cohan was the best trader I ever met.

The good thing about Cohan leaving was that he took Lonnie and all his cash with him.

The bad thing was that we got Joe Olkin.

"Eeereurrreurur guererr woereerrer nerrur."

"Beg pardon?"

Olkin and his gut are standing over me.

"Eeereurrreurur guererr woereerrer nerrur!"

"Oh, sure, we're going to be trading index arb for you now." Is this guy for real?

"Meureurur."

Olkin sounds like he has a pinched nerve. I can barely understand him. He also has no concept of personal space. I can lick his belly button if I want to.

Seems he was the head of program sales before coming down to index arb, but I have no idea how he managed to sell a single trade. He's unintelligible. He's also loud, but friendly, in an overbearing sort of way. And, finally, he's the proverbial bull in the china shop—whenever he walks down a row on the trading floor, he inevitably bumps into every chair, every desk, and every sidecar along the way. He spills coffee, trips over his own feet, and bumbles around aimlessly.

I can't tell if he's smart.

Ingram is happy, though. It seems that Olkin will tolerate mediocrity, up to a point. And this is good, because Ingram and I aren't making any fucking money.

Trading index arb then was like swimming through a Chuck E. Cheese's ball pit. It was clear that the arb had been turned into a robot trade, and we were the last holdouts trying to do it by hand. The Bank One guys had long since left the pit. Not because I put them out of business, like I'd sworn to, but because they were busy writing computer programs to put *me* out of business. I was the fastest motherfucker on the street, but I couldn't keep up with the robots.

I began, once again, to fear for my job. It was a new fiscal year, and all the money we'd made with our fancy interest rate trades was booked and gone. We had to start over from zero, with the same budget as the year before—this, apparently, was the source of the disagreement between Ingram and Lonnie—and there was no conceivable path to meeting our target with robot wars. We had to figure out something.

So I started to figure out what I would do after they fired my dumb ass. Drive to Chicago, maybe, and become a floor trader. I was qualified for little else, and I wasn't about to crawl back on my hands and knees to the military. I'd have been sentenced to a life of people spitting on the back of my neck. And even this wasn't a long-term solution—it was only a matter of time before the floors were entirely shut down, according to Meat's doom-and-gloom predictions.

Every morning, I hit the snooze button as many times as possible, dragged myself to the shower, dressed, didn't bother tying my tie, slept on the bus on the way to work, made my way upstairs, squeezed out a few arbs, and spent the rest of the day feeling sorry for myself. Then I'd return to New Jersey and fill a sixty-four-ounce plastic cup half with Jim Beam, half with Coke. I stopped working out. I stopped running. I stopped being interested in anything at all except for my monster mixed drink and sleep.

I had, by this point, broken down and bought a television. *Off.* I just wanted to turn everything off. Fucking shit. I drove to the Secaucus Best Buy and spent zero time patrolling the aisles, making a beeline for a cheap Samsung flat-screen number—the plasma TVs were, at this point, prohibitively expensive. I struggled to fit the idiot box in the back seat of my car, grunting and sweating, until I finally just tore off the box and left it to blow around the parking lot. There.

The market had, of course, affected me profoundly. Stocks were rallying now, but nobody believed it, least of all me. Had Ben Cohan stayed long from the day he called the Elizabeth Smart rally, he'd have made himself a fortune. I thought the next leg of the bear market was imminent, and I thought it was going to wipe me out first.

I had not, by this point, purchased a cell phone. I was secure in my decision. I didn't want to talk to anybody—ever—for any reason. I didn't want people to be able to contact me. I didn't want them to know where I was.

I thought about taking the car, driving off to Montana, assuming another identity, and starting over as a dishwasher. Nobody would even know *who* I was. Nobody would know about the wasted potential.

If I'd been working in any other role—as a customer trader or a salesperson—someone might have noticed. Someone might have noticed the listless behavior or the weight loss. But I didn't interact with *anyone*. The only person who might have noticed was Ingram, and he and I were in the same boat.

One morning, in December, as the market opened, I tried to peel off a trade. I could not.

That was it.

Index arb was dead.

Completely dead.

Up to that point, I had about a one-minute window to get in a few trades before the robots took over. Now the window had completely disappeared. There was nothing to do.

I left promptly at 1600.

I took the bus home.

I went inside.

I got my cup and emptied most of a bottle in it.

I sat in front of my stereo, played the saddest music I could find, and drank.

I began to scream uncontrollably. My cat came to see what was wrong. I gave him a hug.

I went upstairs and fished around in the medicine cabinet.

Nothing. Absolutely nothing.

A bottle of Tylenol PM.

I ate half the bottle and washed it down. I went to the mirror. I even looked like I wanted to die. I thought about Tom Cruise in *Vanilla Sky*, with his mangled face, waving at himself in the mirror before he kills himself, as if to say, "I'm outta here."

I'm outta here.

I felt a little wobbly. I needed to sit down. Why not log into Bloomberg and see what's going on with Japan?

For the first time in months, I felt great. Hey, look at the Nikkei. Does it always feel this good before you die?

Hey, if I'm going to die, I should probably make a phone call.

I pick up the phone.

I don't know who I'm calling.

She's asking me if I'm okay.

Everything's fine.

## 8

"So, you were out swinging from the chandeliers last night, huh?"

*Go fuck yourself,* I thought, with as much hate as I could manage. If I weren't on the trading floor, I would have choked the life out of him.

It was Paul Kung, the Korean dividends guy. Paul did the work for us that nobody else wanted to do. He maintained a database of dividends so we would know how much futures were worth. My wife had called the office yesterday morning to tell him that I wouldn't be in, and Paul had answered the phone. She left out the part about me almost killing myself.

I was found face down in a pool of vomit. When I regained consciousness, I was furious. I pounded the floor with my fists and tore a towel that had been given to me. If there was a God, He was on my shit list. I could not even kill myself properly.

After I was cleaned up, I sat upright in bed, sobbing, hoping that the sun would never rise, hoping that it would remain dark forever. The day after you try to kill yourself is the worst day in the world. It is the day that was not supposed to happen. It is the day that you were supposed to miss, like trying, and failing, to call in sick to school the day of an exam.

I had somehow talked my wife out of calling an ambulance. She did, however, call a suicide hotline. Up until this point, she had been watching me carefully; my behavior had been causing her concern, and I could feel her eyes on me when I refused to speak and stared off into space. I cried to a sympathetic woman on the other end of the phone, who was probably my age. She told me I needed to get help. I ignored her. There was nothing wrong with me. What I had done, or tried to do, was perfectly rational. Anyone who lives with that much pain has the right to try to get out of it.

I had said some things the night before. Yelled, rather. I had shouted that I hated myself, that I didn't deserve to live, that I deserved to die. I wondered if anybody on the street had heard what was going on.

I was filled with rage. I was angry with God.

The next day, the day that shouldn't have been, I ate a sloppy cheese-burger at a diner down the street, my head still fuzzed. I felt like I was swimming in a dirty fish tank. It was my first day off of work in at least a year. I never took days off—the money didn't make itself.

Now, two days later, I was back at work. The authorities had moved our desk closer to the window. Today there was sun in the middle of winter. It was hurting my eyes.

I had been a failure. I had embarked on a stupid pursuit of free-market capitalism just at the point when it would have been much safer to keep a secure if unsatisfying government job. I had proved that I could not trade; I had no edge. I did not fit in the world of $3,000 dinner tabs. I had no resume. I had absolutely nothing going for me. I was ugly.

I hadn't spoken to Ingram, really, in weeks. What was there to talk about? We were both doomed. We were sitting in the same life raft, and we weren't about to get into a fight about the remaining food. Olkin, for all his clumsiness, had proven to be a decent human being, but I was not comfortable telling him that they might as well shut us down; that there was no more money left to be made. He had enough problems as it was. In his current job as head of program trading, he was punching above his weight. He was the only doofus in a group of a dozen or so managing directors, perfect financial specimens, brilliant minds, and all-around great guys.

In trading, you cannot pretend for very long that nothing is going on. You cannot ignore the fact that you aren't making any money. Someone will figure it out, sooner or later. In another profession, such as teaching, or law, or public service, you can be a buffoon for quite some time without any consequences. There are even bad doctors. Half of all doctors are below average. But the 50 percent of traders that are below average are fired within a year and replaced with another 50 percent. Shit or get off the pot. That seat is an expensive piece of real estate; it costs over $20,000 dollars a year just to keep the Bloomberg terminal running, not to mention the health insurance, and term life insurance, and every other perk, and if you are simply occupying it and stealing oxygen, it makes sense to replace you with someone else.

I had to figure out a way to make money. It was either that or get fired. Jay Knight had done it. Look at him, he was trading from Miami. At some point in Jay's career, he had to make the decision that he was going to accept risk. He had to decide that taking risk—*pursuing* risk—was better than the alternative, which was sitting around and collecting an annuity. He did not want to be one of the legions of traders or salespeople who traded customer flow and made money around the margins. He wanted to take big risk. And it had paid off.

Why not me? It had been in the back of my mind ever since Ingram had told me Jay Knight's story. What if I became a trading hero? What if I traded my way out of the New York office and into a cabin in Vermont? Or a ranch in Northern California? Or an island in Puget Sound? Sure, I could get rich, but it was more important that I bought myself a ticket out of 745 Seventh Avenue, away from all the bad accents and bad ties and politics.

So, there it is. I'm going to trade prop.

Where to start?

I had been working at Lehman Brothers for more than two years, and I still knew next to nothing about financial markets, except for the futures basis and some intricacies about short-term interest rates. There was a lot more to know about proprietary trading.

I got a notebook in which I recorded data. I recorded the open, the high, the low, and the close of every relevant futures contract. I recorded levels of all major worldwide stock markets. I also wrote down the strips of all interest rate futures.

I filled my head with information.

I also spent at least a half hour scanning Bloomberg and the Internet for major market news. I read it. I didn't know what I was reading at first, but I continued to read until it started to make sense. In the beginning, I read everything, but then, over time, I began to learn what was relevant and what was not. I would take more notes in the notebook.

I became a student of the markets.

Then I began to print out charts. In the morning, I would print out the previous day's charts of the S&P and Nasdaq and tape them to a page in the notebook. I would make notes on the chart. I looked for support and resistance. I looked for trend lines and breaks of trend lines. I looked where trends began and where they were exhausted.

I did all this before I placed a single trade.

Meat and I hadn't talked in a while. I felt bad, because the less we traded with him, the more likely it was that he would get laid off too. He needed to trade futures to justify his existence. We were all in it together.

I told Meat about my plan. He'd tried his hand at prop trading at one point too. When he worked for Ben Cohan, Ben set up a small futures account for him to punt around in. Meat was a piker, a cautious gambler. He didn't make or lose very much money, but he was determined to help me in my quest.

It wasn't a good market to be day-trading, in late 2003. All the volatility had gone out of it. In fact, I noticed that I hadn't seen Yoda in a couple of weeks. I asked Sam Grossman where he was.

Sam made the throat-cutting motion.

"Ting's gone?"

"Yup, they blew him out."

"Why?"

"He was losing a boatload of cash. Ting was a trend follower. It was easier for him when the market was volatile and he could hop on thirty-point trends. Now we're lucky to get a ten-handle day."

My first lesson of trading. If the market changes, *you* have to change too, or else you are out on your ass.

That morning, the futures opened flat, around 1120. The previous day's high was at 1122. The trading floor was silent. When there is no volatility, nobody plays. I called Meat.

"Meat."

"Yeah."

"Work ten at two."

"Working ten at two. Oh half bid."

I had noticed that the market encountered resistance at the previous day's high. I was offering futures there, figuring that it would happen again.

"One bid. Twenty bid. Half bid."

"*Filled.*"

Fuck. Now I was short. There was no arb; I just had naked risk. I did not like it. I was tightrope walking, and someone had taken away my balancing pole *and* the net.

Then the magic started to happen.

"Eighty offer now. Half offer. Offered at one."

*Ack. I can't handle this anymore.*

"Meat, work an oh bid on ten."

"Oh bid on ten. At one. At sixty. *Filled.*"

I had just made $5,000 on my first trade. No arbitrage. Fucking magic. I just took money out of the market.

"At a half. At nine. At nine now."

Shit. I could have made more money.

"At eight. At *seven*, now."

Shit.

"At five."

The market was cratering. I had sold the high, but if I had stayed short, I would have made an additional $12,500.

"At *three* now. Jeez, Jared, you sure do know how to sell them."

"Apparently. I just don't know how to cover."

Lesson number two: don't be a pussy. If you are right in a trade, stick with it.

"Meat, work a one bid on ten."

Yesterday's low was 1111."

"One bid, working."

In the first half hour, the market had already traced out the previous day's range. I was trying to buy on the low.

"At eighty. Twenty bid, at eighty. Still twenty bid. Forty bid now, half bid."

*Shit.*

"Two bid. Two half bid. Three bid. *Unable.*"

*Goddamn* it.

Lesson number three: don't get too greedy.

At the end of the day, I had $5,000. Had I traded everything perfectly, I could have had $50,000.

This was a lot more work than index arb, but it was also more fun. On Wall Street, most people play for pennies, for basis points. They pick up the phone and collect commissions. Maybe they work in stock loan and borrow and lend, and earn a spread. Maybe they are an options market maker, and buy on their bid and sell on their offer. Very few people make a living by *taking* liquidity; by actually expressing an opinion on the market. Some of those people went on to run the biggest hedge funds in the world, making hundreds of millions of dollars.

It all starts here.

I had already changed seats at Lehman three times. This time I was sitting in between Ingram and Vikesh, the god of program trading.

There are four kinds of people. There are people who are smart and hardworking, there are people who are dumb and hardworking, there are people who are dumb and lazy, and there are people who are smart and lazy. The people who are dumb and lazy aren't much of a problem: you just have to feed them, and they will stay out of the way. The smart and hardworking people are annoying: they are busybodies; they are the people running for student council and trying to run everyone's lives. The people who are dumb and hardworking are the worst; they fuck things up for everyone, thinking they are helping.

The people who are smart and lazy are the best because they build tools to help people do their jobs so that they don't have to work so hard.

Vikesh was one of these people. It seemed like he spent only a half hour a day doing actual work, which was torturing a spreadsheet so fast that smoke started to come out of the computer; and the rest of the day goofing off with Delee and Herb or thinking up ways to make money.

There was a minor bull market in stocks of companies that trafficked in security equipment. First and foremost was Taser International, which had become a fad stock that was waxing short sellers like a surfboard. But there were others, basically penny stocks that would issue a press release about some new government contract, and the stock would be up 1,000 percent in a single day.

Vikesh and I noticed that before these stocks would spike, there would be a small but noticeable increase in volume. We figured that this was dirty insider buying. Shit like this happened all the time; it was not uncommon for there to be a small increase in volume before a major news event.

I told Vikesh that there ought to be a way to run small cap stocks through a screening tool to detect any small changes in volume. I had no idea how to do it. I was the most computer-illiterate person on the floor. But within five minutes, Vikesh had built a spreadsheet that did exactly that. He came up with five stocks that fit our criteria.

He invested in all five.

The next day, one of them was up 1,000 percent.

Vikesh figured he made about $10,000. He bought lunch for the desk.

He went back to goofing off. Making money, to him, was hardly even a challenge.

Shortly thereafter, Herb announced that he had been invited to speak to a class of incoming interns.

"Not in those pants, you're not," said Olkin.

"Why not?" asked Herb.

"Dude. We can tell what religion you are," said Delee.

It was true. His junk was clearly outlined.

"Were those pants that tight when you bought them, or did you gain weight?"

Herb was visibly embarrassed.

Olkin was hopping up and down. "Tim, check this out!"

Tim Pelliccio looked at Herb's crotch. "Mushroom cap!" he announced.

Tim kept going. He yelled it across the floor. "*Mushroom cap!* Check this out! It's *MUSHROOM CAP!*"

John Smith made his way across the floor without moving his neck. He looked down, then looked up at Herb. "You got an explanation for that?"

"He's supposed to give a speech to a bunch of analysts in two hours," said Olkin.

"Not in those clothes. Jesus." Smith pulled out a handful of hundreds. "Go downstairs and buy some new pants. No, you don't have to pay me back. It's on me."

"But I don't want to—"

"You have no choice in the matter. Go buy some fucking pants."

Delee and I were howling. I wore bad clothes, but Herb was worse. When he was working for Cohan, he was off-limits. He was under the

Cohan umbrella. Now that Cohan was upstairs with his robot wars, Herb was fair game. This was old school—giving someone money so he can change his offensive attire.

I was starting to feel better.

Sam Grossman appears in front of me. He wants to shake my hand. I haven't seen him in months.

"Dude, I made VP."

I had never heard of someone going around congratulating himself for making VP.

"That's . . . uh, great."

I had not made VP.

"Did you get deep selected or something?" I ask nonchalantly. "I thought you had to wait three years to make VP."

Sam smiles. "You know how it is. I'm working for Ben. He thinks I do a good job. We're making money—the stars were aligned."

*Hmm.* "Do you get paid more as a VP?"

"Yes and no. They increase the base salary. The bonus is still discretionary. But I assume it has some effect."

I had just received my bonus earlier that day, in a conversation with Olkin. I was getting paid a $90,000 bonus, not counting my salary. I wasn't happy or unhappy. It was merely a fact. I would save the money, in any case.

I wondered how much Sam got paid.

I knew how much my friends got paid. For the most part, they were crushing it. Adam and Wilson were in the high $100,000s. Brad was a little bit lower. Only happy, friendly Chris, who had probably freaked out everyone on the mortgage desk, got paid less than me.

I wasn't quite at the point of envy, yet. People were going to get paid more than me. I worked in an unimportant, insignificant backwater. I was no Jay Knight. Did I want to be a size hitter and get paid $1 million a year? Sure. But I had no idea how to get there.

I probably wasn't going to get there punting around futures. I'd had some success. I was making $10,000 to $20,000 a day scalping in and out of positions. I never got greedy. I never had a huge day. But then, I was disciplined. I rarely lost money. I had an odd system. Most traders have huge, volatile swings. They make piles of cash one day, then they get rinsed the next. I was treating trading like a nine-to-five job, as a career, not a call option. I might have been able to make more by taking larger positions and swinging it around, but I couldn't stomach the volatility.

I was a piker.

But I was getting the opportunity to trade more size. Olkin had taken me under his wing and was having me trade futures against some of his larger program trades. I had become, for better or worse, the desk expert on trading futures. I became his execution clerk, which I was happy to do, because it was one less reason for me to get fired. In the meantime, Ingram was still scratching around the index arb and waiting for interest rates to move.

The stock market had closed, and I was winding up my day, doing my P&L and closing down the book. Olkin yelled over to me, "*Buy four hundred Nasdaqs!*"

I almost jumped out of my chair. This was the biggest order yet. And since stocks were already closed, this was going to be difficult. None of the locals was going to want to take a position after the close.

"Meat."

"Oh bid at one. What's up, Jared?"

"Got a big one."

"Okay."

"One on *fifty*."

"You said fifty, right?"

"Yes, Meat."

"Bought twenty, bought forty, *filled*. Paid one on fifty."

"Two on another fifty."

"Working two on fifty. Bought twenty-five. At three. Unable on twenty-five. At three."

"Up to three."

"Up to three. Bought ten. *At fourrrrr.*"

"Fuck!"

These locals were *fading* me. To fade is to be unwilling to trade. I hadn't even bought a hundred of the four hundred contracts, and already I was running into trouble.

Olkin: "How's it going?"

I held up the index finger. *Wait.*

"Meat, pay four on the balance."

"Working fours . . . *filled.*"

"Meat, five on fifty."

"Working five on—goddamn it."

"What?"

"*Unable.* At six. No, at *seven,* now."

"Jared, how's it going?"

Index finger again. *Wait.*

"Up to seven."

"Unable!"

I couldn't buy these fucking futures.

"*Jared, how's it going?*"

I answered him. "Not going so well."

"At eight now. At nine. Showing ten on the offer."

*Fuck.*

Olkin was pissed. "Jared, we have *risk* here! What the fuck is going on!"

That was it.

I lifted the phone high, high above my head and smashed it on the desk like I was splitting wood. The receiver shattered into a thousand pieces, raining down plastic on the surrounding desks, tinkling like broken glass. I got up and started to march off the trading floor.

Everyone—*everyone*—was looking at me.

*What the hell*—I pumped my fist triumphantly.

The trading floor erupted in a long, lusty standing ovation. They had never seen so spectacular a phone smash. People were on their feet. Hank Hsu yelled, "It's never too late in the day to break shit!"

It was best career move I would ever make.


Within a month I had two job offers.

Tim Pelliccio wanted me to trade cash. I had heard rumors of this: Lehman was launching a small cap trading desk that would make markets in hundreds of small, thinly traded, illiquid stocks. I thought that cash trading was monkey work, but I thought that small cap could potentially be more interesting.

Tim finally came over to pitch the idea. I had been sitting down awhile, and my nuts were stuck to the inside of my thigh. I stood up, and did a little sidestep to try unsticking them. I was successful. My sac peeled away, and my balls hung in the breeze.

Tim caught all of this and started belly laughing. "What was that, the little scrotum step?" He imitated me, sidestepping.

We had a few good laughs. Nothing like a scrotum joke to break the ice.

Tim told me he thought I could be a good addition to the small cap team, with my program trading skills. I agreed. It is true. It makes no sense to treat small cap as a collection of individual stocks. You treat it as an asset class and trade it all at once.

The poker-playing, sports-betting Johnny B. was the head of small cap. He was a taskmaster. I sat with him for a few days and watched his every move. It seemed like his entire universe revolved around something called VWAP. This I understood to be volume weighted average price. Why it is so important, I cannot say.

Johnny gave me a couple of stocks to trade to try and beat VWAP. There was nothing hard about it; all I was doing was buying stock. But it is a game. If I think it is going up, I buy more early and beat VWAP. If I think it is going down, I buy more later and beat VWAP. It requires you to take a view on the direction of the stock.

It is hard to have an opinion on the direction of hundreds of different stocks.

But I was game. I traded against the VWAP a few times, mostly successfully. If Johnny was pleased, he didn't let on. He had a lot of balls in the air and a lot of sports bets.

In the meantime, while I was dicking around with small cap stocks, I was approached by Mark Ricci, the head of volatility trading. Mark was a shadow on the trading floor. A phantom. He was the most powerful person you didn't know about. I didn't know what his voice sounded like, because he never raised it above twenty decibels.

There were two theories about this. The first held that Mark had been a hothead at one time. A raging lunatic. Stories circulated about the time he climbed over a desk to choke the shit out of one of the sales guys. He had spent the last several years trying to atone for his rageaholic ways. The second held that Mark was fanatical about privacy and didn't want anyone to hear what he was saying. On a trading floor, this is difficult, if not impossible. If you want to say something in private, you go into an office. But Mark was a ventriloquist; his lips would move, and the dummy would respond.

"I k we g h a ortu n e ETF d k, b e d ng it he r t a t I nage, and y u mig be n r e b."

*ETF desk? I think he's asking me to trade ETFs!* I craned my neck to hear more.

"Wi re eri nce in I d x arb age, I a l f t."

"I do think the index arbitrage experience will help! When is this going to happen?"

"We e to der a w ot es, hope lly it w l be hap soon."

If I understood him correctly, he was asking me to trade ETFs. There was an opening. Chandler, having destroyed the Molloy Brothers, was bored and looking for new challenges. He wanted to trade options, and had dragged Mark Ricci into the fishbowl for at least a dozen meetings, trying to make it happen.

The ETF trader, on an equity floor, was like being the bond trader on the Treasury desk. It was ground zero for the biggest risk, the fastest trades, and the most prestige. Jon Corzine was the bond trader and went on to run Goldman Sachs and the state of New Jersey. I would trade ETFs and go on to—never mind. I would be hopping on the express elevator to managing director-land, if that was what I wanted.

I felt terrible for Ingram. He was the one who spent a few weeks sitting behind Chuck and Chandler, trying to get a taste of the ETF magic. Now he was going to be alone. The plan was that he was going to trade prop. I had mixed feelings about this. Ingram was a nice guy and a truly great trader, having made the biggest, baddest index arb trade of all time, but he was no Jay Knight. He knew how to size a bet appropriately, but he had a hard time coming up with the right bet in the first place. I had been the idea guy. We had been a perfect team up until this point. Now he was going to be sitting by himself with a bow-tie-wearing structured vol trader we called Sniffles to run a halfhearted prop effort. I was the opposite of jealous.

I took Tim Pelliccio aside and told him politely that I wasn't interested in being an assistant to a small cap cash trader when I could run the ETF desk.

Tim didn't have much to say to me after that, scrotum joke notwith-standing.

In the meantime, in 2004, Lehman Brothers was making money.

The company had been making money all along, in nontransparent ways. Were it not for the mortgage desk cranking out hundreds of millions of dollars every quarter after 9/11, we might have been in serious trouble. True, much of the success story had to do with us finding temporary space and getting our trading floors up and running. But few people talked about the role that the mortgage and interest rate franchises had in keeping the firm afloat.

This was prime time for mortgages. The Federal Reserve had lowered interest rates to 1 percent, setting off a refinancing boom. Typically, during a recession, home prices suffer or at least languish. In this particular recession, home prices began to lift off. The weird thing was that nobody thought it was weird.

Lehman Brothers was first and foremost a bond trading firm. Equities were an afterthought. Lehman Brothers traded equities like the Colorado Rockies pitched, at least before they figured out to stick the balls in the humidor. They had a pitching staff, just for show, but were too busy conking home runs. If you wanted to trade stocks, you were better off at Goldman Sachs or Morgan Stanley.

The rumors were spilling out of the fourth floor as to how much money these guys made. Managing directors were in the mid- to high millions. Were these guys more talented than your plain-vanilla equities trader? Would any of them have been able to trade S&P 500 futures alone, deprived of sensory input, with no customer flow to speak of? Did they have trading talent, or were they in the right place at the right time?

I was beginning to learn that being in the right place at the right time was a predictor of at least half of the success of someone on Wall Street. Take two associates of equal ability. One of them trades stocks, the other goes into this backwater alphabet soup where they trade things like CDOs, CDS, and other shit you never heard of. One of them rides the wave and builds a solid gold house; the other never comes close to seven figures.

Even Dick Fuld was an example of this. He and his lieutenant, Joe

Gregory, had been commercial paper traders in the old days of Lehman. Today nobody gives a shit about commercial paper traders. Money market trading is for non–Ivy League mooks. A monkey could do it. But back then, when interest rates were close to 18 percent and volatile, trading commercial paper took nerves of steel. There was a lot of money to be made, and lost. If Dick and Joe had come out of their associate class trading sleepy stocks, it is highly likely that today someone else would have been in charge of Lehman Brothers. Not to say that these weren't smart guys, but maybe they were just average guys who happened to be in the right place at the right time.

Then, in another thought: what if Lehman Brothers was led by average guys?

Mark Ricci was sure taking his fucking time moving me over to ETFs. It had been months since our conversation, and I still hadn't heard anything.

I started to pay attention to what was going on at the ETF desk. Chuck had left ETFs and gone back to trading index options, leaving Chandler in charge, with lacrosse-playing D.C. as assistant. Chandler was under a serious amount of pressure. He didn't have the Molloy Brothers to kick around anymore, his margins were being compressed by liquidity and narrowing bid-offer spreads, and his customers were getting more and more aggressive. Chandler was getting downright nasty. A sales trader would ask him for a market on 100,000 SMH.

"Thirty-two, thirty-seven!"

"Chandler, can you tighten that up a little?"

"*That's not the right price*! THAT'S NOT THE RIGHT PRICE!" Hair flopping around, D.C. looking embarrassed. The sales guy would sigh and hang up the phone. Another trade lost. Another customer blown up. Chandler thought he was doing the right thing as the guardian of the sanctity of the market-maker quote, but it is a two-way street, there is give and take, and you can't turn away trades on principle. You have to take some of the bad ones in order to get the good ones.

I was beginning to think that D.C. was some kind of capital markets version of Mother Teresa. He sat there all day and never said a word. He cleaned up messes. He fetched lunches. He never asked for any glory. He was picking them up and putting them down.

After the close, I introduced myself. "What's going on over here?" I asked.

D.C. smiled. "You mean Chandler?"

"Uh-huh."

"You don't know the half of it. The back-office guys won't talk to him anymore. I have to do all the breaks."

"Like which guys?"

"Like Fred Barr. Like Aaron Anderson."

Aaron Anderson was the king of back office. Soft-spoken and perfectly rational, Anderson knew how to untangle any trader screwup. He had told me, in a private moment over a glass of champagne at a wedding, that he really wanted to be an archaeologist. He was not happy with his station in life as a back-office puke, but he was getting paid too much to leave.

"Anderson's the best guy up there! What happened?"

D.C. laughed. "You don't know the half of it."

"How's the P&L?"

"Going down. We used to make about two hundred, two-fifty a day. Now we're down to about one-fifty."

Chandler was close to a meltdown. ETFs were suffering on his watch. "Where is the rascal?"

"Beats the shit out of me."

I walked over to Chandler's desk. For some reason, his desktop had not locked, and all four screens were still displayed. He had an Outlook appointment sitting on top of his spreadsheet showing a meeting at a competitor.

"D.C."

"Yeah?"

"Look at this."

D.C. looked. "*Hoooollllly* shit!"

"He's looking for a job. How long has this been going on?"

"It all makes sense now," said D.C. "He's been getting these weird phone calls and putting them on privacy. Sometimes he shows up around nine, or he'll leave right at the bell."

If you are going to look for another job on Wall Street, it is important that you keep things very quiet. If Lehman Brothers found out about Chandler's extracurricular activities, they could fire him on the spot, leaving him short not one but two jobs. It was careless of him to leave a snail trail of his activities in his email.

I was kind of pissed. Being the head ETF trader was the best job in the world, at least to me, but to Chandler, it wasn't good enough. Lehman Brothers was paying Chandler exactly what he was worth. He wanted more. In my opinion, Chandler lacked imagination. Instead of fighting it out with the sales guys every day over pennies, he should have had a higher vision for the business. There was a lot of work to be done. Lehman Brothers relied on a handful of very large hedge funds for most of its ETF revenues. The company needed to diversify, to make office visits, to wine and dine, and to make tight markets.

I had half a mind to drop a dime on Chandler. He was sitting in my seat. Chandler was burned out on ETFs, and I was just getting started. Chandler was sick of doing trades for negative edge and wanted to do trades for positive edge. He wanted to trade options. And he was going to follow Mark Ricci around like an attention-starved puppy until he made it happen. He didn't know how good he had it.

Personally, I liked Chandler. I thought he was a good kid and that decent people sometimes do unflattering things when they are getting bombs dropped on their head on a daily basis. But until Mark Ricci made the swap, there was nothing to do but sit around and wait for a piano to drop on his head.

There is a popular index of small cap stocks known as the Russell 2000. As the name implies, there are two thousand stocks in the index. They are small stocks. These are not big names like Apple and GE, these are names like 1-800-Flowers.com and Jack in the Box; stocks that are squirrelly and highly speculative. The Russell 2000 is the object of a very large program trade every year.

Each year on June 30, the folks at Russell decide what stocks they are going to kick out of the index and what stocks they are going to put into it. Some of the stocks added are so small they aren't even in the Russell 2000; they are what is known as *microcap* stocks. Some stocks graduate from the Russell 2000 to the Russell 1000, a group of large cap stocks. Some are demoted from the 1,000 to the 2,000. And so on. There are a lot of stocks changing places.

This is important because there are billions upon billions of dollars that are indexed to the Russell 2000. If you own shares in a small cap stock index mutual fund, chances are that it follows the Russell 2000. An index fund is forced to own *every stock in the index* in the correct proportions. If a stock is kicked out of the index, the fund must sell it. If a stock is added to the index, the fund must buy it. This creates opportunities.

A bank, or a hedge fund, can research the stocks that are likely to be added and deleted from the index and then buy, or sell short those stocks well in advance of the actual trade. The profits can be enormous. Ben Cohan had told me privately that he once owned ten thousand shares of a stock, which, days after the Russell rebalance, was to be acquired for cash at $20 a share. On the rebalance, it closed at *$120* a share. On one stock, he had made $100 times ten thousand shares, or $1 million. Multiply that times two thousand stocks, and you can see the magnitude of the money involved.

Why would a stock that is known to be worth $20 close at $120? Because of liquidity. Many of these stocks are very thinly traded and cannot support the kind of volume that comes through on the rebalance. There are zillions of shares to buy and zillions of shares to sell. All kinds of weird things can happen. This gave birth to a cottage industry of "wrong-way" Russell traders, people who put sell orders on stocks to be bought, and buy orders on stocks to be sold. They would try to sell the $120 stock on the closing print, because the next morning, it would be worth $20 again.

Sometimes there were more wrong-way guys than right-way guys. This made the Russell trade difficult to predict.

Ben Cohan was the master of the Russell rebalance trade. Every year, he made tens of millions of dollars for the firm. He didn't do it all himself; it was an effort that was driven first by research, which told him what stocks to buy and sell, and then by technology, to make sure that everything would be working on the day of the trade. Cohan was paranoid in the extreme. He had floppy disks made, with spreadsheets containing the day's buy and sell orders. He would seal them in an envelope and give them to another firm, which were to be opened and executed in the event that our computers went down. If they did not, the disks were to be returned unmolested. On Russell day, an *enormous Star Trek* convention would congregate on the floor, with dozens of programmers, IT guys, and researchers. It was disconcerting. Live long and prosper.

With Cohan upstairs in prop, doing his own rebalance trade, Olkin was to be running the effort downstairs. But there was a third player: Ingram. Mike was going to give it a go. There were to be three Russell rebalance traders at Lehman Brothers, possibly competing against one another, and it was not hard to figure out who would win.

I had been watching Ingram prepare for this for a number of weeks. He had a spreadsheet of the P&L for his basket trades. I thought this was odd: this particular spreadsheet was designed for option trades, not basket trades, which meant that already the firm wasn't giving him the necessary tools for the job. I didn't know if Ingram was piggybacking off of our index research or was doing his own. I didn't know if he was in a right-way trade, or a wrong-way trade, or something in between.

I had little to do on the Russell rebalance. I had a portfolio of Russell stocks, hedged with futures that I needed to rebalance, but all that was necessary for me to do was to dump my positions in a spreadsheet and give it to Vikesh, who would pair it off against customer flows. I couldn't trade, at least in the last hour of the day. In the last hour, Lehman told all its customers to take a hike in order to conserve computing power for the Russell rebalance.

Throughout the day, I watched Ingram. His legs were jiggling constantly, and he was hunched over his computer.

When it was over, Olkin went for a round of high fives with Delee, Herb, and Vikesh. They had done well. I looked over at Ingram.

I knew where to find the P&L number on his spreadsheet. I could see it from a distance. Positive was black, and negative was red.

It was red. And it was seven digits.

Legs still jiggling.

Shortly thereafter, Chuck is standing over me with his blond hair. "Have you seen Chandler?"

"No, why?"

"We have a problem."

I look over at D.C. He is buried under flow, and he looks like he is trying to solve five Rubik's Cubes with a gun pointed smartly at his temple.

Chuck walks away. When things quiet down, I approach D.C.

"Where's Chandler?"

"Doctor's appointment."

*"Where's Chandler?"*

"You know where he is."

"What's the problem?"

"We had a friendly create last night, but we did it the wrong way. We came out long two million shares of something."

D.C. has a chart on his desk. It is down about a dime. That's $200,000.

"So now what? You have to trade out of this piece of shit? Maybe you should give it to one of the cash guys."

"I think we're going to handle it here. You know."

I do know. Goofs like that are handled privately. You don't want to advertise to the rest of the floor that you fucked up.

Chandler is in deep shit. He knew the night before that he was going to come in long two million shares of stock, and he still went to a job interview. Chuck can read between the lines. No trader in his right mind schedules a doctor's appointment at the market open. Doctor's appointment is code for job interview or for midday extramarital tryst.

An hour later, Chandler and his floppy hair roll in. Nobody talks to him.

"e'r ing be m ng yo o er he ETF d ext k."

Mark Ricci is saying that he's moving me over to the ETF desk next week.

"What about Mike?"

"W id e t e ould for h m. W g g o et h go. It wi b an elim on of si ion, so it will look like t l id off."

He's saying that Ingram is getting laid off. I am sad.

"What about Chandler?"

"We're m ng him o er to vol. He g w ed, ut 'll s ing o er, just like he was ociate. He g ng to have to learn over again."

Chandler is moving over to vol. I think. Talking to Mark is always so confusing.

I was going to be an ETF trader, I guessed. I hadn't realized it at the time, but it hadn't been an easy decision for Mark to make. Some of the sales guys preferred that Mark look outside the firm for some proven talent, a hired gun. It wasn't unanimous. Nobody was sure they wanted the insane index arb trader who pounded desks and spit tobacco all over the place.

I had survived 9/11. And a suicide attempt. And my business being taken over by robots. If I could survive that, I could survive anything.

Mark wasn't finished. He leaned closer, so I could hear. "Chuck's already built the systems. We don't need someone to build infrastructure. And we don't need someone to just sit there and make markets. We need someone to grow the business. We need someone to find new clients. We need a marketer."

"A marketer?"

"Put your MBA hat on for a minute. Ask yourself: how do I increase the top line? Because we are already good at maximizing the bottom line.

"Think about it."

## 9

# Aggressive | Summer 2004–Fall 2004

Some young boys dream of being sports stars. They dream of hitting a walk-off home run in the bottom of the eleventh inning in the World Series, chugging around the bases, helmet raised high, and landing on home plate with both feet. Then their jubilant teammates hoist the hero in the air and carry him off the field on their shoulders.

Others dream of being astronauts landing on the moon, or firemen rescuing people from burning buildings.

I dreamed of being a trader.

I had a vision of being the trader, standing in the middle of the trading floor, buying on my bid and selling on my offer, not even bothering to hedge, just trading off of gut instinct, making millions of dollars for Lehman Brothers and getting paid millions myself. I would be the trading hero, the center of attention, the *size* trader. Interns visiting the floor would wonder who the animal in the middle of all the flow was. Customers around the street would know who the axe was. Everyone would want to trade with us, because we were the center of information and liquidity. I would be sought after by CNBC and *Wall Street Journal* reporters to comment on the day's price action. I would give the keynote address at conferences. Headhunters would call me twice daily, trying to lure me away with multimillion-dollar contracts. I would hire a team of the smartest MBAs and undergraduates. D.C. would get rich just by sitting next to me. We would be rock stars.

The reality was far different.

In order to trade ETFs, you need someone to bring *in* the trades. You need a sales force. Our sales traders were a ragtag collection of poorly motivated, well-compensated free agents who did business with the fastest, scummiest hedge funds on Wall Street. There are tensions between traders and salespeople. Sometimes the sales trader knows that the next trade that he is about to bring in will be a massive loser for the firm. Sometimes he brings it in anyway, because it isn't his problem; he gets paid the commission whether the trade makes or loses money. This makes the traders resentful.

Most of the trades that were being brought in were losing trades. Our clients were a school of man-eating sharks, people who would rip off their own grandmother's face for a penny. When they traded, they had either information or momentum on their side. Being a trader wasn't so much about hitting the game-winning home run, it was about being a hockey goalie and making fifty saves. The one puck you let get by you can lose the game.

The solution is to get nicer clients. That is easier said than done. No sales trader likes to cold-call people, and if he has a pad of accounts that pays him $10 million a year, he is not terribly hungry for new business. We wanted big mutual funds, big pension funds that would give us big, juicy steaks; orders with a lot of "edge"; orders that were neither price sensitive nor time sensitive. Getting these customers was entirely out of our control.

After a few weeks, D.C. had informed me that he was going to miss a day of work for doctor's appointments. After years of playing lacrosse, his knees were burger. He was going to have a battery of tests.

I didn't think that it was a terribly good idea to leave me alone in the house after just a few weeks on the job, and I told him that.

I got in at 0600 that day, just to be sure.

It was a quiet day. There were a handful of medium-size trades, which I handled without tripping over my own feet. I hadn't lost any money and even managed to make a couple thousand bucks here and there, plus commissions. That afternoon, I was feeling pretty satisfied with myself.

A disembodied voice yells from D.C.'s turret: "Seven hundred Q's, how?"

Seven hundred means seven hundred thousand.

*Who is that?*

I'm making a market in $30 million in Nasdaq stocks to someone I don't know and can't see.

"Is this D.C.?" asks the voice.

"This isn't D.C., it's *Jared*!"

I'm trying to look at the price of the ETF on the left and yell to the turret on my right. My head is snapping back and forth like a typewriter. "Forty-one, forty-six," I say, leaning over to the turret.

I look at the price. It is trading at thirty-seven.

"*Sold!*"

"*Fuck!*" I pound my keyboard. A few keys pop out.

The market is in free fall. There is a rumor of a terrorist attack or something. I've just been picked off.

I am still yelling at the computer. "Motherfucker piece of *shit!*" I can see a handful of cash guys looking across the floor at me.

I am trying to sell futures, but I cannot sell them fast enough. It is like some carnival game, like the softball-in-the-basket thing, that I can't quite get the hang of.

Chuck walks over. "What's going on over here?"

"Some *asshole* sells me seven hundred Q's over D.C.'s turret. I don't even know who it was."

Chuck laughs. "That asshole is Billy Doyle. He's a fixed-income sales guy. He's worked here for twenty-five years. He covers Broad Street. The hedge fund."

"Great. Tell Billy Doyle that he just sent a cruise missile into my P&L."

I look across the desk. Brian Spychalski is getting a good laugh out of this.

That boy sure does have a sick sense of humor.

D.C. returns the next day. I tell him about Billy Doyle's disembodied voice. He gets a good laugh out of it too.

I like it when D.C. is on the desk. He is a stabilizing influence. He is the voice of reason when I start getting a little wild, and he helps give me confidence in my ideas. "What do you think about shorting some spooz here?" I'll ask him. He'll say, "Yeah, looks pretty good." So I'll put on the trade. I make a lot of money with D.C.'s reassurances that I'd otherwise be too afraid to make.

Jamie Ransom stands up. He is a senior sales trader, bespectacled, clueless, and a grave danger to a trader's P&L. Jamie didn't know what day it was, whether or not it was expiration, nonfarm payrolls Friday, or Christmas. When he stood up to look at something across the floor, he would squint, as if he were peering through a dense fog. Half the time you walked by his desk he would have his shoes off or be curled up seemingly asleep in his chair.

This good-natured slug had cultivated relationships with the big macro hedge funds over the years, and this happened to cover the clients who traded the biggest and the fastest. If the news got out that Brazil was selling $50 billion of dollar swaps, Jamie's clients were the first ones buying EWZ, the Brazil ETF. If something kinky happened anywhere in the world, they were buying a yard of yen with the currency guys, a yard of twos with the Treasury guys, and selling a few million SPYs with me. They were fast and huge. Jamie was neither fast nor huge. He was milquetoast.

Jamie's order-handling skills got worse as the size of the order grew.

He is squinting through fog again, at me. "One hundred BBHs, how?"

"Oh no." D.C. doesn't like this trade.

I have to redeem myself. "I'll take it." Technically, we could pass on trades, but almost never, and certainly not this time.

I look at Chuck's NAV pricer. It was telling me that I should make a very wide market on 100,000 BBH. A dollar wide. *This thing can't be right.* I decide to make it fifty cents wide instead.

"Fifteen at sixty-five!"

Jamie says something into the phone.

I wait.

"Jamie!"

He peers at me again. "Fifteen at sixty-five, right?"

"Yeah, but you'd better hurry up—"

"*Sold!*"

I mutter to myself. I slice off 10 percent of a BBH basket and send it to the market.

BBH has cratered. There is a vertical line on the chart.

"What the fuck?"

I slice off another 5 percent. Sell market.

BBH is down $1.15 in a matter of minutes. We have lost $115,000.

There is a loud noise in my head. It sounds like a jet taking off.

"*What the fuuuuucccccckkkk!*"

It is a scream, coming from a wounded animal. I stand and slam both fists down on the sidecar, as hard as I can. The entire row of desks shakes.

D.C. takes over. "Jamie, what the hell was that?" Jamie looks like he is trying to hide behind the desk.

I have never lost so much money. I stand, staring at my keyboard, hands shaking.

In that moment, I know that something is wrong.

*Nobody else does this. Nobody else feels this way.* Ingram liked me because I had a little fire in my belly. I was going way beyond that. If I had been within striking distance of Jamie, I would have murdered him with my bare hands.

*What is wrong with me?*

I am eating lunch, a charcoal chicken panini from across the street at Majestic. It costs $9 but is worth it, in a guilty sort of way. It is as heavy as lead. I noticed recently that my pants were starting to get tight.

Frank Segal walks up to the desk. "Ya wanna go see the Allman Brothahs?"

D.C. and I look at each other. We look at Frank. "The Allman Brothers?"

"Yeah."

"Isn't that, like, classic rock?"

He laughs, adjusts his toothpick, and pulls up his pants. "Whaddyou—you don't know the Allman Brothahs?"

"No, not really."

"They're a southern jam band." His eyes are moving from side to side, and he is blinking. "You think you know something about music? You know how many guitars I own? I got this collection of guitars. Yeah."

"I mean, no, it's not really my thing."

"Fuck that shit. It's for a customer. The Whitworth guys. We got backstage passes. At Jones Beach."

I look at D.C. again. He looks at me. Whitworth is by far our biggest customer, paying us, the ETF desk, millions of dollars in commissions. This is our way of saying thanks.

I despised analog music. I hated anything with a guitar. Concerts, for me, were watching someone twiddle knobs on a mixer. Frank Segal did not collect mixers. He collected guitars. So off we went to see some banged-up old guys who by this point had blown all their cash on pot and acid and were touring second-rate venues to try to make it back.

I was the opposite of thrilled.

But this was what I was supposed to be doing, at least according to the unintelligible Mark Ricci. Wining and dining. Gripping and grinning. Waving the Lehman flag. You! You, sir, over there! You need to be trading ETFs with us. Not with those other mooks. With Lehman Brothers. The smart guys! We are better than them.

This marketing thing was going to be tough.

I walked across the floor to the bathroom so I could hang a whizz before I had to sit in a car for a few hours. I observed that there were grown men fleeing the bathroom.

I struggled inside, swimming upstream through a flood of traders and salespeople running in the other direction. I turned the corner and saw Frank Segal in his underpants.

My Lord.

Frank was changing into jeans for the concert.

He looked like a mouse in a pillowcase.

This man was worth at least $20 million, and probably more. How could he let himself get like that?

Frank had reserved limousines for the occasion. Not just town cars, but limousines. Limos are actually a rarity on Wall Street. It's an image thing. Limos are for famous actors and rappers. Town cars are for boring guys in suits who made at least as much money as the actors and rappers, and actually saved it.

And then, the only alcoholic beverage available in the limo was Coors Light. *What the fuck is that?* Yellow beer made me sick. At least get a microbrew or something. God, was this terrible.

I was inconsolable.

We pulled up in front of Whitworth's building, and Luigi, the trader, wiggled in. It was me, Frank, and Luigi.

There was silence.

"Jared, say somethin', for cryin' out loud! You're the tradah; staht talkin' about the market or somethin'!"

I had no social skills.

Luigi leaped to my defense. "Leave him alone, Frank. He's new in the job; he doesn't know how this stuff works yet."

I resented his benevolence. I would have liked nothing more than to be full of wit and wisdom on the capital markets. The truth was that I was fresh from a year of trying to eke out a living scalping S&P 500 futures. I knew nothing. To get there, I forced myself to have another beer.

I sized up Luigi, who was in jeans and a long-sleeved T-shirt. I wondered if he wore that to work every day or if this was the concert uniform. These hedge fund guys, you never know. He was skinny, energetic, with an energetic haircut and waistline. He was intelligent, yet warm and down-to-earth. I started to think that the real talent ended up at hedge funds, and I was working on the sell side, at the bank, with all the mutants.

I stared out the window. I was out over my skis. I was going to be a complete failure at this marketing thing. Who was I kidding? I had no social graces. Did Mark Ricci expect me to be a sales guy? Did he expect me to start cold-calling customers? Did he expect me to spend four nights a week out boozing it up with my buy-side counterparts? This wasn't going to work. I was good working alone. I didn't dress right, I didn't look right, and I just stared at my shoes.

"Hey, look, a Bentley."

We were on the Long Island Expressway. You'd think a Bentley wouldn't be all that uncommon.

"Black people," said Luigi. "Must be rappers."

I looked across the lane at the Bentley. The driver, a black man, looked like Heathclifford Huxtable, from *The Cosby Show*. He didn't look like a rapper.

This was going to be a long night.

Jones Beach was an outdoor venue. This was news to me. Long Island, once you get out far enough, is actually kind of attractive. There was sand. There was sky. There were trees. I was pleasantly surprised.

D.C. wasn't saying much. He may have been a world-famous lacrosse stud, but he was still an introvert. And he was twenty-four. This was an older crowd. There were five Whitworth guys and five Lehman guys, and

D.C. and I were easily the youngest. The rest of them were wearing jeans and T-shirts, in a transparent attempt to look cool. D.C. and I still wore our suits. Our ties were loosened. It was August, still.

"So we only have eight backstage passes. You and D.C. are going to sit out in the crowd," said Frank.

This made it easier.

D.C. and I wandered through the crowd of aging hippies to find our seats. We were in the middle of the middle row in the middle section. I was going to be dying for a pisser in an hour, after I finished my beer, and I was going to have to struggle to climb over the knees of the hippies.

The lights dimmed, and the concert began. One hundred spliffs simultaneously fired up. I've never understood how marijuana enhances the concert experience, or, for that matter, why it cannot be experienced without it.

This music sucked.

There was: "Layla." I was about to eat a gun. We were hating this. I almost felt like holding hands with D.C.

Behind the band, I could see a crowd of about forty dudes playing air guitar. I could see Frank Segal pulling up his pants. They were feeling pretty skippy with the backstage passes. I thought I'd gotten the better deal; at least I got to sit down for this nonsense.

I experienced a wave of revulsion for trader culture, sports, and music, and anything that had anything to do with virile, hearty, robust, thoughtless white men. I think that classic rock is the lowest form of music there is. It is music that is so bad, it can be enjoyed only while drunk. Or high. It is undisciplined, yet not free-form. It is vulgar. It aspires to nothing. Wall Street guys listen to it for that very reason.

I hated everything that had to do with Wall Street. I hated the music, I hated the money, I hated the women, I hated the cars, I hated the clothes.

But I loved the trading.

"Two-fifty SPYs, how?"

It's Jamie. He's awake this time. He wakes up periodically for trades. He's asking me for my market on 250,000 SPYs, or the S&P 500 ETF. It's an easy trade, but a fairly large trade.

The market is skidding. The customer is Battalion, which is an un-predictable but usually below-average trader of SPYs. Battalion bought earlier in the day. I think he's about to puke them to me. I bid him in the hole.

"Thirteen, eighteen!"

"Sold!"

*Right where I want him.*

I print the stock in the hole, and the market comes rocketing back out. I hedge with futures a dime higher. I have just made a tidy $25,000, a good day by my old standards, which I have just accomplished in a mere ten seconds.

There is a collective groan from the sales guys. "*Ohhhhhhhhhhh.*"

D.C. and I are laughing. We've just ripped off their faces.

Jamie meekly stands up and comes around to the desk.

"Hey, if you don't mind, we're going to have to give him an improve-ment."

*An improvement?* I have never heard of this. "What do you mean?"

"You know. Like a penny or two better."

"You want me to change the price?"

Jamie shifts his weight. "Yeah, by a penny or two."

"If he wants a better price, then why don't you tell him to step into his time machine and sell the stock thirty seconds ago?"

"C'mon, Jared, there's no need to—"

"I'm being serious. We're big boys here. This is the big leagues. There are no do-overs. No tears."

Frank Segal waddles over. "Jamie's right, you're going to have to give him an improvement."

"Why? Customers don't improve me when I get run over on trades."

There is a crowd of sales guys, a press gang, forming around the desk. I look to Mark Ricci for help.

Mark comes over. Jamie and I explain the situation. "He's a good cus-tomer, blah blah blah," say the sales guys.

Mark says the following: "I I k w hou mai n h cust r nship," shrugs his shoulders, and walks away.

I'm outnumbered. I change the price to fifteen cents, writing a check to Battalion for $5,000.

That night, I finish off a jar of pickles at home, wash it out, and bring it to work. I tape a piece of paper around it, write "Penny Jar—Price Improvements—$.01 = $1,000," and put it between D.C. and me. For every trade where we have to improve a customer, we throw a penny in the jar, with an audible clink. It makes the sales guys roll their eyes.

Within a month, we have given away $136,000 to pay for other people's fuckups.

D.C. and I settle into a routine. He has been in search of a mentor.

Chandler has taught him surprisingly little about futures. I start from the beginning. I tell him what I know about initial margin, about variation margin, about expiration and delivery procedures. I proceed to tell him everything I know about the basis, on interest rate and dividend risk, and how to hedge it. I have brought over about $2 billion worth of stock with me from index arbitrage, and I show him how to rebalance it and how to make index changes. He is grateful.

I also show him how I prop trade. Ten futures here, ten futures there, and I continue to make about $10,000 to $20,000 a day punting around spooz. It adds up. He takes great interest in this. I resolve at some point to set up an account for him to practice in.

In return, D.C. teaches me the grand poker game that is dealing with customers. With Chuck, ETF trading was a matter of pure mathematics: you know what fair value is for an ETF, and you make a goalpost market around fair value, bidding three cents below and offering three cents above. Chandler improved on this process: he had a sixth sense for figuring out whether customers wanted to buy or sell. If they wanted to sell, he would still make a six-cent-wide market, but he would bid five cents below the fair value and offer a penny above, trying to extract every last penny out of the customer. If he could guess right more than half the time, it was a profitable strategy. As it turned out, he could guess right almost *all* the time, and so could D.C.

It really wasn't a sixth sense. It was a matter of keeping track of what customers did. If they bought earlier in the day, and the market went down, they were likely to sell and puke their positions. If they had accumulated a large position two months ago, and the market had rallied significantly, they were likely to want to sell out of their position. But it took some practice.

D.C. got it right every time. To me, it seemed like mind reading. But if you were successful at it, you could save money. And beyond saving money, it was good marketing. If you *knew* that the customer was a seller, you could *lock* the market, which is to say that you could offer to buy it or sell it at the same price. Locking a market is insanity. The whole point of having a bid-offer spread is to earn a little bit in between. You buy something at $10.00 and sell it at $10.03. In between, you are making three cents. Locking a market theoretically earns you no profit.

But even when you lock a market, you still earn commissions. Commissions were three cents a share. This may not sound like much, but if you trade a one million share order, that's $30,000 in commissions. Locking a market is advertising in that you are saying to the customer: "I am a kamikaze. I will trade at a stupid price in order to get you to trade with me. I will do something suboptimal because I want your business." Chandler was making locked markets on his own terms. I will lock it, but I will lock it at *my* price. You can trade at *my* price, or you can take a long walk off a short pier. The customer is fooled into thinking he is getting a good deal, when in reality, he is not.

That's Wall Street.

We were, as a general rule, supposed to be making locked markets on smaller vanilla trades, like 100,000 SPY. I had no experience at it. I was wrong at least half the time. I was costing us money. D.C. assured me that I would get it, after some practice.

There was a whole world outside of index arbitrage about which I knew nothing. I had spent the better part of three years learning everything there was to know about the futures basis. Here I was trading ETFs on the sectors, like the financials, energy, or basic materials, or on countries, like Japan, South Africa, or Canada. There was a lot to know. If you were going to be trading overseas, you had to know about short sales and settlement procedures in different countries. You had to know about hedging currencies. You had to know about *liquidity* above and beyond everything else; you had to understand that financials were more liquid than tech, which was more liquid than energy, which was more

liquid than biotech. Liquidity is *the* most important concept to understand in trading. You need to know how fast you are going to be able to
get out of a position.

I started to pick up on nuances and to follow things like the yield
spread between two-year notes and ten-year notes. If it was wide, it was
good for banks, because banks could lend at higher rates and pay very
little on their deposits. When the spread widened, banks went up. And if
the Federal Reserve was going to raise short-term rates, then the spread
would compress, and it would be bad for banks. I was pretty proud of
myself for learning that one.

There was a lot to learn about interest rates in general. Lehman Brothers had a formidable interest rate group; its trading and research were
consistently ranked number one. I almost got a job in rates, as a matter of
fact, until Wilson James cockblocked me. Trading Treasuries, I thought,
was easy; it was pure mathematics. With stocks, there are stories, there
are whispers, and there are rumors. You are always at an information
disadvantage. With Treasuries, your information was economic releases:
CPI, payrolls, ISM, and nobody had an edge on that. You could take an
outright view on rates, or you could do a *relative value* trade; you could
buy an old ten-year note and sell a current ten-year note against it, hoping that the prices would converge.

The Treasury guys got on the hoot every morning—the "GOVT
HOOT"—and talked about the interest rate market. First the econo-
mists would get on and talk about the data and the implications for Federal Reserve interest rate policy. Then, the 2s trader would talk, then the
guy who traded the "belly," or 5s, then 10s, then bonds. Then the interest
rate option traders would get on and talk about all kinds of arcane things
in terms of "BPvols." I was in love.

Ingram had told me about his days on the rates desk. Far from being
pure mathematical traders, these guys were inveterate gamblers. They
thought nothing of adding to a losing position, doubling down, sometimes tripling down. They booked offsetting dummy trades to fool the
risk managers. I was horrified. This kind of behavior, to me, was beneath
us as professional traders. Professional traders understand that trading
is a living, not a call option. It is the amateurs who think that there is

somehow glory in this profession. It is the dreamers who fantasize about making $10 million for your firm in one day, getting promoted and carried off the trading floor on the shoulders of your coworkers. *No.* Trading is about gutting it out day after day in the trenches, making your $10,000 here, $10,000 there, until it begins to slowly add up.

One morning I noticed a new voice on the hoot. It was Gary Park.

Gary sounded different from the other rates traders. The rest of the team sounded very conservative, and very concerned. They always talked about being "close to home." Gary never talked about being close to home. He talked about swinging it around. Swing it around he did; and on his first day he reputedly had a $10 million P&L swing. The managing directors nearly had a coronary.

Gary was new on the desk and seemed to be suffering from undiagnosed attention deficit disorder. In between taking positions the size of the GDP of Albania, he talked to himself, and to the rest of the firm, via the hoot. When stocks rallied, he would yell "STOCKS!" over the hoot.

I loved it, so I did it too.

I could pretend I was Gary Park, but I was no Gary Park. I would never take a position the size of the GDP of Albania.

Or so I thought.

I got paid a bonus in December 2004. For the year, I was making $290,000. That was a lot of money.

It occurred to me that between D.C. and me, Lehman was getting away with paying the ETF desk less than $500,000. I thought they were getting off easy.

I still did not get promoted. Now Sam Grossman was going to be two years ahead of me. I was legitimately passed over for promotion. Was I doing a bad job?

I asked Mark Ricci. "Mark, I kind of thought I was going to get promoted this year."

"Y hav b radin ETFs th long y . We thought we y a lit mo ."

*Jesus Christ.* Everybody's making VP. What the fuck.

I let it drop. I was, after all, the size ETF trader.

• • •

I am plotting a futures trade. Jamie stands next to me, squinting.

"Want to go to a dinner with the Broadstreet guys?"

I am the marketing guy. I cannot say no.

Broadstreet is a legendary hedge fund. Actually, it is not so much a hedge fund as it is a fund of funds: a hedge fund split up into six or eight different pods. The theory is that if one particular hedge fund manager has *alpha*, or edge over the market, then eight of them working together will have even more alpha and will sometimes offset one another, reducing volatility. It worked well in theory and in practice. Broadstreet had been around for a long time.

I had no idea what they did. All they ever did with us was trade a couple hundred thousand QQQQs here and there. I would be going to dinner with some of the greatest financial minds in the industry. Me, I was a punk ETF trader.

Dinner was at Maloney & Porcelli, on Fiftieth Street. I had not been there before. At the bar, I saw several men in their fifties with collar tabs, pocket handkerchiefs, and brandy snifters. It occurred to me that these people could be seen only in New York City, and beyond that, they could be seen only in a restaurant such as this. I was watching old-school old money at work. I could never be old money. I was new money. But I wasn't the kind of new money to go off and buy a Benz. I was the kind of new money that was going to squirrel it all away in gold, just in case the world came to an end. I was paranoid new money.

Jamie joined me at the bar. "What are you having?"

"Jack and Coke."

"Aggressive." And he ordered a vodka soda.

*Aggressive* can mean only one thing on Wall Street: it means that you are the opposite of cool. If someone tells you that you have an aggressive tie, it means that you are wearing something that is a little loud, a little gauche, and that you are taking a career risk. A goatee can be aggressive. A shirt that is not white or blue can be aggressive. Suspenders are *very* aggressive—off-the-charts aggressive—and are out of the question. I was having an aggressive drink.

The Broadstreet guys took their time showing up. By the time we were all seated, I'd had three or four Jack and Cokes. I was feeling fine.

People were saying things, but I wasn't listening. They were not talking about the market. They were talking about family (which I despised—no desire to have children), and about golf (also despised). I was ordering more Jack and Cokes off the bar, to supplement the expensive bottles of wine.

The Broadstreet guys were smiling. If I were that tall and good looking, I would be smiling too. If I were that rich, I would be orgasmic. These were guys that were getting paid a percentage of what they made. If they made $50 million, and they got to keep 10 percent, they made $5 million. Personally. Some of them had made $5 million or more for several years running. I was having a tough time getting promoted to vice president. I drank more Jack and Cokes.

One of the Broadstreet guys was not tall and good looking. His name was Larney. We were fast friends. Larney had thick fingers and was blue collar. He kept talking about poker. He was talking about entering tournaments and playing cash games. I was as clueless as I was when I sat next to Johnny B. But I listened.

We stood up to leave. Everybody exchanged business cards. The room spun momentarily; I was ten drinks deep. The golf guys with kids were going home. Larney wanted to teach me how to play poker. Jamie tagged along.

We are at a bar on Second Avenue. Larney knows the owner, and we are ushered into a back room. Larney is carrying an elaborate aluminum case full of cards and chips, which he got from the back of his car. Jamie is slurring his speech, and we leave him at the bar. Pussy. He's in no condition to find his way home, but that's no concern of mine.

We are playing Texas hold 'em. Larney explains the rules. We are going to play for chips, not money. I order more drinks. Larney and I are going toe to toe with the booze. He is going to lose.

We play for a while, and drink, and I am bleeding chips. I don't really know what I am doing.

I catch on. I get a big hand. I am slow-playing it.

I take Larney for all his chips. He is pissed.

Larney packs up all his shit in the elaborate aluminum case, and we are back out on the street. Suddenly the case opens, sending chips and cards scattering all over the sidewalk. "Fuck it," says Larney, and hops into the back of a cab, leaving me with the mess. I am standing on the sidewalk in a pile of chips.

I don't remember how I get home. The next morning, I wake up with no jacket, no iPod, holes in my pants, and bruises all over my body. I am a good marketing guy, I think.

Broadstreet never trades with us again.

*Am I getting fat?*

I stared at myself in the bathroom mirror. It was hard to tell, but it looked like I was getting a bit of a gut. It was what a friend of mine from West Virginia would have called a "dunlap," as in My belly "done lapped over my belt." I had been warned that when I turned thirty, my metabolism would slow appreciably. Plus, on a trading floor, it is impossible to stay healthy. When you have people who are making a million bucks a year, they think nothing of dropping a few hundred dollars now and then to buy lunch for the desk. For us, the derivatives guys, it was usually Lenny's sandwich shop. I never passed it up; I always got a "number one," which had corned beef and coleslaw on it. The cash guys with their pocket handkerchiefs were even more outrageous: they routinely ordered $30 hamburgers from Del Frisco's or the Palm. The managing directors, guys like Mark Ricci and Chris Masters, who were always fit and trim, were models of dietary discipline and self-control. Ricci would dine on a lacrosse ball–size blob of cottage cheese, with a constellation of blueberries. If I ate that, I would have been fucking starving and even more irritable than I already was. My days of bringing sparse lunches to work, consisting of a small sandwich and a piece of fruit, were long gone. I was eating like a king now, like the king of Tonga, and I was proud of it. Expensive dinners with lots of steak, lots of creamed spinach and hash browns, and wine. I deserved it. For once, I felt rich, like a champion sumo wrestler. My arms were still defined, sort of. There was a vein in there somewhere.

I brushed my teeth and shaved in the shower, thinking not a little bit about my dream from the night before, in which I was a drug dealer, selling cocaine out of a cheap compact car in a cheerless suburban neighborhood. In my dream, I had difficulty deciding whether I should sell it or use it myself. I stared at the plastic bag, puzzling over it, like a hard math problem, then drove around the block a few times and thought about it some more.

Getting dressed was easy. All my shirts were blue or white, and most of my ties were green, and from Brooks Brothers. I had given up on the discount rack stuff. Rather, I had succumbed to all the teasing. Brooks Brothers was passable attire: it was not *aggressive*, and it would not attract attention. I would allow myself to spend $70 on a shirt, and up to $50 on a tie. The suits were still from Men's Wearhouse, at least the ones that I hadn't worn holes in. I couldn't bring myself to discard them yet.

I went downstairs, grabbed my wallet and keys, and headed out the door, picking up the newspaper on my way out.

I stopped.

*Did I lock the door?*

Of course I had locked the door. I kept walking.

*Did I lock the door?*

I couldn't shake the feeling that I had somehow forgotten to lock the door. I walked back to the house, up the steps, and jiggled the knob. It was locked.

*Oh, good.*

I walked down the street.

On the bus, I read the paper. I read, for the millionth time, that bond prices go down when interest rates go up. Then, in another thought: *did I lock the door?*

*Of course you locked the door, you dummy. You even checked it.*

But I couldn't remember locking the door the first time, and now I couldn't remember checking it, either. I *knew* that I had checked it, but I couldn't remember the physical sensation of checking it.

What if I had left the door unlocked? What if my mailman decided to grow a brain, let himself in, and cleaned me out of all my valued possessions? It was a stretch, given that the only thing I had of value was an expansive CD collection filled with music that nobody but me seemed to want to listen to.

Why was I suddenly so interested in whether or not the door was locked? For years, I just walked outside and did it automatically, without giving it any thought at all. This had never happened to me before.

Well, it was too late to go back and check. The bus was entering the tunnel. I wasn't about to turn around and go back home.

The rest of the day, I wondered if that damn door was unlocked. I could barely concentrate on the market. I was sick to my stomach.

I had thought about sending an email to Larney following the Broad-street dinner debacle, but I let it drop. I tried to piece together what had happened; if I had done or said anything that would have upset him and, more importantly, jeopardized our business relationship. I couldn't, but I also couldn't remember how I got holes in my pants and bruises on my legs, either.

I had been to more than a handful of customer dinners by this point, and the result was usually the same. Before dinner, I was too shy to say anything and stared at my shoes. The sales guys, and sometimes the customers, would wonder aloud how someone so introverted could possibly function on Wall Street. After dinner, I was loaded full of Jack and Cokes and capable only of pounding shots and giving the customer punches to the kidneys. I was not much of a sales guy. There had to be a better way.

I had been toying with the idea of sending out Bloomberg messages. In the financial world, very little of significance ever happens on conventional email; it's for corporate blather, HR stuff, and expense reports. Bloomberg messages, or emails, are for the markets: what traders think about the markets, what positions they are recommending, and what trades they are pushing on their clients. Lots of traders did this, particularly the cash traders, and to an even greater extent, the bond traders, who actually published their "runs," or their pricing quotes, on Bloomberg messages. They were in constant contact with their clients. Up until that point, I never talked to any of mine, unless I was properly lubricated.

I needed to build a distribution list, so I went around to the sales guys and asked them for the names of their clients. This was hard. I got a lot of raised eyebrows—they didn't want to part with the identity of their clients, because they didn't know what kind of crazy shit I would be sending them. They wanted to be the gatekeeper, to control the flow of information. This was understandable; there was a lot more downside to the relationship than there was upside. You can send a hundred passable

Bloomberg messages, but if you send one that pisses someone off—for example, a trade idea that is bullish on a stock that a client is short—then it's game over, pull the light. But I was persistent, and at the end of the day, I had accumulated a list of about forty people.

I had to come up with a name for my Bloomberg list. I was having a lapse of creativity. I called it "SALES." It was, after all, for the purpose of increasing sales. God, what a dunce I am. I was the marketing guy, after all. After entering forty names into the list, I gave my first Bloomberg message a try:

FM: JARED DILLIAN, LEHMAN BROTHERS INC.

TO: SALES


WE ON THE ETF DESK HAVE A UNIQUE TECHNICAL INDICATOR; THERE IS A GOOD CHANCE YOU HAVE NEVER HEARD OF IT. WE CALL IT THE "TEN HANDLE RULE."


IT IS NO SECRET THAT WE ARE IN A DECLINING VOLATILITY ENVIRONMENT. IN THE LAST FEW MONTHS, WE'VE NOTICED SOMETHING; WE'VE NOTICED THAT ONCE S&P FUTURES HAVE MOVED TEN HANDLES ON AN INTRADAY BASIS, THEY TEND TO REVERSE. I HAVEN'T BACKTESTED IT, BUT I HAVE DISCOVERED PROFITABLE OPPORTUNITIES INTRADAY ONCE THE MARKET HAS MOVED TEN POINTS.


UNTIL VOLATILITY PICKS UP, EXPECT THE TEN HANDLE RULE TO STAY IN PLACE. THERE IS STILL SIGNIFICANT RESISTANCE AT 1,150, GOING BACK THE LAST SIX MONTHS. STAY SHORT BELOW 1,150; NEW LOWS WILL PROBABLY OPEN UP THE RANGE.

I couldn't figure out how to turn off the all caps. The default in Bloomberg was all caps. There had to be a way, but it was beyond my comprehension. Looking at it, I decided I liked the military message traffic feel of it. I felt like appending BT NNNN to the end of it.

I was afraid to hit Send. What if people thought I was a moron? I was completely unqualified to write about anything unless it pertained to stock index futures or the Fed. These were guys who were in the business of portfolio management. If they didn't make money, they went out of business. They didn't have time for random bullshit. I didn't think some king daddy rabbit hedge fund trader really wanted to read the random scribblings of some ETF piker.

I hit Send. The world stayed spinning on its axis, at least momentarily.

Bloomberg has a way where you can track who reads the message. I hit "7 Go" to pull up the list. After a few minutes, check marks began to appear by their names, indicating they had read it.

About fifteen out of the forty people read it.

Not a bad start.

"Go sit down."

I looked up. Brian Spychalski, that sick bastard, was really giving it to one of the sales guys.

"Pat, go sit down. Go. Go sit over at your desk and just sit there. Don't pick up the phone, don't do anything. All you do is bring in losing trades. The firm will be better off if you just sit there."

Pat, a new sales associate with perpetually rolled-up sleeves and monkey arms, hung his head. He looked as if he had emptied a cat litter box into a plastic bag, only to watch the bottom of it drop out, leaving litter and turds all over the carpet. But he refused to move.

"Go sit down!"

Pat shuffled back to his desk.

Everyone was looking at Spychalski, by now nicknamed Spike. "Hey," I offered.

Spike looked at me. "What's up?"

"What was all that about?"

"PII."

"PII? What the fuck is that?"

Spike smiled. "Right, that's what I said! Polaris Industries. They make snowmobiles."

Spychalski traded options on industrials, which usually meant that he was the grab bag, the catchall for any options trade that came in the door. If it wasn't tech, if it wasn't health care, if it wasn't energy, it was industrial. For an energy trader, you need to know one thing: the price of oil. Spychalski had to know everything about everything, or at least know when to play defense. Nobody in the world, it would seem, would care enough about a shitbird stock like PII to put an options trade on it.

"Dude. Earnings are tomorrow. It's July. It's July earnings for a snowmobile company, and this jackass wants to buy puts the day before."

I laughed. "Sounds pretty dirty."

"*So* dirty. Come here for a second; let me show you something."

I walked around to the other side of desk and sat next to Brian. He pulled up a series of charts.

"Okay, so this is the first trade I did today." There was a vertical line on the chart going straight up, pornographically.

"And this is the second trade I did today." There was a vertical line going straight down.

"And this is the third trade. And so on."

"So these guys are in the stock when they are quoting you?"

"Yes. It's like that with my whole pad. All these scumbags are either in the stock, or they know someone who is, or they have some other information. It is *impossible* to make money like this."

What Spike was saying was that his customers were frontrunning their own options trades. It's just unethical, and a bad business practice. If you make it impossible for your broker to commit capital for you, after a while he is going to get pissed and tell you to trade somewhere else. But the reality was that competition between the brokers was so fierce that someone, somewhere, would be willing to do that scumbag's business. If we turned it away, we would lose market share and never get it back. Spike was trapped; if he took in too many bad trades, he would lose money, but if he turned too many away, we would lose clients. "Now I know why you get so upset all the time," I said, which sort of failed to capture the enormity of the problem. Spike was the only other person on the floor who would throw temper tantrums at least as big as mine. His usually were lower in volume but sharper, with acid personal attacks. Whereas I thought the sales guys were essentially good people who sometimes did stupid things, he thought they were just stupid people who did malicious things.

He was partially right. Trading tended to attract more intellectual firepower. There were a few bright bulbs over in sales, Kevin Rodman, a motormouth Dartmouth graduate—sort of a cross between Vince Vaughn and Jared, the Subway spokesman guy, who had moments of brilliance when he wasn't too fucking hungover to bring in a trade, but aside from that, it was a long trip on the short bus.

"You ever see that *Beavis and Butt-head* where they're working at the fast-food place?" Spike asks me.

"Uh, yeah."

"Where Beavis says, 'Thankyoudrivethru'?" he says, affecting a Beavis voice.

"Yeah."

"Check this out."

Spike plays a sound file on his computer: "*Thankyoudrivethru.*" He is cracking himself up, giggling like a fourteen-year-old. "That's what this place is, a fucking drive-thru window. Drive thru and pick up your bag of money at the next window."

As I walk back to my desk, he is still playing the file and laughing to himself. "*Thankyoudrivethru. Thankyoudrivethru.*" It occurs to me that all of us on the trading floor are essentially grown children, but Spike is more a child than most of us. He laughs, he throws temper tantrums, he makes a scene when people try to take away his toys.

Over time, "drive-thru" becomes part of the Lehman lexicon. Anytime D.C. and I get picked off, we say, "What a drive-thru."

With his sick sense of humor and scorched-earth policy, Spychalski is having an indelible impact on the derivatives business.

D.C. and I were starting our own drive-thru window.

Frank Segal appeared at my desk. He adjusted his toothpick and pulled up his pants. "Ya ever hear of Observah?"

"Observer? Yeah, I've heard of them." A hedge fund.

"We got a meeting. Tomorrow. You're comin'. D.C. can stay here. They want to trade SMH." SMH was a semiconductor ETF, and years after the tech bubble, people still traded it. A lot.

"Aren't they a tech fund?"

"Not really. Sort of."

"What's this all about?"

"What's this all about? These guys pay six million to the street in ETF commissions alone. They're one of the biggest payers. We need to be involved."

I hadn't heard good things about Observer. All I had heard was that they were fast and dirty.

The next day, I was sitting in a crosstown cab with Frank Segal. We were going three long blocks away. We were stuck in midday traffic. It would have been faster to walk, but that might have put too many miles on Frank's designer shoes. Hell, it would have been faster to drag ourselves with our lips.

Every hedge fund in New York looks exactly the same. There are frosted glass doors; there are unoccupied conference rooms, ostensibly for the purpose of raising money; there is beige-colored wood paneling and desks; there is a trading floor, quieter and more sinister than a bank's trading floor; and there is the fancy-pants name on the door. Observer.

I did not envy the hedge fund traders on the trading floor. Unlike at a bank, hedge fund traders make no asset allocation decisions. They have no discretion on what to buy or sell. They have discretion only on *when* to buy or sell. A portfolio manager decides what stocks he wants to trade and gives them to the trader to simply execute. There is ample opportunity for Monday morning quarterbacking, because if the trader buys at the highs of the day or sells at the lows, he has to deal with an irate portfolio manager. If the portfolio manager sucks, he blames all his problems on the trader, and the trader doesn't get paid or, worse, gets fired. The hours are longer, and the pay is worse. It is a thankless job.

Frank and I are escorted into a conference room with a sweaty, seething professional wrestler. His forehead is gleaming; I can't tell if it's the hair gel that has slowly drained out of his hair over the course of the day, or if it's sweat. It's hot in here. Frank seems to have known this guy for a while, or at least he is pretending to.

The professional wrestler's name is Liam. He's sitting across the table from me, and he's talking to me, but I can't hear a thing. I'm looking at the veins popping out of his neck, and the sweat, and the size-too-small shirt. He's on steroids. He's on *something*. And he's angry, in a way that suggests that he is angry all the time. I am hardly a model of serenity, and I sense that he is trying to pick a fight. I am game. I roll up my sleeves too.

"So what we want to do is to be able to trade SMH at the NAV." That means no profit for me, at least before commissions.

"How many?"

"Up to one hundred thousand. And we want to trade it at the *Bloomberg* NAV."

I look at Frank. No help.

"Bloomberg only publishes NAV once every fifteen seconds."

"So?"

"So. So SMH can move a lot in fifteen seconds."

"That's how it's going to be. You don't want the business, we can find someone else." Sweat is pouring off his forehead, and his armpits are drenched.

I look at Frank again. He interjects, "Jared wants the business, don't worry; he's just going to have to find a way to make this work."

What Liam is proposing is that we trade at a price that updates only every fifteen seconds. When D.C. and I make markets, we are looking at a pricer that updates *continuously*. SMH can move as much as a nickel in fifteen seconds. On 100,000 shares, that's $5,000. For Liam, this will be like shooting fish in a barrel. He can wait for SMH to make a quick move one way or another and pick us off.

What I want to say is, "Fuck you, you sweaty goon, I'm out of here." But I don't. I shake his hand, tell him I agree to his terms, and Frank and I walk out.

"You what?"

"D.C., I had no choice in the matter. This guy Liam was about to rip out my spleen and show it to me, and Frank the Tank was going to stand there and watch."

D.C. is upset, but not so much at me. He knows that we have zero influence. Politically, we have about as much pull as Frank's left nut. Frank has to come up with some revenue. Given lemons, we are going to have to make lemonade.

"A hundred smash, how?"

It's Frank. "Smash" is shorthand for SMH.

"Here we go," says D.C.

I look down at Bloomberg. SMH is at $32.33. But according to our model, it is at $32.30.

"Thirty-three cents!" I yell.

"Sold!"

Of course.

Liam has just arbitraged us for a clean $3,000, and we haven't even hedged the trade yet. SMH starts to take a dirtnap; he's right on momentum too. The trade costs us $10,000. Spike plays Beavis's *"thankyoudrive-thru"* over the hoot.

Twenty minutes later, Frank stands up again. "A hundred smash, how?"

D.C. takes it. "Eleven cents!" Our model has it at fifteen cents.

"I buy!"

We lose an additional $10,000 on that trade.

*"Thankyoudrivethru."*

If you could make $10,000 by pushing a button, how many times would you push the button?

For weeks, D.C. and I write checks to Liam at Observer. Free money. Spike gets more creative, switching to barnyard noises and zoo animal noises, and settles on a text-to-speech converter that allows you to type things in, and replays them in robot voices. "MY NAME IS D.C. COLLINS, AND I WEAR SOAP ON A ROPE AROUND MY ANKLES FOR OBSERVER."

It all comes to a head. Observer hits me on 100,000 SMH, and it goes off the cliff. "Fuck! Goddamn it!" *"Thank youdrivethru."* I grab my mouse and start clubbing it over and over on the desk until it explodes like the Death Star. Like a pit crew, D.C. reaches into his drawer, pulls out another one, and plugs it in.

"Fuck if I hedge this trade." But it keeps going lower and lower. The chart of SMH looks like the first hill on the Millennium Force roller coaster at Ohio's Cedar Point amusement park. Soon we are out $50,000 on a lousy hundred smash.

With my new mouse, I stubbornly call the bottom and buy 500,000 shares of QQQ, an enormous trade. The market rallies, QQQ goes up ten cents, and I sell it, making back the $50,000.

If it had continued to go lower, we would have lost hundreds of thousands of dollars. I was being forced to take huge, unnecessary risks, just to try to make up the lost money to Observer, which not only was arbing us on the NAV, but was clearly frontrunning its own trades. Jesus H. Christ on a popsicle stick. But this is what we were getting paid for—not to make money but to prevent losses. It was demoralizing.

Observer and Liam eventually got bored, like a cat that has spent the better part of an hour toying with a mouse, finally leaving it for dead. He went on to bully someone else.

We were tired, pissed off, and grateful.

Years ago, as a clerk for my market-making firm out in San Francisco, I went on a ski trip with the traders to Lake Tahoe, Nevada. I was riding with Courtney, the mad chess genius who had made a multiple-six-figure day trading Qualcomm options.

Courtney was giving a lecture on the markets. "There's so much to know," he said, "and you can spend a lifetime learning. What happens in the Nikkei affects what happens in the DAX. What happens in the DAX affects what happens here. Then there are currencies. Then there are interest rates. It is all connected; it is one massive linear programming problem that nobody is smart enough to figure out." Courtney was trying to learn. At the time, I barely knew the difference between gamma and vega.

But finally, after the four years I had spent at Lehman Brothers, it was starting to happen. *I was starting to see relationships.* I was starting to see relationships between things that nobody else could see. Not just first-order relationships, like those between basic materials stocks and the weakness of the dollar, but second- and third-order relationships.

It is generally true that people who scored high on the SATs did not know the answers to all the questions. They knew enough to eliminate wrong answers from the multiple-choice questions, which was enough. So even though this might not have been an indication of raw intelligence, it meant that there was still some unquantifiable, sophisticated reasoning going on. As it turned out, I had high SATs. So did a lot of other people on Wall Street. Though we may not have known the right answer, we knew how to pick it out of a lineup.

Jay Knight, making ten sticks a year down in Miami, was who he was because he could see relationships. He could see relationships between bonds. He could see things that nobody else could see. If other people could see these relationships, they would be putting on the same trades and making the same kind of money. But they weren't.

This doesn't mean that all traders are geniuses. In fact, most of them aren't. I was smart but not a genius. I could see these relationships, but it wasn't an act of cognition; instead, I *felt* them. When you are sitting in front of a Bloomberg screen, and you have hundreds of prices in front of you, you begin to develop an animal instinct of how things are related and how they are going to move when something happens somewhere in the world. It was if I was attached to a living, breathing organism, like a fetus being carried by a woman, or like Neo, in his embryonic state, plugged into the Matrix, floating in a pod filled with organic goo.

What surprised me most was that nobody else could see the same things that I could see. Most of my colleagues sat passively, dumb to what was going on around them. Through the noise on the trading floor, the trades my customers made, the prices of stocks and bonds, I could sense that the market had a soul. I felt it emotionally. Stocks going down was death, a destructive act. Stocks going up was life. I experienced the market in an emotional way; my moods and feelings were tied to the market.

I also realized, after a time, that ideology plays a role in markets as well. The market is not Democratic or Republican, statist or libertarian. The market is *capitalistic*, and threats to the market, from either political party, were a threat to the wealth being stored by every man and woman in the country, and by me, and my livelihood.

I began to write about that.

FM: JARED DILLIAN, LEHMAN BROTHERS INC.
TO: SALES


EXAMINING THE DOLLAR BILL IN MY HAND, WHICH IS DEPRECIATING BEFORE MY VERY EYES, MY EYES ARE DRAWN TO THE TEXT: "THIS NOTE IS LEGAL TENDER FOR ALL DEBTS, PUBLIC AND PRIVATE." THIS MEANS THAT I AM LE-GALLY BOUND TO ACCEPT THIS "FEDERAL RESERVE NOTE" AS PAYMENT FOR

MY SERVICES, INCLUDING THESE CLOUDY BLOOMBERGS. SINCE I CANNOT LEGALLY REFUSE DOLLARS, I WILL MAKE THE BEST OF THEM ON MY OWN TIME.

THAT'S TOO BAD, BECAUSE THE MARKET HAS RENDERED ITS DELAYED-REACTION VERDICT ON THE H-H TESTIMONY, AND "CONUNDRUM" DOESN'T APPEAR TO HAVE BEEN A SATISFACTORY ANSWER TO THE KOREANS OR GOLD BUGS OR OTHER DOLLAR SHORTS. IN ALAN GREENSPAN'S MEMOIRS, HE WILL NOT LIST THE LIQUIDITY INJECTIONS OF 1997, 1998, AND Y2K AS HIS GREATEST ERROR. RATHER, THE GREATEST ERROR FROM THE STANDPOINT OF THE FED WAS RAISING RATES IN 1994 TO HOLD OFF "ANTICIPATED" RATHER THAN REAL INFLATION. THE INFLATION WAS A PHANTOM, BUT THE HURRICANE FORCE BOND BEAR MARKET IT UNLEASHED WAS NOT. *THAT* IS THE MISTAKE THE FED CHOOSES NOT TO REPEAT.

INFLATION, AS MEASURED BY THE CPI AND PPI TO WHICH WE ALL GENU-FLECT (AND WHOSE INNER WORKINGS AND HIDDEN MECHANISMS WE ARE HOSTAGE TO), HAS HERETOFORE BEEN NONEXISTENT. INFLATION, AS MEASURED BY THE RAPID EXPANSION OF MONEY AND CREDIT, HAS BEEN "CREEPING." AN INTEREST RATE HELD BY GOVERNMENT UKASE LOWER THAN IT WOULD STAND IN A CENTRAL BANK–FREE WORLD DOES MORE TO IMPERIL THE CURRENCY SITUATION. A FEDERAL RESERVE NOTE IS REDEEM-ABLE FOR NOTHING. YOU CANNOT TAKE IT TO THE WINDOW AND RECEIVE GOLD, OR FOREIGN CURRENCIES, OR SCOOBY SNACKS. LIKEWISE WITH THE PAPER PROMISES OF THE ECB AND BOJ. RATIONALLY, WE SHOULD HOLD LESS OF PAPER AND MORE OF THINGS.

I FIRST RECOMMENDED GOLD ON 9 FEB. IT IS UP A GOOD 6-PLUS PERCENT SINCE THEN. I CONTINUE TO RECOMMEND IT, AND I RECOMMEND BUYING IT LUSTILY, PAYING THROUGH THE OFFER IF NECESSARY. GRANT POINTS OUT THAT THE LAST COMMODITY BOOM ENDED, AMONG OTHER THINGS, IN THE ACQUISITIONS OF PHIBRO AND J. ARON IN LATE 1981 (WHICH HAPPENED TO BE ONLY THE BEST TIME IN AMERICAN HISTORY TO BUY BONDS INSTEAD). I AM STILL SEEING BILLBOARDS FOR DITECH.COM BUT NONE FOR THE WORLD GOLD COUNCIL. WE ARE NOWHERE NEAR THE TOP.

My distribution list, by this point, was up to a few hundred people. I was getting better. I had been learning more about the markets and had ventured beyond commenting on day-trading futures.

1) 2/22 11:35 JASON LAREDO/Can I get on your list?

Another subscriber. They were starting to pile up, both inside and outside the firm.

I liked writing about the market. It helped to crystallize my thoughts. If I couldn't decide whether to take a position in something, I would write a Bloomberg, and the decision would be made for me.

I started to develop a peculiar fascination with words. I wanted to write the best trader commentary possible. Since I couldn't sell, this was my way of advertising for the business. If I could produce something that people wanted to read, they could receive it, but the implication was that they would trade ETFs with us. Many didn't; they just freeloaded, but that was fine, because it was still great publicity if they forwarded my material around.

I knew that I wasn't the greatest financial mind, but I also knew that nobody else on the street could write worth a damn. I gave up reading street research after only a few tries. It was abhorrent. Financial people are the worst writers in the world. I had won a writing award in high school, and two in college, without really trying. I seemed to have a natural talent with words, even though I had disregarded it and studied math instead. In the short to medium term, it had been a good decision. I was making a lot more money with a math degree.

What I wanted to do was to create a product that people would derive pleasure from reading. Nobody cared if there were buyers of U.S. Steel or sellers of Philip Morris. They'd heard all that shit a million times before. People wanted to read things that were insightful, and entertaining, and tragic, and funny.

It became an obsession. Along with trading, I spent all my time thinking about the next Bloomberg. I had received a blank diary for Christmas, and I started to carry it around with me, along with a pen, to jot down notes whenever something would come to me, say, on the bus.

Then, at my desk, I would wordsmith the fuck out of the thing until it smelled like petunias. Then I would hit Send and get more subscribers.

Within a short period of time, we actually started to get some business.

I was orgasmic. Six years earlier, I had taken a tour of a dingy trading floor and ducked a water bottle, which led to my first job running tickets for traders. Now I was the head ETF trader at the third-largest investment bank. When I stood in the middle of the floor and yelled out trades, all eyes were on me. I had engineered a recovery in our ETF business, and we were swimming in order flow. My opinions may not quite have been moving markets, but our customers were reading them, and more were signing up by the day.

A year ago, I'd tried to take my own life. If I'd had a gun at home, I probably would have been successful.

That seemed like a long time ago.

I wasn't so much willfully ignoring it, I just couldn't remember why I did what I did, why I felt so terrible, or even what it felt like. I was, after all, euphoric. I got into work early, and I left late. When I got home, I drank, and read books about trading, and then worked on my Bloomberg messages for the following day. I was living, breathing, eating, and sleeping the financial markets. The possibilities were endless. I had arrived.

I was deliriously happy. It almost felt like I was short of breath. I might have been too, because I had really put on weight. I felt like a man who knows that he is in the right job, at the right place, at the right time in history; a man who is doing exactly what he was put here on earth to be doing. With my head full of numbers, I was entirely useless as a sailor. As a trader, I was part mathematician, part behavioral scientist, and part bully.

D.C. and I were having fun together. We had our little routines: at three o'clock, every day, a willowy thing, flat chested, with chestnut hair, would descend the stairs behind us. We sat and watched, hunchbacks with cleft palates, looking for a wet nurse to change our drool cups. We said it was the best part of our day.

I turned into a prankster. I would take pieces of thin cardboard, cut them into the shape of spurs, sneak up behind people (usually Herb), and tape them to their heels. I would stuff fish into the mouthpieces of their phones. I threw things at people all day long: packets of soy sauce, ketchup, and balled-up pieces of paper. I farted, and would run to the door as D.C. yelled, "Doorknob!"

I still had bitter clashes with the sales force. To me, it was never bringing in the right trades at the right time. Too often we were haggling over pennies. At the end of my profanity-laced tirades, though, I would usually acquiesce. I didn't mind letting the customer have his way on a medium-size trade as long as the flow kept coming. I wasn't going to be another Chandler. But the sales guys had to know that if they were going to challenge me on price, they had a fight coming—otherwise they would take advantage of me all the time.

It seemed that we were blundering into new business opportunities on a daily basis. D.C. was approached by a craggy bond salesman with a thick wick of hair named Matthew Cook. They knew each other somehow: lacrosse, Garden City, some rich-white-guy network; I couldn't figure it out. Cook had a client, arguably Lehman Brothers's *biggest* capital markets client: a large commercial bank that wanted to trade ETFs. Cook was nervous as hell, because any fuckups on the second floor, where we worked, could have a direct impact on his sales credits. After all, the bank paid Lehman Brothers *tens of millions* per year. So Cook came first to D.C., and then to Frank Segal and any managing director that would listen to him, to ask that we would provide this whale tight, fair markets on anything they wanted to trade.

I was intrigued. This was the type of customer we had been looking for: big, slow money that would trade in monstrous size and spread commissions on us like Crisco. What could be so hard about it?

They gave the account to Eric Savitz, a Morgan Stanley retread that Frank Segal had shipped over shortly after he arrived. For the past two years, we had been trying to figure out what Savitz did for a living. He was a sales guy, but he seemed to cover nobody, and he was partly deaf, so most of the time he sat there, stunned. He would listen to people's conversations and nod slowly. He was a great guy, with plenty of warmth to go around, but appeared to serve no purpose. Frank Segal assured Cook that Savitz had safe hands, and that D.C. and I were trading athletes, and that his coveted, special relationship would not be in any jeopardy.

Weeks went by, and I thought the whole thing had been a hoax. We got that a lot—new client, it pays the street a lot, yada yada—and then nothing happens. Our business was full of disappointments, some large, some small. I wasn't about to lose any sleep over it.

"Dillian."

I looked over. It was Savitz. He had the phone to his one good ear. "It's them," he mouthed silently.

I put down my corned beef sandwich and readied myself. I waved D.C. back to the desk; he'd been off talking to his lacrosse buddies.

"One point seven million DVY, how?"

"DVY?"

"Yes."

I had never traded DVY before. I looked it up. It was a dividend ETF. It had stocks of companies that paid lots of dividends. Seemed like an odd choice of something on which to spend $70 million.

I pulled up DVY in the impact pricer and entered 1,700,000. It said we had to make a fifty-five-cent-wide market.

"You see that?" I asked D.C.

"Yeah."

"Is that right?"

"Beats me."

"I'm going to cut it in half just in case." I had no idea what I was trading. It was a shot in the dark.

"Eighty at ten!" I yelled over to Savitz.

Savitz whispered into the phone. He held the phone away from his good ear, like it had puked sand into it, and hung up.

"What happened?"

"They hung up."

"Why?"

"They said it was disgraceful."

"What was?"

"Your market."

Oh boy. We were going to hear about this one.

Within minutes, Cook is on the floor, darting around like a hummingbird. His client is pissed. He's not even talking to me and D.C. He's gone straight for Chris Masters, and Mark Ricci, and Frank Segal. Soon they are all huddled around our desk. I explain what happened.

"Look, the impact pricer said fifty-five cents, and I cut it in half. I'm not sure what else they want. That is a very tight market."

"W you m ne d to rad ev tighter at," says Mark.

Now Cook is at Savitz's desk, talking to the bank himself.

"Ask him what price he wants to trade it at," says Mark, audibly this time.

Cook whispers into the phone. "Ninety-eight," he says.

"Mark," I protest, "that's two cents above the offer. We're going to get steamrolled."

"Put it up," he says.

I sigh and sit down, waving in the trade. It is done.

The trade is too big to trade out of in a matter of minutes, so I calculate what I need to hedge it and lift a huge slug of futures off the screen. The market doesn't take it well: it starts to run higher.

Well, time to start trading this thing. I figure I'll start with 5 percent of the basket—about $3.5 million—and send it to the market.

The price rips from .98 to .03.

"What the hell?" exclaims D.C.

"What the fuck is in this thing?" I open up the basket and look. *Oh no.* I had heard about this one: an index weighted by dividend yields. The number one name is Philip Morris, MO. The number two name is PBCT, or People's Bank of Connecticut.

PBCT ordinarily traded 60,000 shares a day.

We have 180,000 to buy.

My stomach flip-flops and gurgles. Not only are we not going to get out of this in a matter of minutes, we aren't going to get out of it in *days.*

There are about two hours left. I put 30 percent of the trade in the VWAP algorithm, which is essentially like autopilot—I'm letting the computer take over. I take a basket of S&P 500 stock of comparable size and put it in the VWAP on the sell side, to gradually take us out of our hedge. All that's left to do is to watch helplessly.

DVY is full of little-pieces-of-shit stocks. I pull up charts on all of them. Our customer is ripping all these little dividend stocks by buying an ETF. The funny thing is that the people who trade the stocks and the research analysts who cover them are going to get all excited. Little do they know that it is just some gorilla that's buying a dumb dividend ETF.

I sit hunched over my desk, legs jiggling, frozen like some Rodin statue. I'm not accustomed to being in a trade that I can't get out of. They say that liquidity is the biggest risk: not being able to exit a position in the same manner that you put it on. Today we are barely going to make a dent in this thing. We might not even finish trading it *tomorrow*. If I'd wanted to trade something it would take me a week to get out of, I would have taken a job trading emerging market bonds. ETFs weren't supposed to be like this.

That night, I slept even less than usual. My brain was full of charts of little-pieces-of-shit stocks shooting off into infinity.

The next day, I spent the morning frozen in the same position, getting my shit pushed in by DVY. It began to slowly occur to me that if there was a way to lose money off of this trade, there had to be a way to make money off of this trade too.

*What the fuck index is this?* The Dow Jones Select Dividend index.

"D.C., you ever hear of this index before?"

"No."

"You think this thing rebalances?"

"No idea."

I bounced across the floor to talk to Michelle Beatty. Michelle's purpose in life was to answer stupid fucking questions. About indices. Technically, she was a research analyst, but on an average day, she had to field about a hundred questions on this or that index from this or that sales trader who was trying to find an answer for his or her client. While I talked to her, she fired off about three or four emails, one-word responses.

"Does this index rebalance?"

"Yes. All the Dow Jones indices rebalance at the same time, and it's coming up in about six weeks." *Zap!* Off went an email.

*Money.*

"Can you send me the index changes?"

"Sure." *Zap, zap, zap* in an email, and it was mine.

I spent that afternoon poring over the spreadsheet she had sent me.

"Oh no," sighed D.C., "what are you up to now?"

"I'm going to do the DVY rebalance trade. We're going to make back all the money we lost on this thing, and then some."

"You know what you're doing?"

"Not really."

I spent a few days constructing the trade. I made a list of the piece-of-shit stocks that were going into the index, and a list of the piece-of-shit stocks that were coming out. I was going to buy the ones that were coming in, and sell the ones going out. This was the same as the Russell rebalance trade, but I figured that this one would be a lot more successful because it wasn't as well known and wouldn't be full of scumbag hedge funds. The chance of a wrong-way trade was very small. It should be very straightforward.

Once I had built the baskets, I fed them to the machine and put them in the vwapper. Autopilot. Chug, chug, chug. The robot bought these pieces of shit, a hundred shares at a time, all day long. After the first day, I had bought $10 million worth of shit and sold $10 million worth of shit. I was long and short shit, and stood to profit handsomely.

*How big should I make this thing?* "Go big or go home," Ingram had once told me. If there was one thing in the world that guy knew, it was how to size a trade. I was sure on this one, and I would not be accused of being a piker. So I plowed more and more shit into the trade.

Finally, I was long and short $50 million worth of shit.

When a rebalance trade works, it works. People have stock to buy, and people have stock to sell. They have no choice in the matter. They have to buy the stocks I just bought, and they have to sell the stocks I just sold. I didn't know anything about these names; they were mostly just pissant regional banks. It didn't matter, because I knew which way they were going.

"D.C., look at this."

"*Hooollly* shit."

Within a few days, I had made $1 million.

It was time to take the trade off.

I did the same thing in reverse; I started to sell the pieces of shit I had bought and buy the pieces of shit I had sold short. But I had encountered a problem. Other people were doing the same thing.

There were other smart guys in this trade, after all, and we had come to the same conclusion at the same time: it was time to get out. We were each conspiring to limit the others' profits. My money was disappearing. The green number had changed from $1,000,000, to $950,000, to $900,000.

Fuck.

I couldn't watch this.

I walked around the desk.

"Hey Mark."

I leaned closer so that I could actually hear him.

"I've been working on a cool trade. Want to check it out?"

At the end of the day, Mark was my boss, though he was typically too busy to care much about what D.C. and I were up to. The ETF desk was supposed to run itself. He had bigger fish to fry, like his political wars with the sales guys.

Mark and I walked around to my desk, and I explained the mechanics of the DVY rebalance. He listened and nodded his head. "This is really good," he said. "How much money have you made on it?"

"Well, it looks like I'm down to about $875,000 right now."

Mark nodded his head some more. "This is *outstanding*," he said, and disappeared.

It never occurred to me to ask permission to put the trade on in the first place.

At another bank, if I had pulled a stunt like that, I would have been taken out back and horsewhipped. I was using a huge amount of firm capital to put on a trade that I really had only a vague idea would work out. I was but one step removed from a floor monkey. They say it is better to ask for forgiveness than to ask permission. But at Lehman Brothers, it was almost never necessary to ask for forgiveness. You were *trusted* to put on trades that you thought would make money. If you biffed one, it was no big deal. If you biffed two, it was no big deal. If you had a history of biffing trades and you were leaking cash, then that was a different story. In the meantime, you could continue to do whatever you wanted.

This was the beauty of working at Lehman Brothers.

After a few days, the market let me out with $700,000. It was the most money I had ever made on one trade. I made that money because I was paying attention. I made that money because, in my unusually heightened state of awareness, I saw a pattern that nobody else was seeing. Two things happened: I was trading something out of my comfort zone, which enabled me to see something that I wouldn't have seen otherwise.

It was an argument for trading everything I could get my hands on.

"Spike, grab a drink?" Spychalski was usually good for some fun. When that kid got going, he started talking really loudly about how dumb the sales guys were, which I found endearing.

"Compliance meeting, dude. You get the email?"

Oh, that thing.

I thought that compliance was placed on the trading floor to figure out if anything fishy was going on. The guys from the department sat in the corner by themselves and did Lord knows what. Many of them were aspiring lawyers. They were nice, but they didn't see the world in the same way that we traders did. We were engaged in commerce. If there was a novel or creative way of doing something, we wanted to do it. We didn't want to ask anyone's permission. D.C. and I had a heated discussion with one of them about our order-handling procedures. He said we were doing it all wrong. I told him to eat it.

All the traders on the floor filed into the auditorium. Everyone was represented: cash, derivatives, converts, programs, quants. It was a lot of people. It was a lot of people who wanted to get the hell out of there and go have a drink.

There was an Ice Queen in the front of the auditorium, waiting for everyone to get settled. It is a Lehman custom that every meeting starts exactly five minutes after the designated time. I thought it was a nice civilian touch.

The Ice Queen was holding a few sheets of paper. She was telling us about some enforcement action, some case that was supposedly a turning point in NYSE regulation. We are moving from a more lenient regulatory regime to something more strict, she said. I scratched my balls.

Few people understand the degree of regulation to which traders are subjected. They aren't regulated by the Securities and Exchange Commission per se; the SEC delegates its regulatory powers to "self-regulatory organizations," or SROs, such as the New York Stock Exchange or the National Association of Securities Dealers. Most people know the NYSE as the friendly trading floor that they see on television, but what they do not know is that it is also a mean-spirited regulatory bureaucracy.

Ice Queen starts reading the details of the case, an enforcement action involving a trader at another bank. "On April 4, 2002, Carl Garber approved a customer facilitation for approximately 4.8 million shares of XYZ Corp. (XYZ) at $9 per share. The price was at a premium to the market, since the stock at that time was trading at approximately $8.95. Subsequent to the customer facilitation, the price of XYZ began to decline, and Ryan entered a series of $9 limit orders via SuperDOT to purchase XYZ at Garber's instruction. The multiple $9 limit orders had the effect of artificially influencing the price of an Exchange-listed security. In addition, one of the orders entered by Ryan was a market order which was executed at $9.03, on a plus tick higher than the price at which the block was acquired by the Firm that day, thus causing a violation of Exchange Rule 97(a)(iii)."

None of this was making any sense. But as Ice Queen continued, I slowly figured it out. The trader bought a bunch of stock on a block. His boss told him to keep buying stock at a specific level. Someone had noticed and called the stock cops. The specialist thought that the trader, Ryan, was manipulating the stock by holding up the price. The enforcement action said that this was "inconsistent with just and equitable principles of trade."

*Now, that is awfully subjective*, I thought, as I felt a chill. You mean, there are people out there who might think that what I am doing is not consistent with just and equitable principles of trade? That if you don't like what someone else is doing, you blow the whistle, and he gets hauled off to compliance jail?

And, worse, the orders that someone had complained about were being entered in *electronically*, not verbally. Someone was watching supposedly *anonymous* order flow and drawing conclusions.

I did a mental review of every trade I had ever done. Had I done anything illegal?

The exchanges weren't going to play nice anymore, said the Ice Queen. The trader in question got a censure and a $75,000 fine. The money was nothing—but he might never get a job again.

As we left the auditorium, I found myself standing next to Chuck. "You hear that?" I asked him.

"It's serious. These people can take away your livelihood. They have the power."

My trading would never be the same again.

## Piker | Spring 2005–Fall 2005

There was a nerd sitting in front of me.

It takes one to know one. I had spent the beginning of my adult life trying to escape nerdism by joining the military and lifting weights and shaving my head. In my seventeenth year, I was sick of being a nerd. I joined the wrestling team and put people in headlocks. I hung out with anti-intellectuals and farted. Up until that point, I thought that the only sensible purpose for the body was to carry around the brain. I wanted big guns, and as a by-product, I wanted girls.

What I failed to consider was the types of girls that I would be attracting.

But on Wall Street, I needed to grow my brain back, not having used it for nine years. Money is made through intellect, not with muscles, and it is a much higher compliment to be called "smart" than a "stud." Wall Street was filled with smart people, most of whom had not taken a nine-year detour shouting military cadences.

This man before me was, unmistakably, a dork. Not a nerd in the traditional sense: no glasses here. He was shortish, with hair that implied he didn't care, with a shirt and tie that implied he cared even less. He was concentrating on his computers so much that he was oblivious to the fact that I was standing there staring at him, sizing him up. I gathered that he had been stuffed into more than one locker in his time, if he could have fit in one.

This was my new supervisor.

The benign and happy Chuck had been my old supervisor, and Chuck had reported to Mark Ricci. But Chuck had been busy with other things in the last year or so. He had his hands full trading index options, and he was starting a new business venture for the firm: he was building a swaps desk. Chuck was a builder, and he was using his talents for good, building pricers and software and everything a team of swaps traders would need to do their jobs. As a consequence, he hadn't paid much attention to me or D.C. He had let us do our thing, and the results had been good. Now it was going to be a new regime.

The nerd's name was Marty Korenkiewicz. Buzz had been building around Marty for weeks; we were hiring a former MIT-trained engineer who had fallen just short of getting a PhD. Marty had a big brain, and he used it to get within one question of getting a perfect score on his GRE. He looked like an MIT guy; like he'd had one too many Mountain Dews staying up in a computer lab all night.

Marty was coming from a broker-dealer like us. That was where the similarities ended. His previous firm was a private partnership, not a publicly traded company, and dispensed with the formalities of even having an investment banking division for the purposes of doing deals and having primary issuance. These guys were all gamblers, cardsharps, poker wizards. They were traders; professional traders. They hired raw mathematical talent, taught them gambling theory, and let them trade. It was one of the street's rare success stories of a man with a vision who had built a fantastic organization.

The problem for Marty was that he had signed an onerous noncompete agreement, which meant that when he quit, he had to wait a year to take another job. Marty hadn't traded for a year, and he was rusty. There he was in front of me, trying to get the hang of things.

I introduced myself. *Nice guy. I can work with this guy.*

Things were about to get a little more exciting.

They were exciting enough as it was. My Bloomberg emails were attracting more business, but it was the wrong kind of business. Lehman Brothers, historically, had associated with what you might call a faster breed of client. These were not big, slow pension funds. These were fast hedge funds, aggressive traders. D.C. and I were trading athletes, and so were our customers. Every day was like a hockey game, and we were the goalies.

We started to learn that certain salespeople attracted the dirtiest kinds of clients. There was Ray Perkins, a managing director with tenure, who looked like he was about twenty-seven years old. Reptilian, he scowled. Years ago, I watched him hurl paper tickets at one of my associate classmates with disgust. He was a dick, allegedly.

Ray was moving up in the organization. It wasn't so much that he was getting more clients, it was that he had lucked into getting the *right* clients: because all of them were growing, they were attracting more assets; the more they grew, the bigger the trades they did, and the more they traded. Ray was looking like a genius for picking up a fund called Spartacus back when it was nothing.

I knew nothing about Spartacus except that it was a big pain in my ass. A few times a day, Ray would slither out from under a rock and lob in some big Spartacus trade, hissing, which inevitably always blew my head off.

"Two-fifty SPY!"

"Thirty-three, thirty-six!" I would say.

"SOLD!"

Before I had time to hedge, the market would correct, and $25,000 would be gone.

"*Oooooooooooh*," the trading floor would say.

They got us again.

Spychalski fished around the internet for more sound effects. He came up with a rattlesnake sound.

"SOLD!"

"*Oooooooooooh!*"

"*Sssssssssssss.*"

Fucking Ray. It wasn't so much that he kept putting us in losing trades, it was the way he did it. He did it with anger, like we deserved it, like we had original sin for being traders, or something. I couldn't figure out what this guy's problem was. He seemed to using Lehman as a platform for world domination. A year later, I would have a disaster of a dinner with Ray and a redheaded mutant client who played with his BlackBerry the whole time we ate sushi in silence. Ray covered some low-quality human beings.

We also had to deal with Sneaky Bill, a blond who had come over from Morgan Stanley. Sneaky Bill played dumb at just about everything, so it was impossible to be angry with him without simultaneously feeling sorry for him for being so clueless. Sneaky's wife apparently dressed him up in fashionable clothes, including flat-front pants.

"Who the fuck wears flat-front pants?" asked Spychalski.

"He looks like Eurotrash," I added.

Sneaky had a way of asking for price improvements:

"XLE, two-fifty!"

"Forty-two, forty-five!"

Pause. "Does forty-four work?"

"Who's asking?"

"I'm asking?"

"No, I mean, you or the customer?"

"Huh?"

"I'm out!"

"Wait, does forty-three work?"

"Make it stop," pleaded D.C.

"Fine." I sighed.

"Man, that guy is dumb," said D.C.

If he was really dumb, we would have been able to exploit it somehow. Sneaky knew what he was doing.

Jamie, the mouse, comes up to the desk. D.C. and I look at him.

"Jared," he says, "we need you to go to dinner with Battalion."

"Why? Don't we already do their business?"

Jamie shifts his weight. "This is different. We only trade SPYs for one part of the fund. They actually do a lot more ETFs, and we don't see any of it. We should try to win that business."

I am interested. "How much do they do?"

"It's a lot. Probably five times what we are seeing right now."

I turn to D.C. "See, this is what I am talking about. There's so much flow that we're not seeing right now. This is the kind of stuff that we need to be doing." I am high up on the assjack. I have been preaching this to everyone who will listen: that we need to get aggressive with our customers.

I had decided that I was going to be the king of ETFs on the street. When hedge funds asked one another about ETFs, they would say, "Do you trade with Lehman?" I wanted to be the primary source of liquidity and the center of attention. I wanted people to associate ETFs with Lehman Brothers and, by extension, me. I would shrug off my previous failures at client dinners and attempt to close the deal with Battalion. I figured that it had the potential to pay us several million dollars a year.

The dinner was to be held at Nobu 57, the uptown location. It was the hottest ticket around. Kevin Rodman had camped out there when it first opened, paid the maître d' $500, and earned himself reservations whenever he wanted them. It was an astute business decision. Every account wanted to go there, and for good reason: Nobu 57 was filled with celebrities. I kept hearing reports about how people were bumping into Derek Jeter and A-Rod. Much later, I would have a broker dinner there and be seated not more than ten feet away from Alyssa Milano, who was even better looking up close than she is on television. I tried and failed not to be creepy.

I was goddamn thirsty. By this point in the evening, I usually had a few drinks in me. The bar was crowded, and I was having a hell of a time getting in my drink order, lacking large breasts. I turned to recent hire Del Miller, a blond Berkeley kid with a head for derivatives, who was a half foot taller. "Del. I need a Maker's and ginger. I can't get their attention."

By this point, I had graduated from Jack and Cokes to Maker's Mark and ginger ale, at the prodding of a broker who insisted that I stop drinking such dark, macho drinks in the middle of the summer. Once I tasted a Maker's and ginger, I was hooked. It was velvet, and it was a fucking hammer. The weak ones tasted delicious, and the strong ones were toxic. I needed to drink them all the time, or I would get irascible.

Del wasn't having any luck with the bartender, either, some penis who was probably making $1,500 a night in tips. Del was saying *yo* and flapping his arms around like a pelican, and still no drink. After five minutes, I lost my cool.

"Will you hurry up and get the fucking drink?"

Del turned to me and said, "Do you need me to hook a hose up to your mouth?"

I quieted down.

I always felt a hopeful tension before these dinners. The truth of the matter was that there was a lot more money at stake in a client dinner than there was in any individual trade. A good dinner could result in millions. A bad one could lose a client forever, like what I had done with Broadstreet. Yes, I had no people skills. I was a trader, and all the salespeople like Del and Jamie told me that I had zero sales ability. But I was determined to try. I was determined to make this work. I ordered another drink, letting the feeling wash over me. Try and smile, you fuck. Don't be a creepy loser.

The Battalion guys arrived late. One was wearing a *T-shirt*.

I was a bit more conservative about dress than most people. I had, after all, spent half a career wearing a military uniform. To me, a tie was no big deal. When Lehman Brothers had gone back to suits, there was a lot of pissing and moaning. To me, it was fine. I thought we should look like professionals, even if it didn't mean that we would necessarily act like them.

There is an unwritten rule that when you are at a hedge fund, you do not wear a tie. You do not wear a suit. After all, you are in the business of portfolio management, which is a hard business; you don't need something around your neck strangling you while you work. Ties were for sell-side losers. I had never heard of a hedge fund where you had to wear a suit. But I had not, up until this point, ever heard of one where you could wear a T-shirt. These guys looked like bums.

*Whatever*, I thought. Battalion had enjoyed a run of extraordinary luck, including some eye-popping years earlier in the decade, and I figured they were entitled. The three of them that just sat down with us were probably each worth over eight figures.

I felt terribly insecure. It was not the first time I had broken bread with people who were richer than me. Hedge fund guys tend to be richer because they get paid on performance. If a $1 billion fund is up 30 percent on the year, that is $300 million, and the partners get to keep 20 percent of that, or $60 million. If there are only a handful of partners, well, they get disgustingly rich. We got paid good money, but it was not hedge fund money. We were pikers, peons, barely qualified to be sitting at the same table, begging for scraps, for $1,000 commissions on stock trades. It was demoralizing.

Jamie, for being a wuss, is not a bad sales guy. He is talking up the Battalion guys, name-dropping, and they are all having a good laugh. I wonder where he learns this. I order another drink.

On my left is Garrett, a beefy, fast-talking portfolio manager. He seems to be in charge of the other two goons. The conversation centers around what people are doing for the summer. Inevitably, to a man, everyone is going to the Hamptons. God, what bastards. I saw absolutely no utility in sitting in some of the worst traffic imaginable to live in a house that I spent $10,000 on renting for a week to hang around with the same douchebags that I saw at work every day. The prospect was not appealing.

Garrett turns to me. "What do you have planned for this summer?"

I have a response ready; I have been thinking about it. "Well, I am going to a wedding in Scotland, so my wife and I are going to spend a week there. She's a little outdoorsy, so we're going to bring a tent and spend the week driving around and camping."

Garrett fires back, "So when you say 'outdoorsy,' you mean she likes to eat mushrooms and take it up the ass?" He makes a fist-in-the-ass motion with his hand.

Conversation stops, like an electromagnetic pulse just went off. Jamie and Del look at me nervously, waiting for the explosion. Then, nervous laughter.

It takes a few minutes to sink in. *Did he really say that? Am I imagining things?* I am not the kind of person who has a witty response to any put-down. But I am at the precipice of drunk, and I allow myself to fill up with rage. *Who the fuck says something like that?*

The Battalion guys get a big laugh out of it and go back to acting like jackasses. The other two goons, including the one with the T-shirt, are playing footsies under the table. They are jabbing each other, and poking each other, and basically fucking around. They are getting louder. Jamie is trying to ignore them.

*Wham!*

The goon not wearing a T-shirt goes down. The chair spins out into the middle of the aisle, and he is rolling around on the floor, drunk, unable to get up. The other customers are looking on in horror. The maître d' whispers something in Jamie's ear and takes him aside for a private conversation. A scene is developing. Everyone is staring.

Jamie comes back, and he is clearly flustered. "So let's talk about ETFs." He turns to Garrett. "What are you guys typically seeing for ETF markets these days?"

"Half a million locked, for a penny commission."

*That does it.*

"I'm sorry, but we're not going to be able to do that business for you. Sorry if the dinner was a waste of time," I say.

Jamie starts out of his seat as if he had just received a prostate exam. "Whoa! What Jared means is that I'm sure we can work something out. He can make tight markets; he does it all the time."

"No," I say calmly, "that's not what I mean. I am saying that *I* am not going to do this business. Period."

Jamie fumbles some more. Garrett recovers. He is smiling. "Jamie, it's okay. If he doesn't want to do the business, we'll find someone who will."

I wasn't going to be a whore for these guys. For these Battalion guys, it was a game. They were rich as hell. They could have a game where they were as rude as humanly possible and see if they could still get the whore broker-dealers to do their business. It was offensive. These were *bad* guys. These were despicable human beings. I wasn't going to have anything to do with it.

I got up from the table. I was more drunk than I thought. The conversations, the music, the air, was blending into a singular sensation: *let me out of here. I need air.*

I burst out onto the street. It was no better out there. I was wearing one of my better suits, and it was soaked against my skin.

As I walked, I thought about what had just happened. I was probably going to be in deep shit. I was probably going to be in big trouble for blowing up a huge account. After all, it wasn't just the ETF business that I had jeopardized, it was the options business, the cash business, the relative value business—everything. It was probably worth $20 million a year to the firm. What, was I supposed to stand there and let this guy announce to the room that my wife was an anal whore? Is this what it means to be a broker? Am I supposed to put up with this crap?

I needed another drink. I ducked into Shelley's Crab House, walked past the garish seafood display, and went upstairs to the bar.

I was honored with a Maker's Mark and ginger ale in a glass the size of a pail. And it was strong. I paid with cash. I had $40 left in my wallet.

I was completely fucked. I had just traded my way out of a job. Mark Ricci tells me to market the business, to bring in new clients, and I lose existing ones. I was a complete and utter failure. If I did manage to keep my job, they should never put me in front of another client again.

*Gosh, this drink tastes good. And it's nice and cool in here.*

I wished I were Jay Knight. Jay Knight doesn't have to put up with any of this bullshit. He doesn't have to deal with big mooks talking about pounding his wife in the ass. He sits down in Miami and mints Kruger-rands, wearing flip-flops. Where had I gone wrong? The days of putting on big Eurodollar and spread trades with Ingram seemed so long ago. If I had kept at it, I might have been rich by now. I might have been in Miami, with Jay, laughing it up.

I needed to trade more.

I ordered another drink.

The one thing I missed about working in the military was working with *good people*. People who were going to stand up and tell you the truth. They didn't have an angle. They weren't out to get something. They weren't going to stab you in the back. These people I associated with now, these overeducated, smart-assed pricks, these were the worst human beings in the world. They had no concept of *fairness*. To them, fairness was getting what they wanted at the expense of everyone else. They wanted me to lock markets and then to run over my ass. They didn't care about me. It was all about how I was going to help them get rich.

I ordered another drink.

What was I going to do in this ETF job, anyway? What was the career path? If I was ambitious, I could hope to have Mark Ricci's job someday. But that wasn't going to happen, because I didn't trade options. Only the volatility traders got to have that job. I was going to be stuck in ETFs, putting up with this bullshit forever.

I ordered another drink.

Fucking bastards.

I ordered another drink.

I looked down at my watch. Funny, I couldn't *see* my watch. I literally could not make out the hands. Was it eleven, or was it one? I couldn't tell.

I needed to get out of there.

I had a car waiting for me, somewhere on Fifty-seventh Street, I knew. There was a line of black cars on the street. I forgot what number was mine. I started opening passenger doors and asking the drivers if they were supposed to bring me home. They looked at me, annoyed.

I couldn't see my car. I couldn't see anything. I was literally blind. Blind drunk.

I started to walk.

• • •

"Buddy, time to get off."

I look up at a three-hundred-pound man in a bus driver's uniform.

"Time to get off," he says again. "Last stop."

It occurs to me that I am on a bus.

I have sobered up, small. I step off the bus, and it roars away.

*Where am I?*

None of this looks familiar. There are streetlights and storefront windows. There are no cars, no pedestrians. The place is deserted. It is a moonscape.

I look around for a phone booth. I curse myself silently for not having a cell phone.

A shitbox car, a real gravedigger, pulls up at the stoplight. I tap on the passenger window. The driver rolls it down.

The driver is wearing a do-rag on his head and has a tattoo on his neck and face. He looks dangerous.

"Where am I?"

He looks at me.

"Where am I?" I repeat.

"Ridgefield Park."

"You know how to get to West New York?"

He nods.

"Give you twenty bucks to take me there."

He opens the door.

I get in. There is no way that this car passed inspection.

The driver speeds away, through the stoplight.

"Let me know if you see any cops," he says.

He is running red lights and stop signs left and right.

"Let me know if you see any cops," he says again.

This guy is out of his mind.

He drives onto and off of a curb, then onto grass. The car is bottoming out in the ditch. He is going seventy in a twenty-five.

"Let me know if you see any cops," he says a third time.

We are home. Foolishly, I let him drop me off in front of my house. With grandiosity, I pull out a business card. "In case you need anything," I say.

"What, are you a lawyer?"

I wave at him with my left hand and get out.

My hangovers were never that bad. In a way, it was dangerous: I could drink as much as I wanted and not have to worry about the consequences. At least, not those including being driven home to your doorstep by a gang member.

I locked the front door and headed down the street to the bus.

*Did I lock the door?*

*You dummy, of course you locked the door.*

*I'd better go check.*

I went back and checked the door, which had become routine. It was locked. I decided to lock it again.

*Maybe if I lock the door in a specific pattern, I'll remember.*

I locked the dead bolt one, two, three times, and the doorknob one, two, three times. I checked it again.

*Locked.*

I sit at my desk in silence. I am hoping nobody notices me. Jamie is already at his desk. He pretends I do not exist.

Mark Ricci materializes next to me.

*Here it comes.*

"I heard what happened last night."

*Here it comes.*

"You did the right thing. We stand by you one hundred percent."

There were good guys, after all.

The compliance meeting had found space in my mind, and occupied it, rent free. I was dimly aware that I was regulated. It never occurred to me that someone might be analyzing my trading activity.

I supposed that it made sense. After all, the SEC had to have ways to figure out if there was insider trading going on. If there was a spike in volume in a stock before a big deal, I was sure that it went into the trading records to figure out who was buying and who was selling. For some reason, in the past, the possibility of anyone looking at what I was doing seemed very remote. Now the threat was real.

It wasn't that I was concerned about insider trading; I never had inside information, and I didn't anticipate having any. But there is a rule on stock exchanges that says that you cannot trade ahead of customers. On the New York Stock Exchange, it is known as Rule 92. The idea is that if a trader, like me, is aware of the presence of a large customer order, he could trade ahead of it to try and make money. The regulators routinely audited trade data to look for signs of any Rule 92 violations. If they saw that you had traded a lot of stock, and then a customer had traded a lot of stock right afterward, it was a potential Rule 92 violation, even if it had been inadvertent.

I felt like I was being watched. I felt like there was a Big Brother that took note of every trade I did, and that if I ever screwed up, I was going to be hauled off to compliance jail, or worse. What happened if you violated exchange rules, anyway?

I shuddered as I thought about Ben Cohan. He'd had a public hearing at the exchange, the results of which it published on the internet. The NYSE was kind to Cohan, only fining and suspending him. But it could have been a lot worse. He could have been fined more, or he could have been barred from the industry *permanently*. Once you are barred, that's it; time to find a different career.

I became exceedingly careful. When we got a trade, we agreed on a price, I printed it to the tape, and I hedged it, in that order. I made sure not to hedge it before I printed it, because, if I had, it would look, at least to the regulators, like I was trading ahead of the customer.

One time I screwed up; I hedged first.

"God*damn* it!" I said in despair.

"What?" asked D.C.

"Nothing."

"No, what?"

"*Nothing.*" That was it. It was on the historical tape. Forever. If anyone wanted to look at it and find the Rule 92 violation, he could.

I started to calculate probabilities. What was the probability that the regulators would audit that particular piece of data? Twenty percent, I decided. What was the probability that, if audited, they would find it? Fifty percent, I decided. What was the probability that it would lead to a hearing? Thirty percent, I decided. What was the probability that I would get barred from the industry? Thirty percent, I decided.

I did the arithmetic. I had about a 1 percent chance of getting barred from the industry for life.

*It's okay. It's only 1 percent.*

*Jesus Christ, 1 percent. A one-in-a-hundred shot. That's a pretty high chance.*

How long would it take for this to happen?

Three to six months, I decided.

*So I have three to six months to live, before they kick me out.*

I can't enjoy anything until six months pass, when I am out of the woods. Until then, I am a dead man walking.

Meanwhile, Marty Korenkiewicz, my boss, had made a splash trading index options. His markets were several orders of magnitude better than Chuck's, and Chuck, though a nice guy, was not considered to be especially customer friendly. Marty came in and started putting up customers left and right at ridiculous prices, and greatly increased the amount of risk that he was carrying.

Marty loved trading. He simply couldn't stop trading. He came to Lehman with a bit of an uneven history: he was rumored to have blown sky-high at his previous firm. There was another rumor floating around that, during the morning of 9/11, when planes were flying into buildings, Marty was sitting quietly at his futures terminal trading it up while his colleagues were running around like decapitated chickens.

Marty was also an addict, like many traders. He was, deep down, a gambler whose game of choice was the market. He would binge, trading thousands of contracts, losing millions of dollars, and vowing never to trade again. He would turn off his computers and swear off speculation completely. But the old desire to win would always come back.

Most traders have an aversion to large trades. They get an inquiry on a couple hundred million dollars of delta—putting them in a position that's moving at around the rate of $100,000 a second—and they go weak in the knees. The voice cracks, and the hands shake. Stress is a perfectly normal reaction to lots of risk, but some people adapt better than others. Furthermore, dealing with risk is like ass stretching. If you shove an object in your rectum, it is painful, but the more you do it, the bigger the object you can fit up there, until one day you are comfortable with, say, a peanut butter jar.

Marty was wired differently from most traders. His stress was inversely correlated to the size of the trade. He was more concerned with small trades than he was with large trades. Any trade that was worth doing was worth doing big. If you want to trade the front-month-straddle five thousand times, why not ten thousand times?

Del Miller comes over to Marty's desk. "I've got a new customer," he says. "Pretty small account, one hundred fifty million dollars, based out of Atlanta; says he wants to trade some OEX."

The OEX is the S&P 100 index, or an index of one hundred of the largest companies in the market. Back in the eighties and nineties, the OEX was the most widely traded option complex in the world. But since more money was indexed to the S&P 500, its SPX options had become more popular over time. Every once in a while, you would get an odd duck who wanted to play in the "O," which was American style and P.M. expiry, making it a bit exotic.

But Del has no idea how big of a fish he has landed. The OEX guy starts trading five thousand, six thousand, eight thousand options at a clip. We are all looking at one another, wondering how a $150 million account trades that size in OEX options.

Del stands up, attracting a lot of attention to himself. "OEX, APRIL 580 CALLS, FIVE THOUSAND UP!"

Marty does a little shuffle around his desk and plays with his mouse. "THREE AT THREE FORTY!"

Del shouts, "I BUY!"

When a salesperson asks a trader for a price on an option, by default he's asking for a two-sided market. This means that the trader must respond with two prices: a price at which the customer can buy, and a price at which the customer can sell. In this case, Marty responded by telling Del that the customer could buy at $3.40 or sell at $3.00. The difference, or spread, is theoretically how the trader makes a profit.

Marty starts hedging with S&P futures. He has a habit of not hedging all at once; he trades in odd lots because he has a paranoia about robots and algorithms and trade sniffers figuring out his trading activity. *Buybuybuybuybuybuybuybuybuybuybuybuybuy.*

This has the effect of making the market run away from him. The machine-gunning of little trades is only pissing off the market. "*Fuck!*" yells Marty.

Del stands up again. "OEX, APRIL 565 PUTS, SEVEN THOU-SAND UP!"

"BUT I HAVEN'T GOTTEN MY HEDGE IN YET!" protests Marty.

"SEVEN THOUSAND UP, MARTY. C'MON!"

Marty figures that the OEX guy is going to sell puts, since he bought calls already, and it's likely that he's going to add to his position. He skews his market a little lower than it should be.

"EIGHTY at TWENTY!"

Del yells back, "I *buy!*"

This guy is chopping himself to bits. So is Marty. He starts hedging again. *Sellsellsellsellsellsellsellsellsellsell.* The market starts to fall out of bed. "FUCK!" Marty yells again.

This goes on all afternoon. People stop what they're doing and stare. Everybody is watching Del and Marty maul each other with puts and calls.

At the end of the day, Del comes around to our desk. Nobody has any idea what their positions are, or what the P&L is. All we know is that we have a big pile of commissions. Marty and Del are standing there, pink and flushed, sweaty, and out of breath.

"You guys look like you just had sex with each other!" I proclaim.

Mark Ricci comes over. "W r y nee to ke back and f re o t at t guy's ive s. ep le y t ade l e this if a d t y ng to m it fast."

He's saying that the OEX guy is a maniac, and we should put a hold on trading with him until we figure out his situation.

A couple of years later, the OEX guy hangs himself in his prison cell. He had stolen money from his hedge fund and was trading up a storm to try to make it back.

We wonder aloud why we didn't take more money out of him while we could.

• • •

In spite of my efforts, our volumes were increasing robustly. Every day it seemed we had new clients who wanted to trade ETFs in bigger and bigger sizes. When I started, we were doing, on average, about a $100,000 a day in commissions. Now we were up to $200,000 a day, and growing.

Part of the attraction of ETFs was that they were a clean way to trade. A trader at a large hedge fund, if he wanted to, could easily trade futures electronically. Point and click. But some of them found it to be a hassle to chase the bids and offers all over the screen. It was easier to pick up the phone and trade one million shares of SPY, the S&P 500 ETF, which basically accomplished the same thing. It was more expensive—we charged three cents a share—but it was more fun than blasting futures. We were the grateful recipients of a great deal of this flow.

Over the past month or two, the market had gradually been turning to poo. People were suddenly fearful of credit. The automakers hadn't been doing well, and there was a great deal of apprehension that the credit rating of one or more of them was going to be downgraded to junk. A ratings downgrade in and of itself doesn't really mean anything, except that certain funds are restricted from buying bonds rated lower than BBB. Once the rating falls below that level, all funds restricted to buying investment-grade securities are forced to sell it. It is a huge liquidity event, and, though we didn't see it at the time, it was a powerful statement on the direction that credit was heading.

When hedge funds run into trouble—when they start losing money on their positions—they have to take action. If they hold a half million shares of a stock that trades a quarter million shares a day, they cannot sell it all at once. But they need to hedge the exposure and immunize the portfolio from risk. So they trade ETFs instead. Our business began to pick up dramatically.

It started when we walked in the door in the morning and didn't let up until we left at the end of the day. It was a constant barrage of trades; with our trading software, the makeshift stuff that Chuck had built, we were falling behind. We had so many trades that we couldn't keep up. We were keeping a mental inventory of what our positions were.

We started to learn that we were inversely correlated with the market:

When stocks were going up, nobody needed to hedge. When stocks fell, people needed to hedge *fast*. People needed to sell, and they didn't care about the price. They needed to *get it in*.

On the day of the downgrade, the selling reached a fever pitch. They sold all day, right up until the last few minutes that the markets were open. Salespeople were yelling at me from across the floor.

*"A million SPYs, how?"*

*"Eighty-one!"*

*"Sold!"*

*"Sell three hundred SPY?"*

*"SPYs, show me a bid on seventy-five!"*

*"Seventy-six!"*

*"Sold!"*

*"SPYs, how now?"*

*"How many?"*

"TWO POINT FIVE MILLION!"

It was Kevin Rodman. He covers The Big One. D.C. and I looked at each other. There were ten seconds left in the day.

"SIXTY-SIX!"

"SOLD!"

I was hammering futures as fast as I could. At this point, all the cash people were standing up and watching what was going on. It was a sell-a-thon, both hands out. In the span of three minutes, we traded almost $1 billion worth of stock.

Suddenly it hit me.

I had been presented with a clear buy signal. *When everyone is selling, you should be buying.*

I bought four hundred mini futures, which was a big trade for me. After the close, the futures began to tick higher and higher.

I turned to Marty. "That was it."

"What was it?"

"That was the low."

"Why?"

"Did you see that? *Everyone* was selling."

Marty shook his head and smiled. He had been told by this point that I was the paranoid lunatic. If you ever want people to listen to what you say on Wall Street, you need to say it calmly. He was, by now, accustomed to my histrionics.

*Fuck it, I'll buy some more.* I added to my position. It was the biggest trade I had ever done. I was now long about $30 million worth of stock. And I was going to hold it overnight, unhedged.

I couldn't sleep—again. My thoughts raced. This trade was going to be the beginning, I thought. I would be the king of Wall Street. I was going to displace Jay Knight. I was going to move to Miami and start a hedge fund. I was going to make $15 million a year.

Then, in other thoughts, I thought about the regulators. They were watching. Only a few months had passed since my fuckup. Were they going to audit that trade? I still hadn't heard anything from the compliance guys. They didn't seem too worried about it. But I was going to be standing tall before the man. I would lose everything and end up working at Starbucks, where I would be happy with a fifty-cent tip.

I spent most of my time alternating between making $15 million and working at Starbucks. I thought that either of these outcomes was equally probable. I thought that either of those outcomes was the process of rational thought.

I was at it again. My mind was racing; I knew every chart of every index in the world. I had memorized all the news in the market. I knew what stocks were going up and what stocks were going down. I could *feel* the market. My muscles tensed, my neck hurt, and I could smell myself; I had been too preoccupied to shower. My wedding band was tight.

The next morning, the market was up nine points. I declared victory and sold my position. I had made $180,000—my biggest futures trade yet.

"You see that shit?" I asked D.C. in between bites of a bacon, egg, and cheese. "Hundred and eighty large. Booyah."

D.C. was looking at me funny.

Almost immediately, I experienced regret. The market lurched higher in the morning, to up thirteen handles on the day. It was a slow, gradual rally, as everyone who had sold the day before was gradually being sucked back in.

I couldn't bear to watch. I thought it was going higher, but I was powerless to buy more, having already exited the trade.

A disembodied voice came out of the government hoot: "STOCKS!"

Everyone was all smiles. Mark Ricci was backslapping with his two lieutenants, John, a former DEA agent, and Vivek, an options whiz. Chuck came over from swaps to laugh it up. Spike was playing his animal noises over the hoot. Even Chandler, exiled to options, was smiling. The market had been spared execution. Everyone was happy, except for me.

If I had held on to my position, I would have made $700,000.

Suddenly Marty had all the answers. "You know what your problem is? You trade too small."

"Come again?"

"You trade too small. In my entire career, I have never seen someone as right about the market as you. Your batting average has to be close to eighty percent. But you trade piker size."

"I know." It was true. "And I take profits too early."

"You need to trade bigger. Double your position size. Quadruple it. And don't take profits right away, let them run. Better yet, *add* to your positions when they are winners."

"I know."

"You can't get rich by cutting your winners."

"I know."

Marty was turning out to be a good boss. He was right. I *was* a piker, a cautious gambler. I was right about market direction more than anyone else I knew, and I was making very little money on it. I should be crushing it.

Piker. If the shoe fits, wear it.

*Piker.*


If I had held on to my position for the day, I would have made $700,000. If I had held on to it for a week, I would have made millions. If I had held on to it for six months, I would have been Jay Knight.

The market ignored the auto downgrades and marched higher in the spring of 2005. That wasn't the interesting part; the interesting part was *how* it marched higher. It moved, on average, less and less each day. The *volatility* of the market declined.

In finance, volatility is an important concept to understand, because it dictates how options are priced. If, say, GE is at $20, and you own the $25 strike call options, you think that the stock will go above $25 within a certain period of time. But if volatility is low, there is a smaller chance of that happening than if volatility is high. When volatility is high, things move around a lot. When things move around a lot, they have a higher chance of making an option go *in the money.*

Volatility dictates the price of an option. If volatility is high, you will pay more for the option, which is said to have a high *implied volatility.* But since the volatility of the market was decreasing, since it was moving less and less each day, nobody wanted to buy options anymore; they wanted to sell them. Options on stocks, on futures, on indices were getting cheaper and cheaper.

For options traders, this can sometimes be problematic. It is generally true that most people, most customers, and most hedge funds buy options rather than sell them. When banks like Lehman Brothers sell options, they are said to be *short* volatility; they don't want the market to move around very much. They would prefer that it stays still. But as options get cheaper and cheaper, banks are not getting compensated very much to protect against what could be a very large move. When you sell cheap options, you are asking for trouble.

We blamed the French. There was a rumor going around the desk that the French banks booked all the profit for selling the option at the time of the sale; they did not amortize it over the life of the option. The more options they sold, the more money they made.

Spychalski tried to illustrate the point: "Remember the *Simpsons* episode where Homer has to press the button at the nuclear power plant every day to make sure they didn't have a meltdown?"

"Uh, no."

"Come *on*, that was the best episode ever! Homer gets lazy and doesn't feel like pushing the button anymore, so he gets the Incredible Drinking Bird to do it."

"What the hell are you talking about?"

"You've never seen the Incredible Drinking Bird?"

"No."

Spychalski immediately turned to his computer and logged onto eBay to buy an Incredible Drinking Bird. Within a week, it arrived.

"You've never seen this before?" Spike was holding a test-tube-shaped bird with red tail feathers and a blue hat with a green feather on it. It had googly eyes.

"Never."

"It's like a perpetual motion machine. You put it next to a glass of water, and you dip the beak in the water. The water evaporates off the beak, and does some chemical shit that makes the bird stand up again. Eventually, it starts to get heavy, and it dips back down. It will go on forever."

"So?"

"So! This is going to be the sell vol bird. I'm going to put it next to my keyboard, and it can hit the sell vol key all day. I'll be a millionaire."

"Ha! Let me try that thing."

I had a Bernie Williams pencil holder cup with the number 51 on it, which I got for free at a Yankees game. I went to the bathroom, filled it with water, and set up the Incredible Drinking Bird. Sure enough, it worked.

"Isn't it great?"

It was great. It proved what I had suspected about markets all along: you didn't have to be smart to make money; all you needed was the Incredible Drinking Bird. Buy stocks. Sell vol. It will work forever.

Everything was going up.

It wasn't just the markets. It seemed like everyone, everywhere, had money. My esteemed colleagues were spending hundreds of dollars to get into restaurants and clubs, where there were waiting lists of weeks or months. They were spending thousands more on strippers. Apartment prices in the city, and house prices in the suburbs, began to skyrocket. There was, in case anyone hadn't noticed, a housing bubble.

Sitting among the sales guys were two characters who were the liaison to what we called PCS. It stood for private client services, which meant, essentially, rich people. There were some people who had so much money that we treated them in the same way that we would treat a hedge fund or other institution. One of them was Morton Baxter.

Baxter, a secretive septuagenarian, had started out with $25 million, which is a lot of money under any circumstances. He had turned it into

$250 million through his investments in homebuilder stocks, which he bought lustily, along with call options. Spychalski was on the receiving end of all of his trades.

Spike didn't appreciate any of it. Options have something called gamma, which means that if you own it, you don't necessarily care whether homebuilder stocks go up or down; you just want them to move a lot. But by selling these options to Baxter, Spychalski had gotten himself short quite a bit of homebuilder gamma, which meant that he wanted the stocks to stand still. They didn't. They kept going up and up, forcing Spychalski to buy stock at higher and higher prices to hedge.

I, personally, took a dim view of the homebuilders. I had, at one point, sold short a basket of them, only to get stopped out of my trade a week later. These stocks were animals. They were a bubble, to be sure. I couldn't understand how anyone couldn't see that. Take a trip outside of New York, where land is scarce and developments were going up all over the place. It was a clear case of overinvestment, and you couldn't drive anywhere without seeing billboards for mortgage bankers offering low, low rates.

Then there was the thing known as the negative amortization mortgage. Otherwise known as an option ARM, this was an adjustable rate mortgage that allowed the borrower to dictate the terms of the payment. He had to pay back the interest, but paying back the principal was optional. If he didn't, he had to pay it back later. And anything he didn't pay back was added to the balance of the mortgage, meaning it amortized negatively—he could owe more than the house was worth. I began to see that option ARMs, combined with down payments approaching zero, meant trouble.

How much trouble, I wasn't sure. I was concerned only with the first-order effects: that is, what it meant for homebuilder stocks. I thought they were going to go down. They kept going up. We could not be reconciled.

One day, though, homebuilder stocks stopped going up. They lurched lower.

Even if I hadn't been watching the stocks, I would have been able to tell, because Randy Clarke kept hanging around Spychalski's desk. Randy was the PCS sales guy and managed Morton Baxter's trades.

Suddenly all the options that he had rolled up premium neutral were about to finish out of the money. If these stocks didn't start going up again, and soon, Baxter was going to get a margin call. Unbelievably, he owed more to Lehman Brothers than his stocks were worth.

Spychalski had waited months for this. He was sharpening his knives, waiting for Baxter to puke his positions.

Eventually he did. Millions of shares of stock and tens of thousands of options were being sold into the market at fire-sale prices. Clarke, with this thick *Noo Yawk* accent, was barking out orders to Spychalski, who sat there dumbly.

"What's the matter?" I asked.

"I can't take the other side of any of these trades," he said. "Strict orders. Mark Ricci. Worried about liability or something. All I can do is hit the bid."

I shuddered.

"What kind of liability?"

"Beats me, but we are giving away free money to these scumbag hedge funds."

Sure enough, calls were coming in from across the trading floor to sift through the wreckage of Baxter's busted trades. They were buying steadily on the way down, and putting in offsetting orders for market on close. In stocks, and in all markets for that matter, when there is a liquidity event—when a major player is forced out of the market—it is usually profitable to take the other side of his trades. Baxter, the housing market's most leveraged player, was the first to suffer the consequences.

There was that noise again. I had heard it back in 2002: that aircraft engine noise that the market makes when it is cratering. There was a whoosh of orders, a chorus of yelling and screaming, a flurry of activity that accompanies someone getting carried out.

Baxter got rinsed. He had turned his $25 million into $250 million and back to $25 million again. Round-trip.

I was thinking about Spychalski being unable to trade. *Legal. Regulators. Someone is watching.*

The worst part of my day was dealing with EFP brokers.

There are all different kinds of brokers. When most people think of the word *broker*, they usually think of a retail stockbroker, the local yokel who handles trades for people in town. But there is such a thing as an interdealer broker, otherwise known as a "broker's broker," who brokers trades *between banks*.

Sometimes banks have to trade not just with the public, with hedge funds, and with mutual funds, but with one another. It is a lot easier to trade with another bank if there is an intermediary. The interdealer broker knows everyone at all the relevant banks, knows who wants to buy and who wants to sell, and can match up trades. For my purposes, I needed to be able to trade EFPs.

An EFP is an exchange for physical. It's a concept that is well known in the futures industry; it means that you are swapping the futures contract for the underlying commodity. In my case, I was sometimes swapping out stock index futures for the underlying baskets of stock, or vice versa. The reasons for doing this are complex. Sometimes I simply had too much stock on my balance sheet and needed to get rid of it, trading it for futures. Sometimes I had a particular view on interest rates or dividends. And sometimes I was bored, and lonely, and I traded an EFP just to make the broker happy.

The broker was happy because he got paid on a per-contract basis: if the trade was five hundred futures contracts, and he got paid $2 a contract, that was $1,000 from me and $1,000 from the counterparty—not bad for a day's work. His overhead was low: literally, a telephone and a Bloomberg, so for him it was all free cash flow. It was true that most brokers are overpaid, but I did not envy them in the least. They had to make outgoing calls to grumpy, pissed-off ETF traders all day.

I had two brokers: a neurotic named Ronnie and a laid-back creature of New Jersey named Andy. They were at war with each other. There were two big brokers in EFPs, and they were constantly fighting it out for market share. If I traded with Andy, I got angry phone calls from Ronnie. If I traded with Ronnie, I got angry phone calls from Andy. I stopped taking their calls. I had caller ID, and I could see their phone numbers light up, and I ignored them, watching the light on my turret blink over and over again. They were infuriating, and they were both probably making more money than me.

I was picking a hangnail, ripping the skin away from my finger and watching the blood well up, then run down my hand, when the phone rang. It was not a phone number that I recognized. I answered it.

"Lehman."

"Is this Jared?"

"Yes."

"This is Jason, from Forward Markets. You have a second?"

"Yes."

"I'm Jason. I'm from a broker that's based in the UK, and we're looking at building up a presence in equity derivatives in the US. I'm going to be covering EFPs. You interested in getting out sometime?"

"Actually, yes." I was sick of Ronnie and Andy. Anything was better than this.

"See you at Bryant Park tomorrow night?"

"Okay. See you by the bar."

I was going to get free drinks out of this—my favorite. Delicious Maker's and ginger. Fantastic.

It was a fucking gorgeous day; one of the best days I had ever seen in New York City. I hadn't been to Bryant Park in the afternoon. Yes, it was the usual Wall Street douchebag crowd, but there was something else: the women were phenomenal. There was a ridiculous amount of ass here. My philosophy was that it didn't matter where I got my appetite, as long as I came home to eat.

"Jared?"

"How did you recognize me?"

"I had an idea of what to look for."

All pissed-off ETF traders look alike.

Jason was handsome as hell. I fell in love with him. Three inches taller than me, with a muscular neck and a broad smile, he was unlike anything you would ever see in New York. New Yorkers look at the ground and sulk. He held his head high and smiled. He looked like a winner. More accurately, he looked lucky; like someone who fell ass-backward into pussy on a daily basis. This was going to be good.

"What are you having?"

"An extra-large Maker's Mark and ginger ale."

Within seconds, he'd navigated the bar and produced a bucket of the delicious stuff.

"You're not from around here," I said.

"No, I'm from L.A."

"What are you doing here?"

"I actually used to be an energy broker—did most of my time in natural gas—and I'm switching over to equities."

"Why?"

Before he had a chance to answer, two blondes materialized next to us. Rather, they materialized next to Jason. Blondes never materialize next to me.

"What's up, guys?" He was all smiles.

The blondes turned out to be pharmaceutical sales reps. One was outgoing, with a freckled neck, drinking beer and laughing like a lumberjack, *haw haw haw*. The other was cute as hell and sipped chardonnay silently, peering over her glass at Jason. They were—in the strictest definition of the term—cougars. But they were friendly.

The conversation was inane; rather, I have no ability to participate in inane conversation. I find the business of selling pharmaceuticals to be interesting, if a little smarmy, and I was getting a charge out of listening to the blondes talk about how they seduce doctors into buying their shit. But I was lost in thought about work, my trades, and when the regulators were going to come and get me, which I figured should be any day now.

For a brief moment in time, though, I managed to be completely present. I could taste the Maker's and ginger, I could feel the sun on the back of my neck, I could see the pretty faces, I was just the right amount of buzzed, and for once it felt good to be a trader. Being a trader should mean that I get free, delicious drinks and access to hot females. For a moment, life did not suck.

Then I looked at Jason and I was filled with envy. *Sex comes easy to this guy*, I thought. *All he has to do is stand there, and he is flocked with women. I am medium handsome, but I am a brooding loner; I am as unapproachable as you can get. Smiling requires great effort and feels contrived. This bastard can get laid on command. I hate myself.*

It was suggested that we head somewhere downtown. The blondes had a car. I was, by this point, fully loaded, and volunteered to sit in the backseat, in between Jason and a human drool bucket.

"Who's this guy?" I asked the blondes.

"He's a doctor."

The doctor's head was drooping low, bobbing. He was wasted, letting out soft belches. "Surgeon, actually," he managed.

"One of your clients?"

"Yes. Honey, you have surgery tomorrow?"

Drunk doctor nodded.

Soon we arrived at another bar, filled with people. There were colors and lights and lots of laughing. Loud music. I was fucked up. There were leis hanging from the ceiling, and someone put one around my neck. I smiled for a picture with Jason. I pushed my way back to the bathroom to drain the lizard, and in doing so, I lost track of the pretty blondes. They were gone. Jason was here, though, and he had plans.

We went off to a club called Duvet. There was a velvet rope and a long line. Jason knew the bouncer, and we were inside.

There were beds.

Duvet. Bed. I get it. There was a long bar, and people were sitting on beds, chatting. Jason and I found one and sat. Within seconds, he was surrounded by women.

One was a pixie brunette who said that her husband worked at Morgan Stanley. Her friend looked dangerous.

Jason departed with the pixie. I was left with Dangerous.

We were Dangerously close.

Jason returned and tackled Dangerous. She rolled him over on the bed, kissing him. He reached around and—

—and began to finger-bang her through her jeans.

*This is too bad.*

I grabbed my bag and headed out into the summer air.

*Fucking bastard.*

I was dangerously close to an affair. I didn't want to have an affair, but I wanted *her* to want to. Instead my broker, the sperminator, swooped in and molested her.

I threw my bag on the ground, and started kicking it, with futility. I kicked it all the way up Seventh Avenue for at least ten blocks.

That is all.

• • •

I should have known better. When I go out, I lose time—wide spaces of time, gone forever. I had no recollection of what happened. The last I remembered, I was kicking my bag up Seventh Avenue.

The next morning, I arrive at my desk. It is covered in brown liquid.

*What the fuck?*

I try to piece together what happened. I find a tipped-over bottle of soy sauce. Who the fuck spilled soy sauce on my desk?

My computer is on.

*Oh no.*

I look at my futures terminal in horror and disgust. This didn't happen. This can't be happening.

In a blackout, I had come back to Lehman Brothers, logged onto Bloomberg, read some articles on Japan, checked the Nikkei, and did Lord knows what else.

I am pretty sure that you can get in trouble for coming back to work drunk.

Of course, the firm's security system would have registered me coming in at midnight.

And the security cameras would have seen me at my desk.

*People are watching.*

## 12

# Everything Is Not Going to Be OK | Winter 2006

FM: JARED DILLIAN, LEHMAN BROTHERS INC.

TO: SALES

I ONCE MET A TRADER FROM AN ANTIQUE LAND

WHO SAID: THE CARRY TRADE, ONCE MADE OF STONE

STANDS IN THE DESERT. NEAR IT ON THE SAND,

HALF SUNK, A SHATTERED DOLLAR LIES, FALLEN DOWN,

WHOSE INFLATION AND SNEERS FROM THE SOUTH AFRICAN RAND

TELL THAT ITS CREATOR WELL THOSE PASSIONS READ

WHICH YET SURVIVE, HOUSES, CONDOS, AND THINGS

THE FED WHICH MOCKED THEM AND THE BUBBLE IT FED

AND ON THE PEDESTAL THESE WORDS APPEAR:

"MY NAME IS GREENSPAN, KING OF KINGS:

LOOK ON MY WORKS, YE MARKET, AND DESPAIR!"

NOTHING BESIDE REMAINS: ROUND THE DECAY

OF THAT COLOSSAL WRECK, WHERE VOL SELLERS DARED,

THE WASTELAND OF P&L STRETCHES FAR AWAY.

"Are you insane?"

I laughed.

"No, I'm serious, have you completely lost your mind? Shelley in Bloomberg messages?" Marty thought that I had finally lost the dots on my dice. D.C. was laughing his fool head off. A buzz was propagating across the floor, as people read my creation.

I was at it again. I had a head full of poetry, and I was up all night the night before, thinking of a way to adapt "Ozymandias" into a Bloomberg message. I was happy with the results.

My in-box was filling up with mail, half of it cheering me on, half of it wondering from which asylum I had escaped.

I was pleased.

Comp day.

I never understood what everyone was so worried about. I had plenty of things to worry about, and one of them was *not* how much I was going to get paid. No matter what I got paid, it was going to be enough. I had fallen just short of $300,000 last year, and it had been more money than I could ever expect to see in my life. Of course, I hadn't done anything with it; I had just saved it, you know, just in case. I had lived through one bear market, barely, and while I figured myself to be a survivor, there was no telling what would happen the next time around. I needed a cushion.

Comp day is the worst day of the year. Nobody does any work on comp day; nobody puts on any trades, nobody makes outgoing calls. Everyone just sits, staring at the screens, waiting for his name to be called, to go into a back office. A certain lifelessness descends on the floor. In good years, most people are unhappy. In bad years, nearly everyone is unhappy. This had been a good year, relatively speaking; the first good year since the bull market several years ago. Lehman Brothers had been killing it, fixed income had been killing it, mortgages had been killing it, and even equities had been killing it. It was the sweet spot for financial markets. Everyone was making money.

Still, there is often a gap between what people think they are worth and what they are actually worth. Sometimes that gap is dictated by the market. If a cash equities trader is worth $500,000, even if he is exceptionally good, it is hard to argue that he should be paid $1 million no matter how much money he makes or how much business he brings to the firm. People on the customer side of the business, like me, are tethered to market-dictated replacement-cost prices. People on the proprietary side of the business, like Jay Knight, have no such restrictions. If they were to leave, the money wouldn't make itself. If *I* were to leave, Lehman would inevitably find someone capable to take my place.

I was determined not to get involved. I had come from a lower-middle-class upbringing, wearing secondhand clothes and narrowly missing the school's free lunch program. For my grandmother to give me two quarters to go play video games was a very big deal. If she was feeling rich, she would give me a third quarter. That was how it went—not quite poor, not quite middle class. No matter what the outcome was, I was going to walk away from this discussion a lot richer than I was before.

I was sitting in an office with Mark Ricci. I was three feet away from him and still couldn't hear what the fuck he was saying. "Y'v d a fan ob this year," he began, and I was not the least bit nervous. All these other jerks had spent the last month tying themselves up in knots, trying to angle for more money. I figured that if I did my job, good things would happen.

I was right.

"Last year, your total compensation was two hundred seventy-five thousand dollars, and this year it will be six hundred fifty thousand dollars."

*What?*

Mark slid a piece of paper across the table toward me.

$650,000.

*That is an insane amount of money.*

"I assume you're happy with the results."

"*Oh* yeah. This is great." $650,000.

*What the hell am I going to do with all this money?*

I had heard stories of people going bananas with their newfound wealth. People spent money like they were going to the electric chair and found themselves with debt problems. That wasn't going to be me. I was going to save this bonus, just like I had saved all the other bonuses. There were things I wanted to do with it, for sure. I wanted to buy some gold. But beyond that, this was getting squirreled away.

I walked out of the office not feeling my feet. I couldn't hear the noise of the trading floor; I walked past the rows of desks, past the televisions, past the sliding tickers, to Kevin Rodman's desk. Kevin, or K-Rod, was the best sales trader at the firm. He knew how to read people, how to empathize, how to make a joke, and how to extract a trade. He knew how to read body language and inflection. He had copious people skills.

He looked at me. "Good number?"

"How did you know?"

"You're *glowing*, that's how I know. You look like you just spotted yourself. That's cool, you deserve it."

"What about you?"

"Haven't had it yet." He left it at that; we both knew he'd had a good year.

I returned to my desk. Before I had a chance to sit, Rodman yelled over, "A million SPYs, how?"

I fumbled. I was lost in space, thinking about all my money, and I hadn't looked at my screens.

"Immediate!" he said.

"Ten, fourteen!"

"*Sold!*"

Suddenly, the market lurched lower. Phones were ringing, everywhere. Something had happened somewhere in the world, and I did not know what it was. I had been *picked off*.

"GODDAMMIT, MOTHERFUCKER!" I punch the turret, cracking the screen, spraying droplets of blood all over my desk. "NICE FUCKING PICKOFF!"

*Beep!*

I picked up the phone. It was Rodman.

"Dude, are you bipolar or something?"

"What?"

"Are you bipolar?"

"I don't even know what that means."

"One minute, you're flying, you're as happy as you can be, and the next minute, you want to kill someone. I have never seen mood swings like that before."

"I'm a trader."

"Dude, you need to get yourself checked out. It's not normal."

He hung up.

I knew it was not normal. I just didn't know what to do about it.

Shortly thereafter. Delete, delete, delete.

Every day, my in-box filled up with crap. It filled up with research, which was crap, it filled up with human resources stuff, which was crap, and it filled up with stuff from the back-office guys, which was crap. I spent at least twenty minutes a day deleting crap. Then, I saw this one:

ATTN: NYSE REGULATORY INQUIRY #81A90

The bottom dropped out.

My heart raced as I opened the email.

The NYSE Surveillance Division is opening an inquiry into the following trades:

B CAT 65 54.01
B CAT 131 54.01

Summary trade data is provided in the attachments.

Please provide the following information:

The name and date of the baskets;
Whether the program trades were firm or agency, and
Please provide an explanation of the strategy.

Please provide this information by the close of business tomorrow.

Jim Matson Esq
Legal Counsel

This is it.

I had no idea what these trades were. "D.C., I need you to take a look at something for me."

He looked over my shoulder as I opened the attachment. There were hundreds of executions, with the CAT trades highlighted.

"Doesn't look like a big deal."

"But what the hell trade was this?"

"I can't remember."

"Me either." I was sweating.

Great: we were getting an inquiry on some of our trades, and we couldn't even remember what the hell they were. I was definitely going to jail.

I gathered that it was a basket of S&P 500 stock, so it had to be a SPY trade. I looked at the time of executions; they were first thing in the morning, so they had to be market on open trades. But the trade was from a year ago—I couldn't possibly remember what the context was.

"Do you remember doing any kind of market on open trades about a year ago?"

"Sure, we used to do cash open for Red Hills all the time, remember?"

*Oh yeah.* "Ahh, I remember."

"So that's it. Reply to the email and tell them what the trade was."

"Is it firm or agency?"

"Well, it was for a customer."

"But the basket is marked firm."

"So tell them firm."

"But it was for a customer."

"So tell them agency."

"Dude."

"I don't know, tell them both. Call up the lawyer and explain it to him. It's not a big deal."

"It *is* a big deal."

"Why is it a big deal?"

"Don't you remember that compliance lecture? These guys can take your livelihood away. Or worse."

"Stop."

"I'm *serious.*"

"Stop. This is not a big deal. Call up the lawyer and ask him what it's about. Right now you are getting worried about nothing."

*Goddamn it.*

I called the lawyer.

"Jim speaking."

"Hey, this is Jared from the second floor."

"Hey, Jared."

"I just got this email from you about the inquiry."

"Okay, did you have some questions?"

"Well, first of all, is this a big deal?"

"Probably not. We get these inquiries from the exchange all the time. We probably get fifty of them over the course of the year. We talk to the traders, we get the information, and we give it to the exchange. Forty-nine times out of fifty it turns out to be nothing."

"What about the fiftieth time?"

"Well, then it leads to something else."

"Like what?"

"Look, there's no reason to get concerned about this right now. All the exchange is doing is looking for information. This might not even be the focal point of the investigation; they might be trying to get information for another investigation. It could be anything. It could be insider trading, it could be an exchange rule. We just don't know. And chances are that we'll never know; I submit these to the exchange, and most of the time I never hear back. It just goes away."

"If you were to hear something, how long would it take?"

"Three months, six months, it all depends."

"You don't know."

"I don't know."

*I am in deep shit.*

"You sound worried. Look, there's nothing to be worried about. This is probably nothing. Just send me back the email, and everything is going to be fine."

That morning on the way to work, I had walked by a movie poster for *A Scanner Darkly*. The tagline read, "Everything Is Not Going to Be OK."

I identified strongly with that.

What the hell could the exchange possibly want with two odd-lot CAT trades? I didn't see how this could possibly have anything to do with me. I put down a basket of stock, market on open. I put it down well before the open. I got executed. I got my fills back. What was this about?

Maybe it is a fishing expedition. Maybe they are trying to get me to slip up, so they can come in and investigate my other trades. Maybe they'll find my other Rule 92 violation. Who knows what they will come up with?

I wrote in my email that the basket was marked "firm," but that it was actually "agency." Could that have been confusing? Could that have opened up the door to the regulators? It said, Is it agency, or is it firm? I had given them a half-assed answer. What if they needed to talk to me more?

I had heard about depositions, on-the-record interviews. Two regulators come in and put down a tape recorder in front of you. This is not the criminal justice system; you are not afforded the same legal protections against self-incrimination. You have to answer every question, and answer it truthfully. If you refuse to answer a question, they can revoke your license. Guys had to go down to the exchange, in their suits, in the morning, and give testimony. It was the worst experience of their lives. Some of them had narrowly missed regulatory action.

I guessed that maybe a third of my colleagues had been caught up in some regulatory problem at one point or another. It wasn't that everyone I worked with was a crook; quite the contrary. It is just that working at a large investment bank, it is easy to get tangled up in conflicts. I learned that most of what happened in the regulatory arena had less to do with the letter and the spirit of the law and more to do with people feeling wronged in one way or another, and reporting it to the authorities. When you are playing with big trades, big tickets, sometimes people get their feelings hurt. Then they go tell on you.

The odds of me escaping standing tall before the man over the course of a long trading career were very slim indeed, which I was slowly beginning to realize. If something did happen, though, I wouldn't be walking into a hearing armed with a peashooter. The firm employed dozens of lawyers who helped keep the traders—and, more importantly, the firm—out of trouble. If you were acting in good faith, the firm could be expected to back you up. But if you were a lone wolf, the firm was going to hang you out to dry.

It all seemed so horribly unfair. How was I supposed to remember a trade that I did a year ago? A few hundred shares of stock out of the millions and millions of shares that I traded every day?

I was walking home in the cold. I was drowning in fear. Fear, which turned into pain, which I felt in every cell of my body. How was I going to make it for the next six months? How was I going to live knowing that every day could be my last on a trading floor?

I didn't want to stick around to see how this turned out.

As I walked up the hill to my house, I saw a car parked in front of it. Inside was a man wearing a suit. He was reading a newspaper. As I walked by, he appeared not to notice me until I had passed his quarter, at which point he turned.

I hurried up the steps and opened the door, locking it behind me.

I pushed aside the blinds. The man was looking at me.

I closed the blinds.

I was staring at the screens, paralyzed with fear.

"Hey Needman," said D.C. "what the hell happened to you?"

I looked up. It was Needman, our back-office guy. He looked like he had received a prison beating. He had a black eye, cuts all over his face, and a divot in his head.

"Uh, I fell down."

"Well, we all know you got your ass kicked, so you need to come up with a better story than that."

Needman meekly took our tickets and headed back upstairs.

Chuck comes over. "Did you see that guy? What happened to him?"

"He 'fell down,'" says D.C.

Chuck is smiling. "It looks like he went to a shovel fight and forgot to bring his shovel."

I try, and fail, to smile. It has been a week. Twenty-five more weeks to go.

I look over at Spychalski. He looks like he is asleep.

"What's going on?"

He pulls up a chart of some stock that had gone straight up. "50 Cent."

"What's that?" (Spychalski named all his stocks after rappers.)

"They got taken out. I was short calls."

"What's the damage?"

Spychalski shrugs. "About six million."

"*Six million?*"

This, coming from a guy who would flip out over ten grand, pound the desk, rip off his tie, and throw it in the trash can. Six million dollars is incomprehensible. It is too big to be pissed off at. He has given up.

"Let me talk to you for a second," he says, motioning toward the end of the aisle. "This is a problem."

"Why?"

"Every month these guys would come in and roll their calls out, on a calendar spread. I kept waiting for it this month—nothing. They didn't roll. Why? Because they knew it was going to get taken out."

"So?"

"So I'm thinking about calling the cops."

This is the last thing I need.

"Why, because they didn't roll their position?"

"Yeah."

"You can't really hang your hat on that."

"Dude, I was short gamma out the wazoo. This is fucking catastrophic. I am going to get fired."

"You're not going to get fired," I insist. "That's ridiculous. You're supposed to facilitate customers. This is going to happen every once in a while."

"I have a bid in on a one-stick house. Better go tell the wife that we can't buy it."

Everyone wants to call the cops on everyone. Lose money, it is someone else's problem. I don't like how this is shaping up.

A few weeks later, the phone rang. It was a number I didn't recognize.

"Hello?"

No answer.

The number had flashed for a second before I picked it up. It was an 860 area code, but I didn't memorize the rest of the number. I knew 860 to be Connecticut. But who would be calling me from Connecticut?

Well, the New York Stock Exchange wouldn't be calling me from Connecticut. Maybe it was the NASD. I looked online to see if the NASD had a field office there, and I couldn't find anything. Then it occurred to me that it might be suspicious if I was looking up NASD offices, so I deleted my web history. I vowed never to use the internet ever again at work.

*Maybe it was a lawyer*, I thought—some lawyer that the NASD had contracted out. And then, in another thought:

*Maybe it was the FBI.*

Surely the FBI had field offices in Connecticut. I cursed myself for not remembering the number; if I had, I could do a reverse phone lookup and see who was calling me.

But why would they call me and then hang up? Well, to see if I was there, I suppose. Why would they just call my number to see if I was there?

*Maybe they are coming to get me.*

I looked at the clock. There was an hour left in the day.

I started packing my shit.

"Where are you going?" asked D.C.

"Doctor's appointment."

"You didn't tell me about a doctor's appointment."

"Just remembered."

"You looking for a job?"

"No. And there's no doctor's appointment. I'm just getting the fuck out of here."

"Why?"

"If anyone comes looking for me, tell them I'm not coming back."

"What?"

"See you later."

And with that, I was out onto the sidewalk with the street vendors.

I was filled with fear. What good was leaving early going to do? *If the FBI comes, and you're not there, they're just going to go to your house, if they're not there already.*

*Now you're being ridiculous. The FBI isn't looking for you over a few hundred shares of CAT.*

*Just because I'm paranoid doesn't mean they're not out to get me.*

I walked up the hill to my house. The man in the car was there again. This time he was talking into a cell phone.

*Don't look.*

He wasn't looking at me.

*Don't look.*

I went upstairs, into the house, getting the mail out of the mailbox.

I pushed aside the blinds and looked.

We made eye contact.

I dropped to my knees.

My heart was pounding through my chest, so hard that I could hear it. This couldn't be a coincidence, seeing the same man in front of my house two nights in a row. He was clearly staking out my house. I cursed myself for not looking to see if there were any communications vans on the street, with antennae sticking out. I resolved not to use the phone or the computer, in case the car could pick up the signal.

I went upstairs with the mail. It was the usual pile of bills and credit card applications, with one exception: something from something called Market Research. I opened it, revealing a letter from Karen Smith of Northbrook, Illinois, with a survey asking my opinion on a variety of financial publications.

*How did they get my name and address?*

*This is it,* I thought: first the NASD, and now the FBI. They were trying to get me to fill out something so I would leave my fingerprints on the page, then send it back to them. Clearly this was a shell company that was set up by the feds to try to get me to incriminate myself.

I threw it in the trash, then thought better of it. *Might need that,* I thought.

The next morning, I went into work armed with the letter. I hadn't eaten in days.

I started searching on Google for Market Research of Northbrook, Illinois. There was nothing—not a thing. I knew it was a sham.

Then I had an idea. I started looking up addresses adjacent to Market Research, LLC.

Bingo.

Moore & Feldstein. Attorneys. In the suite next door. I called them.

"Moore and Feldstein."

"Hello, I'm calling from New York. Do you by chance work next door to Market Research?"

"Yes, they're right down the hall."

"What do they do?"

"Well, it's not really 'they,' it's just Karen Smith; she runs the business by herself. She outsources marketing activities from bigger companies."

"What kind of companies?"

"Well, I know she works with the *Wall Street Journal*. What is this all about?"

"How well do you know her?"

"I know her very well. She's a nice lady."

"You're sure she does marketing."

"Yes, quite sure. What is this about?"

"I got a piece of correspondence from her yesterday. It was very unusual. I was wondering how she got my information."

"I'm sure it's all very aboveboard."

"She doesn't work for the FBI?"

He laughed. "Not to my knowledge. I think I would know." He added, "You have a very active imagination."

"Okay, thanks."

I hung up.

I was glad that Lehman Brothers didn't record its lines like most banks do.

I tried to come up with the worst-case scenario.

I knew that if I was found guilty of breaking some exchange rules, I could be fined, censured, suspended, or barred from the industry. I figured that it would probably be the latter. But what if it went criminal? What if it violated some antifraud statute? I spent hours at work looking up federal law, breaking my promise not to use the Internet at work. I was leaving a trail of evidence they could use to convict me. I finally found that I could be sent to prison for twenty-five years.

When I thought of prison, I got pain in my bowels. I wouldn't do well in prison. Effete banker snobs do not do well in prison. There was an economist at a rival bank that had been sent away for insider trading to a very rough medium-security prison. It had shown up on the news that his lawyer was begging—yes, begging—the judge for him to be sent to a different prison.

Why did prison have to be so inhospitable? Why couldn't the authorities spend money on increasing security so that assault and rape wouldn't happen? I would serve a sentence if I knew I would be left alone. Maybe I could ask to be left in isolation instead of living with the general

population. I knew what would happen, then. I had seen *25th Hour.*
Edward Norton had told me. They would knock out my teeth so I could
give frictionless blowjobs. As soon as they turned out the lights at night,
that's it. I could deal with having a cellmate, but if I got stuck in one of
those prisons where it's row after row of bunk beds, I would be doomed.

What would I do in prison? Would I work out? Would I be forced to
join a gang? Would I have to undergo a gang initiation? Would I have to
kill someone? I knew what would happen: I wouldn't have the stomach
to do any of those things, and I would be gangless, a stateless vessel,
subject to everyone's jurisdiction. I might as well not eat, go on a hunger
strike, and let them put me in the hospital. Maybe I could attempt suicide and be sent to a mental ward instead. Hell, maybe I could actually
commit suicide and get it over with.

"You okay?"

D.C. was looking at me.

I had ravaged one of my fingernails, and blood was pooling on the
desk.

"I'm fine."

"You look terrible. You sure everything is okay?"

"Fine, really."

D.C., for the moment, was satisfied. But I felt his eyes on me. I had
been lifeless lately. Instead of ranting and raving, screaming and yelling,
pounding the desk and threatening to kill clients, I had sat helpless to
do anything but watch the screens. I knew that he knew something was
wrong. I knew I could trust D.C.; I knew he hadn't been wired by the
feds, but I didn't think he would be capable of understanding the inten-
sity of the fear that I was experiencing. He thought that this was no big
deal, the regulatory thing. He had long since forgotten about it, while I
walked, shoulders hunched, eyes hollow, feeling hunted. They were closing in, and I could feel it.

My clothes were falling off of me. I had made a conscious effort to lose
weight ever since a client dinner in Connecticut where I was forced to
unbuckle my belt in the backseat of a town car afterward. But now the
pounds were disappearing. I was literally sublimating. I wasn't hungry,
ever. I didn't eat breakfast, I didn't eat lunch, I would have a few bites for
dinner, and consume the rest of my calories in alcohol. I had taken to

filling my plastic cups halfway with Bacardi, halfway with Diet Coke, and sitting and watching television, getting slowly stoned. I spent my days at work paralyzed with fear, going home as quickly as I could so that I could make it disappear. And I was sleeping. I slept to escape. I used to want to spend every hour awake; I could not get enough of life. Now, instead of life, there was only pain. Any time spent asleep was time free from pain.

It was February. My wife wanted to go grocery shopping.

An impatient, sudden realization hit me: they were coming. I knew they were coming. I could hear the car doors slamming outside. One, then two, then three. I heard the voices. They were talking on their radios. They had guns. They had handcuffs.

"Are you okay?" my wife asked.

I fell to the ground, clutched my knees, and began to sob.

"What's wrong?"

They were right outside, now. They were wearing dark sunglasses. There were six of them, maybe eight. There would be no escape. There was nowhere to run.

I cried louder, heaving, snot running out of my nose onto the hardwood floors.

"What's the matter? Get up!"

I could hear them breaking down the door. It slammed once, then twice. They couldn't open it.

They were coming through the windows now. They were crashing through. I heard the glass around me. I heard a helicopter outside.

I screamed.

I was on an exam table in the emergency room. A nurse was talking to me. I couldn't hear what she was saying.

"What's the matter?"

"I don't know," I heard myself say.

"Are you sad?"

I nodded. *You'd be sad too if you were going to prison for twenty-five years.*

"You can't tell me what's going on?"

I looked at her. So much for privacy of medical records. I couldn't trust her. If I told her that federal agents had tried to get in my house, she would just pass along the info to the FBI. I had to keep it secret.

"It's just work stuff."

"You're sad about something at work?"

"Yes."

She looked at me with an expression that conveyed that she was getting nowhere. She sighed and handed me a piece of paper, which told me everything I needed to know about anxiety attacks. She handed me two pills.

"These are Xanax. They help with anxiety. I'm giving you only two because—you'll need to get a prescription if you want more."

I got it. She thought I was trying to con her for some pills.

"They will help with the anxiety. Take one this afternoon and one tomorrow morning. If you don't feel better after that, you need to go see a psychiatrist."

A psychiatrist. Like hell. I wasn't crazy, I was going to go to prison. It was an important distinction.

The next morning, at work, I understood why the nurse had been so hesitant to write me a prescription. This was great stuff, this Xanax. It really took the edge off. I felt like a record player at 16 rpm. I was still pretty sure that I was going to get raped in prison, but the Xanax made the possibility seem a little bit more remote.

The Xanax, however, was making it impossible to trade. I felt like most people felt when they faced five computer screens full of charts and financial data: confusion. Numbers moving everywhere. It was incomprehensible. And my writing had suffered since I was being hunted by the stock cops; I hadn't put out a decent Bloomberg in days. But at least I was functioning. At least I wasn't waking up in terror. I thought about seeing a psychiatrist, then reconsidered. I had, at one time, a security clearance. They asked me questions about whether I had ever seen a mental health professional. Maybe going to the doctor would disqualify me from getting a security clearance someday. Maybe it would disqualify me from a lot of things. I was going to have to learn to do without the Xanax.

I thought about what would happen when it all went down, when they raided my house and hauled me off in handcuffs. Of course, my picture would be in the *Wall Street Journal*. It would be all over the internet. I wouldn't be making it to high school reunions, and people would know why. They would talk about me. After I served my sentence, I would have to get a landscaping job somewhere. No more being rich and famous. I would live out the rest of my life in anonymity, not talking to anyone, not even in the nursing home where I would sit alone at my table in the corner with my soup.

I thought about how fragile life is, how careers, and networks, and friends are built up on trust and reputation, and how it can all be lost in a minute. I thought about how random and arbitrary life is: one day I could be trucking along, making money, happy, and by trading a few hundred shares of CAT incorrectly, I could be sent away for years. I needed to live in a universe that made sense. But nothing made sense. *Life* didn't make sense: bad people got rich, and good people went to jail. There was no rhyme or reason. Some people feared physical harm; they would step into an elevator and get a sense of impending doom, that the cables would snap and they would be sent plummeting to their death. I didn't fear physical harm, I feared reputational, financial, and legal harm. I thought that bad shit happened randomly, and it happened to me most of all.

Human beings are not well equipped to deal with randomness. We want to live in a universe that makes sense. People trade this way too; they think that it is possible for a stock to move 5 percent or 10 percent, but not 50 percent. In the markets, I could compute probabilities and feel safe. With the law, there were no probabilities; nothing made sense. I had received a regulatory inquiry. Why? Randomness.

It got worse.

It was as if the fear had thickened my blood and grown in me like a cancer. I refused to answer the phone, to send emails, or to place trades. I sat and stared at the screens, doing nothing.

D.C. was looking at me.

*They're not going to get me,* I thought, *because there is not going to be anything left to get.* I was going to kill myself, and I was going to do it right this time.

No pills. I was going to cut my wrists.

A broker had sent me a Christmas gift of steaks and steak knives from Omaha Steaks. These were exceptionally good knives, and one, in particular, would be perfect for slashing my wrists.

I looked down at my wrists. The veins seemed awfully small.

There had to be a better way than this. I wanted to bleed to death, but I was squeamish about cutting tendons (as if I would ever need to use my hands when I was dead).

Here it came. I was going to cry on the trading floor.

Chuck walked by.

"Chuck."

"Yeah, what's up, man?"

"I need to talk."

"Sure, let's get an office."

I followed Chuck across the floor. We entered a conference room, and I sat down.

I started to cry.

Chuck was not expecting this. "Dude, what's wrong?"

I told the truth. "I don't *know* what's wrong!"

"Is anything happening?"

"Yes. And no. I don't know."

"What is it?"

I told him about the NYSE.

"That's what you're upset about? This stuff happens all the time. It's no big deal."

I cried harder.

"I don't know what's real anymore," I said. "I can't tell what's real and what's not. Doesn't that mean you're crazy?"

"Look, if you need help, the firm can put you in touch with all kinds of people you can talk to."

I wiped my tears. "Maybe. I'll let you know."

"Seriously, man, this is no joke. This isn't just a place to work. People take care of each other here. This is a family. Lots of people care about you."

"Thanks."

I wiped myself off again. No crying on the trading floor.

As I walked back to my desk, K-Rod playfully called out to me, "Hey, Dillian, get over here!"

I walked over. He and Jamie looked at me.

"Jesus, you look terrible."

I looked down at myself. I was cold, so I was wearing my coat indoors. My clothes were hanging off of me like curtains. I had lost a lot of weight.

"Dude, you need to get something to eat," said Eric Savitz, who was by now a good friend.

I had lost forty-two pounds.

"Yeah."

"Is something wrong?"

"It will be fine."

I walked away and went back to my desk. I couldn't handle any more of the third degree.

There was an FOMC meeting in about an hour. I was determined to make some money.

It was Ben Bernanke's first FOMC meeting as Fed chairman. The Fed had been hiking rates for some time, and everyone knew that they were going to hike another twenty-five basis points. What was unknown was whether they would indicate that they had an inflation bias or not. I figured that they would not. What most people don't understand about Fed meetings is that it is not usually a matter of whether or not the Fed will hike or cut rates, or by how much, it is a matter of what kind of bias they had, and what kind of language they had in the directive. People read the directive for clues as to what the Fed was going to do in the future. The Fed was very careful about what kind of language they used in order to guide the markets. It was one big game—a game that I was typically very good at playing.

The release was scheduled to come out at two fifteen. I watched the clock.

One minute to go.

Thirty seconds.

Ten seconds.

It was out.

No inflation bias.

*Buy!*

I bought two thousand minifutures, my biggest trade yet.

The market rallied momentarily. For a second, I had made $100,000.

Then it began to decline.

I had lost $100,000.

I had lost $200,000.

*Stop yourself out.*

$300,000.

*Stop yourself out, damn it.*

I could not bring myself to sell.

I didn't want to get help. I just wanted to end it.

$400,000.

I knew what I would do. I would go home and get the kitchen knife.

$500,000.

I would stand over the sink.

$600,000.

I wouldn't fuck around, trying to slice it open. I would plunge the knife in, as hard as I could.

$700,000.

Blood would spurt all over the walls and all over the floor. I would sit on the floor and slowly bleed to death.

$800,000.

My wife would come home and find me in a pool of blood.

$900,000.

*Stop yourself out.*

$1,000,000.

*I need to get out of here.*

I quickly looked up a psychiatrist—any psychiatrist—in New York. Natasha Zhuraleva, on Fifty-second Street.

I left, leaving the position open. I could lose $5 million, and I didn't care.

I needed to save my life.

*What if today's the day they come and get me? What if they're headed to the building right now? They won't find me there. They won't be able to track me, not unless they're watching the security cameras along the street. Maybe they are watching the security cameras. Don't touch anything; you'll leave fingerprints. Walk fast, now, don't stop. Keep moving. As long as you get to the doctor, everything will be fine.*

*What if they look at my internet activity? What if they find out that I had spent the last month looking up laws and prison sentences? They will know for sure that I saw this coming. Can't they increase sentences for that? Can't they send me to a higher-security prison? If they just put me in solitary, everything will be fine. Don't make eye contact with the cops. Yes, I know they are looking at you, don't look back. There is probably a warrant out for you; they probably saw your picture and they are looking for you. Please, don't talk on your radio. Don't call it in.*

*Walk faster.*

*Why not end it now? Just don't look when you cross the street. The traffic is coming from the right. Look left and walk out into the street. Let the bus hit you. That might not do the job; they don't move very fast. Try it anyway. Walk into the street. Don't look. See what happens. If nothing happens, then you were meant to live.*

*Nothing happens.*

*They are probably breaking into your house right now. They are probably tearing the place apart. The neighbors are gathering outside, watching the SWAT team enter the house. You know, they are probably following you from the building. They probably know where you are going. Don't look back, keep walking. Don't run. If you run, they will stop you. Pretend like everything is fine.*

*I never should have talked to Chuck. They are going to get to him first. I told Chuck that I was worried about the inquiry. He won't know not to tell them. He will tell the truth, which will mean the end of me. You asshole, you're supposed to be able to keep a secret. There are some things you should just take to your grave.*

*What are you going to tell the psychiatrist? I am going to tell her I need help. She is going to ask you what is wrong. Can I tell her what is going on? Isn't what you tell a doctor private? They will get to her somehow. Tell her that you want to kill yourself, which should be reason enough for her to give you something. All I want is for her to give me something that will make this go away. Even if it doesn't go away. I want to take something to make me feel better. Maybe I can be on drugs throughout the duration of a trial, and not feel anything.*

*How am I going to be able to survive through a trial? How am I going to be able to defend myself? Will I plead not guilty? Or will I accept some kind of deal where I have to go to prison for three or five years or something? If I go to prison, it will be a death sentence—I have to stay out of prison. There is no way that I can survive in there.*

*Wait a minute, you don't even know what you did yet. All you did was put down a basket of stock market on open. But they will find something. They will find something that I did. And if it's not that, it will be something else that they find in the course of their investigation. They are going to get me, one way or another.*

*It's a good thing I don't have a cell phone. It is easy for them to intercept communications. I have heard of that before. It's a good thing I haven't been using the phone, anyway. I haven't left a trail of evidence. They don't have anything on me.*

*But what if they do? What if they talk to my friends? What if they go back to high school and college? They will find someone, somewhere to say something bad about me. They will use it against me.*

*What is that guy looking at? I saw him looking at me. He just turned around. Was that something in his ear?*

*Keep going, you're almost there.*

*I can't take this anymore. I need help.*

*I need help.*

*God, help me.*

I was panting.

I went into the lobby, up the elevator to the third floor, pressed the buzzer, and collapsed in a heap on the couch in the waiting room, sobbing. I clutched myself, shaking.

A tall woman who might have once been a model motions for me to go into her office. I am still crying, wiping my nose.

"What seems to be the problem?" she asks in a thick Russian accent.

"I don't know."

"Are you depressed?"

"I don't know."

"Are you suicidal?"

"Yes."

"Have you been thinking about it a lot?"

"Oh yes, all day."

"Do you know how you are going to do it?"

"Yes."

"How long have you been like this?"

"A few weeks."

"What about before that?"

"I was fine."

"Were you happy?"

"Oh yes, very happy. Everything was great."

"So you had a lot of energy?"

"Oh yes."

"Were you sleeping?"

"No, I never sleep."

"What about now?"

"Now I sleep all the time."

"Have you been eating?"

"No."

She takes notes.

"I'm afraid," I offer. "I'm afraid all the time."

"What are you afraid of?"

*Do I tell her?*

"I've run into some trouble at work."

*Good. If you tell her about the federal agents, she'll think you are crazy.*

She takes more notes.

I look at her.

"Well," she says finally, "I would say that you are bipolar and that you should be prescribed lithium."

"Great!" I catch myself from holding out my hand for a prescription.

"But you have to go to the hospital."

"What for? Like, just for a visit? Sure."

"No, not a visit."

*This doesn't look good.*

"How long?"

"I don't know, probably awhile."

I am trying to process this. I can't see myself being away from work for a long time, but at the same time, I don't think that federal agents will be able to get to me inside a hospital. Could they? They would never take someone out of the hospital.

"I'm not so sure," I say.

The Russian model is getting agitated. She looks like she is about to press some sort of big red emergency button. "You cannot go back out there—you have to go to the hospital. I can have the police take you there, but it would probably be best if you got someone to take you."

*Not the police.*

I'm not too sure about this. I'm not thrilled about going to the nut-house. I wasn't crazy, after all; there really *were* people out to get me. Maybe I could just hang out for a while until the storm passes.

*You can't go back to the way it was,* I think. *You can't go back out there.*

"Are you sure there is no other way?"

"Yes."

*Okay. This is it.*

"I'll go."

*I surrender.*

## 13

## I Remember |

"Have you thought about hurting yourself or others?"

"Yes."

That was the second time that day I had answered the question in the affirmative, and I quickly learned that it was the one surefire way to gain admission to a locked psychiatric ward. There was no going back now. There was no, "I didn't mean it!" What I had said, I'd said. The words were there, placed on the counter, for the two of us to see. I had thought about hurting myself; I had thought seriously about it. I admitted it, out loud, to the nurse in the emergency room.

I learned quickly that there are not one but two emergency rooms in the hospital. There is the regular ER, and there is the psych ER. Nobody gets to see what goes on in the psych ER. It is in the interior of the hospital, with no windows; nobody wants to see what goes on in there. The room was split in half. On one side were the patients; on the other, the nurses. They were separated by a thick plate glass window.

I gave my valuables to the security guard, a hulking black man who did not look me in the eye. Wallet, containing three $100 bills and a variety of credit cards. A bus pass. An iPod. Keys. A handful of change. I was instructed to undress. As it turned out, I had worn my best suit that day. I didn't care what they did with it. For all I knew, I wouldn't be needing it again. I stood and undressed, donning a hospital gown. The nurse led me to a room, where I was told to wait.

The room contained nothing except for a bed—if you could call it that. It was a flat surface with padding, covered with some kind of material that was impossible to tear. There was nothing else in the room. The lights were on, and there was no switch; no way to turn them off. A large window faced out into the hall. There I could see the faces of the nurses looking back at me.

I stood at the doorway and looked around at my new surroundings. This was unlike anything I had ever seen. The nurses' station seemed to be some sort of command center—they sat in darkness, with a row of computer screens, looking back at us, the patients. We seemed to be under observation. They were watching to see what we were doing; whether we would pound our heads against the walls or scratch out our eyes. But there was nothing *to* do, except to wait.

Periodically, a nurse would enter my room and ask me a series of questions. I told her everything, except for the part about the federal agents, which she wouldn't have believed anyway. She seemed very wary around me, like I could potentially be violent or something. "Hey, I'm just a regular guy," I wanted to say. "Just like you. I'm just having some problems, is all." But to her, I was not a regular guy. I was to be treated with extreme caution. If I was capable of hurting myself, I was capable of hurting anybody. The muscular security guard was never too far away.

I decided that the psych ER wasn't such a bad place to be. I was safe here, after all. I could worry about other things; I could worry about whether they were going to have a bed for me upstairs. I could worry about whether they were ever going to bring me a sandwich. I could worry about whether they were going to bring me any drugs.

On cue, the wary nurse arrived with pills. I didn't even look at them.

This was the worst place in the world, but I was content here, at least for the time being. I was content because, instead of worrying about losing a million bucks and having the FBI after me, I could worry about when I was going to get food and when I was going to get a bed. I could worry about whether any of these other patients was going to flip and gouge out my eyes. By going from a bad place to a worse place, I felt better. I left some dystopian world where every trade I made was recorded electronically, to being monitored behind plate glass. When people actually do jump out of the frying pan and into the fire, trading one form of misery for another, it is usually a good trade.

My insides matched my outsides.

I wasn't ashamed. Some people might be embarrassed by being in a psych ward; they might be embarrassed and worried that other people thought they were crazy. Well, I already knew other people thought I was crazy. But I wasn't crazy, I just wanted to lock myself in here to get away from the federal agents. That was perfectly rational. If other people wanted to think I was crazy, well, they could think whatever they wanted. I was perfectly sane.

There is a commotion. A new patient in the psych ER is making a scene. *"I graduated from Harvard!"* she screams. *"Who the fuck do you think you people are?"* If she did indeed graduate from Harvard, I think, she has fallen a long way down. Her clothes are rags. Her hair is matted. She looks like she has come from the street. And, she is on *something*. She is having a complete fucking breakdown right in the middle of the hallway. The nurses are letting her yell it out. It's disturbing, but for some reason the noise doesn't bother me. Her screams are only an echo of what is going on in my own head. I can feel what she is feeling. The world doesn't make sense to her—well, it doesn't make sense to me, either.

I begin to get a little agitated. I have been down here for a few hours now, and there is no sign of moving me to a bed. *How long are they going to keep me down here?* The wary nurse has stopped coming by. I can see them looking at me through the glass. I figure I am part of some vast behavioral experiment. What do the nuts do when they are left to their own devices for a few hours?

I try to communicate with the security guard to ask him what is going on. "Hey."

He gives me the right-hand wave. *Nuts are not allowed to talk.*

*Fine.* I leave him in peace. I figure he has the worst job in the world.

There is another commotion. The nurses and the security guard are hustling one of the patients back outside, giving him his clothes. He was seeking medication. "At least give me my cigarettes back," he says.

For lack of anything else better to do, I decide to lie down on the bed. It's really uncomfortable. I lie on my side, staring at the wall. I figure that if the pills they gave me do what they are supposed to do, I will fall asleep soon.

*More screams.*

I don't know what time it is; they took my watch. It is impossible to tell. The light has been on the whole time. They have brought in another young woman on a stretcher, in restraints. She is screaming like she is being tortured. Children will get bored of screaming after a few minutes and stop. This woman goes on forever; she screams and screams for at least an hour. I am encouraged. Someone is in worse shape than me. I am almost an impostor, I think. Some people have real problems.

I go back to sleep.

In the morning—I guess that it is morning—there is a new nurse in the room with me. She is apologizing, telling me that I should have had a bed by now, but they are still making room upstairs. Whatever. I have all the time in the world.

I am groggy as hell. *What the fuck did these people give me?*

At last, I am in a hospital bed. I have no idea how I got there. People bring me pills. When it gets dark, periodically someone will wave a flashlight at me in the room.

I sleep for an entire day.

I awake with an interesting problem. I have an erection.

It's not what I expected, after having being admitted to a psych ward. But I figure that I have been asleep for most of the last twenty-four hours and that perhaps the magnitude of morning wood is somehow correlated with the length of time spent asleep.

I make my way to the bathroom. It's a big bathroom. The first thing I notice is that there is no shower curtain rod. The shower curtain is attached with Velcro to a track. *No way to hang yourself in here,* I think.

I unceremoniously bang one out in solitude.

It will be the last time for over a year.

I surveyed the damage.

These were my new peers, these people. I found that I had little in common with the Wall Street cake eaters with their Hermès ties. I had more in common with these people—the lunatics—like this guy over here; the bearded Jewish guy leaning up against the wall.

*What is that guy doing, anyway? He stands there all day.*

A psych ward can be disconcerting. I was in a hospital gown. But there were few people in hospital gowns. Most of them were in civilian clothes, walking around like they would on the street. Street clothes were a privilege to be earned. I was a new nut, so I got the hospital gown. I wasn't sorry. It suited me, for the time being.

I liked the place. On the outside of the floor (I did not know what floor I was on) were patients' rooms. On the inside was the nurses' station. Nobody was allowed in there. Also in the interior were supply closets, where I learned you had to get permission to get a razor; and a room for drugs, where people would line up at certain times of the day. At the end of the wing, on the north end of the building, there was a vista overlooking the FDR Drive.

There wasn't much to explore, but I shuffled around in my socks and my hospital gown, and did laps around the wing. Nobody was particularly interested in how I spent my time. I was primarily concerned with trying to stay away from the television, the idiot box, which was on throughout the day. It was right outside my room, which annoyed me. The other patients watched cartoons, the Home Shopping Network, anything that was on. A few years ago, I had bought a television to become a vegetable. But I at least watched programs that had a point. These nuts would watch anything. Over time, I got up the courage to change the channel to CNBC. I was missing a lot. Gold was going through the roof. Maybe this was the ideal way to observe the markets, I thought: from a nuthouse.

I hadn't heard anything about the FBI since I had been admitted. There were two possibilities; either they saw me come in, and they were going to wait for me to come out, or they had contacted the hospital staff, which had told them to bugger off, and they weren't about to wound me with the information. Either way, I was safe for a while. I wondered how long I could keep up the act, how long I could pretend to be crazy so that the feds would eventually get bored and go away.

I still had no idea what medications they were giving me.

Four times a day, they came with pills. It occurred to me that some of them were vitamins; one of the questions they had asked me was whether I was taking any. But I had no skills at pill recognition. Weren't they supposed to tell you this stuff, anyway? I felt like I was being left in the dark, but I did not have the energy to do anything about it.

I had my answers in time. I was napping in my room when a startlingly attractive Indian woman with wide, expressive eyes appeared at the foot of my bed. Had I not been a patient in a mental ward, I would have felt compelled to hit on her. She was my doctor, she said, and she would be taking over my care. She said her name was Dr. S——.

*Come again?* "What did you say your name was?"

"Dr. S——."

Unpronounceable. I was never going to get this right. In my mind, I referred to her as S+12.

S+12 started asking me more questions. *All I get around here are questions. Questions about what I eat, about how much I sleep, what my moods are.*

"Do you have racing thoughts?"

I thought about it. *Yes, I couldn't stop thinking about being pursued by federal agents.*

"Yes."

"Does it happen often?"

"All the time."

"Do you have feelings of elation, like you're on top of the world?"

"Not right now."

"Not now, but in general."

"Absolutely."

"Has anyone ever told you that you talk faster?"

"Yes."

"What about at work? Is your behavior different from other people at work?"

"I'm a trader. Everyone's like that."

"Well, what about your trading? Do you trade a lot? How many orders do you put in, in a day?"

I thought about it.

"A couple thousand."

"How many does the average person put in?"

I thought about it.

"Maybe twenty."

S+12's eyes got even bigger, and she started scribbling on her clipboard. I said something magical, I guessed.

"How often do you get depressed?"

I thought about this one for a long time.

"Not very often. Once every couple of years. But when I do, it's really awful."

"What does it feel like?"

"Like I can't move. Like I don't have any energy at all. Like I want to just die."

"Do you use alcohol or drugs?"

"No drugs. I drink."

"How much?"

"Well, a lot, I guess."

"When you're feeling good or when you're feeling bad?"

"Both."

S+12 sure was friendly. She had that luxury, I suppose. The nurses have to deal with all the patients' crap, and the doctors can just waltz in and ask all the softball questions.

"Do you have any questions?" she asked me.

"Yeah, what is the medicine you're giving me?"

"Well, we started you off on Depakote, but I think we're going to change you to lithium."

I had no idea what she was talking about.

"What does that do?"

She sighed. "We think you have bipolar disorder. There are two types: bipolar I and bipolar II. Bipolar I is the most severe. That's what we think you have."

"And the lithium helps with that?"

"Lithium is a mood stabilizer. You have transitions from periods of mania to periods of depression, and the lithium helps with that. We're also giving you risperidone, which is an antipsychotic."

"Antipsychotic?"

She looked at me. "You won't have the racing thoughts anymore."

*She knows.*

S+12 gave me a sweet smile, then left me with my thoughts. *Bipolar disorder. That was what K-Rod thought I had. Interesting.*

I didn't know anything about it.

All mental illnesses, to me, were lumped together. Bipolar disorder. Schizophrenia. It was all the same to me. It was all the same to most people, I suspected. I would receive my diagnosis, and it would not occur to me to go to the patient information center so that I could read about it, not even once. I went there to use the computer to check on the market instead.

Six years ago, while I was working in the Coast Guard, my supervisor, the lieutenant, was giving me a mild lecture when I snapped, pounding on the desk, sending full coffee cups and soda cans flying. I expected to be disciplined, yelled at for insubordination.

Instead everyone wanted to know if I was okay.

I was starting to find that I had little in common with most of the other patients—at least, socially speaking. Interestingly, a plurality of them were Hasidic Jews, including my roommate, who turned out to be the guy who leaned up against the wall all day. He would stand motionless unless it was time to eat or time to play Ping-Pong, at which point he would turn into Forrest Gump and start slashing the ball all over the place. There was one other clean-cut-looking white male. I struck up a conversation.

"What are you in here for?"

"Depression."

I didn't know that plain-vanilla depression could land you in the hospital.

"Is it bad?"

"Well," he said, "last year I attempted suicide by eating an entire jar of pills, and I spent the next three months in a coma. When I woke up, I'd lost years of memory. It's taken me all of this time to piece everything back together. I started getting depressed again, really bad, so I checked myself into the hospital."

*Holy crap.*

"What are you in here for?"

I let it slip. "Well, I'm really in here to get away from the FBI, but they tell me I have bipolar disorder."

He let that one sink in for a second.

"Name's Jared." We shook hands.

"John."

"Good to meet you, John."

I was starting to feel better. It occured to me that I should take a shower, since it had been four days. I bothered the orderly for a razor too. He made a pretense of watching me shave.

I felt like a new man.

• • •

From time to time, there are activity periods on the psych ward. I hadn't participated in any yet. I hadn't been in the mood. After my shower and shave, I was starting to feel like I should interact with people more. I was also starting to get the sense that I was being observed carefully, and that if I didn't show signs of socialization, they wouldn't let me out anytime soon. I thought that would be a good thing, and then I caught myself—I needed to get out of here eventually.

There were a lot of reasons why I didn't want to participate in any of the activities. First of all, I wasn't nuts. Second of all, I just liked being alone. Third of all, I liked to read. I was tearing through books since I had been admitted, including the crappy donated ones that were at the end of the hall. And finally, deep down, there was a part of me—an elitist part of me—that felt that I was better than these people; that I wasn't like them. Not just because I wasn't crazy but because I was an important person with an important job. *No time for yoga; I have shit to do.*

There is a painting class, of sorts. Rich white ladies from the Upper East Side volunteer their time to bring things to do for all the nuts. Today they have brought miniature potted plants, and we, the nuts, are going to be able to paint the pots. *Sounds pretty stupid,* I think, *but what the hell.*

I sit down at the table, and a nice lady presents me with a potted plant, some paint, and some paintbrushes. I go to town, forgetting momentarily that I am a terrible artist. I glob thick splotches of paint on the pot, first blue, then green, then gold, then yellow, then silver, then red. It looks hideous. But for a brief moment in time, I forget myself, and it is freeing to paint this fucking pot a million different colors. For once, in the last few months, I am in control of something, even if it is as inconsequential as a potted plant.

She wants to talk to me.

"What are you making there?"

I frown. "I'm not very good at painting. I'm just making a design."

"How long have you been here?"

"About four days."

She can't decide whether to ask. "What do you do—you know, out there?"

I smile. "I'm a trader at Lehman Brothers."

She looks at me in horror. Wall Street jerks don't deserve charity.

*Yeah, that's right lady, the poor nutjob painting a plant just got paid $650,000.*

She moves on to the next patient. I allow myself to feel smug.

There was no violence in the psych ward. There were no straitjackets, and to the best of my knowledge, there were no padded rooms. There was one patient that they kept under lock and key, with a guard posted outside his room, but that was the only potential menace.

I decided that a psychiatric ward was one of the saddest places in the world. There was a woman who couldn't stop crying. There it went again: in the middle of the day, the screaming and crying. The nurses would come and try to put her back together, to put her in bed, to give her something for the pain. I didn't know what was wrong with her. I didn't want to know what was wrong with her; in these matters, I minded my own business. But the crying would come and go, day and night; it was always present.

These were people who were broken. Something was wrong upstairs; connections weren't being made, or they were being made in ways that shouldn't be made. There was an educated, well-spoken woman in her sixties who told fantastic stories about her husband boinking the maid and lifting skirts. When he came to visit, he looked like an accountant and held solemn conversations with the doctors. When he left, she would scream after him. She was a paranoid schizophrenic. She was seeing things that weren't there; she believed things to be true that actually weren't. And she didn't seem to be getting any better.

Was I getting better?

I started to wonder if I really *was* like these people. I entertained, for a moment, the possibility that I actually was crazy; that there were no federal agents looking for me. It seemed unlikely. It had all seemed so real. I really believed, when I was rolling around on the floor of my house, that a SWAT team was crashing through the windows. I could hear them. I could feel their presence. But they weren't actually there—which didn't make the experience any less real. My experiencing it made it real. Twenty people could have told me that it wasn't real, and I wouldn't have believed them.

They say that the definition of insanity is doing the same thing over and over again and expecting a different result. Well, that's one kind of insanity, as it usually pertains to addiction. But the medical definition of insanity is more like this: believing things to be true that aren't true. Seeing things that aren't there, hearing things that don't exist. That's insanity. Was I insane? Maybe I was—I didn't know. I still wasn't able to tell what was real and what was not. I still didn't know if the federal agents existed or if I had imagined them. But, for the first time ever, I was actually wondering if I had imagined them. Was this progress?

Then, in another thought: if I really was like these people, what did that mean? It meant that I was crazy. I started to think about how I must sound to other people. If I heard myself talking, I'd call myself crazy too. Looney tunes, wacked out, certifiable. My heart sank. People had called me crazy for most of my life, but I never believed it to be true. Being crazy meant that everything you said was discountable. *Don't mind him, he's just crazy.* It was important that nobody would ever find out.

I had visitors.

It was Mark Ricci and Vivek, Mark's number two. I was happy to see Mark—Chuck Monaghan had clearly told him; he had to, Mark was his boss—but I was unhappy to see Vivek. It meant that word was spreading on the trading floor.

Mark read my face. "Don't worry—nobody else knows."

I trusted him.

I was in good spirits. I told him about my roommate, who leaned against the wall all day and occasionally shredded the other lunatics in Ping-Pong. I told him about the nice lady with the potted plant. I told him about the interpretive dance and yoga I had been doing. I told him that I had been making friends. I told him that, yes, after about a week, I was starting to feel better. I didn't tell them about S+12, who was mine, and I didn't want them horning in on her.

"How are things back on the floor?"

"Things are fine," Mark said. "D.C. has everything under control. He's doing a great job."

"Yeah," said Vivek, "except we don't have anyone to yell 'STOCKS!' and scream at the sales guys all day long. It's kind of quiet, actually."

I laughed. It seemed like a long time ago—and it seemed like they were talking about someone else.

I couldn't believe that Mark had actually come to visit. Mark, who was impossible to track down in the middle of the day, being busy with meetings and empire building; Mark, who was impossible to understand even in the best of circumstances. Here he was, sitting in a chair in my room. I thought that I would have been shunned. I thought that I would have been disowned. You never know how people are going to react to crazy. I had been told by my wife, a long time ago, that a distant relative had been hospitalized. I reacted with revulsion. Now here I was, talking to two Lehman Brothers managing directors in a psychiatric ward. They weren't running the other way. Mark's mouth was moving, and he was telling me that I was part of the team. For the first time, I listened. Look across any Wall Street trading floor: a sea of white and blue shirts. But there is mental illness, maybe, and there are drug addictions, and alcohol addictions, and broken marriages, and messy divorces. Maybe Wall Street people know better than most that people are fallible, and what is important is their minds.

Chuck really hadn't been kidding about all this Lehman Brothers family bullshit. It really was true. Yes, Wall Street is a cutthroat environment. Yes, there are a lot of unpleasant politics. True, people often don't like one another. But at the end of the day, Mark reminded me, we are all on the same team, and we look out for one another. Who knows? Maybe if I had worked at some other bank, they would have let me rot in here. Maybe I wouldn't have a job when I came back out.

D.C. came by too. He had watched my meltdown on the trading floor, and he had been concerned. We had sat next to each other for a few years now. We knew when we were happy, when we were upset; we knew the sound a bad trade makes and the smell of our farts. He was my wingman. Me checking myself into the hospital had inadvertently thrust him into the limelight.

He painted a different picture from Mark. Since I had left, the markets had gone apeshit. Everything had gone straight up, and he was getting buried under a massive pile of ETF trades. Plenty of people had come by the desk asking about me, and he had been telling people quite simply that I was sick. He didn't come out and say it, but he needed me to come back to work.

I assured him that wasn't going to happen anytime soon. That was what I really wanted to do: come back to work and start getting my head caved in on trades again. Losing hundreds of thousands of dollars at a clip. Giving away price improvements for other people's fuckups. Dealing with salespeople. Getting ripped off by unsavory customers. Yeah, that sounded like a fucking picnic. Let me pack my picnic basket with my paper plates and my mustard right now.

What could be better? I was getting three squares a day. I was reading books. I was relaxing. I couldn't go *outside*, but I didn't care. I had to deal with the occasional meltdown from one of the other patients, but I didn't care. Already I was putting weight back on. Already I was feeling better. I kind of liked it here.

"You know, you should really join us for yoga," she said.

I didn't know her name. I hadn't learned many people's names. She was this nameless woman who came up to me every day to try to get me to do queer things.

I thought of my roommate. He had confided to me that he was being held against his will. One morning, he was home in bed, and a team of paramedics scooped him up and took him to the hospital. That was it. He'd had only one visitor. As much as I didn't want to end up in a federal prison, I wasn't sure I wanted to be locked up in a nuthouse for the rest of my life, either.

I followed her to the south wing. On the south side, the people were a lot more active. There was television, yes, but people were walking around socializing. People were happier, smiling. I wondered if they had put me on the north side with all the hard cases. I figured that they had.

We stood in a circle. We were instructed to bend over and touch our toes. I did, and felt all the blood rush to my head. We had to stand up and breathe in deeply, and breathe out. Arms to the side. Arms in the air. Breathe out.

This didn't seem much like yoga. I started to realize that doing simple things with my body was healing, in a way. I commanded it to breathe in, and it did. I commanded my arms to go out to the side, and they did. Maybe, after all, I actually was in charge of what I did. Maybe I was actually in control.

A woman started to cry in the middle of it and had to be consoled.

*This is just what I needed*, I thought. I had to start over. Reboot. I really was crazy. Maybe this is how crazy people heal.

Maybe I do have bipolar disorder, whatever that is.

The next morning.

"Are you going to the writing workshop today?" It was the nameless lady, again.

"Uh, pass."

"Come on, you really should."

I didn't even know what she was talking about, and it already sounded terrible. Some of these nuts were on some heavy-duty medications, and I didn't imagine it would do a whole lot for their writing.

"You really should do it," she continued. "Siri Hustvedt is a great writer, and she has been volunteering here for a long time."

"I'll think about it." *Not.*

"In the meantime, there's a book that you need to read. I notice you're reading all the time, so you should learn about your illness." She handed me a piece of paper and pointed at *Touched with Fire*, by Kay Redfield Jamison.

I thought about my poor roommate again. There was a strong correlation between standing around and staring off into space and not being let out. As much as I hated to admit it, there were a lot of creepy things about being in a nuthouse, not least of which was this idea that you're not well unless you socialize with everyone. It was very authoritarian, in a sinister kind of way. I was being observed. I needed to do something.

I found myself seated at a rectangular table with a few of my esteemed colleagues. A complicated woman sat at the other end.

She began. "Today we're going to write in the style of Joe Brainard's *I Remember*."

*Ah, I see, a writing exercise.*

She read excerpts: "I remember the first time I got a letter that said 'After Five Days Return To' on the envelope, and I thought that after

I had kept the letter for five days I was supposed to return it to the sender."

"I remember the kick I used to get going through my parents' drawers looking for rubbers."

"I remember when polio was the worst thing in the world."

"I remember pink dress shirts. And bola ties."

"I remember when a kid told me that those sour clover-like leaves we used to eat (with little yellow flowers) tasted so sour because dogs peed on them. I remember that didn't stop me from eating them."

And so on.

"You have twenty minutes."

So I wrote:

*I remember the ancient tree in the playground between buildings 111 and 112. There were four levels—level one, level two, level three, and level four. We kids would sit in the branches at our assigned levels— Kyle at level four, Kirk at level three, Vern at level two. I was at level one—I was chubby and did not climb well. There we sat.*

*I remember the swimming pool and its own system of little kid hierarchy. A white tag meant you were a novice swimmer, red meant advanced, and a blue tag meant lifesaving skills. I swelled with pride on receiving my white tag. I still have it somewhere.*

*I remember the strips of metal that would fall off the golf-cart-like government vehicles. You could spring them fifty feet in the air. We called them Twinese Twingers.*

*I remember Billy. He was a bully. His mother committed suicide.*

*I remember exploring Castle William with Kyle. It is a famous historic structure overlooking New York Harbor. It was mostly full of trash and debris. We howled when we found that somebody had used a broken toilet and left something for posterity.*

*I remember going to see* Clash of the Titans *at the theater next to the enlisted club. The two seats front and center had been defaced. When you sat down, you were the proud owner of graphically illustrated female and male sex organs. I always got the female seat because I was younger.*

*I remember playing T-ball on the Dodgers. The team's star first*

*baseman, handsome and athletic at six years old, was named Mike*
*Lavache. He might as well have been Robert Redford. We won the*
*final game in spite of his absence.*

I read it aloud. "Good!" she said.

After it was over, she cornered me in the hallway. "You know," she said, "you should really think about being a writer. What things do you read?"

"Well," I said truthfully, "I really like short stories, so, for example, the Best American Short Stories series."

"I was in that!" said Siri.

"I don't remember—"

"In 1991."

"Oh, I have it going back to 1992." I remembered.

I also remembered that at one point, I had wanted to be a writer.

In high school, I had Wally Lamb as an English teacher. He had finagled a sum of money and built a writing center in the basement of the high school, outfitted with Apple IIc computers. He was more than just an English teacher; he was teaching a writing seminar for high school students as an aspiring writer himself. He wore knit ties, squared at the end, with plaid shirts, and wallpapered the classroom with his rejection letters from publications like *Playboy* and *Vanity Fair* and various literary journals, almost proud of his failure. This was before *She's Come Undone.*

Mr. Lamb had organized a writing contest, kind of, and made all of his students participate. I wrote something deeply personal, distant, with diminished affect, and I felt *alive.* I was spending late nights at the home computer, the PS2.

I thought I was sure to win.

The Coast Guard Academy was not known for its humanities, but I took a writing class there and managed to win a writing award for a short story about an act of shockingly callous infidelity. Again, I wrote it in the middle of the night, when the corps of cadets was asleep. Here I started to seriously think about being a writer. I went and bought the 1997 edition of *Writers Market* and told everybody of my plans. I was going to quit the Coast Guard and write literary fiction.

They told me I was being an idiot.

"Make some money first," they said, "then go be a writer." So that's what I did. I got an MBA instead of an MFA, and my life took a wild de-tour onto Wall Street. I forgot about what it felt like to write, to commu-nicate, to change the way that people feel. I buried it under fixed-income mathematics and managerial accounting and decision theory.

Had it all been a big mistake?

Probably not. Money is important. Being a starving artist is a hell of a lot easier if you're not starving. Toiling in poverty and obscurity is way overrated.

But I remembered. I remembered like the father, once the pitcher on the high school baseball team, who goes to college and finds work and never throws a baseball again until his son gets old enough, and he throws the ball, and says, "Man, this is fun." That writing exercise—my brain hadn't felt so *alive* in years. I wanted more.

That night, I was having trouble sleeping for the first time since being admitted. I was thinking about what Siri had said to me. A real writer was telling me that I could be a writer.

For the first time, I wanted to get out.

I had no idea when they were planning on letting me out. It occurred to me that it might be a lot easier to get in than to get out.

I'd checked myself in on my own accord, and, theoretically, I could leave anytime I wanted. This is where the law gets a little murky: if the doctors decided that I was not quite well, that I was a threat to myself or others, they had the legal means to keep me inside. I couldn't just walk up to S+12 and say, "Hey, let me the fuck out." It would raise all kinds of red flags.

I started to drop not-so-subtle hints. "I'm feeling much better," I would say, and it was true. I also said that I felt "stable," which I thought was an-other key word. No, I wasn't having any racing thoughts. No, there were no more thoughts of suicide. Everything was peachy. Now let me out, I have to go back and trade. I also wanted to get back to my wife, who was probably thankful for the vacation from her husband's insane behavior.

During my daily session with S+12, I finally came out and told her point-blank that I was ready to leave.

Her eyes darkened.

"When you came here, your symptoms were very *acute*," she said, letting the word hang in the air. "We are acting in your own best interests. You haven't been here that long," she added, "so please be patient."

S+12 was hot. But she had turned on me, doing a Jekyll and Hyde from friendly, helpful doctor to stern taskmaster. I was thrown off, and worried. Things weren't looking good.

I did not have the whole story. I would learn eventually that the docs were waiting for the level of the medication to stabilize in my bloodstream. Lithium isn't a magic pill; you don't take it and suddenly start feeling better. You take it over time, and it builds up in your blood. There is an optimal level for bipolar people, and it takes a while to get the lithium up to that level. All I could do was wait.

I was no longer any good at waiting. I had blood tests every other day or so, and the lab staff was famously disorganized. Sometimes they would forget, and other times they would be hours late. I would spend the day doing laps around the north wing, from the television to the windows overlooking the FDR Drive, and back again. I wanted freedom, and I was being held up by incompetent jerks.

*Everything is moving so fast.*

I was outside for the first time in two and a half weeks. Cars, people, talking, moving, walking; everything was moving impossibly fast. And it was bright outside—an unseasonably warm day. I tugged at my pants; my clothes were a bit tighter, as I had put some weight back on.

Checking out was both easy and difficult. I had to have a blood test before they would let me leave, to make sure that the lithium level in my bloodstream was acceptable, and it was a giant clusterfuck trying to get it scheduled. The hospital, I learned, is a dysfunctional bureaucracy. But after that, I got the clean bill of health from S+12, they gave me back my stuff, and I packed it in a bag and walked out onto the street.

I felt good. I felt good enough to forget to check the street corners for parked cars with men inside. I felt good enough to not look over my shoulder at who was following me. I had, quite literally, forgotten everything—all of it. This is what the medication was helping me to do. The antipsychotics were helping me to forget. What had all the fuss been about? I could not say.

I didn't feel any particular shame at becoming a mental patient. I was a sick person, not a bad person. It was all chemical. There was an imbalance in my brain, and all it took was a simple correction, and I was fine. Having bipolar disorder is no different than having high blood pressure or diabetes. I wasn't going to want to kill myself anymore, but I wasn't going to want to stay up all night and write poetry, either. Yes, I was probably never going to get a security clearance. Yes, I was probably never going to be able to own a firearm, but when I thought about it, that didn't seem like such a bad thing. If I'd had one before, I might have actually gone through with it.

I got on the subway with my wife, feeling profoundly happy for the first time in what might have been years. I looked at the people around me; I could hear their thoughts, their fears, their worries—they were thinking of nothing but themselves. For the first time in my life, I had found out, finally, who I actually was. I had bipolar I, severe. I was capable of wonderful, creative things. I was capable of being a huge pain in the ass. And I was living in a universe that finally made sense.

I was me.

## 14

Top Tick | Spring 2006–Winter 2007

Much to D.C.'s disappointment, I decided to take even *more* time off after leaving the hospital. It would be just too jarring to go straight from the hospital back to staring at the screens. I spoke to Mark Ricci about it. He said to take as much time as I needed, but poor D.C. was stuck in the meat grinder all by himself, doing the work of three people.

Home alone, I watched the market. I turned on the television, CNBC, the bubblevision, and fired up Bloomberg on my home computer. There was a lot going on. People were buying *things*. They weren't buying paper, they were buying things, they were buying anything that wasn't nailed down: houses, gold, copper, lumber. It was a bull market in everything. The stock market had gone crazy too.

I had been pretty much right about everything as it had pertained to the housing market, and yet success was, for the most part, elusive. I had shorted homebuilder stocks too early, only to watch them go straight up a pink orifice, and then missed them on the way down. Being early, in trading, is the same as being wrong. I had been telling anyone who would listen that we were headed for a housing apocalypse, and yet I had been unable to make any money off the idea. The only thing worse than being rich and dumb is being smart and poor.

Yes, I was making good money. In fact, if it were even possible, I was making more money than the year before. But it wasn't about money; I had no use for houses or cars. I got satisfaction out of being right, and I wanted a job where I could get satisfaction out of being right over and over and over again. Being the ETF trader meant that I was the missile sponge for customer trades; I was getting paid not to lose money rather than to make it. Psychologically, it is an important difference.

I never met Jay Knight. I only had Ingram's stories, which he still told me from time to time, about his top-secret trading operation. To Jay, I'm sure it wasn't about the money, either. Prop traders like him, all they want to do is to have fun. It is fun to be right and smug and derive satisfaction from watching your opponents get steamrolled. It is fun to turn a small number into a big number. It is fun, for once in your life, to be able to sell the top tick. It is fun to look at a printout of all the year's trades and pick out all the winners and the losers. It is fun to come up with ideas and to express those ideas with money.

It is fun to win.

It is fun to be a part of history, to remember the trade you put on during the Russian debt default or the tech bubble. It is fun when people ask you for advice. It is fun to be one of the richest people that nobody knows about.

To be a flow trader means that you must suffer occasional—no, constant—indignities. It is not fun to be constantly asked for price improvements. It is not fun when people say "refresh." It is not fun when customers talk about having anal sex with your wife. It is not fun to not be able to leave your desk to go take a piss. It is not fun to have to deal with compliance. It is not fun to be tied to a discretionary bonus. It is not fun to be told that your markets suck. It is not fun to watch things trade away.

It was not fun, but I wouldn't have traded it for anything.

I was doing what I could to make it fun. I was writing, which was fun. My Bloomberg list had grown quite large, and people were asking to be added to it every day. People wanted to read what I wrote. They wanted to hear what I had to say. I was becoming an oracle, of sorts. It was a strange experience.

It seemed that most of the street were in the same position that I was in. They knew that the housing market had problems. They knew that subprime was a problem. They knew that there was a possibility that the banks could be in trouble. They just didn't know how to make money off of it. The market kept going up, except for homebuilder stocks, which had croaked. They were the canary.

In my mind, it wasn't just residential real estate that was the problem, it was commercial real estate too. There was an exchange-traded fund that tracked commercial real estate, called IYR. It was filled with REITs, or real estate investment trusts, tax-advantaged entities that held income-producing property.

IYR was pissing me off.

It mocked me. It went up day after day. But people had gotten themselves into the same jackpot with commercial real estate that they had with residential real estate: they were borrowing more and more money, paying ever more stupid prices, with no possibility of ever being able to service the debt with rents received. They were buying for price appreciation.

I noticed that there was a divergence between commercial and residential real estate. How could residential real estate be in trouble, while commercial real estate continued to go up? They were connected, inextricably linked by the credit markets. At some point, the credit markets would simply be unable or unwilling to finance the marginal acquisition. Then the gig would be up.

I was going to be a hero. I wanted to be like Jay Knight. And this trade was going to buy me the Don Johnson suit and flip-flops.

I was going to short IYR.

Not short, mind you, because if I was wrong, I didn't want to have my head blown off. If commercial real estate continued to rally, I would be faced with potentially unlimited losses. I wanted to construct a trade where if I was wrong, my losses would be limited. I was going to buy *put options* on IYR. That way, there was only a limited amount of money that I could lose: the premium I paid for the options.

If I was going to be on the next plane to Miami, I was going to have to do this trade big. Really big. Big enough that people around here noticed. I had observed that the people who rose to the top of the organization, the people who really got ahead, weren't necessarily the people who traded the smartest. They were the people that traded the biggest. Wall Street doesn't distinguish between good risk and bad risk; it distinguishes only between big risk and small risk. I had been trading successfully for quite some time, but it made no difference, because I was trading too small to be noticed. I needed to trade big enough that I attracted attention to myself, even if I lost money on the trade, because bad attention was better than no attention at all.

Korenkiewicz, my boss, was the perfect example. Marty was a loose cannon, in the nautical sense of the term. When he traded, he traded wildly, taking massive positions in both futures and options. His daily

P&L swings were sickening; he was, on average, up or down a couple of million dollars a day. In the long run, he had made a decent amount of money, but he had made it with very high volatility, which meant that he had a very poor Sharpe ratio, a measure of reward-per-unit risk. Had he been a hedge fund, he would have found it very difficult to raise money with his track record. But he was not a hedge fund; he worked at an investment bank, and at an investment bank, nobody cares about your Sharpe ratio. They care about the bottom line: how many dollars there were at the end of the day. Korenkiewicz made good money, but he used up a lot of capital in the process.

This made no sense. Imagine a hedge fund with $10 billion of assets. Over the course of a year, it makes $100 million. The investors are pissed, because they have received only a 1 percent return. But the hedge fund managers say, "Wait! We made one hundred million dollars! That's great!" I could not understand the focus, to the exclusion of all else, on dollars and cents, when the rest of the world operated on return on capital or return on equity. Nobody talked about Jay Knight's percentage return. They talked only about how much money he made, which was, at last rumor, over $100 million a year. But he could have made it off of $100 billion in capital, for all I knew, which meant one thing: go big or go home.

I decided to buy four thousand IYR put options, slightly out of the money. I figured that would be big enough.

When I finally walked back onto the trading floor, I wondered, *How on earth did I ever work at this place?*

It was the same sea of white and blue shirts that it always was. But something was different. I was seeing, for the first time, that everyone was interested only in himself. I expected something like a hero's welcome or a standing ovation, but people were busy talking on the phone or looking at computer screens. Nobody had noticed that I was gone. They were inherently self-centered. *Good*, I thought, *this is going to be easy.*

On my way to my seat, I bumped into the imperious Chris Masters, now the head of equities.

I looked at him. He looked at me.

"You all right?" he asked.

"Yup."

"Good." He slapped me on the shoulder. "Get back in the game." *Rub some dirt on it.*

D.C. was glad to have me back, and said so.

"How are things?" I asked him.

"It was *insane* while you were gone."

"What?"

"Totally insane. We were doing four hundred thousand, five hundred thousand a day."

"Dude, you never told me."

"We didn't want you to worry. It got handled okay."

This was incredible. Doing $400,000 in commissions was a lot even for two people. For one person, it was impossible.

D.C. went on. "I didn't know where my risk was half the time. I was flying blind. It was awful. You are never allowed to check into a mental hospital again."

We both laughed.

I wanted to pick up where I left off. I wanted to start printing money. But the screens were moving way too fast.

*This is a problem.*

The medication was not helping me trade. There was a sea of numbers, and I wasn't making sense of any of it. I was swimming in a pool of wet cement. My brain had gone soft. I wasn't just rusty; the medication was screwing with my trading. I couldn't imagine how I had ever done this before.

*Am I going to be able to keep taking the medication?*

*You are going to need to take the medication. You want to end up back in the hospital? You want to start thinking that federal agents are after you?*

*But this is awful. I can't even make one trade.*

I was going to have to figure out a solution to this.

"SPYs, two hundred?" It was Kevin Rodman.

"I got it," I said to D.C.

"Forty-four, locked!"

"Buy 'em!"

*Okay, step-by-step. Accept. Print. Hedge. Book. Cross. Done.* I broke down the trade into pieces, concentrating on each individual element. Back to basics. I had to relearn how to do everything.

Then there was the fact that I had no ideas. I had been out of the market for about three weeks, and I didn't even know what was going on. The financial markets are a story. If you skip ahead fifty pages in a book, you are going to be lost. You are going to have to pick it up through inferences, by what is going on around you. It takes a great deal of time to catch up.

I felt like I didn't fit in—even worse than I felt before. Now I wasn't just the poor kid with bad suits. I was the poor kid with bad suits who was a mental patient.

*First things first.* Concentrate on flow trading. People get paid plenty of money to just be an ETF trader. *Don't try to do it all at once. It will come back to you.*

*I hope.*

I was filled with gratitude for my new life. Every day I was given a gift: the gift of the next twenty-four hours. What I did with that time was the most important decision of my life.

My trading was coming along in fits and starts. The medication proved to be an obstacle at first, but a few months after my hospitalization, my Russian model psychiatrist mercifully lowered the dosage, and I was feeling fine. Instead of trading a few thousand times a day, I was trading twenty times a day, if that. I was more deliberate, more thoughtful, and more rational. Trading, before, was an effort. I put on positions irrationally, sometimes with anger. I wanted to prove to the market that I was right. Now I had realized that the market is always right, and I am fortunate if I am able to hitchhike on it for part of the way.

We were still dealing with the same dirty hedge funds as before. I had been unable to cajole our sales force to produce any new customers in the United States, so I became more ambitious: I would look outside the United States for business.

Lehman Brothers had a group of people who did just that. They were sales traders, but they covered institutions overseas, focusing mostly on Western Europe. One guy covered Scandinavia, or as we called it, "the

Skandis." One covered the United Kingdom. A warm, gregarious SVP named Adam Rosello oversaw the operation.

I told him about my idea. I told him that our competitors, other banks, were seeing a lot of ETF trades from across the pond, and we were getting virtually none of it. In America we were almost number one in ETFs, but outside of the United States, Lehman Brothers was virtually unknown.

Rosello and I arranged a marketing trip, where I would go overseas and see as many money managers as I could, to try to drum up some business. I would bring two things: a stack of marketing materials and me. I would market myself as a source of knowledge; by this time, my writings had attracted over a thousand readers on Bloomberg. I was a little nervous about the trip, given my previous history as a salesman and the fact that I'd recently had a Velcro shower curtain.

I brought an extra suit, some T-shirts and underwear, and little else. My schedule was full; I was hitting five cities in five days: Zurich, Geneva, Amsterdam, Stockholm, and London. At the age of thirty-one, it was my first trip in Continental Europe. Zurich I found to be flat and cautious, Geneva was drenched in old money, Amsterdam was untamed, and Stockholm—well, everything they say about the women in Sweden was true. In London, I held court in the Sanderson hotel, playing pool and telling dirty jokes with the inverse of Rosello's team, the London guys who sold US stocks to UK clients. It seemed like they needed little excuse to go out. I returned triumphantly, high-fiving Rosello, doing a victory lap around the floor, and telling Mark Ricci how much business my trip was going to bring in. Then I sat down with D.C. and Steve Rodriguez, the new associate from the Wharton School of Business. Steve was introverted, considerate, and a deep thinker, though we hired him primarily for his computer skills. D.C. and I were sick of being spreadsheet jocks and wanted someone to do the dirty work for us.

I sit down at my desk and smile.

*Beep.* It's Rosello.

"Pick me up," he says.

I pick up the phone.

"Where can you show a bid on four hundred thousand EEM? It's Silvermine."

"Silvermine?"

"Bro, you just saw these guys in London. Big hedge fund. Remember?"

I do remember. I sat across a conference table from a heavyset trader named Terry, who was a perpetual motion machine. He tapped his feet, played with the papers I gave him, and shifted his weight.

"EEM pre-market—that's a hell of a way to start off." This trade had major hair on it. Under the best of circumstances, 400,000 EEM was a monster. It was an ETF made up of emerging markets stocks, filled with stocks from places like Brazil and India.

"I don't need to tell you what you have to do."

"I know." I had just seen these guys.

I draw in a breath. S&P futures were down eight points overnight. The ABX, a credit derivative based on subprime mortgages, was cratering. China had raised reserve requirements last night. The markets were looking awfully shaky.

"Show a 116 the figure bid."

"I'll be back," says Rosello.

"What's going on over there?" asks D.C. Both he and Steve are looking at me.

"Silvermine. I just saw these guys in London."

"400,000 EEM pre-market?"

"I know. I'll handle this."

*Beep.*

"Pick me up."

"Yeah."

"*Sold* at 116."

"Send me a ticket."

I fill the order with a sense of dread. I'm an experienced trader, but this time I am in over my head.

*I have to hedge.* I line up a pile of futures and let them drop. The market doesn't take it well; it drops another three points, stabilizes, and invites me to sell some more.

I look back at EEM. It is now *offered* at 115.50. Someone is trying to sell it fifty cents below where I had just bought it.

I am out a quick $200,000.

D.C. is looking at the screen silently. He can see the 115.50 offer, just like I can. He knows what is going on. Technically I am in charge, but in practice, we are a team.

"What do you think here?"

"There's no bid."

"I know there's no bid."

"I wouldn't have done the trade," he says.

"Okay, tough guy, but we had to do the trade. I just saw these guys. We can't pass on their first trade."

Now there is a 115.00 offer. Down $400,000, and the market is still not open. There is still no bid, no way to trade out of it even if we want to.

114.50 offer. Then $600,000, and we haven't sold a share.

Finally the market opens, and EEM begins trading around 114. I lay out a quick 50,000 shares, and it acts poorly: 113.50.

We are out almost $1 million, and it is the first five minutes of the day.

"SPYs, a million!"

It is Jamie.

"Thirteen bid!" says D.C. He doesn't even show an offer.

"Sold!"

"That'll help," I say sarcastically.

Throughout the day, the market grinds lower and lower and lower. We are buried under an avalanche of selling. They are selling everything in sight: SPY, XLF, XLB, QQQQ. I can't bring myself to sell all of the EEM. *It has to come back. This isn't happening. This can't be happening.*

By three o'clock, I have sold the balance of the position, the last piece at 107.

We have lost $1.6 million.

I'm not ready to give up, though. We have been selling off all day, and the market is down over 3 percent. The market hasn't been down over 2 percent in six months. What is everyone freaking out about? Subprime, supposedly, and this China reserve requirements thing. I fail to sense the urgency. This market is bound to rally.

*Wait for it.*

*Wait for it.*

At three thirty, I know it is time to buy. With grandiosity, I stand up, puffing out my chest, pick up the phone, and announce over the hoot: "I AM A SIZE BUYER OF SPYs. OFFER-SIDE BID TWO MILLION

SPYs." I am telling all our customers that I will pay any price just to get long.

*Fuck it. I'm not going to get a trade.* I go into the futures and buy as many as I can: three thousand.

I am going to make it all back.

I am right, momentarily. The market ticks up a few handles. I've made about $250,000.

*On the comeback trail.*

Then, suddenly, the bottom is out. The market tumbles off a cliff.

Everyone on the floor sees it at once. You can hear people say, "Whoa!" and "What the fuck?"

The futures screen is a mess of free fucking electrons. There are no bids and offers, just a jumbled soup.

Then it stops—the screen is frozen.

*Fuck.*

I click on it. It's broken.

The electronic futures are down, but the open-outcry, pit-traded contracts are still trading. I pull up a chart.

They are in free fall.

For the first time ever, I fear for my job.

There is nothing left but space, the open air of a vacuum where no trade is taking place, where positions are being marked aggressively lower. In a few minutes, the futures are down an additional twenty points.

I have just lost $3 million, on top of the $1.6 million I lost on EEM.

If I sold here, I would surely lose my job. All I can do is hope and pray that it will come back.

Under normal circumstances, hope is not a strategy, but it is all I have.

Suddenly, the market begins to rise again; slowly at first, then turning into a furious rally. The futures screen reboots and comes to life. I can now get out of my trade at the same point I got into it.

I sell the entire position, escaping with a loss of only about $200,000.

"Hooollly shit," says D.C.

I learn two things from that experience:

One. Do not fuck with the market.

Two. You are the worst salesman in the world.

• • •

*What if the refrigerator is open?*

Every morning, on the way to work, I would grab two cans of soda out of the fridge; my effort to save a buck here and there instead of buying it from the trader pantry. Every morning, I would close the fridge and head out the door to work. This morning, I couldn't remember closing the fridge.

*What if I left the refrigerator open?*

Well, the food would go bad, but more importantly, the cat could get inside the fridge, and should the door happen to swing shut, he would be trapped in there and suffocate.

*That's completely irrational. The door won't open on its own, and it won't close on its own.*

Still.

I went back up the steps, unlocked the door, and went inside. The refrigerator was closed.

In that moment, I understood what was happening: in addition to having to check and recheck to make sure that the door was locked, I was going to have to check the refrigerator every morning. It would become part of my ritual.

I locked the dead bolt five, three, and one times. I locked the door handle five, three, and one times. I then locked the dead bolt three times, then once more. I locked the door handle three, then one time. I locked the dead bolt one more time, then the door handle one more time. I checked it again.

*Ready.*

This was getting annoying. All of my other symptoms had disappeared. The mood swings, the anger, the irritability, the lack of sleep, the depression, all gone. Within a month of leaving the hospital, I was as good as new. But the obsessive-compulsive behavior was still there—in fact, it had gotten worse, not better. *Where does this shit come from?*

I got to work and did some reading on the internet. I learned that obsessive-compulsiveness was part of a class of anxiety disorders. It could be treated through therapy and sometimes with medication. Pah. The last thing I needed was more medication. Already I felt like a chemistry set; the Russian model liked to tinker with the dosage.

I had work to do:

FM: JARED DILLIAN, LEHMAN BROTHERS INC.
TO: SALES

IMAGINE A TIME SERIES. A LINE, CONNECTING THE DOTS. IT FORMS A TREND. LET'S ALL SIT AROUND AND TRY TO FIGURE OUT WHAT, OUT OF HUNDREDS OF FACTORS, HAS CAUSED THE TREND.

WHAT CAUSED 9 MONTHS OF GRIND IN THIS TIME SERIES FOLLOWED BY A MELTDOWN? IT IS THE WORLD'S BIGGEST UNCONSTRAINED MULTIVARIABLE EQUATION. THE YEN CARRY TRADE? MAYBE, MAYBE NOT. MAYBE IT WAS PERCEPTION OF VALUATION. MAYBE IT WAS RATES. MAYBE IT WAS FED EXPECTATIONS. MAYBE IT WAS MY CONCEPT OF "GRAVITY," THE IDEA THAT CREDIT AND VOLATILITY ARE NOT "MATTER," BUT INSTEAD, A FORCE. MAYBE IT WAS A LITTLE OR NONE OF THESE THINGS. BUT THE YEN CARRY TRADE SEEMS TO BE OUR COLLECTIVE CONSENSUS FOR WHAT WENT WRONG LAST WEEK. WHICH MEANS IT WAS PROBABLY IN ERROR. IS IT? WE WILL NEVER KNOW FOR SURE.

CONSIDER ANOTHER IDEA. INNOVATION, AND GROWTH, AS EXPRESSED BY THE STOCK MARKET, OCCURRED IN SEMICONDUCTORS IN THE 1980S, AND IN INTERNET IN THE 1990S. IN THE 2000S, IT IS FINANCE. FINANCE HAS BEEN THE MOST RECENT TECHNOLOGICAL INNOVATION, WITH ALL THE COLLATERALIZING, DISINTERMEDIATION, TRANCHING, SWAPPING, AND HEDGING THAT WE HAVE ALL LEARNED TO DO. SOME OF THIS MAGIC, THIS ALCHEMY IN WHICH WE TURN WATER INTO WINE, IS SHOWING ITS LIMITS IN IRVINE, CALIFORNIA. FINANCIALS ARE DOWN THE MOST IN A MONTH OF ALL THE SECTORS.

IS THIS THE END OF THE BULL MARKET IN FINANCIALS? WILL FINANCIALS NO LONGER BE THE BIGGEST WEIGHT IN THE S&P? OTHERS HAVE BEMOANED THE PERCENTAGE OF OUR GDP THAT IS DEVOTED TO FINANCIAL ALCHEMY. THEY HAVE OBSERVED THE TRANSITION OF GE, AN INDUSTRIAL CONGLOMERATE, TO A FINANCE COMPANY. I THINK THERE IS A STRONG POSSIBILITY THAT THIS TREND IS RUNNING OUT.

IF YOU MUST BE LONG ANYTHING, SHORT FINANCIALS AGAINST IT.

I paused to play with my pet IYR trade. It had been doing well—the legendary real estate investor Sam Zell had puked all his holdings at the top, and I was sitting on about $1 million in profit. It was not going to get me to Miami, but it was a good start, and if I was patient with the trade, I might make more.

It is a natural human tendency to want to look at winning trades more often than losing trades. When IYR was going my way, which is to say, down, I recalculated the spreadsheet repeatedly, hitting the F9 key: F9, F9, F9. IYR was my little baby animal, and I was caressing it to sleep. Get down there, you bastard.

I was pretty fucking proud of myself. Not long ago, I was in a place with no razors, no plastic knives, and no shower curtain rods. Now I had taken aim and blown the head off of the biggest, baddest, bubbliest bull market, and I had a good lead on the trade if I wanted to add to it.

"Lehman on the tape!" someone yelled from across the floor.

I pulled up the hot news on Bloomberg. It said:

BN 11:49 ARCHSTONE-SMITH BOUGHT BY CONSORTIUM FOR
   $19.8B


BN 11:50 LEHMAN BROTHERS BUYS ARCHSTONE-SMITH

*Fuck.*

This meant that, while I was selling REITs, somebody else at Lehman was buying them.

In fact, someone had made a bet on REITs so large that it was half the size of our market cap.

*This is not going to be good*, I thought. I was pretty sure I was right on my trade, and REITs were going to keep going down. I was pretty sure that buying Archstone—an absolutely gigantic REIT—was a bad idea. I was pretty sure that whoever was in charge of real estate at Lehman Brothers was a complete buffoon.

His name was Mark Walsh.

Most of us had no idea what went on in real estate. If we knew, we would have hit the bid on our stock and hit the bricks.

The firm was swimming in money. In the not too distant past, Lehman had been very disciplined about expenses—not saving paper clips in the mold of Bear Stearns, mind you, but people flew coach on short flights, and the administrative people were appropriately annoying about getting expenses approved. Now, it seemed, the firm was defecating money. I was sent to a firm-wide vice president leadership program (I finally did make VP in January, anticlimactically), where I did goofy shit like crawl around on the floor blindfolded under the instruction of some FDNY fire chief mook, and did ballet moves with the prima ballerina Susan Jaffe, clenching an imaginary marble in my butt cheeks. It was followed up by a massive reception at a nearby hotel, with the keynote address given by Bill Clinton, whom we had reportedly paid $150,000 for the privilege. Dick Fuld presented him to us with a startlingly partisan introduction, and Clinton followed up with an hour-long condemnation of Bush-era policies. It was surreal.

Meanwhile, on the trading floor, people were spending money like there was no tomorrow. Marty Korenkiewicz had become the king of variance swaps and was paying brokers so much money that they were practically buying him lunch every day. Barbecue, sushi, Lenny's—there was always a gargantuan feast parked at the end of our row. I found it difficult to resist. Then the cash guys, who were constantly trying to one-up one another on who could buy the fanciest lunch, were spending up to $40 a meal, having burgers and steaks delivered from places like Bobby Van's, the Palm, and Del Frisco's—places that would actually include complimentary steak knives with the meal.

It was surreal.

I had, a month or two ago, found out my compensation for the year, and it was absurd. I was getting paid $850,000, which was an insane amount of money. Once again, I had no plans for it. I was saving it. Someday it might be necessary.

People were getting paid a lot of money, but it is important to not be deceived by the pornographic numbers. Not all of the money is paid in cash; a lot of it is in stock that cannot be sold for five years. In five years, a lot can happen. The stock might be worth a lot less. As a VP, I was getting about 25 percent of the money in stock, and when I mentally added up all my wealth, I didn't even include it in the calculation. It wasn't liquid. I couldn't sell it. To me, it was worth zero.

However, I was able to sell the stock that I had received five years ago when I got my first bonus, back in early 2002. It was thirty-six shares. The day it vested, I sold it at a price of $84.51, netting me $3,042.36 before taxes.

Without knowing it, I had practically top-ticked LEH.

## 15

## Grace | Spring 2007–Winter 2008

The housing market was fucking out of control.

FM: JARED DILLIAN, LEHMAN BROTHERS INC.
TO: SALES

A FRIEND OF MINE (A MORTGAGE PROFESSIONAL) AND I WERE RIDING RENTED ONE-SPEED BIKES UP AND DOWN THE STRAND IN HERMOSA BEACH. WE FOLLOWED SOME SIGNS POINTING TO AN OPEN HOUSE LIKE MOTHS TO A BRIGHT LIGHT. TWO OR THREE HOUSES BACK FROM THE BEACH WAS A PIECE OF NEW CONSTRUCTION, WHAT WE ON THE EAST COAST WOULD CALL A DUPLEX. FROM THE FRONT, THE BUILDING WAS A GRAY, STYLISH ATTEMPT AT MODERN ARCHITECTURE, MUCH LIKE MANY OTHER HOUSES IN THE AREA.

WE KICKED OFF OUR SHOES AND WENT IN THE FRONT UNIT. WALKING UP THE STAIRS TO THE LIVING ROOM, WE FOUND THE REAL-ESTATE EQUIVALENT OF GLENN GUGLIA, DREW BARRYMORE'S FIANCE IN *THE WEDDING SINGER*. MR. BROKER WAS CHANNELING GLENN, A SYMBOL OF 1980S BOND MARKET EXCESS, BOTH IN APPEARANCE AND DEMEANOR AND IN HIS SKIMPY RATIO OF INTELLIGENCE TO NET WORTH. THE REAL GLENN GUGLIA, ACTOR MATTHEW GLAVE, IS TRAINED IN THE MARTIAL ART OF SOO BAHK DO MOO DUK KWAN, FORMERLY KNOWN AS TANG SOO DO MOO DUK KWAN, IN LAKEWOOD, OHIO, UNDER THE GUIDANCE OF MASTER MARLENE KACHEVAS DURING 1984–1985. YOU CAN'T MAKE THIS STUFF UP.

"THE BACK UNIT'S THE ONE THAT'S FOR SALE," MR. BROKER TELLS US. "I SOLD THIS [EXPLETIVE] THIS MORNING." HE IS DRAPED OVER A CHAIR IN THE LIVING ROOM NEXT TO THE FRONT WINDOW. "THIS ONE SOLD FOR TWO-FIVE. THE BACK ONE'S FOR SALE AT ONE-SEVEN." MR. BROKER IS TOSSING OFF SEVEN-FIGURE PRICES CARELESSLY, LIKE THROWING A PAPER GLIDER. HE LOOKS LIKE HE CAN'T WAIT TO GET OUT OF HIS SHIRT AND TIE AND DO

WHATEVER GLENN GUGLIA DOES WITH HIS FREE TIME. "THE PLACE ON THE CORNER WENT FOR SEVEN MIL. AND THE ONE DOWN THE STRAND WENT FOR EIGHT-THREE." I TELL HIM WE'RE GOING TO CHECK OUT THE BACK UNIT. "BUY THE [EXPLETIVE], WILL YA?"

WE WALKED AROUND IN THE BACK UNIT AND FOUND IT SATISFACTORY. WE RETURNED LATER TO SEE THE FRONT UNIT AND FOUND MR. BROKER STRETCHED OUT ON THE BED, IN THE MASTER BEDROOM, TRYING TO CATCH SOME Z'S.

IN ANY BOOM-BUST CYCLE YOU FIND PEOPLE MAKING HAYSTACKS OF CASH COMPLETELY OUT OF PROPORTION TO THEIR INTELLIGENCE, ABILITY, OR WORK ETHIC. MR. BROKER/GLENN GUGLIA MADE $175,000 LITERALLY IN HIS SLEEP, AND HIS SALES PITCH AT A SECOND $119,000 COMMISSION WAS "BUY THE [EXPLETIVE], WILL YA?" WHILE I FOUND HIM LOATHSOME AND OF-FENSIVE, I CAN AT LEAST USE HIM AS A COINCIDENT INDICATOR. I WILL CALL HIS BROKERAGE ONCE A MONTH TO SEE IF HE'S STILL WORKING. WHEN HE'S GONE, IT WILL BE A GREAT BUY SIGNAL. AND HE WILL BE OFF BUILDING ETHANOL PLANTS.

I had been visiting with Chris Vincent, my friend from the Lehman associate program and the cabin in New Hampshire. Vincent was living the good life, working as a portfolio manager for a mortgage firm in Southern California, and spent a not inconsiderable amount of time enjoying the scenery on the beach. At the time, it seemed like a fantastic trade.

I had been full of wisdom on the forthcoming housing crunch to my clients in the form of my Bloomberg messages, but I hadn't been very good at taking my own advice. The market was impossible to trade. No matter what I did, stocks refused to go down. It was demoralizing. I was bearish, and wrong, just like a lot of other smart people on Wall Street. I no longer had the certainty of my convictions. Being right *eventually* was no consolation; by then, I would have lost too much money.

Lehman Brothers Equities, however, was in full swing. We were growing. We hired some additional traders, including a Val Kilmer dop-pelgänger we called Hollywood, and a pale, brainy trader dressed in dark shirts we called Circuit City. Marty had hired his own pet, a neurotic former structured-vol trader named Louis Hamilton. Structured volatility is a fancy way of saying exotic volatility, which is a fancy way of saying that he traded options that were unusual and difficult to price. Structured vol was for the real geniuses, the rocket scientists that were socially incapable of working with anyone else on the floor. But Louis, a reasonably good-looking Harvard MBA, was the most presentable out of the bunch.

Louis knew how to price options, but he knew next to nothing about markets. Sitting behind me, he was continually asking me what I thought the market was going to do.

"What's the market doing here?"

"Going up."

Inevitably, I would be right. And I would have failed to take my own advice.

Then there was Happy, a shambling mess of a human being who we had hired to trade higher-order derivatives. Happy was a mad genius, having graduated from MIT, but he weighed north of three hundred pounds and slouched around the floor with his shirt untucked. He was, perhaps, the single most unpresentable banker that existed anywhere in the universe. He sat in a pile, drinking Diet Coke directly out of two-liter bottles, which he consumed at a rate of about three a day. He looked like a forty-foot python that had just swallowed something big, like Louis Hamilton. He was one of God's creations, like John Coffey in *The Green Mile*: a great, gentle man, and one of the few decent human beings on Wall Street.

Together, along with D.C. and Steve, and a few other analysts I hazed from time to time, we formed the index desk. We traded anything in the stock markets that had anything to do with an index. Steve, D.C., and I traded ETFs, or what was known as the delta, and Marty, Louis, and Happy traded the options, the nonlinearity. We were a lacrosse god, a writer, a mute, two fat geniuses, a Harvard snob, and a couple of mascots. I joked that we were the island of misfit toys. But these misfit toys were making a lot of money for the firm.

We developed a system where I came up with trade ideas that would inevitably make a lot of money and fed them to Marty, who would put them on in massive size. I learned that I was too chickenshit to use any of my own ideas, so I gave them to Marty; he would make money on them, to the benefit of the firm and, ultimately, me. For me, the system worked. I didn't care so much about making money as I did about being right. Marty cared more about making money and would put on just about any trade that I suggested to him, no matter how outlandish. After a few months, we had trades on in just about every asset class, including credit, credit volatility (options on CDX), energy, gold, interest rates—just about everything except for mortgages. Marty even got long cotton, after I had urged him to do so. I was the idea man for a macro portfolio manager, but Marty was taking most of the credit.

Working at a place like Lehman Brothers provided certain perks. The firm offered us disability insurance that enabled us to retain a certain percentage of our earnings should we become incapacitated in any way. This was interesting to me, because I had been locked up once already, and though I felt more stable than I had in years, who knew what was going to happen in the future? I wasn't so much worried about getting crippled by a deliveryman on a bicycle as I was worried about going out of my gourd. But when I met with the disability insurance broker, he told me that I was disqualified because I had been in the hospital in the past year.

Louis told me about his meeting with the disability insurance people.

"Did you notice that those guys know your comp?" he asked.

"Come again?"

"Your comp. He had my comp on a piece of paper."

"So?"

"So. That is supposed to be confidential."

"Well," I said, "the firm probably releases that information to those guys. They need it if they are going to be calculating premiums."

Louis frowned. "Anyway," he continued, "so I asked him, 'If you have my comp, do you have everyone's comp?'"

"And?"

"And he says yes. So I ask him, how much does a managing director make? He hedges a little bit and says it's a really huge range, but says that pay can vary from one million on the low end to multiple millions on the high end."

"Wow."

"So then I ask him, 'How much does a VP make?' And he says any-where from a few hundred thousand up to four million."

"Four million?" I exclaimed. "What the fuck VP makes four sticks a year?"

"Right? That's what I said. I told him it has to be in structured credit or mortgages or something. You know what he said?"

"What?"

"Nope: *real estate.*"

It all made sense now. These drunks who went and bought Archstone, the drunks who had risked the entire firm, were getting paid assloads of money. The traders thought that the bankers were getting rich. The bank-ers thought that the traders were getting rich. They were both wrong: the people in real estate were getting incredibly rich. How much talent does it take to buy a building and wait for it to go up in price?

If you want to spot the next big bubble, all you have to do is follow the money. Look around you, and see who is getting paid more than the professional athletes. In the early eighties, it was the oilmen. In 1999 and 2000, it was the technology bankers. Now it was the real estate guys. I was hearing anecdotes of Europeans calling up New York City real estate brokers and buying million-dollar apartments *sight unseen.* The subprime lenders, like New Century and Accredited Home Lending, had already gone tits up. Subprime was dead. But commercial real estate was imper-vious to reason or logic.

I had busted my ass to get to Wall Street. I had gone to business school, working two jobs at the same time, but while I was getting paid reasonably well, I was still having trouble getting promoted, being po-litically deaf. For once, just once in my life, I wanted to fall ass backward into money. Just once. I wanted to blunder into some job that was going to pay me millions of dollars a year.

Then, in another thought, I probably *still* wouldn't be happy.

If you have been around the markets long enough, you know intuitively when the market is healthy and when it is sick. You know when it is paranoid, and you know when it is complacent. You know when it is am-bitious, and you know when it is meek. Suddenly, in the middle of July, for no apparent reason, the market got AIDS. Everything went wrong at the same time. Credit, as represented by the spreads on corporate bonds and the price of credit default swaps, began to widen. Emerging market equities were hammered. Carry trades—the act of borrowing in one currency with low interest rates and investing in another currency with high interest rates—began to unwind. And most of all, financial stocks were taking a beating, including Lehman Brothers stock.

It is what I had been expecting for years, but I failed to anticipate what it would look like when it actually began to happen. Suddenly, the realization had hit the markets that people were too leveraged, whether it was hedge funds, banks, or individuals; that too much money had been borrowed; and that it could not possibly be paid back in full. In the financial markets, something isn't a problem until it is a problem. People had known for years about excessive leverage, but nobody did anything about it until they had to. The markets, and the people in it, have a tendency to look past structural defects as long as everyone is making money in the short term.

From our standpoint as ETF traders, things suddenly got a bit more interesting. Hedge funds use ETFs to hedge, for the most part. If they like a bank stock, like Citigroup, they will buy it and short a financials ETF, such as XLF, against it. If they hate a utility stock, like Duke Energy, they will sell it short and buy a utilities ETF, like XLU, against it. Suddenly every trade began to move against everyone at the same time. To the extent that hedge funds had to liquidate their trades, like Citigroup and Duke Energy, they also had to take off their hedges, like XLF and XLU. With everyone taking off his hedges all at once, D.C. and I suddenly found that we had a lot of business.

It was a miserable time to be making markets. When things are good, there is a lot of competition for business, and traders like us made very *tight* markets—with a nonexistent spread between bid and offer. But suddenly there was a lot of volatility—things were moving around a lot—and people still expected the same tight markets. We made, on more than one occasion, $1 million of commissions in a single day, but we were losing half of it, if not more, in trading losses. We did the best we could to minimize the damage, but we were getting pummeled by our customers.

Meanwhile, every hedge fund in the world wanted to trade on instant messenger. Salespeople didn't even pick up the phone anymore; they were tippy-tapping away on the keyboard to their clients. On the phone, trades can be done quickly—get a market, buy or sell. With instant messenger, there was a delay. We found ourselves doing $200 million trades in the middle of a cratering market over instant messenger. For the hedge fund client, it was like shooting fish in a barrel. Ask for a market, wait, wait, wait for it to move. If it moves in your direction, you sell. If it moves against you, ask for a refresh. A hedge fund client could get three simultaneous markets from three different banks and trade on the best one. Instant messenger had given free options to all of our clients. Options have value, and we were selling them for free.

Tradingwise, I didn't know what to do. I had some trades that were working out well (I was long volatility, in the form of call options on the VIX), but I was too busy to sell financials or play the carry unwind, where investors sell high-yielding currencies in favor of low-yielding ones. I was too preoccupied by customer trades to trade proprietarily, which was too bad. *Jay Knight must be making a fortune,* I thought. In any case, most of the trade ideas I had given to Marty were making a fortune.

I began to think about the possibility of a crash; the market felt like it could fall to pieces at any moment. In general, a crash is defined as a multi-standard-deviation event—a move in the market that is so large that it is unexplainable by any fundamental event. A crash is a liquidity phenomenon; there is a burning theater with one small exit. At various points in the month of July, I felt one coming—I felt that we could be down 10 percent in a single day, and all the market required was a little push.

FM: JARED DILLIAN, LEHMAN BROTHERS INC.
TO: SALES


IT IS NOT A MIRACLE THAT THE MARKET HAS CRASHED SPECTACULARLY, TWICE, IN 20 STANDARD DEVIATION MOVES. THE TRUE MIRACLE IS THAT IT HAS NOT CRASHED EVEN MORE. FORGET THE PROBABILITIES AND THE FAT TAILS FOR A SECOND. IT (THE MARKET) IS AN INHERENTLY UNSTABLE SYSTEM POPULATED WITH PEOPLE WHO ARE MORE VOLATILE ON AVERAGE, WHO ARE GOVERNED BY THE 95 PERCENT OF THEIR BRAIN THAT IS SUBCONSCIOUS, WHO ARE IRRATIONAL, WHO DEAL IN CONVEXITY BUT FAIL

TO UNDERSTAND IT, ET CETERA. THE TRUE MIRACLE IS THAT THE MARKET DOESN'T CRASH ONCE A YEAR—AND THAT IT ALWAYS SEEMS TO RECOVER.

TAKE FEB. 27, 2007, FOR EXAMPLE. WE HAVE CLEARLY DOCUMENTED WHAT CAUSED THE MINICRASH: CHINA AND THE EARLY HINTS OF SUBPRIME. BUT WE HAVE NO RATIONAL EXPLANATION WHY THE SITUATION DID NOT GET WORSE. WE HAVE NO IDEA WHY THE STOCK MARKET RECOVERED. IN A PARALLEL UNIVERSE, 2/27 TURNS INTO A MASSACRE. PECK SAYS, IN THE CONTEXT OF MENTAL HEALTH: WE KNOW PRECISELY WHY PEOPLE BECOME MENTALLY ILL. BUT WE DON'T KNOW WHY OTHER PEOPLE SURVIVE TRAUMAS AS WELL AS THEY DO. WE KNOW PRECISELY WHY SOME PEOPLE COMMIT SUICIDE. BUT WE DON'T KNOW WHY OTHERS DO NOT COMMIT SUICIDE.

THE MARKET IS LIKELY TO GO DOWN, PERHAPS CONSIDERABLY MORE. I MAY EVEN LOSE MY JOB. YOU MAY EVEN LOSE YOUR JOB. BUT WE ARE NOT LIKELY TO SEE A REPEAT OF '29 OR '87. THE MARKET HAS A TRACK RECORD OF BEING ACCIDENT RESISTANT. YOU MAY ASCRIBE THIS PROPERTY TO THE SUPERNATURAL. OR YOU CAN CONTENT YOURSELF WITH SOME RATIONAL EXPLANATION. AFTER READING THIS BLOOMBERG, SHOULD YOU STILL FEEL THE NEED TO BUY SOME CRASH PROTECTION, LEHMAN IS AS GOOD A PLACE AS ANY. BUT EVEN THOUGH ONE OR MORE OF US MAY BELIEVE IN THE SUPERNATURAL HERE, WE ARE STILL GOING TO DYNAMICALLY HEDGE YOUR TRADE.

We know why some people commit suicide. But we don't know why other people do not commit suicide. I didn't know why I didn't commit suicide; why I decided to gallop across town to a psychiatrist in the middle of the trading day instead of going home and butchering myself. I *should have* committed suicide. I was *destined* to commit suicide. But something, somewhere, intervened.

The financial markets had the same self-destructive instincts. They *should have* crashed. They *wanted* to crash. They were *destined* to crash. But they did not. Someone or something, somewhere, intervened. Crashes happen so rarely that people think they are extreme events. But they are not. *Not* crashing is the extreme event. Markets are made up of people who are irrational and unpredictable, and all of them—all—will eventually fail.

Every morning, when I woke up, I had to listen to a voice in my head. Every morning the voice told me two things: One, everything is not going to be OK. Two, you don't deserve any of this. This was my base-case scenario every day, and I have had to build myself up from there. I allowed myself to feel gratitude for my diagnosis, my lifesaving medication, my job, my wife, and all of my friends. I had to tell myself that everything was going to be okay.

Even when it wasn't.

The financial system was under a great deal of stress. It suddenly became difficult to borrow certain stocks. LIBOR had come unhinged from its usual spread over Fed funds. And there was a great deal of debate as to whether the Fed should lower interest rates.

I had strong feelings about this. This "subprime crisis," which is what people were calling it in 2007, was a result of people borrowing more money than they could ever possibly pay back. I saw them do it. We all saw them do it. From sophisticated housing speculators to people whose eyes were bigger than their stomachs, everybody was getting in on the act and taking out negative-amortization mortgages with no money down. I was offended.

The debate, which had already turned political, then focused on monetary policy. Certain congressional members, like Sen. Chris Dodd of Connecticut and Rep. Barney Frank of Massachusetts, wanted the Fed to cut interest rates in response to the crisis. But Congress—or even the White House, for that matter—isn't supposed to have any influence on monetary policy. If they wanted to speak about it as a matter of public policy, I supposed that they were entitled, but it was bad form. Federal Reserve independence was sacred. There was not even supposed to be the impression that lawmakers had any influence on interest rates. If they did, it could have disastrous results. Every hyperinflation in human history can be traced back to a situation where the central bank was being operated for political ends.

Going into the September meeting of the FOMC, the interest rate policymaking body of the Federal Reserve, nearly everyone universally thought that the Fed was going to cut interest rates at least a little bit; the question was how much. At a minimum, people believed it would cut twenty-five basis points, or a quarter of a percent. Others thought they would cut interest rates by fifty basis points. I didn't know, but I knew that if they indeed went fifty basis points, it would have nothing to do with economics and everything to do with political pressure from people like Barney Frank.

I watched.

I waited.

Fifty basis points.

I wrote:

FM: JARED DILLIAN, LEHMAN BROTHERS INC.

TO: SALES

THE ONLY RATIONAL THING TO DO HERE IS BUY EVERYTHING THAT ISN'T NAILED DOWN. BUY OIL. BUY GOLD. BUY WHEAT, CORN, AND BEANS. BUY COPPER, LEAD, AND TIN. BUY THE WHOLE DAMN COMMODITY INDEX. BUY IT UNTIL YOUR HEAD CAVES IN. BUY EUR, CAD, AUD, AND NZD, AND FINANCE IT BY SELLING THE BOLIVAR, ER, I MEAN THE DOLLAR. BUY GE, MSFT, PFE, XOM, AND CSCO. BUY THE SPX. BUY THE NDX. BUY THE S15HOME. SELL PUTS ON HOMEBUILDERS AND USE THE PROCEEDS TO BUY A HOUSE. BUY POT. BUY AGU. BUY SEVERAL 50-POUND BAGS OF FERTILIZER AND KEEP THEM IN YOUR BASEMENT. BUY 100 PROPANE BOTTLES AT HOME DEPOT. BUY HOME DEPOT, HOME EQUITY LOANS ARE BACK IN STYLE. BUY A BALL-PEEN HAM-MER. BUY AN AIR COMPRESSOR. BUY A CHEESE GRATER. BUY A GERMAN SHEPHERD. BUY A RACEHORSE NAMED "CURRENCY DEBASEMENT." BUY ONE OF THOSE THINGS YOU SHAKE UP AND IT SNOWS INSIDE. BUY ONE OF THOSE THINGS YOU PUSH AND YOU MAKE THE LINES ON A BASEBALL FIELD. BUY A BASEBALL TEAM. BUY THE WASHINGTON NATIONALS AND RENAME THEM THE "DIRTNAPS." BUY MADONNA'S *RAY OF LIGHT.* WE ARE LIVING IN A NOMINAL WORLD, AND I AM A MATERIAL GIRL. BUY A WEBSITE, A BANKING LICENSE, AND START SELLING MORTGAGES. BUY A DANCING ALIEN IN A BIKINI. BUY SCRAP METAL. BUY MY CLASS RING AND SMELT IT. BUY GILLETTE FUSION AND 20 YEARS SUPPLY OF RAZOR BLADES. BUY A GRAVEL TRUCK. BUY ALL

THE VILLAGE PEOPLE COSTUMES. BUY THE BARRY BONDS 756 BALL, BRAND IT WITH AN ASTERISK AND SEND IT OUT INTO SPACE. BUY SEVERAL COPIES OF *ATLAS SHRUGGED* AND SEND THEM TO THE HOUSE AND SENATE FINANCE COMMITTEES. BUY FARMLAND. BUY DIRT. BUY EVERY LAST FREAKIN' ELEMENT IN THE PERIODIC TABLE. BUY A PARTICLE ACCELERATOR. BUY THE CHUNNEL. BUY LICHTENSTEIN. BUY A COMMERCIAL FISHING PERMIT AND EXPLOIT ONE OF GOD'S CREATIONS. BUY A LENNY'S SANDWICH SHOP. BUY A SPOOL OF NETWORKING CABLE. BUY ME SOMETHING NICE FOR CHRISTMAS. BUY ALL OF THESE THINGS, BECAUSE SOON THE PRICE IS GOING TO BE HIGHER. BUY WHATEVER YOU WANT, JUST MAKE SURE YOU SPEND ALL YOUR MONEY AND GO DEEP INTO DEBT, TAKING OUT A MORTGAGE, A HOME EQUITY LOAN, A LEVERAGED LOAN, AN INVESTMENT GRADE BOND, A HIGH YIELD BOND, REG T MARGIN, OR CREDIT CARD DEBT. IT'S THE AMERICAN WAY, MAN, GET WITH THE GOSH DARN PROGRAM.

My phone was ringing off the hook. My email in-box was filling up.

I had touched a nerve. Without really knowing it at the time, I had spoken directly to the fears of a lot of people in the market, the fears of what the central bank would do to extricate itself from the mortgage problem. What we were experiencing was the beginnings of a *debt deflation*. The economy slows, prices fall, and since there is a lot of debt, it becomes hard, if not impossible, to pay off the debt absent any inflation. The correct solution to a debt deflation is to do nothing: the economy will recover on its own if given enough time. But that is too painful a solution for most governments and central banks to pursue; instead they want to create *inflation* because when the aggregate level of prices is rising, it becomes cheaper to pay back the debt in real terms.

The problem is that inflation is the enemy. The problem is that inflation, once it begins, is very difficult to control. Inflation can do a lot more damage to an economy—as well as to the entire social fabric—than deflation can. Look at Japan: after twenty years of deflation, things are still pretty good. I think that most countries would be happy to have what Japan has after twenty years of deflation. But inflation inevitably leads to hyperinflation, which can rip apart a society—and start wars.

What did I know? I was just the ETF trader.

• • •

I had managed to make about $1.5 million off the IYR trade. I still was not in Miami.

Marty was still giving me a hard time about my trading. He told me that my hit ratio on my trade ideas was higher than anyone that he'd ever seen, and that I should take advantage of it by trading as big as I could. I listened momentarily. It was good, sometimes, to take advice from Marty.

If there was one thing that Marty had done well, and Ingram had done even better, it was to appropriately size a bet. This was something I found very hard to do. The idea was to determine which of your trades were the "better" trades, the ones with the higher expected values. You wanted to allocate the most money to your best trades. I was terrible at that; I bet small on everything, even my best ideas.

I had an idea: I wanted to put on a curve steepener.

There are all different kinds of interest rates. There are thirty-year interest rates, there are ten-year interest rates, there are five-year interest rates, there are two-year interest rates, and everything in between. If you plot these on a graph, the shape of the line connecting the points is known as the *yield curve*. The yield curve can be flat (all interest rates are basically the same), or it can be steep (long-term interest rates are higher than short-term interest rates). There are economic implications to this; when the curve is steep, banks tend to make money because they are borrowing at a lower interest rate and lending at a higher one. When the curve is flat, it usually means that a recession is coming, because the Fed has raised short-term interest rates to the point where they are going to begin to inflict pain on the economy.

The yield curve was relatively flat. But I knew that this fifty-basis-point interest rate cut by the Fed was not going to be the last; actually, it was going to be the first of many. My view was that short-term interest rates were going to be brought lower by the Federal Reserve, and long-term interest rates were going to remain higher because of anticipation of the inflation that the Fed was about to set off. It was a fairly obvious idea, but sometimes the obvious trades work the best.

Marty told me, "Don't even talk to me until you get that thing above one hundred thousand dollars a basis point." What he meant was that I should have the trade so large that I would make or lose $100,000 if the spread between two-year interest rates and ten-year interest rates changed by a single basis point, or a hundredth of a percent. That sounded like a lot, but I was game.

I was sure on this trade.

First I had to figure out the correct ratio at which to trade two-year note futures and ten-year note futures. I had to look it up; I was not, after all, a government bond trader. Then I started to piece out the trade to Meat, who was putting the spread into "the machine" to trade for me automatically.

"I got it up to fifty thousand bucks a basis point," I told Marty.

"Don't talk to me."

I went back to work.

The market had found an equilibrium after the first roller-coaster drop and was now muddling along, giving me time to focus on this steepener. Already the trade had moved a few basis points in my favor, giving me a couple hundred thousand dollars.

"Up to eighty thousand," I announced.

I got the right-hand wave.

There was something I liked about this. The more of the trade I put on, the more it went in my favor. This is what traders are supposed to do: to add to a winner. I kept feeding more and more futures to Meat's machine, and the P&L went higher and higher.

"Up to one hundred thousand," I announced to Marty.

"Okay, now make it two hundred thousand."

"What?"

"I want you to double every trade that you put on, starting with this one. Get it up to two hundred thousand a basis point and then talk to me."

Fuck.

Already this was a big trade. In fact, I was long *a half billion* dollars' worth of two-year notes. The Treasury traders don't even trade this big, I thought.

I fed more futures to Meat's machine.

I found that I wasn't even paying any attention to D.C. and Steve anymore. I was too busy fucking around with my steepener. I couldn't take my eyes off of it; every time the market moved, I made or lost a few hundred thousand dollars. This was getting massive.

Finally: "Okay, Marty. Two hundred thousand dollars a basis point."

"Really?"

"Really."

"How much are you up on the trade right now?"

"One point four million."

"Now, don't take it off until you make five million."

What the fuck. I was long a *billion* worth of two-year notes.

I thought about this. Here I was, an ETF trader, and I was cruising around with a billion worth of twos. How does this happen? Is this how Wall Street works? Aren't I supposed to get permission for something like this? I'd never had a directional bet on a billion worth of anything before. This was intense. This was Warren Miller skiing-off-a-cliff trading.

That was the magic of Lehman Brothers, I suppose. It is better to ask forgiveness than it is to ask permission. Look at the things you can do without bureaucracy. Look at the growth you can achieve. Can you imagine what the world would be like if I had to ask permission to put on every single trade?

It would be pretty fucking boring indeed.

I made $5 million on my curve steepener.

Jay Knight would be proud. Nineteen more trades like that, and I would move to someplace cool, like Manhattan Beach, California. Yeah, that would be cool.

Once I had made $5 million, I took the trade off immediately. All $1 billion worth of twos. The whole thing. I'd had enough. I had spent the last two months of my life just staring at that fucking trade tick for tick, not even talking to people, just sitting there staring at one number on the screen—one number that was going to dictate how much I would get paid this year. Meanwhile, I had to lock the door and check the windows a million times before I left for work. This was my first significant year trading proprietarily; between my IYR trade and the curve steepener and a few others, I had put together about $8 million, to go along with $40 million or so in net ETF commissions. I was responsible, at least in part, for about $48 million of revenue for the firm. How much of that would accrue to me?

Paying people on Wall Street is an art, not a science. The $8 million that I had made trading prop—now, I could take just about all the credit for that. If I hadn't had those ideas, if I hadn't put on those trades, Lehman Brothers would never have made that $8 million. Now, one could argue that Lehman Brothers creates the environment that is conducive to making the $8 million; it has all the technology support and the back office and the Bloombergs and the information and everything else. How much is that worth?

Pure proprietary traders, like Jay Knight, get to keep about 10 percent to 15 percent of what they make, if they work at a big bank. If I had been a pure proprietary trader, I would have been paid about $800,000 for my efforts.

But then, I was functioning as the head of ETF trading, and I was managing the customer trades in every ETF under the sun. I was dealing with big risk—big delta risk—on a daily basis. There was nobody that could do it better than me and D.C. We were the best at what we did. How much was that worth?

This is where things get tricky. There are salespeople who *bring in* the trades, and the firm is paid a commission for their efforts. It doesn't matter *how* they bring in the trade—whether it is through the force of their personality or the amount and quality of strip clubs they have frequented with their customers. They are responsible for bringing in the trade, and they like to think that they are entitled to that commission.

Not so fast. Sometimes customers, like hedge funds, trade with a bank not because of the sales coverage but because of the trading desk. If the trading desk gives them superior service—such as in quality or speed of execution—or if the trading desk gives them the best prices, then it is the traders who are bringing in the trades.

In our case, we had actually been paid about $65 million in commissions, and we had *lost* $25 million of it, leaving us with $40 million. That sounds terrible, and is terrible, but it is the nature of equity trading on Wall Street. Most trades are not priced to be winners; you expect to *lose* money on the trade and retain a fraction of the commission. So for every three cents per share of commission that we were paid, we kept a little less than two cents of it.

*This* was the standard for how we were measured: whether we had a good or bad *loss ratio*. If our loss ratio was high, we were shitty traders and were paid accordingly. If our loss ratio was low, we were stud traders and were paid accordingly. We were somewhere in between. Besides, it was notoriously difficult to get accurate loss-ratio information from the other banks; if we talked to one of our counterparts from across the street, he had no incentive to tell us the truth. He had no incentive to tell us if he was getting steamrolled on trades.

I figured that a good ETF trader, with six or seven years of experience and with a 35 percent to 40 percent loss ratio, should get paid in the high six figures. Say, $700,000.

But then there was the fact that my Bloomberg writing had attracted so much attention over the last year or two; it was an undisputable fact that my written commentary had attracted a great deal of customer flow. I had become the de facto voice of Lehman Brothers Equities, and we had written evidence that people were trading with us because of the things that I wrote. I figured that was worth at least another $200,000.

So if I got paid $800,000 for prop, and $700,000 for flow, and $200,000 extra for writing, that was $1.7 million.

Now, I was sure to trade at a discount to that. How much of a discount?

Absolute worst-case scenario, I should get paid about $1.1 million. That would be disappointing but acceptable.

Only on Wall Street would $1.1 million be disappointing.

I was feeling it. I was feeling what everyone feels on comp day in December.

In the past, I didn't care what I got paid. I figured that if I did a good job, things would work out in the long run. But this year, things were different.

The managing directors had been *managing expectations*. This is common in any given year, but it was rampant this year. The subprime crisis had damaged the firm; to what extent, nobody could say, because our earnings seemed to be fine and we weren't taking any write-downs. But we all knew that things weren't right. They couldn't be right—with financial firms blowing up all over the place—unless the fixed-income guys had everything perfectly hedged, unless they were wizards, like the guys at Goldman Sachs.

The managing directors had been letting it slip that the bonus pool was not as high as people originally thought it would be, and that we could all expect to be paid less. This is what happens every year; the managers talk you down, lower, lower, and lower still until you are so despondent about the measly paycheck that you are going to get that when it finally comes, you are happy. I had expectations. I wanted to have my first seven-figure year, and I deserved it.

But there was something else I wanted. More than anything, I wanted to be promoted to senior vice president, or SVP, having made vice president two years earlier. I figured that since it had taken them four years to promote me to VP, they should make it up to me by deep selecting me for SVP.

There are ranks in finance, like there are in the military. But instead of first lieutenant, captain, and major, there are analyst, associate, and vice president. Above vice president is senior vice president, and above that is managing director. Managing director is the end of the buffet. You get all the pay, and all the perks, and, according to the insurance guy for Louis Hamilton, no managing director in the entire firm makes less than a stick a year.

Since I had an MBA, I came into the firm as an associate, like everyone else with an MBA. If you have only an undergraduate degree, you come in as an analyst. But it took me four years to make VP, when it takes most people two or three. I had always been told, by people like Mark Ricci, that I was doing a fantastic job, but I just hadn't been visible enough to get promoted. This made sense when I was trading index arbitrage in the corner with Ingram. But now I had as much visibility as you could get trading ETFs. There was no reason for me not to make SVP. I had single-handedly built the business into a powerhouse.

It had taken me so long to get promoted that I was being lapped by my peers: guys who were analysts when I was an associate were now coming up for SVP too. It was embarrassing.

*Maybe you should just relax and be happy*, I thought. *You are getting paid a shitload of money to play games.* I should have been glad that I wasn't under lock and key. I was doing great—well enough that I had almost completely forgotten how bad things were, and now I was fighting for money, power, and prestige.

I wanted to get promoted more than I wanted to get rich. Much more. I would trade a few hundred thousand dollars in pay for a business card that said "Senior Vice President" on it. I would give my left leg, my left nut, or the left arm of my firstborn son.

Lord knows the nut wasn't doing me any good. I carried it around like a useless prop.

Fucking medicine.

I am in an office with Marty Korenkiewicz, my boss.

He slides a piece of paper over to me and starts talking. "You know it was a tough year for us, but . . ."

That is all I hear.

| | |
|---|---|
| Name: | Jared Dillian |
| Unit: | Flow Volatility |
| Division: | Equities |
| Title: | VP |
| 2007 Total Comp: | $850,000 |
| 2008 Salary: | $175,000 |
| 2008 Bonus: | $675,000 |
| 2008 Total Comp: | $850,000 |

*What the fuck?*

Marty is still going on. "Blahbetty blah blahby blah blah blah."

"Hey." I interrupt. "It says I'm a VP."

There is a question mark on Marty's forehead. "Um, is that a problem?"

"YES. I should have made SVP this year."

"Well," he begins, "we tried to pay you what we could."

"It's not about the money"—though I'm not thrilled with the money, either—"but this is embarrassing. You have guys half my age making SVP. This makes me look like a fucking moron." I am shaking like a dog trying to shit a razor blade.

Marty is in a bad spot. He starts fumbling and bumbling. "Uh, I don't remember your name coming up on the list this year. I guess we just forgot."

"Forgot?" Holy shit. There are guys getting promoted three years ahead of me. I try to salvage this. "That's inexcusable."

I am filled with rage. *Another year of being VP. By the time I make SVP, it will have been eight years.* This is a complete goat-fuck, an unmitigated fucking disaster, a total loss. I need to get something out of this.

"Look, I need you to do something for me. One thing."

"Shoot," he says. He really wants to help.

The one thing to remember about comp day is that it's too late to change what you get paid. It's already been decided. You have to accept it, no matter how much of a turd it is.

"Someday, in the future, I might need a favor. I don't know what it is right now, and it's not worth talking about until then, but I need you to promise me that when the time comes, and I need you to back me up, that you'll do that."

Marty squirms a little. He's unbounded short volatility now—the danger has passed—but he knows I got screwed, and he has to agree.

"Okay," he manages, "anything you need."

"Good."

*Right where I fucking want him.*

Marty, without knowing it, has just promised to help get me set up like Jay Knight in a year's time. I will do nothing but trade prop for a year and build up enough of a track record to get firm capital. Then I will go out on my own.

Nobody needs a title when he is trading from Miami.

FM: JARED DILLIAN, LEHMAN BROTHERS INC.

TO: SALES

SINCE IT IS YEAR-END AND BONUS SEASON AND ALL THAT, I AM SPENDING MORE TIME THINKING ABOUT MY FUTURE. I MEAN, DO I KEEP WHIPPING AND DRIVING ETFS? OR LOOK FOR A CAREER CHANGE?

I HAVE ALWAYS THOUGHT ABOUT LEADING A CULT. AN ETF CULT. IMAGINE A TOUR BUS FULL OF OHIOANS DRIVING THROUGH HOLLYWOOD, THE TOUR GUIDE ON THE MICROPHONE ON THE FRONT OF THE BUS. "AND ON YOUR LEFT, YOU WILL SEE—MY GOD! WHAT IS THAT?" AND ALL THE OHIOANS WILL

LOOK OUT THE WINDOW AND SEE ME IN THE PARKING LOT OF THE MCDON-ALD'S, NEXT TO THE DRIVE-THRU SIGN, WEARING WHITE ROBES, ARMS RAISED TO THE SKY, CHANTING OUT TICKERS OF OFF-THE-RUN OBSCURE ETFS AND SPEAKING IN TONGUES. "DGG PRFF CMF USL RJN TDX SIJ GAF PLANSTIBL TRONGIX MEFT UN TORP." THRONGS OF FOLLOWERS IN BOWLING SHIRTS RESPOND "THE NIGHT TIME IS THE RIGHT TIME," GENUFLECT, AND SHOWER ME WITH TINY PICKLES.

THAT WOULD BE COOL.

## 16

## Bad Trader | Winter 2007–Summer 2008

There are a lot of insults that you can hurl at people on Wall Street without pissing them off. *Jerk.* Big deal, there are a lot of rich, successful jerks. *Scumbag.* Everyone needs to bend the rules once in a while. *Bad guy.* There are cokeheads, philanderers, backstabbers, and worse. And they all make money.

About the worst thing that you can call someone is a *bad trader.*

There are all kinds of bad traders. There are guys who take profits too early, only to watch their trade triple in the next six months. There are guys who never take profits, only to give back all their gains and then some. There are guys who are too cautious. There are guys who are too reckless. All of these mistakes stem from psychological failings, usually related to fear. Fear of missing the trade that everyone else is in. Fear of failure. Fears about acceptance, self-worth, and material well-being. When you call somebody a bad trader, it is a particularly sharp criticism because it implies that there is something fundamentally wrong with that person. He's unfit. He's weak. And worst of all, he's a mook. A loser.

On the second floor of 745 Seventh Avenue, there were lots of *good* traders. A good trader is very exceptionally paranoid. A good trader always takes into account liquidity when looking for the outtrade. A good trader pays attention to sentiment. A good trader pays attention to trend. A good trader knows enough to be contrarian and not to do the same thing that everyone else is doing.

Not everyone at the firm was contrarian.

Lehman Brothers had been around for a long time—158 years, in fact. But it had been through several near-death experiences along the way. The collapse of the firm and the sale to American Express in 1984. The Russian debt default and the financial crisis of 1998. The terrorist attacks of September 11, 2001. Each time, the firm not only emerged unscathed but stronger. Every Wall Street bank had incredibly bright, talented people. So did Lehman Brothers. But Lehman employees were survivors. They were cockroaches, having lived through plagues and famines and nuclear winters.

This was a highly functional aspect of the firm's culture. The senior executives, on up to Dick Fuld, would tout the performance of the franchise after the firm was blasted out of its headquarters on 9/11. "We are survivors," they said consistently. But Lehman Brothers employees harbored no illusions that they were blessed; they simply had confidence in their ability to survive any downturn, any crisis, any bear market.

This confidence was somewhat misplaced. As they say on Wall Street, the one-hundred-year flood comes once every ten years.

The volume of real estate deals that Lehman Brothers was doing was absolutely staggering. We had a nearly $40 billion portfolio of buildings, single-family homes, malls, hotels, and land. Rumors were beginning to swirl that the Lehman real estate folks weren't even visiting the properties—they were just crunching numbers in Excel spreadsheets and buying shit sight unseen.

If you are a risk taker, this is not terribly irrational behavior. You are B. F. Skinner's pigeon in a box. Push lever, eat food. Push lever, eat food. If you made $1,000 every time you pushed a button, how many times would you push the button? I spent three years in index arbitrage doing just that.

It is easier for someone to get away with this if he trades very liquid instruments such as stock and bonds, like me. If you buy one hundred S&P 500 futures, then buy another one hundred, and another, and another, soon you have a large position, but one that can be easily liquidated if the market starts to turn lower. However, $40 billion worth of apartment buildings is not easy to liquidate in a distressed sale.

The real estate people were behaving rationally because, in general, Wall Street people have call option–like returns. A call option is the right, but not the obligation, to buy something at a certain price before a certain date. The most money you can lose is the price you pay for the option. But if you entered into an agreement to buy GE stock at 20, and it actually goes to 40, you get to buy it at 20 when the market is much higher. You have potentially unlimited upside.

And that is how a Wall Street career works. It is rational to take more and more risk because if you lose money, all you lose is your job. The firm eats the loss—it doesn't take it out of your paycheck. Meanwhile, you can make tens of millions in upside. Most people don't actually behave this way, because they have some sense of responsibility and judgment that prevents them from taking stupid risks with other people's money. Most people are careful, even when it is irrational to be careful. But with Lehman Brothers, you had a scenario where a group of employees had option-like returns and took excessive risk, while ignoring liquidity (the ability to get out of the trade). Management too had option-like returns. In the past, Wall Street firms were partnerships, meaning that partners had to share in the losses. The shareholders of a publicly traded corporation that goes bankrupt have no such recourse. Meanwhile, if management fails to understand kurtosis, power-law distributions, and what are known as "fat tails"—and the concept that the market moves in cycles—you have the perfect storm: a blinding display of incompetence. You have people who call themselves professionals but lack even a basic understanding of risk.

I liked to think of myself as a good trader. D.C. was a good trader. Marty was a good trader. We all were good traders.

We didn't know it, but in 2008 we were being led off a cliff like so many lemmings by a cadre of bad traders.

FM: JARED DILLIAN, LEHMAN BROTHERS INC.

TO: SALES

I JUST WANTED TO SAY THAT IT IS THE NEW FISCAL YEAR, AND I FEEL TER-RIBLE. I MAY TALK A BIG GAME IN THESE BLOOMBERGS, BUT IF YOU TRAINED A WEBCAM ON ME, AT ANY POINT IN THE DAY YOU WOULD SEE ME SWEAT-ING OUT SOME POSITION, SITTING PARALYZED IN FEAR, OR BACKSLAPPING ABOUT SOME MINOR WIN THAT IS ALMOST CERTAINLY GOING TO GO IN MY MUSH SOMETIME IN THE NEXT HOUR.

I STRUGGLE WITH BET SIZE. I HAVE MORE BAD IDEAS THAN GOOD IDEAS, AND I TEND TO ALLOCATE CAPITAL EQUALLY TO EACH. AND WHEN I DO HAVE A WINNER, IT IS A HERCULEAN EFFORT TO REALLY BE A PIG IN THE TRADE.

I TRADE MORE WHEN I'M BORED AND LESS WHEN I'M BUSY. THIS LEADS TO CHAOS WHEN THINGS START MOVING.

SOMETIMES I MAKE MY INITIAL POSITION TOO LARGE, WHICH MEANS I HAVE NO AMMO LEFT IF THE TIME COMES TO ACCUMULATE MORE.

I AM RESPONSIBLE FOR MY ACTIONS. MY LOSSES ARE MY OWN DOING, BUT IF I LOSE TOO MUCH, I GET DEMORALIZED EASILY, AND I WON'T TRADE FOR A MONTH.

I HAVE BIASES. I AM PERPETUALLY BULLISH ON AIRLINES, GOLD, AGS, AND MEGA CAP, AND I AM PERPETUALLY BEARISH ON HIGH-BETA TECH, REITS, UTILITIES, AND CHINA.

I ALSO HAVE MEAN-REVERSION BIAS; I SHORT THINGS THAT GO UP AND BUY THINGS THAT GO DOWN. I SNEER AT TREND FOLLOWERS AND SNORT SOMETHING LIKE SELLING THINGS AT HIGHER PRICES AND BUYING THINGS AT LOWER PRICES. BUT IT MEANS I LACK THE IMAGINATION TO SEE A MASSIVE TREND DEVELOPING.

I DON'T LACK DISCIPLINE, I LACK VOLITION. I ENTHUSIASTICALLY WHACK SOME LOSERS, BUT OTHERS I CONVENIENTLY FORGET ABOUT.

I F9 A LOT MORE ON GOOD DAYS AND LESS ON BAD DAYS.

SOMETIMES I BELIEVE A LITTLE TOO MUCH IN MY CHART-READING ABILITY.

I SHOULD TRUST MY GUT A LOT MORE THAN I DO.

I HAVE A BIAS TO INACTION. IF THINGS ARE GETTING SQUIRRELLY, I HAVE A HARD TIME PICKING UP THE PHONE.

I HAVE BEEN IN WAY OVER MY HEAD SEVERAL TIMES. I AM LUCKY TO STILL BE SITTING HERE.

AND IN GENERAL, I TRADE TOO SMALL. MY BOSS IS RIGHTLY JABBING ME
WHEN I AM BEING TOO MUCH OF A WEENIE, WHICH IS BASICALLY ALL THE
TIME.

YEP, IT'S A NEW YEAR, ALL RIGHT. ANOTHER YEAR OF TRYING TO STAY OUT OF
MY OWN WAY. I HAVE THE DEEPEST ADMIRATION FOR ANYONE WHO CAN MAN-
AGE A PORTFOLIO AND MANAGE IT WELL.

*This is the last time.*
*Eight-five-three-two-one-one.*
*Eight-five-three-two-one-one.*

I was having a bad morning. It was eight o'clock, and I was still trying
to leave the house. I had checked the basement door, the front door, the
back door, all the windows, the refrigerator, the coffeemaker, and every
other appliance in the house. I had resorted to using the Fibonacci se-
quence as a pattern for locking the door. I had been through everything
four times, made two trips on to the bus, and had to run back to the
house. I was exhausted.

*I can't go on like this.*

I had once seen a television show about a man with an anxiety disorder that compelled him to constantly pull his car over to the side of the
road to check the bumper to see if he had hit anybody. It would take him
hours to drive anywhere; he would have to stop at least a hundred times.

I could relate.

I had been told that there were medications for this, the obsessive-
compulsive disorder. I had asked my doctor about it. I was crippled by
this thing. Unfortunately, they interact badly with the bipolar medication, so I was basically screwed.

Furthermore, it had started to work its way into other aspects of my
life. I found myself having to log off my computers in a certain way when
I left work, counting and staring at the screens. First screen: *five-four-
three-two-one*. Second screen: *five-four-three-two-one*. I knew people were
looking at me. I had to do it anyway. I was turning into some kind of
freak show.

I was feeling a little similar to the way I felt prehospital—like I was out of control. I was powerless to stop doing the things that I was doing. For just once in my life, I wanted to feel like everything I did, I did for a reason.

I was told that any anxiety disorder is simply the mind trying to distract itself from something it doesn't particularly want to face. So what was it that I didn't want to deal with? On the surface, everything was fine. I was stable on my medication, and happy. My marriage was as good as it had ever been. I was trading up a storm. So what was there to worry about?

It was a mystery.

During March, I had been trying hard not to pay attention to the Bear Stearns thing. Like a cat, I had an incredible capacity to ignore.

If you had asked me what was going on with Bear Stearns, I couldn't have told you. Subprime something or other. It was my job to know these things, but I made it my job *not* to know. I didn't want to know. I never once pulled up news on Bear Stearns. Truthfully, I *liked* guys from Bear Stearns. They were resourceful. They had to be resourceful, because nobody ever gave them any resources; they had to build shit themselves. They were outgoing in an eager sort of way. And they were not snobs. It wasn't funny to make fun of someone's misfortune. Everyone was having a good laugh at Bear Stearns's expense, and I was having none of it. *Na na na na, I can't hear you.*

Bear Stearns had tried to hire me once. I got a phone call on the desk from a number I didn't recognize. "Are you on privacy?" the voice asked. I hit the privacy button. The guy introduced himself as a senior trader for Bear Stearns—Murray Foreman—and asked if we could meet for drinks. It was all very secret squirrel. I liked the sound that subterfuge made, so I went along with it.

The surreptitious meeting was to be held in the lobby bar of the W Hotel in Times Square—just a short walk for me. The W had been one of my favorite hangouts, a terrific place to catch some eye candy, with lots of professionals—a friend had been the recipient of a brumski from a female bodybuilder there—and $14 drinks. The cocktail waitresses wore these tight dresses that were just the right length; they came down to the divider between leg and ass. If someone was buying, I was there.

Foreman shows up with a Joe Pesci doppelgänger named Louie, who apparently was the man in charge; an option trader and a good one at that, if I was to believe what I was hearing. Foreman was and played the straight man, former Air Force pilot with the driest sense of humor that I had yet encountered.

These two characters wanted me to trade ETFs. I was going to tell them no, but not until I'd had my fill of Maker's and ginger. These guys just seemed too unstable; they didn't have their shit together. Foreman told me about how they had such a large tolerance for risk that he would have 100,000 SPY against 100,000 DIA—and I couldn't tell if he was being funny, and Louie was just, well, being himself. Abbott and Costello. Penn and Teller. This was more vaudeville than trading. They said that they would pay me more money than I ever thought possible, but I had just been paid $650,000 from Lehman, and that was already more money than I had ever thought possible. I sucked down my eighth or ninth Maker's and ginger and bid Mutt and Jeff adieu.

*Good miss.* A month later I was in the nut hut.

About the only thing that I had learned from the financial crisis was how to bid for XLF, the financials ETF. Now it was trading around 23 bucks, whereas before, it had been close to forty. All everyone wanted to do was to sell XLF. *Fine.* What is this Bear Stearns thing about, anyway?

I pull up a chart.

Holy mother.

The stock is in free fall, on its way to being cut in half, from 120 down to 60 in a single day. Toward the end of the day, people are buying the 30 strike puts; in essence, a bankruptcy bet. It's mayhem. To date, I haven't seen anything like it in the markets, and by this point, I have seen a lot.

I begin to think: What if this is an opportunity? What if this is one of these opportunities that come along once every few years, one of those rare buying opportunities? Sentiment is what drives markets, and sentiment has been so bearish, so negative, that on any given day, our customers have five times more sell orders than buy orders. They've taken the market capitalization of all the financial stocks to almost 50 percent of their value. Sure, there is a financial crisis, and it might consume Bear

Stearns, but the markets tend to overdo things just a little. They are as irrational on the downside as they are on the upside.

On Sunday night, as I was getting out of the shower, I received an email from Jeff, a former colleague from the floor of the P. Coast and now a variance swap broker, attaching a story about Bear Stearns.

It was true. The company was essentially bankrupt; it was getting bought for $2 a share.

*Sell*, wrote Jeff.

*Buy*, I wrote back.

I sat there and thought to myself, *What would I do if I were a hedge fund trader and Bear Stearns had just blown up? I know: I'd sell short Lehman with both hands.* It made sense, even if you didn't know anything about Bear *or* Lehman. You could make money trading without knowing anything. Monkey see, monkey do, and right now, the monkeys were all over Lehman.

The stock started out the day around 40 bucks, which was the lowest it had been for years. It traded lower, on heavy volume, first to 36 and then to 32. By this point, everyone on the trading floor had stopped working and was watching the chart. Some people had just lost a few million, personally. I, for one, had lost about $50,000 in that spell. But we all stood to lose much more than that if Lehman went out of business.

The managers spent the morning huddled in their offices. That was what happened anytime something big was going on—we could see them in their all-glass offices, and were left to wonder what the hell was happening.

I walked over to Adam Rosello's desk. He had his Lehman chart up. By this time, the stock was down to about 27 bucks.

I didn't know what to say, so I said this: "Dude, what do you think?"

"Are you fucking kidding me?" he replied. He had kids. This was harder on people with kids. If I went to zero, I could go flip burgers.

"Who's doing it? We're not seeing any of the flow here, are we?" It was permissible for us to take an agency order in our own stock.

"Hell no. Bro, these are our own clients that are shorting our stock.

There's no loyalty here. There's no relationship. These guys are trying to make a buck, and they want to bring us down."

Investment bank stocks are very fragile instruments. Technically, they shouldn't exist at all, because their degree of leverage is so high. They are all built on confidence. If confidence in a firm evaporates, like what had happened with Bear Stearns (or Drexel Burnham Lambert or Bankers Trust before it), then the firm ceases to exist. Sometimes this relationship works in reverse: instead of the stock price being an indication of confidence, confidence becomes an indication of the stock price. By ganging up on, say, Lehman, and forcing the stock lower, you can actually put a bank out of business as its counterparties demand more collateral. Pretty fucking ruthless. Put a few thousand people out of work, just so you can make a buck. If I wasn't such a capitalist, I would have been appalled.

The stock was down to 24 bucks.

"Oh God!" said one of the sales guys, standing up, grabbing his hair. The whole joint was silent, except for CNBC, which was turned up full blast, going on and on about how there was a run on Lehman. The televisions were echoing across the floor. I had forgotten to eat my lunch. It was spooky.

The stock hit 20.

Lehman Brothers had been through this before. There was a run on Lehman, big-time, in 1998. The street thought, correctly or incorrectly, that Lehman was in possession of a ton of Russian debt that had just defaulted, or had exposure to it somehow. Same thing was happening—they were taking the stock to zero. That's when the famous "Ronnie Lott trade" was executed. The corporate bond traders gave out an award annually for the ballsiest trade of the year. They named it after football Hall of Famer Ronnie Lott, who had famously lost a finger and gone out to finish a football game. Rumor had it that they would bring him to the firm to give out the award.

We had been through it again in 2001.

This firm was a survivor. We weren't going anywhere, not without a fight.

The stock began to rally, up to 24.

The firm wasn't going anywhere because I was an employee. I was a survivor if there ever was one. I had survived mental illness and lived. I was here because I was no quitter. To a man, if you asked anyone on Wall Street for a word to describe Lehman Brothers, the word was *scrappy*.

The stock was up to 28. The squeeze was on.

There were hundreds upon hundreds of millions of shares of Lehman on the tape thus far in the day. People were very, very short, and they needed to cover. There is nothing so nasty in trading as an ass-ripping short squeeze. Hedge funds had sold hundreds of millions of shares in the morning, and they had to buy it all back in the afternoon. Somebody was going bear hunting, and we couldn't figure out who.

The stock was back above 32.

People were starting to get excited. Some high fives were exchanged. There were smiles across the trading floor. We were going to make it after all.

36.

This was going down in history of one of the all-time great Lehman Brothers comebacks, like ten years ago with the Ronnie Lott trade.

40.

*Lehman on the tape.*

We had announced a large convert deal, which meant that we were selling our own bonds convertible into common stock directly to the public. Except that we weren't selling them to the public: we had pre-placed the entire deal with friends of the firm. Oftentimes, when hedge funds are short a stock and they are trying to cover, they will try to participate in a stock offering to try to get shares they need to flatten themselves out. Lehman knew who all the dirty hedge funds were that were shorting its stock, and we weren't going to help them out. In fact, we were going to squeeze them even further.

When the deal was announced, the stock traded even *higher*. It was now up on the day. The market was happy because not only was Lehman not going out of business but it also had the ability to raise a seemingly limitless amount of capital. With that much access to capital, how could we ever go out of business? The hedge funds were getting ass raped.

I was proud to be an employee of Lehman Brothers. Why? Because when it came down to it, we could beat any other bank in a fight. We could pummel the Goldman guys, who were too rich to have rage. We could clobber the Morgan Stanley guys, who didn't want to get dirty. We could stomp the frogs from BNP and FrogGen. Bear Stearns might have been a challenge, but now it was gone. We could pretty much kick anybody's ass that we wanted. We were loaded with athletes, and we fought dirty. You come at us, we are going to crush you. Back the fuck up.

Yo.

There was work to do. I wanted to move to Miami.

I was sure that the market was going higher, and I had to find ways to express my bullish opinion. The great thing was that all the bullish bets were very cheap because most people thought that the end of Bear Stearns meant the end of the financial system and the world as we know it.

I was bullish, but to a point. I didn't think that the market was going to return to the all-time highs. I just thought we were going to get a bouncy-bounce, a medium-size one.

There are trades for that. I sized up the 1350-1400-1440 call tree in May. Basically, I wanted the SPX to finish between 1400 and 1440 on May expiration. If it finished between 1350 and 1400, I would make a little bit of money, and I would make more money the closer it was to 1400. If it finished above 1440, I would gradually begin to lose money. I could put on the entire trade at *zero cost*.

There were a lot of reasons why this trade made sense. First of all, it was highly unlikely that the market was going to rally through 1440 by May. It was still a bear market, and bear markets don't make higher highs. Second of all, if the market did rally, the options that I had sold, the 1400 and 1440 calls, would lose value due to a decline in volatility. The trade had the potential to be a massive winner.

In baseball, hitters talk about being able to "see the ball." The ball actually *looks* bigger. It looks big, and slow, like the pitcher is lobbing a basketball. Underhand.

That was how I was trading.

For the first time in my career, I could genuinely *see* the ball.

I had sold long-dated risk reversals on Citigroup, Countrywide, First-Fed Financial, Freddie Mac, MBIA, and MGIC, and I immediately sold the puts and stayed short the calls.

328 | Jared Dillian

I bought Ford stock.

I began to trade Fed funds futures.

I sold a call spread on Apple.

I bought Archer Daniels Midland.

I sold puts on AIG.

I bought a put spread on AK Steel.

I traded a one-by-two put spread in Caterpillar.

I shorted Chipotle Mexican Grill.

I bought Cummins Inc.

I bought a put spread on CSX.

I bought Dean Foods, and eBay.

I traded the 145-150-155 call tree in EEM, the emerging markets ETF.

And so on. I put on dozens and dozens of trades.

Not all of them were winners. But when a trade started to go against me, I religiously whacked it out. I did exactly what I was supposed to do. I cut my losers and let my winners run. I *added* to my winners.

I was putting on trades that made no economic or fundamental sense. I would trade anything. Just give me a position—*any* position—and I will make it work. I could make money with any stock, any security.

I was making a ton of money.

I was going to catch Jay Knight.

FM: JARED DILLIAN, LEHMAN BROTHERS INC.
TO: SALES

IN MY DESK I HAVE A THREE-YEAR-OLD CAN OF HAGGIS. I GOT IT ON A TRIP TO SCOTLAND IN 2005. I DON'T THINK IT WOULD TASTE VERY GOOD ANYMORE. I'M PRETTY SURE POSSUM MUSHED UP INTO POI WOULD TASTE BETTER.

THE LOW IN THE SPX IS 1256.98. IF WE TRADE DOWN THERE IN THE NEXT MONTH, I WILL EAT THE HAGGIS. ON THE DESK. WITHOUT NEEPS AND TATTIES.

I thought the haggis bet would be a fun thing to do. I had no idea the response that it would generate.

Everyone wanted to take the other side of the bet. Everyone was still bearish after the Bear Stearns blowup. It was actually easy to model the likelihood that I would be forced to eat the haggis. Basically, this was what was known as a "one-touch" option, meaning that it immediately went in the money and returned a fixed payout when a price level was reached. The haggis one-touch. Probabilistically, there was about a 30 percent chance that I was going to have to eat the haggis. But in my mind, there was a 0 percent chance.

I was seeing the ball. I *knew*—which is different from believing, thinking, or feeling, or guessing—that the market was going higher. I just knew. How did I know? I just knew. I had a lot of money riding on that outcome, and it was working out swell.

The market would occasionally lurch lower. I would get a flurry of emails from my clients and other people in the firm. *Haggis! Haggis!* Personally, I thought haggis was delicious, but probably not straight out of a three-year-old can.

I was having fun.

FM: JARED DILLIAN, LEHMAN BROTHERS INC.
TO: SALES

I GOT A CALCULATOR WATCH FOR CHRISTMAS, WHICH I AM CURRENTLY WEARING. I'LL PAY EVEN MORE HOMAGE TO THROWBACK NERDISM AND TALK A LITTLE BIT ABOUT DUNGEONS AND DRAGONS.

WHAT CHARACTER CLASS IS YOUR STYLE OF TRADING?

FIGHTER:
—A WARRIOR WITH EXCEPTIONAL COMBAT CAPABILITY AND UNEQUALED SKILL WITH WEAPONS.

—A TRADER WHO SLUGS IT OUT, HACK AND SLASH, PUSHING PEOPLE AROUND, DAY AFTER DAY.

MONK:
—A MARTIAL ARTIST WHOSE UNARMED STRIKES HIT FAST AND HARD—A MASTER OF EXOTIC POWERS.

—A TRADER WHO STILL WRITES TICKETS AND ESCHEWS COMPUTERS ON HIS WAY TO MAKING MILLIONS.

PALADIN:
—A CHAMPION OF JUSTICE AND DESTROYER OF EVIL, PROTECTED AND STRENGTHENED BY AN ARRAY OF DIVINE POWERS.

—THERE ARE NO PALADINS IN TRADING.

ASSASSIN:
—A KILLER AND SPY, ADEPT IN THE DARK ARTS.

—LOOKS FOR SECURITIES WITH EXCEPTIONALLY HIGH SHORT INTEREST AND INITIATES A SQUEEZE.

DRUID:
—ONE WHO DRAWS ENERGY FROM THE NATURAL WORLD TO CAST DIVINE SPELLS AND GAIN STRANGE MAGICAL POWERS.

—BUYS SOCIALLY RESPONSIBLE ALTERNATIVE ENERGY AND SUDAN-FREE ETFS.

ILLUSIONIST:
—ADEPT IN A SCHOOL OF MAGIC PERTAINING TO THE SEEN AND UNSEEN.

—CREATES ILLUSIONS OF SIZE AND VOLUME IN ORDER TO INFLUENCE OTH-ERS' TRADING DECISIONS.

MAGIC-USER:
—A POTENT SPELLCASTER SCHOOLED IN THE ARCANE ARTS.

—CARRIES WITH HIM AN ARRAY OF SPELLS (THE EARLY EXERCISE SPELL, THE INDEX REBALANCE SPELL) TO CONJURE P&L OUT OF SEEMINGLY NO-WHERE.

RANGER:
—A CUNNING, SKILLED WARRIOR OF THE WILDERNESS.

—USES TIME AND SALES AND OTHER TRADE FORENSICS TO TRACK DOWN WHO IS RUNNING HIM OVER.

CLERIC:
—A MASTER OF DIVINE MAGIC AND A CAPABLE WARRIOR AS WELL.

—A TRADER WHO DILIGENTLY BUYS PROTECTION, OVERWRITES, USES STOPS, AND OTHER LOSS-MITIGATING TECHNIQUES.

THIEF:
—A ROGUE, CAPABLE OF SNEAKY COMBAT AND NIMBLE TRICKS.

—SELF-EXPLANATORY.

WHAT CHARACTER WOULD I BE? A BARD, OF COURSE. A PERFORMER WHOSE MUSIC WORKS MAGIC—A WANDERER, A TALE TELLER, AND A JACK-OF-ALL-TRADES.

I was going to get paid. I was going to get promoted. I had made $20 million in the first half of the year.

Of the $20 million, $5 million of it had come from my call tree. The market improbably climbed right in between 1400 and 1440, leaving me with $5 million from an initial investment of precisely $0. I had managed the chaos that was the rest of my portfolio and massaged many more millions out of that.

I had made, by that point, about $6 million simply day-trading S&P futures. After seven years, I had finally solved the mystery. Trade only when you have an edge. Otherwise, don't trade. Out of the first 125 market days of the year, I had traded on perhaps 10 of them, and made $6 million. I didn't have to be involved in the market all the time. This was a learning process, and I had to learn that I was not omniscient, that I had very little control over what happened in the market, and that if the market allowed me enough visibility to make a little money off of it about once a month, then I should consider myself fortunate. I had gotten myself to the point that I rarely, if ever, lost money day-trading. Retail punters spend entire lifetimes trying to figure this out. Maybe I could teach some high-priced seminar to day-traders in Fort Lee, or something, one of those things they advertise in infomercials on CNBC.

For the first time, I felt like a professional. More importantly, I felt like I could do this on my own. I was ready for Miami. I was ready for Jay Knight.

## 17

## Those Bastards | Summer 2008–Fall 2008

I stood on the street corner, trying to cry. The medicine wouldn't allow it.

I had just spent the last hour and fifteen minutes trying to leave my house. I was impossibly late for work. I had gone to check the windows, the locks, the refrigerator, and everything else in the house five times. I was standing on the sidewalk, trying mightily to fight off the urge to go back a sixth time. Somehow I couldn't remember checking the window in my office to see if it was locked, even though I had undoubtedly checked it five times already.

*Don't go back. Just go to work.*

*Don't go back.*

I went back to the house. I couldn't resist. I caved in—again.

This was fucking awful. This was beyond debilitating. If this got much worse, I wouldn't be able to leave my house *at all*. Now I knew why there were people such as recluses and shut-ins. The outside world was just too fucking complicated and scary.

I had no answers.

Things had not been going well. As I walked back to the house, I thought about what I was going to do for a job. Lehman didn't look good, and I was slowly realizing that we were going to go tits up in the end.

Tango uniform.

Some time ago the Dickler and Joe had hired a new chief financial officer named Erin Callan. She was hot and bitchy. Up until she went on CNBC wearing only a summer dress, I hadn't seen her, or at least I thought I hadn't, until I left the building late one evening, and there was a photo shoot going on in front of the main entrance. A blonde woman in her forties was being photographed getting out of a town car, bare leg exposed. Was it her? I didn't know for sure, but until now, I hadn't made the connection.

Lehman had reported earnings through the Erin Callan mouthpiece, and, much to everyone's surprise, there were no write-downs. *Write-downs* were becoming the new buzzword on trading floors, marking the extent that investment banks wrote down the value of their impaired financial assets. We had hardly written down anything at all, and both investors and employees thought that was really, really weird. *I* thought it was weird. We knew we were big in mortgages and all that toxic stuff. We should have been writing things down left and right.

We all shrugged. Maybe those guys are geniuses. Maybe they hedged.

I didn't know what the Ira Sohn Investment Conference was until David Einhorn spoke at it. Apparently it is where all the bigshooter hedge fund managers go to talk about their best trades. Einhorn was the owner of a hedge fund that masqueraded as a publicly traded reinsurer, or vice versa. He had added credibility because he'd entered the World Series of Poker on a lark and ended up finishing in the top twenty, donating his winnings to charity. Einhorn's favorite trade? Short Lehman Brothers stock.

It is hard to overstate the impact that his speech had at the conference, but the next day, it was in the papers, and everyone was talking about it. He had shaken the financial world to its foundation by implying that a large, leveraged investment bank might not be as sound as the financial statements said it was. Einhorn spent a lot of time going over accounting details, including the valuation of a Lehman Brothers asset in India, and income associated with it. He really missed the larger issue, which was the fucking ridiculous real estate exposure, but in trading, it is acceptable to be right for the wrong reasons.

Lehman had to respond or not respond, and Erin Callan responded. It wasn't what she said but how she said it: she dismissed Einhorn's criticism as those of a dirty, deranged short seller. It was a profoundly bad move. Everyone knows that when a firm starts criticizing the short sellers, it has something to hide. The stock promptly took a dirtnap.

Lots of people were getting freaked out. I'm sure that hundreds of therapists all over the city got to hear plenty about Lehman Brothers potentially buying the farm. One might think that I would have been worried enough to have another breakdown, resulting in a second hospitalization, but I felt fine. I was worried not so much about losing my job, or financial insecurity—because I had saved plenty—I was just worried about *change*. I wanted to be Jay Knight, but that might not happen. I wanted to get promoted, but that might not happen. I wanted to get a bonus at the end of the year, but that might not happen. Things were going to change, and I wasn't exactly ready for it. During this period of time, it was the writing that was keeping me going. Without the writing, I would have been a mess, just like everyone else.

If I was awake, I was thinking about writing, I was thinking about the next email I was going to send out. If I was on the bus on the way to work, I was thinking about writing. At night, watching television, I was thinking about writing. There was this stuff inside me that had to get out, there was a limitless supply of it, and if I hadn't been busy managing my own creativity, I would have been obsessed with whether Lehman Brothers was going to go bankrupt or not. For once, I was psychologically better off than everyone else, except for the inexplicable obsessive-compulsive behavior.

So, that summer, I set out to try to find a job. I was going to have to trade at a hedge fund.

*Window: closed.*

I was not excited by this prospect. I was insane, and I know insanity when I see it, and everyone in the professional money management industry is completely insane. Running money is a notoriously tough business, and it attracts some notoriously tough people. Arguably, the pressure is worse than at an investment bank because you are only as good as your last trade; it is a constant battle for performance. You start losing money, you go out of business, and fast.

I wanted to run money, but I was a little too green to start out as a portfolio manager. I wanted to find someplace where I could be the head execution trader and maybe have a little pile of capital on the side that I could manage. Being an execution trader at a hedge fund is a pretty thankless job, but in some cases, it paid reasonably well, and the alternative was to go trade ETFs at a smaller bank with shittier technology and less capital.

"That job doesn't exist," my hedge fund friend Vern told me. "It's a unicorn. It's a mythological creature." I was having a Diet Coke at Heartland

Brewery. "That job where some old guy takes you under his wing and shows you the ropes, that job doesn't exist anymore. It's a fiction."

Still, I gave my resume to headhunters. "Why do you want to leave Lehman?" they asked. "Well," I said, "it has nothing to do with the rumors. No. Yes. Yes, I'm concerned, but it's not the main reason I'm leaving. I'd just like to do something else with my career."

They eyed me suspiciously.

I was working with two headhunters. One was a brainiac of indiscernible nationality who primarily handled quants and program traders. The other was a pair of greasy-haired cell phone salesmen from a firm called Futures Group, the preeminent recruiting firm at the time, the guys that always gave quotes to the *Wall Street Journal* about the piles of money that people were getting paid.

I waited for their calls. None came.

*Concentrate on the Goddamn locks.*

I could start the newsletter.

*Concentrate.*

Ever since that moment in the hospital when I learned that I could actually *be* a writer—that it was actually possible—the idea of having my own publication had been in the front of my mind. It was those stupid Bloomberg messages that were keeping me going. If someone had told me that I couldn't write anymore, I would have stopped going to work. I would have, well, gone home and written a book, or something. What was stopping me was pure greed. If I stayed a trader, and if I was successful, I could make several orders of magnitude more money. I could get rich. I could not get rich writing.

But I could be happy.

I walked away from the house for the sixth and last time, with a plan: if Lehman went tapioca, I was going to start my newsletter.

FM: JARED DILLIAN, LEHMAN BROTHERS INC.

TO: SALES


FROM THE BOOK "HOPE FOR THE FLOWERS" BY TRINA PAULUS: "STRIPE WAS A CATERPILLAR. 'I'M HUNGRY,' HE THOUGHT, AND STRAIGHTAWAY BEGAN

TO EAT THE LEAF HE WAS BORN ON. AND HE ATE ANOTHER LEAF, AND AN-
OTHER . . . UNTIL ONE DAY HE STOPPED EATING AND THOUGHT, 'THERE
MUST BE MORE TO LIFE THAN JUST EATING AND GETTING BIGGER.'"

I WANTED MORE. AND SO I BEGAN TO LEARN HOW TO SPECULATE. IF I HAD A
CHOICE BETWEEN MAKING 10X THROUGH ARBITRAGE OR X THROUGH SPEC-
ULATION, I WOULD CHOOSE X. I DIDN'T WANT TO BE A SNAIL. I WANTED TO
BE THE RED OSCAR THAT WENT AROUND EATING ALL THE OTHER GOLDFISH.
SCRATCHING AROUND FOR A TENTH OF A BASIS POINT IS BORING. GETTING
ONE OVER ON EVERYBODY IN THE MARKET WITH MY OWN IDEAS NEVER GETS
OLD.

ONE DAY STRIPE SAW A TRAIL OF CATERPILLARS CRAWLING TOWARD A GIANT
COLUMN THAT WAS SO HIGH IT WENT INTO THE CLOUDS. IT WAS A GIANT
PILLAR OF CATERPILLARS, ALL TRYING TO CLIMB HIGHER. STRIPE ASKED
THEM WHAT THEY WERE DOING. 'WE'RE TRYING TO GET TO THE TOP!' THEY
REPLIED. 'WHAT'S AT THE TOP?' ASKED STRIPE. 'WE DON'T KNOW, BUT IT
MUST BE GOOD!'

SO STRIPE DOVE INTO THE CATERPILLAR PILLAR AND STARTED TO WORK HIS
WAY TO THE TOP. IT TOOK DAYS, AND WEEKS. IT WAS HARD WORK. HE WAS
PUSHING AND SHOVING THE OTHER CATERPILLARS OUT OF THE WAY. HE HAD
TO CONTROL HIS RISK AND COME UP WITH NEW IDEAS EVERY DAY.

ONE DAY, AS HE GOT CLOSE OT THE TOP, HE HEARD SCREAMS. IT TURNED
OUT THAT THERE WAS NOTHING AT THE TOP AT ALL. THE CATERPILLARS ON
TOP WERE TRYING TO STAY ON TOP. THEY WERE HOLDING ON FOR DEAR LIFE.
BUT THE CATERPILLARS BENEATH THEM WERE THROWING THEM OFF THE
PILLAR, WHERE THEY WOULD PLUMMET TO THE EARTH AND SPLAT.

THERE ARE A NUMBER OF CATERPILLARS WHO PLAYED THIS CATERPILLAR
PILLAR GAME AND ROSE TO THE TOP BY BEING SHORT FINANCIALS AND
LONG COMMODITIES. BUT NOW THOSE CATERPILLARS ARE GETTING THROWN
FROM THE TOP BY FRESHER, MORE DETERMINED CATERPILLARS WHO HAVE
OTHER TRADES IN MIND. AND THE CYCLE WILL CONTINUE ON FOREVER.

IN THE BOOK, STRIPE BECOMES DISILLUSIONED, CRAWLS DOWN THE CATER-
PILLAR PILLAR, GOES OFF AND BUILDS A COCOON, AND BECOMES A BEAUTI-
FUL BUTTERFLY.

I THINK ABOUT THAT EVERY DAY.

Louis Hamilton: "Uh, guys, check this out."

I don't like the tone of his voice. I turn around and look at his screen. He has a form displayed as a PDF.

"What's that?" I ask.

"Look, see."

It is a complicated form, with boxes and bars all over the place. Slowly, I figure out that it is a claim for relocation expenses from someone at Lehman Brothers. The someone is indeed a someone: a managing director. There is a box for his comp.

It says $6 million.

There is an itemized list of moving expenses, broker fees, and so on. At the bottom of the form is the amount reimbursed:

$652,150.

"Who the fuck gets reimbursed six hundred grand for moving expenses?"

Marty is looking at it too. "Who the fuck makes six million dollars a year?"

"Where'd you get this?" asks D.C. Steve is looking over his shoulder.

"Dude, it was just a freak accident, I got emailed some dude's expense reimbursement form."

"Where does this guy work, anyway?"

We all look at the form. It doesn't say his division.

Louis types his name into the People Finder application on the computer.

Up it comes: *Real Estate.*

"What the fuck," we say in unison.

This guy isn't even the head guy in Real Estate. This is some mook MD. Shit MD out your ass. This guy is a nobody, and he's getting paid six sticks. Nobody here in equities gets paid six sticks. *And* they're paying him more than half a stick just to move his house.

Louis is perky. "I should send this form to everyone on the floor, huh?" He thinks about this. "Or maybe that would be a bad career move."

"Maybe there's a way that you can take a picture of your screen with the cell phone," I say.

"We are in deep shit," says Marty.

"They're going to let this thing go all the way to zero, aren't they?" Louis asks me.

"Yes they are. All the way to zero."

It was posturing. I didn't really believe that they would let the fucker go to zero. Nobody did.

But in July and August, they were sure acting that way.

In my Bloomberg emails, I had to act as if. I had to fake it to make it. I had to pretend that Lehman was sound, that everything was okay. My clients helped perpetuate the illusion; none of them ever challenged me.

It was during this time period that I was doing some of my best work. I was hardly even trading anymore; D.C. and Steve were doing all the heavy lifting. All I was doing was punting around some stocks in the prop account and writing. Technically, we were already bankrupt, but I was having the time of my life. The last seven years, after watching the World Trade Center vaporize above my head, I had to believe in something. What I believed in was Lehman Brothers, that I worked at this perfect meritocracy that hired smart people that did great things, and that was eventually going to overtake Goldman Sachs. If I couldn't believe in that, I couldn't believe in anything.

The more cynical I got, the better I wrote.

In high school or college (I can't remember), my yearbook quote was from Pearl S. Buck: "Life without idealism is empty indeed. We just hope or starve to death." At age thirty-four, my idealism had been completely extinguished. All that was left was a blind, inconsiderate desire to survive and win. For the first time, I didn't believe in something else, because there was nothing else to believe in; instead I believed in myself.

I knew one thing: when I woke up in the morning, there were ideas in my head. There were ideas in my head that nobody else had, and my ability to put pen to paper and communicate them separated me from everyone else. As long as the ideas kept coming, I had a job.

FM: JARED DILLIAN, LEHMAN BROTHERS INC.
TO: SALES


O XLB! O BASIC MATERIALS!

YOU CLOUD MY MIND LIKE BEIJING'S SKIES

YOU OBFUSCATE MY COMPREHENSION

WHY DOST THOU REFUSE TO DIRTNAP?

IN 2004 STALWART SALES TRADERS

DISSEMINATED DELICIOUS CHARTS

OF CORRELATION

AMONG SUCH THINGS AS EURUSD, XLB, AND LETTER X

YOUR CORRELATION HAS VANISHED LIKE LOST LOVE

XLB, I WANT TO SMITE THEE WITH MY TRADING APPLICATION

BUT YOU ARE FILLED WITH STRENGTH

AND SUCH THINGS AS MON, DD, DOW, AND PX

AND OTHER CA-CA

WHICH DOES NOT SELL OFF.

SHORTING YOU IS LIKE CROSS-COUNTRY SKIING

IN PEANUT BUTTER

TOGETHER,

LET US CLIMB THE PUT TREE

OF OUR LOVE


Lehman was going to need a buyer.

I was not an investment banker, or an accountant, or a security analyst, so I really didn't understand how the mechanics of it worked. But once your stock gets down to a certain level, the firm cannot survive on a sliver of capital. It needs to be taken over by someone, a tasty snack.

The Dickler was never going to sell.

If Lehman Brothers employees were cockroaches, Dick Fuld was one of the monster cockroaches they have in Singapore that you can walk around on a leash. Fuld had a relatively unassuming academic background, like many of his employees. Like me. He had an undergraduate degree from the University of Colorado, Boulder, where he was an

ROTC cadet, and a business degree from Stern. The mythology is that his military career was truncated by an altercation with a senior officer.

Fuld was known as the "Gorilla," and it wasn't one of those nicknames that required explanation. It wasn't an inside joke. He was just a tough bastard, and he didn't suffer fools. He was a winner. It was once said that if you were standing behind Dick Fuld in line to buy lottery tickets, you could just save your time and hand him your money—that son of a bitch was gonna be the one to hit it big.

This thing was Fuld's baby. No *way* was he going to sell the company. He owned a shitload of it. He could have sold it on the highs, and now it was one-fourth of the price. Nobody sells because he wants to; he sells only because he has to.

D.C., Steve, Marty, Louis, Happy, and I had plenty of impassioned discussions about who was going to buy us. Barclays said it might want us, but the British bank had its own issues. It wouldn't be JPMorgan, because it was still digesting the acquisition of Bear Stearns. HSBC would be good, we thought, because it didn't have much of a US franchise, and we would get to keep our jobs. Bank of America was the most likely candidate, but nobody was happy about that, because if we merged with it, there would be a lot of overlap, and it was very likely that a lot of guys would get laid off.

The more time went by, the more it became clear that nobody particularly wanted us.

If history was any precedent, we weren't going to be sold at all.

Ken Auletta's book *Greed and Glory on Wall Street* is about the sale of Lehman to American Express in 1984. This was a combination that turned nasty almost instantaneously. When you buy an investment bank, you don't buy anything tangible. You don't buy the employees; you don't buy the client relationships. You buy the building, you buy the balance sheet, and the accumulated goodwill, and you hope that the employees come along for the ride. Quite possibly you have to pay them a lot of money to do so. And even if you do pay them a lot of money, that doesn't prevent them from being resentful. Even at the end, years into the deal, employees were still answering the phone "Lehman Brothers," which used to piss off the Amex folks to no end. Amex decided that Lehman and its gorilla head honcho had an indigestible corporate culture and spat it out in 1994. Dick Fuld decided then and there that the firm would be independent forever more.

Lehman Brothers people are a big pain in the ass. It is like conquering some land of barbarians, some dissolute race. What is the point?

Nobody knew what the hell was going on. Everyone kept talking about us going bankrupt, or worse, but from our vantage point on the second floor, things were fine. Yes, we were having trouble retaining clients; salespeople were constantly on the phone, telling our story. We're not like Bear Stearns, you see. Bear Stearns had a liquidity problem. We do not have a liquidity problem. They had a liquidity problem because they funded themselves with their prime broker balances. We do not fund ourselves with our prime broker balances. If people pull their prime brokerage, it has no effect on our firm's capital position. And so on.

The head of sales was a stocky former bond salesman named Mike. Mike couldn't have been more than a year or two older than me, but he was one of these anointed people, the type who would go on to run an entire Wall Street firm at the age of forty. Mike would sit in the middle of the trading floor and tell the bullish story on Lehman Brothers to anyone who would listen, picking apart our balance sheet, showing that we were solvent, discrediting all the analysts paraded across CNBC. Mike had, or appeared to have, complete faith in the leadership of Lehman Brothers to figure this thing out. He walked the walk and talked the talk. On most days, he would attract a crowd of about twenty analysts and associates, young bucks who were not yet cynical enough to disbelieve the hype.

Mike disturbed me. He was an indisputable control freak. Upon arriving on the second floor, he engineered this system of allocating sales credits called *attribution*, which tangled up everyone's lives in bureaucracy for months. The idea was that many people touch an outside client, from the research salesperson to the sales trader, and the revenues the client provides should be divided up accordingly. When the system was in place, the sales traders were at war with research sales. Friendships that had been built up over many years were being torn apart.

Everyone was fighting about money. Nobody fought about money when nobody really kept track of it and just assumed it was all going to work out in the end.

I had a sense Mike was full of shit. He talked too much.

It was time to go home. I logged out of my computers, and then I checked each of them six, four, and two times, then looked over my shoulder as I walked off the floor to make sure they were logged off.

Damn it.

In September, Dick came down to the trading floor.

Richard S. Fuld never came down to the trading floor. He was not one of these management-by-wandering-around types. Seeing Dick anywhere in the building was like catching a rare glimpse of an arctic tern.

The two or three times Dick had ever made an announcement on the floor, he was warmly received. This time, as he made his way to the phone, he was met with nothing but silence.

"I know some of you are unhappy with the performance of the stock." Pause. Pause. Dick had mastered the pregnant pause. "And so am I. As you know, I own a lot of stock." Pause. "And this has been just as painful for me as it has been for you."

*Contrition. Not a bad start.*

"But we're going to beat these guys. Einhorn and his little monkeys. We're going to get all the shorts off our back. And we're going to get the stock back up to eighty-five bucks."

*Um. The only way the stock is going up 400 percent is if somebody learns how to shit gold coins.*

Dick's repeatedly stated goal was to get the stock up to $150. For it to happen now, for the stock to have a 10X return, would require twenty-five years and the most fantastic bull market ever.

"And don't think I forgot about that one-fifty!"

*Now he's lost it.*

"The management team has a plan in place." Pause. "And we are going to execute that plan." Super pause, for effect.

"AND WE'RE GONNA GET THOSE BASTARDS!"

Applause is expected. So people clap, like droids. They can't believe their ears. *Our CEO is out of his tree. Bastards? What bastards? You're the bastards! You're going to get you?*

Louis leans over. "Going to zero?"

"That's right."

I was going to have a tough time becoming Jay Knight if the firm went tits up. I didn't think any other firm was going to let me trade from Miami. I was pretty sure that just about any other firm on the street was going to think that was a bad idea. Then again, what was Jay Knight going to do?

Jay Knight was always going to have a job.

In the last two months, I had scratched together another $2 million. That made $22 million for the year. That meant that I was on pace to make about $30 million—just barely Jay Knight material. It hadn't been easy. After Bear Stearns, I knew that the market would rally, but then I was like a dog who, after chasing a car for miles, caught it, and didn't know what to do with it. I had hedged some of my bullish bets, and some I had not. My book was a mishmash of shit that I hadn't yet untangled, and it was all losing money except for a large short position I had taken in the Australian dollar.

I hadn't heard anything from my retard headhunters. There was no demand for ETF traders who traded macro prop and wrote Bloombergs.

I spent a couple of weeks working with the P&L people to see if they could get me any kind of statistics on return on equity or return on capital. I needed something other than a big number to take to potential employers. They had nothing.

Getting a buy-side job was going to be a lot harder than I thought. I needed to think about plan B. I needed to think about starting my own business, the financial newsletter, which was looking better and better as time went on. Before, I worried about running out of ideas. Now I knew that I never ran out of ideas; that I could write 1,500 words on a topic, any topic, any day of the week.

How the hell did this happen? How did someone who was a writer end up taking a twelve-year detour through the US military and Wall Street? I didn't care. I was glad that I was finally starting to figure out where I belonged after all these years.

Some people never found out.

Suddenly Louis crashes my daydream. "They're taking it to zero, right?"

"Yup."

And then it was all up to the Koreans.

Toward the end, someone leaked to the *Wall Street Journal* that we would be bought by Korea Development Bank.

KDB was only the fifth-largest bank—in South Korea. Being the fifth-largest bank in South Korea is like being the fifth-richest person in Oconomowoc, Wisconsin. Even the largest bank, Kookmin Bank, would have difficulty taking down Lehman. The difference here was that KDB was state owned, and theoretically would have a blank check to buy us.

All the yuks and jokes started. I played the Korean national anthem repeatedly over the hoot. People handed out business cards with "Lee Brothers." Sung Kwak, our biotech cash trader, did the Korean happy-happy dance around the trading floor. Gallows humor abounded.

And then—the talks were called off.

Rumor had it that when Dick sat down at the table with the Koreans, they offered us two times book for the whole company. That came out to about $40 a share, about three times our stock price. That was an outrageously high bid. KDB could have gone down to the floor of the stock exchange with a buy ticket stapled to its forehead and bought every last share of stock for cheaper.

Rumor had it that when Dick heard the offer, he got up from the table in disgust.

I once had a friend who was in the Coast Guard who used to make frequent trips to Haiti. One time, a Haitian entrepreneur set up shop on the pier selling mahogany figurines, accosting sailors as they went by. "You buy something? You buy something today?" Nobody gave a rat's ass about mahogany figurines.

The following day he was still out there. "You buy something?" He had sold precisely zero mahogany figurines.

As the ship was leaving, and the nonrates were casting off the lines, the Haitian figurine retailer was jumping up and down on the pier in a fit of rage. "*Next time the price will be even higher!*" he shouted after them.

That was Dick Fuld.

The history books will show that it would have been wise to hit the $40 bid, because when the news hit the tape that the deal had been scuttled, Lehman's stock traded down to $7. The following day, $3.

Friday came and went without a deal, and we went into the weekend needing a Hail Mary pass—or else bankruptcy.

I decided not to stick around. I had seen enough bullshit for one week. I needed to go blow off some steam for a weekend and think about my next career.

I knew what I was going to do. I was going to walk away from everything, the money, the prestige, and take a chance at something new.

I was in Atlantic City at the Showboat, playing craps.

I was a piker. A cautious gambler.

I loved to gamble, but I hated to lose. The most I ever allowed myself to lose in Atlantic City at one time was $200, which pretty much restricted me to $5 tables. After a while, blackjack became too expensive, so I stuck to craps.

I always played the don't.

Not the Dickler. He was a right-way bettor. And craps is a game of money management. You can press your bet, or you can take your money down.

Dick and Joe had been pressing and pressing and pressing their real estate bet, and their mortgage bet, and hadn't realized any gains. I mean, really? How rich do you have to be?

I was crestfallen. Lehman had been good to me. It was the one firm that would dare to hire someone with a resume like mine, which probably partially explained why I wasn't getting any interest through the headhunters. It was the one place on earth where a smart kid with a second-rate education and a big-ass chip on his shoulder would be allowed inside to dream up ways to make money.

Nobody ever said I couldn't do anything. Nobody specifically told me to *do* anything. The only rule was to be as profitable as humanly possible.

There was no place on earth like Lehman Brothers. There was no bureaucracy, no stupidity, no *Dilbert*-like nonsense. It was intellectually free and more or less a meritocracy.

It was time to move on to something new.

• • •

Sunday night, I came home from Atlantic City and checked the news.
It was the end. We were done. The bidders had walked away.
I wrote this:

FM: JARED DILLIAN, LEHMAN BROTHERS INC.
TO: SALES

THIS IS MY FAVORITE STORY. I THINK HERE IT IS APPROPRIATE. IT IS FROM M.
SCOTT PECK'S "FURTHER ALONG THE ROAD LESS TRAVELED."

*HE WAS A RABBI WHO LIVED IN A SMALL RUSSIAN TOWN AT THE TURN
OF THE CENTURY. AND AFTER TWENTY YEARS OF PONDERING THE
VERY DEEPEST RELIGIOUS QUESTIONS AND SPIRITUAL ISSUES IN LIFE,
HE FINALLY CAME TO THE CONCLUSION THAT WHEN HE GOT RIGHT
DOWN TO ROCK BOTTOM, HE JUST DIDN'T KNOW.*

*SHORTLY AFTER REACHING THAT CONCLUSION, HE WAS WALKING
ACROSS THE VILLAGE SQUARE ON HIS WAY TO THE SYNAGOGUE TO
PRAY. THE COSSACK, OR LOCAL CZARIST COP OF THIS LITTLE TOWN,
WAS IN A BAD MOOD THAT MORNING AND THOUGHT HE WOULD TAKE IT
OUT ON THE RABBI. SO HE YELLED, "HEY, RABBI, WHERE THE HELL DO
YOU THINK YOU'RE GOING?"*

*THE RABBI ANSWERED, "I DON'T KNOW."*

*THIS INFURIATED THE COSSACK EVEN MORE. "WHAT DO YOU MEAN
YOU DON'T KNOW WHERE YOU'RE GOING?" HE EXCLAIMED IN OUT-
RAGE. "EVERY MORNING AT ELEVEN O'CLOCK YOU HAVE CROSSED
THIS VILLAGE SQUARE ON THE WAY TO THE SYNAGOGUE TO PRAY,
AND HERE IT IS ELEVEN O'CLOCK IN THE MORNING AND YOU'RE
GOING IN THE DIRECTION OF THE SYNAGOGUE AND YOU TRY TO TELL
ME YOU DON'T KNOW WHERE YOU'RE GOING. YOU'RE TRYING TO
MAKE SOME KIND OF FOOL OUT OF ME, AND I'LL TEACH YOU NOT TO
DO THAT."*

*SO THE COSSACK GRABBED THE RABBI AND TOOK HIM OFF TO THE LOCAL JAIL. AND JUST AS HE WAS ABOUT TO THROW HIM IN THE CELL, THE RABBI TURNED TO HIM AND COMMENTED, "YOU SEE, YOU JUST DON'T KNOW."*

CLIMBING DOWN THE CATERPILLAR PILLAR, ONCE AND FOR ALL. ONTO MY NEXT ADVENTURE. UNLESS I COME ACROSS A FANTASTIC OPPORTUNITY, I AM GOING TO START A NEWSLETTER. I CAN PRODUCE COMMENTARY THAT IS A HELL OF A LOT SMARTER, FOR CHEAPER.

WON'T YOU JOIN ME?

IF YOU ARE INTERESTED IN SUBSCRIBING, PLEASE WRITE BACK. YOUR INDICATIONS OF INTEREST WILL HELP ME DECIDE HOW AGGRESSIVELY TO PURSUE MY DREAM OF HAVING THE BEST MARKET NEWSLETTER IN THE WORLD.

TOMORROW I WILL GO IN AND EAT THE HAGGIS.

I didn't feel like I belonged at Lehman, or on Wall Street, in the summer of 2001. I didn't feel like I belonged there after 9/11. I didn't feel like I belonged there as an index arb trader. I didn't feel like I belonged there as an ETF trader. I didn't feel like I belonged there with bipolar disorder. But now that the wheels were coming off, and people were losing tons of dough on their stock, and nobody knew what the fuck to do, finally, I felt like I belonged. We were all broken people now.

It wasn't as bad at Lehman as it was at Bear Stearns. Those poor bastards, there was this culture over there that dictated that people reinvested their bonuses in company stock. No kidding. When Bear got bought for $2, it literally destroyed guys with tens of millions of dollars. At Lehman, selling your stock wasn't just okay, it was practically encouraged. It was dumb, people said, to be walking around with 70 percent of your wealth parked in one ticker. When the five years passed, people sold it lustily. I did. But there were people who hadn't, and you could spot these people from across the floor. They had a pinched look.

Wall Street is different. Sure, I had friends. I didn't make friends easily, but when I made friends, they were good friends. But Wall Street friends were different kinds of friends. There are close friendships, but not that close. Wall Street friends don't hug, not really. High school friends, military friends, *they* hug. They have been through some stuff. Wall Street friends have been through stuff too, but it is different. Everything is at arm's length; everyone is looking out for himself. I liked the people I worked with, and I felt sorry for them, but if they hadn't planned for a day that their stock would disappear and they would be out on their ass, it wasn't my problem. The stock *vested* over a period of five years. Before that, you couldn't sell it. Anything you can't sell isn't money. You can't turn it into food. But some people blew through their (million dollar) salaries on wine fridges and golf clubs and penthouse apartments and leased BMWs, "saving" only the stock. To me, these were unsympathetic characters. On Wall Street, nearly everyone makes enough money that he can be socking it away for a day that something catastrophic happens.

I had found what I was meant to do. I was a *writer*. For the first time in my life, someone told me what I was. Siri told me, back in the hospital. It was because my busy bipolar brain was always thinking up new tricks and schemes, and instead of thinking up trades and ways to make money, it was thinking up Bloomberg messages to write. Instead of thinking about the next covered call, instead of thinking about the next spread trade, I was thinking up the next piece of magic that I was going to put into an email. I loved to make people *feel* a certain way. I loved to take them out of their day for just a few minutes and transport them somewhere off the trading floor.

It sucks to have to take medication for the rest of your life, medication that makes you fat and sleepy. It sucks to have to get blood drawn every six months to check lithium levels. It would *really* suck to get a kidney stone after my kidneys fill up with lithium over the course of fifteen years. But I finally became comfortable with who I was; *this* was who I was, good and bad, and I wouldn't trade it for anything. I could be wildly creative, one of those rare right-brain people in a left-brain world, and I could take a couple of pills every day, and things would be cool. Before, I had to make excuses for why I was the way I was. I no longer needed excuses; you don't need to excuse the way you are.

I would start out as a financial writer, at first. But there was a time when I wanted to be a short story writer, there was a time when I wanted to get into an MFA program at one of the leading schools for creative writing, like the University of Iowa. I wanted to master the art of literary fiction. I was crazy enough to do it. Then there was the matter of money, and the fact that I wouldn't be making any of it, and reality set in, and it started to make more sense to go off and make a pile of money *first*, then write later. I hadn't ever considered being a financial writer—that seemed awfully dull—but that's because people weren't doing it correctly.

Financial writing isn't supposed to be like this. It's not supposed to be fun. Financial writing is supposed to be boring as hell. You aren't supposed to have an emotional response when you read research. Nobody laughs out loud at research. Nobody gets angry at it. At worst, people ignore it. But nobody ignored me, because nobody knew what I was going to write next. *I* didn't know what I was going to write next.

What if financial writing didn't have to be so horrible to read? What if street research didn't have to put you to sleep? What if it was a joy to read? That would be my business model: I was someone with a good financial mind but also with some writing ability, and I could produce a product that would get people to think about the market in ways they'd never thought about it before. A product that didn't so much provide answers as it asked more questions. A product that valued the thought process instead of the solution. A product that valued thinking for its own sake. A product that was so much fun to read, people would actually pay for it, over and over and over again.

The obsessive-compulsive tics were particularly bad that morning. Four trips back and an extra hour. Made no difference—there was no job to be late to. It was an odd feeling.

I could see the television trucks from a mile away as I walked up Seventh Avenue. Were Britney Spears, Paris Hilton, and Lindsay Lohan Jell-O wrestling in front of our building? As I got closer, reporters were following me up the street, shoving microphones in my face. Man, I thought, these people really are jackals.

It was a scene on the second floor. Girls crying. Dudes walking around aimlessly. We were bankrupt, for sure, but, oddly, nobody was going home.

I didn't need an invitation. I yanked off my tie—*Won't be needing that*—feeling like Tim Robbins in *The Shawshank Redemption* after he crawls a half mile through a muddy tunnel to freedom. *I'm outta here.*

I was stopped by Mark Ricci, who dispensed with his customary spy-speak. "You might want to stick around," he said. "There still might be some kind of deal. It's a low delta, but . . ."

*Sigh.* I sat back down at my desk and watched my positions get point-lessly nuked for the rest of the day.

The next day was more of the same. These dumbasses still had on their ties.

There was a lot of scurrying around in the managing directors' offices. To be perfectly honest, the last thing I wanted was for us to get bought. I finally had a good excuse to get the hell out of here, and now perhaps we were going to get swallowed up after all.

Barclays, which had wisely passed on buying the entire bank, was now just trying to buy the US broker-dealer operation. To do so, it had to convince the bankruptcy judge that the creditors would get a lot more money for selling the broker-dealer now than if they waited for a month while all the employees scattered to the wind. The argument worked. A few sour-grapes hedge fund creditors registered complaints, but sav-ing part of Lehman Brothers was better than letting the whole thing go down the toilet.

Late that afternoon, all the big shots came onto the trading floor in a phalanx, with a medium-size, wire-haired man in the middle. This man picked up a phone and started broadcasting to the floor that he was Bob Diamond, the CEO of Barclays, and he was buying the Lehman broker-dealer.

The trading floor erupted in cheers.

*Well, fuck me running.*

I sat at my desk and stared off in the distance while my colleagues were whooping it up.

"Dude, didn't you hear, we all have jobs!"

Holy shit. This was the worst-case scenario for me. Had we gone bankrupt, I could have just walked away.

Nobody ever actually *leaves* Wall Street. People get paid too much money. How the fuck do you just walk away from a job that pays you $1 million or $2 million a year to do something else, to diddle around with some newsletter? Nobody does that. People only leave Wall Street *ungracefully*. People don't leave Wall Street, they are pushed. They get too old, they lose their edge, they start losing money or clients. It's the same with professional athletes. Baseball players in their forties, embarrassing themselves, too poor to quit, too proud to retire. Lehman Brothers going bankrupt gave me an out. I could leave gracefully, without giving up any money. Now I was going to have to *quit* voluntarily, to give up even more money, because it was likely that Barclays was going to start handing out retention bonuses.

Furthermore, Lehman was all I knew. I had been doing the same thing, day in and day out, for the last seven years. I had been occupying the same piece of real estate, on the second floor of 745 Seventh Avenue. Some of the faces had changed—Ingram was gone; Dave Lane too—but these were my friends, and I was going to miss them. Seven years is a long freaking time. This place was some kind of hell, filled with money and Hickey Freeman, but it was my home.

I had a lot to be thankful for. I was lucky. If I am working in the widget factory and I turn up bipolar, do they take care of me? Probably not. I was well now, as long as I stayed on the medication, and I had *no* intention of ever going off of it. There was this unresolved matter of the obsessive-compulsive disorder, which had been resistant to medication or any technique I used to try fixing it, but I guessed that I was going to have to live with that.

"Are you staying for this?" asked D.C.

"Nope. I'm out of here."

Louis and Steve were incredulous. "You're going to turn down the offer?"

"I'm going to quit right now."

I wasn't kidding.

I walked over to Mark Ricci's office and knocked. I could barely feel my feet. He was in a personal fast market, dealing with merger stuff.

"Hey, Mark, I quit."

"Okay, great," he said, and walked past me. He had shit to do.

*That was easy.*

I was actually doing it.

Wall Street is different from other jobs: If you're quitting, there's no two weeks' notice. If you're not mentally committed to working there, they don't want you handling their money. You quit, you have to get the hell out of there as fast as possible. Once I walked out the doors onto the street, I would never be coming back.

I walked out of Mark's office, through the crowds of people congratulating themselves, and I took the elevator up to HR to finish the job, which was a wasteland. They knew they were all getting axed. I sat with a serious woman who told me about my medical benefits and other details. I would get no severance, because I was quitting.

I went downstairs, said some good-byes, and then headed downstairs, through the lobby, and out into Times Square.

After seven years.

Leaving forever.

For the first time in memory, I felt comfortable in my own skin. Lehman Brothers was collapsing around me, and I didn't care, because I knew who I was, and I knew where I was meant to be. My self-esteem was no longer tied up with the firm; I didn't get a charge out of telling people I was a trader from Lehman Brothers anymore; I thought I would get a charge out of telling them instead that I was a writer. I wasn't meant to be on a trading floor anymore, I was meant to be on my own, writing.

My diagnosis and the medication had made it all possible. It was fucking scary to think about. I could have easily spent the last two years in a hospital, involuntarily committed. Or, even worse, I could have stayed out there, living my life in misery, lurching from mania to depression, until one day, I finally did myself in, nothing left but teeth, hair, and eyeballs. I thought about all the people that never get diagnosed. It wasn't obvious that I had bipolar disorder. I'm sure some people simply thought I was an asshole.

Now I was getting a full eight hours of sleep every night, not more, not less. I got tired at ten and went to bed. I was up at six. No more all-nighters. No more drinking. No more fifteen hours of sleep. No more paranoia. No more looking for security cameras and federal agents. Before, I was either filled with rage, laughing uproariously, pounding the desk, or at home, dreaming up poetry late at night, or crying myself to sleep in bed. Now I was calm. Lose money on a trade? No big deal. Don't get promoted? Get 'em next year. I wasn't exactly unflappable, but I was close. *This is how normal people must feel*, I thought.

It turns out that even normal people didn't always feel this good.

# EPILOGUE

It was nice not to have to get up so damn early.

In the past seven years, I had lived through 9/11, a suicide attempt, a stay in a psychiatric hospital, the bankruptcy of Lehman Brothers, and plenty of insanity along the way. I had made well over a $100 million trading, and was paid very little of it. I had gotten a job on Wall Street at the worst possible time—buying the highs—and left it at the worst possible time—selling the lows. I made both friends and enemies. I had surprisingly few regrets.

*Not checking the windows.*

This morning, I am getting up to go to work. Not Lehman Brothers, but my new job, writing a newsletter. I have to go find office space. There is a lot of it in the city, with real estate being what it is. This is the beginning. There are other things to do, later: buy computers, get a Bloomberg. Then start sending out free content and waiting for the subscriptions to come in.

*Not checking the refrigerator.*

Now, instead of untangling outtrades, dealing with compliance, or arguing with sales traders, I can finally concentrate on what I do best. How many people in the world get to match their vocation with their avocation? How many people spend eight hours a day doing what they really enjoy?

*Not checking the coffeemaker.*

I am not thinking about the last seven years. I am not thinking about what could have been. I am not thinking about my career cut short, the money lost, the worthless stock. I do not feel that I have been wronged. I have no resentments. It is what it is.

*Not checking the back door.*

I didn't care if the newsletter lasts four months, four years, or forty years. Who knew what the hell was going to happen? I could be back in the hospital within months. I didn't care. I was living for today.

*Not checking the locks, six, four, two times.*
*Not checking the locks, six, four, two times.*
*Not checking the locks, six, four, two times.*
I closed the door, locked it, and walked down the street to catch my bus.

# ACKNOWLEDGMENTS

*Street Freak* is a black swan—a highly improbable event. It was a one-in-a-billion shot, though it is starting to seem as if these kinds of things happen all the time.

Thanks are in order to every teacher of writing I have ever had. In particular, I would like to acknowledge Jordon Pecile at the United States Coast Guard Academy, who had the unlikely and underappreciated task of trying to teach aesthetics to anti-intellectual young cadets. You all helped me immeasurably.

Without my chance meeting with Siri Hustvedt in the hospital, I would never even have conceived of this project. She validated me and my work, encouraging me in a way that nobody had, up until that point. And to think—I could have been sulking in my room instead.

Then there is Santosh Sateesh, the ultimate agent of randomness—without his forwarded email I might still be hating myself on a trading desk.

I would like to thank my literary agents at Writers House, Stephen Barr and Dan Conaway, who saw something other people couldn't or wouldn't see and then tracked me down after I disappeared for six months and prevented me from wasting an incredible opportunity. Their vision and determination made *Street Freak* possible.

Thanks to my publisher, Stacy Creamer, and my editor, Lauren Spiegel, for recognizing the importance of the subject matter and finding the project a worthy artistic pursuit. Lauren's safe hands protected me from my own worst instincts (in most cases) and made the manuscript what it is today. Thanks also to publicity director Marcia Burch and publicity manager Shida Carr for their hard work on behalf of *Street Freak*.

Thanks to my mom and dad for being proud of me.

And most of all, thanks to my wife for sticking with me through years of insane and unpredictable behavior and for supporting me in everything I do.

When you come to a fork in the road, take it.